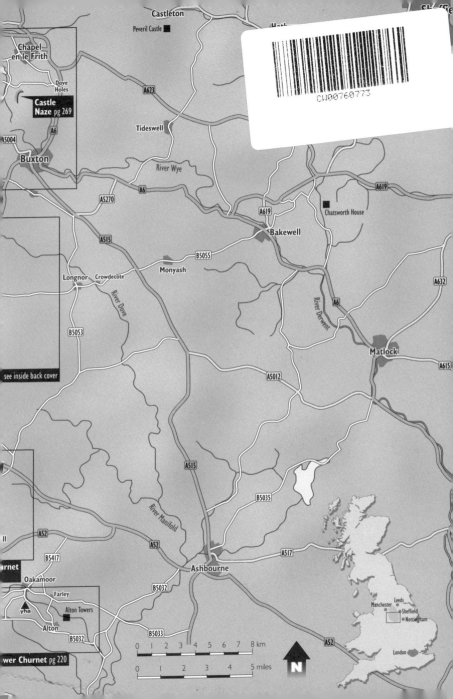

Nancy,

Happy Birthday, have fun!

Clare x

STAFFORDSHIRE GRIT
The Roaches
The definitive climbing guide
to routes and bouldering
on Staffordshire grit

British Mountaineering Council

177–179 Burton Road, Manchester M20 2BB

BMC

STAFFORDSHIRE GRIT
The Roaches
The definitive climbing guide
to routes and bouldering
on Staffordshire grit

Volume Editor: Dave Garnett
Series Editor: Niall Grimes
Researched and compiled by
a team of guidebook volunteers

Staffordshire Grit –
The Roaches
The definitive climbing guide to routes
and bouldering on Staffordshire grit

Copyright © 2004 British Mountaineering Council

Published by:
British Mountaineering Council,
177–179 Burton Road,
Manchester M20 2BB.

First printed 2004

ISBN 0-903908-67-0

Cover photo: Sam Whittaker on Paralogism, E7 6c (page 43).
          Photo: David Simmonite.

 Vertebrate
Graphics

Designed and typeset
by **Vertebrate Graphics**, Sheffield,
www.v-graphics.co.uk

Printed in Slovenia by Compass Press

Previous Editions
1913 **Some Gritstone Climbs**   John Laycock
1924 **Recent Developments on Gritstone**   Fergus Graham *et al*
1951 **Climbs on Gritstone Volume 3**   Allan Allsop
1957 **Climbs on Gritstone Volume 3**   Revised
1957 **Climbs on Gritstone Volume 4**   Eric Byne and Wilf White
1968 **Rock Climbs on the Roaches and Hen Cloud**   North Staffs MC
1968 **Guide to the Staffordshire Roaches and Hen Cloud**   John Smith
1973 **The Staffordshire Gritstone Area**   David Salt
1981 **Staffordshire Area**   Mike Browell *et al*
1989 **Staffordshire Area**   Gary Gibson
2003 **The Staffordshire Roaches** (reprint)   Gary Gibson

BMC Participation Statement
The BMC recognises that climbing, hillwalking and mountaineering
are activities with a danger of personal injury or death. Participants
in these activities should be aware of, and accept, these risks
and be responsible for their own actions and involvement.

Table of Contents

Introduction ix
Acknowledgements xi
Climbing Notes xii
Ⓥ Bouldering xiv
Access and conservation notes xvii
Guidance for groups xxi
Other useful information xxi
Mountain Rescue and First Aid xxiii
Geology xxiv
History xxvii

I The Roaches I
The Lower Tier 5
The Left-Hand Section 6
Ⓥ Lower Tier Boulders 8
Ⓥ Spring Boulders 10
The Right-Hand Section 14
Bengal Buttress 15
Raven Rock 16
The Swan Wall 18
Smear Test Slab 20
Elegy Slab 22
Kestrel Buttress 23
Piece of Mind Slab 27
Ⓥ Piece of Mind Boulders 28
Lower Tier Girdle Traverses 31
The Upper Tier 32
Left-Hand Section 32
West's Wallaby Area 34
Maud's Garden Area 35
The Central Massif 38
Black and Tans Area 39
The Great Slab 41
Ⓥ Upper Tier Boulders 44
Blushing Buttress 49
Ⓥ Cellar and Attic Bouldering 50
Calcutta Buttress 52
Ⓥ Calcutta Problems 53
Ⓥ The Cube 54
The Skyline Area 55
Condor Buttress 56
Trio Buttress 58

Tower Buttress 60
Cave Buttress 61
Skyline Buttress 62
The Pinnacle 64
Alpha Buttress 65
Ⓥ Doxey's Pool 66
Not So Far Skyline Buttress 68
Ⓥ Chasm Boulders 69
Far Skyline Buttress 70
Very Far Skyline Buttress 71
Ⓥ Art Nouveau Boulders 50
Hard Very Far Skyline Buttress 75
Ⓥ Very Far Boulders 50
The Five Clouds 79
The First Cloud 80
The Second Cloud 80
The Third Cloud 82
The Fourth Cloud 85
The Fifth Cloud 87
The Nth Cloud 89
Swivel Finger Wall 90
The Main Face 91
The Roaches First Ascents 92

2 Hen Cloud 100
The Aiguille 105
The Pinnacles 105
Black Wall 108
Delstree Area 109
Central Area 112
Amphitheatre Walls 117
Bachelor's Area 119
Thompson's Buttress 123
The Inaccessible Pinnacle 123
The Boxing Gloves 123
The Lower Buttress 125
The Bordello Area 126
Magical Bouldery Wood 126
The Bottom Buttresses 127
Biscuit Buttress 128
Hen Cloud First Ascents 128

3 Ramshaw Rocks ... 132
  The Main Crag ... 136
  South Buttress ... 142
  The Lower Tier ... 144
  Dangerous Crocodile ... 146
  Ⓥ **Dangerous Crocodile**
    Bouldering ... 147
  Ramshaw Buttress ... 150
  Flaky Buttress ... 151
  Magic Roundabout Buttress ... 152
  Roman Nose Buttress ... 153
  Winking Eye Buttress ... 153
  Ⓥ **Magic Roundabout Boulders** ... 154
  The Pinnacle ... 155
  The Lady Stone ... 157
  Ramshaw Rocks First Ascents ... 158

4 Newstones to Back Forest ... 162
Newstones and Baldstones ... 164
Newstones ... 166
  Charlie's Overhang ... 166
  Uppermost Outcrop ... 167
  Hazel Barn Buttress ... 169
  Scratch Buttress ... 171
  Rhynose Buttress ... 171
  Sly Buttress ... 172
Baldstones ... 174
  Baldstones Pinnacle ... 174
  Gold Rush Buttress ... 177
  Ray's Buttress ... 178
Gib Torr ... 181
  Lower Tier ... 181
  Gibbon Buttress ... 183
  The Upper Tier ... 184
Gradbach Hill ... 185
  Cynic's Buttress ... 186
  The Pinnacle ... 186
  Square Boulder ... 187
  The Yawning Stone ... 187
Wolf Edge ... 190
Outlying Crags in the Gradbach Area ... 192
  Ludchurch ... 192
  Castle Cliff Rocks ... 192
  Gibbons Cliff ... 192
  The Ballstone ... 192
  Flash Bottom Rocks ... 192
The Hanging Stone and Back Forest ... 193
  The Hanging Stone ... 194

  The Western Outcrop ... 194
  The Rostrum ... 195
  The Main Crag ... 195
  Broken Nose Buttress ... 197
Newstones to Back Forest
First Ascents ... 200

5 The Churnet ... 202
The Upper Churnet Valley ... 204
Sharpcliffe Rocks ... 206
  Sharpcliffe Rock ... 207
Belmont Hall Crags ... 210
  Left-Hand Buttress ... 210
  Right-Hand Buttress ... 211
Flintmill Buttress, Consallforge ... 213
  Price's Cave Crag ... 213
  Wetley Rocks ... 213
Harston Rocks ... 213
  Devil's Rock ... 214
  Gib Buttress ... 214
  Biscay Buttress ... 214
  Pinnacle Buttress ... 215
  Cave Buttress ... 215
  Technician's Wall ... 215
  Harston Rock ... 215
Oldridge Pinnacle ... 218
Garston Rocks ... 219
The Lower Churnet Valley ... 220
Stoney Dale Quarry ... 222
  The Little Quarry ... 224
  Lion Rock ... 224
  Well Hidden Buttress ... 224
Cotton Bank Crag ... 224
Great Gate Buttress ... 225
Peakstone Rock ... 226
Castle Crag ... 227
Park Bank Crags ... 229
Ina's Rock ... 231
Rakes Dale ... 232
  Austin's Crag ... 232
  Rakes Dale Wall ... 232
  Toothill Rock ... 234
Dimmings Dale ... 236
  Smelting Mill Buttress ... 236
  Lord's Buttress ... 236
  Long Wall ... 237
  Gentleman's Rock ... 239
  Hermit's Rock ... 240

Rainroach Rock 240
Wright's Rock 240
  The Main Crag 241
  Painter's Rock 243
Peakstone Inn Amphitheatre 244
  Left-Hand Side of the Amphitheatre 244
  Right-Hand Side of the Amphitheatre 244
Ousal Dale 245
  Cottage Rocks 245
  Lone Buttress 245
  Ousal Crag 245
  Ⓥ Cottage Rocks Bouldering 248
Wootton Lodge Crags 250
  Left-Hand Buttress 250
  Right-Hand Buttress 250
The Churnet First Ascents 251

6 Outlying Crags 256
Windgather 258
  North Buttress 260
  Middle Buttress 263
  High Buttress 264
  Buttress Two 264
  Buttress One 265
  South Buttress 265
Oldgate Nick 268
Castle Naze 269
  The Crack Area 273
  South Buttress 275
  The Cluster of Ribs 275
Castle Naze – Surrounding Crags 276
  Western Combs 276
  Allstone Lee Rocks 277
  South-Western Combs 277
  White Hall Rocks 277
  Buxton Boss 277
  Short Edge 278
  Hob Tor 278
Bosley Cloud 279
  The Nose 280
  North Buttress 281

Summit Rocks 283
Secret Slab 284
Chockstone Buttress 285
The Catstone 285
Timbersbrook Quarry 287
Mow Cop 287
  The Old Man of Mow 288
  The Folly Cliff 288
  Hawk's Hole Quarry 288
  Millstone Quarry 289
  Nick I' Th' Hill 289
Knypersley Rocks 289
  Little Slab 290
  Green Slab 290
  The Pinnacle 290
  Hermit's Buttress 291
The Wicken Stones 291
  Garden Buttress 292
  ERF Rocks 292
Rudyard Pinnacle 294
Heighley Castle Quarries 295
  First Quarry 295
  Second Quarry 296
  Third Quarry 296
  Fourth Quarry 297
Outlying Crags First Ascents 298

Graded List 302

Ⓥ Graded List – Bouldering 304

Ⓥ Bouldering Index 305

Crag Index 307

Route Index 308

Chris 'Gus' Hudgins on Acid Drop E4 5c (page 62).
Photo: Niall Grimes.

Introduction

I was introduced to climbing, as a schoolboy, on a trip to the Roaches and Gradbach in the summer of 1975. It was an exciting and memorable event that was to influence the whole of the rest of my life. I treasured and still have my copy of Dave Salt's 1973 guide with its underlined routes and pencilled comments and although I subsequently climbed in many beautiful and impressive venues all over the world, this area retained a special place in my affections. And so, when many years later we were looking somewhere where we could combine work and family life with easy access to climbing, it was only semi-accidentally that we found ourselves living within a few minutes drive of the Roaches. It was a smart move and becoming involved in the production of a forthcoming guide seemed a natural development.

Of course, producing the 10th guidebook to climbing in the Staffordshire gritstone area over what is now a 90-year history carries a worrying level of responsibility, but the enthusiastic help of the whole community of local activists and climbing friends, old and new, has made it thoroughly enjoyable. The hard work and creative ingenuity of Niall Grimes, as BMC guidebook co-ordinator, made it both a pleasure and a practical possibility.

We have tried to capture not merely the bare bones of route descriptions and grades, but something of the atmosphere and experience of the area, its climbs and (an important extension) its bouldering. The result is rather different to previous BMC Peak guides in terms of style and presentation but, although I hope this helps to present the content in a fresh and interesting way, the changes are superficial compared to the content. What is unchanged is the aim to provide an accurate, definitive record of climbing in this very special corner of the Peak. Here is climbing as good, as varied and as memorable as any in the country and I can only hope that we have managed to do it justice.

Dave Garnett, Rudyard, December 2003

This **book**

This book covers all the main gritstone crags of the Staffordshire area – the Roaches, the Five Clouds, Nth Cloud, Hen Cloud, Ramshaw, Baldstones, Newstones, Gib Torr, Back Forest, Hanging Stone and Gradbach Hill. It also covers the multitude of smaller outlying crags in the region – the Upper and Lower Churnet Valley, Bosley Cloud, Mow Cop, Knypersley Rocks, The Wicken Stones (Rock End), Heighley Castle, as well as the attractive outcrops of Windgather and Castle Naze in the Buxton area. It is a definitive guide to all the routes and bouldering to be found on all these crags, as well as a history of the climbing in the region.

How it works

This guide makes extensive use of colour illustrations to supplement written text. They are designed to work together. Lines on the diagrams will give a good general idea of where a route goes. Where

needed, text will help with the finer details. The text is also used to help to give an idea of the character of a climb, and will be very useful in choosing one's route. Whilst every effort has been made to get them right, do not rely solely on where the line is drawn, nor try to follow it at all costs. Use your judgement. The lines are there as guides.

Important note

The inclusion of a crag or route in this guide does not imply a right to climb. Descriptions are recorded for historical purposes only. Great effort has gone into this book to ensure all grades and descriptions are accurate, but always climbers must still use judgement to ensure difficulties are within their abilities, and accept the consequences of these decisions.

Neither the BMC nor anyone else involved in the production or distribution of this guide accepts any responsibility for any errors it contains, nor is liable for any injuries or damage arising from its use. Climbing is a dangerous pastime.

Acknowledgements

A debt of gratitude is due to the many people who made this guidebook possible. The most humble apologies for anyone who belongs on this list but does not appear.

Crag Writers (and everything else)
Dave Bishop, John H Bull, Dave Garnett, Gary Gibson, Niall Grimes, Chris 'Gus' Hudgins, Martin Kocsis, Robert Lavin, Stuart Millis, Richie Patterson, Paul Smith, Andi Turner, Sam Whittaker, Simon Wilson.

A special thanks to other people
who gave constant support and input to the guide
Steve Clarke, Justin Critchlow, Luisa Giles, Julian 'The Judge' Lines, Lynn Robinson, Mark Sharratt, Richard Taylor.

Illustrations
Vertebrate Graphics, John Beatty, Dave Bishop, Duncan Bourne, Mark Crampton, Nick Dixon, Alex Ekins, Colin Foord, Dave Garnett, Niall Grimes, Adam Long, Alex Messenger, Ian Parnell, David Simmonite, Paul Smith, Andi Turner, Ben Tye. All crag photography, illustrations and uncredited photos, Niall Grimes.

Script checking and proof reading
Helen Bush, Kate Cooper, John Cox, Neil Foster, Jane Garnett, Graham Gedge, Dave Gregory, Brian Griffiths, Pat Horscroft, Simon Jacques, Graham Lynch, Ian Smith, Gordon Stainforth, Ken Wilson

And **all the people** who made general input, by contributing written sections, selfless route checking, advice and support
Tom Briggs, Percy Bishton, Clare Bond, Gary Cooper, Ross and Ray Cowie, Jules Cox, Simon Davenport, Rupert Davies, Nick Dixon, Colin Foord, Mark Goodwin, Damian Haigh, Peter Harding, Paul Higginson, Roger High, Mick Hill, John Horscroft, Dave Musgrove, Simon Nadin, Ged O'Sullivan, Simon Panton, Jon Read, Gordon Stainforth, Dave Turnbull, Richard Wheeldon, Ken Wilson.

A very special thanks to all those involved in securing access to the crags in this book
Dave 'Rock On' Bishop, Clare Bond, Bill Brocklehurst, Suzanne Fletcher, Graham Lynch.

BMC Guidebook Committee
John Horscroft, Mike Hunt, Dave Musgrove, Dave Turnbull, Richard Wheeldon.

A particular recognition is due to all those individuals involved in the production of volunteer based guidebooks over the years, without whom the information would not exist.

Finally, a heart-felt thank you to Jane, Kate and Adam who have had share the house with this guide throughout its protracted gestation and put up with the frequent absences and preoccupations of its editor.

Quotations from EA Baker's *Moors, Crags and Caves of the High Peaks* are reproduced by permission of Halsgrove Press.

Climbing notes

Route grades

The system of grading for routes in this volume is the traditional British style, a combination of adjectival and technical grades, and assumes the leader has a normal rack, including standard camming devices, nuts, slings, quickdraws etc., sticky rubber, and no more than two of each limb. The adjectival grade is the first part of the grade, and attempts to give a sense of the overall difficulty of a climb. This will be influenced by many aspects, including seriousness, sustainedness, technical difficulty, exposure, strenuousness, rock quality, and any other less tangible aspects which lend difficulty to a pitch. It is an open-ended system, and currently runs from Easy, which is barely climbing, to E10, which has been barely climbed. Along the way, and in ascending order, are Moderate (**Mod.**), Difficult (**D**), Hard Difficult (**HD**), Very Difficult (**VD**), Hard Very Difficult (**HVD**), Severe (**S**), Hard Severe (**HS**), Very Severe (**VS**), Hard Very Severe (**HVS**) and Extremely Severe, the last category being split into **E1**, **E2**, **E3** etc.

The second part of the grade, the technical grade, is there to give an indication of the hardest move to be found on the route, irrespective of how many of them there might be, how strenuous it is, or how frightened you are when you do it. They come onto the scale somewhere around 4a, a savage example of elitism that must have 3c merchants foaming at the mouth, and currently run thus; **4a, 4b, 4c, 5a, 5b, 5c, 6a, 6b, 6c, 7a, 7b**. By the time you get to **E10 7b**, you should start to have an idea of how the system works.

Bouldering grades

The system of grading in this guide is the V system. This originates in the USA, and is used to give an idea of technical difficulty, strenuousness and sustainedness of any problem. To help with comparisons and to aid anyone unused to the system, English technical grades are also included for each problem. See the bouldering section for further information.

Stars & daggers

For those who need them, stars (none, one, two or three) have been used in this guide to indicate quality. However, on most of these crags, every route is worth doing. Where this is not true it will be clearly stated in the text. An un-starred route is by no means a bad route, and can give as good an experience as a three-star route. Route descriptions also point out the best features of any climb. Read through these and see what appeals to you. Try not to be too guided by stars alone.

Certain routes will have a dagger † symbol by them. This indicates a route where the guidebook team may have doubt about some aspect of the route, such as being unsure of the line, or having an unconfirmed grade due to insufficient repeats.

Ethics & style

The two most basic rules here are be honest, and don't damage the rock. Beyond that, it's entirely up to you, although in terms of style, some ascents are considered better than others. The best is still the on-sight flash, climbing the route first try with no falls and no helpful information. Few hard routes are done in this fashion, many higher grade routes being completed after some form of top-rope practice. However, this is currently acceptable, as long as the final result is a clean lead of the route, ideally placing protection *en route*. Many routes have also become established with side runners for protection. Where this is so, it will be mentioned in the text, and the grade will reflect this fact. And finally, on a happier note, aid points and rest points have now disappeared from the areas covered in this book, and it is unlikely that a new route containing either would be seen as acceptable.

Fixed protection

Fixed protection, in the form of bolts, pegs, threads or hammered wires is, thankfully, virtually absent from this guide. Never, ever, think about placing any, be it on a new route or any subsequent ascent.

For some historical reason, however, the sandstones of the Churnet Valley have escaped this rule, and pegs are to be found on some crags. As with all fixed protection, treat with care.

New routes, first ascents etc.

Details of first ascents, including name, grade, individuals involved, date and style of ascent, as well as contact details, should be sent to: guides@thebmc.co.uk. Another first ascent resource can be found at www.ukclimbing.com.

Another new feature in this guide has been an attempt to record early repeats of major routes, and more importantly, any improvements in style over that of the first ascent. The growing trend of on-sighting hard and bold routes has been reflected in this guide. See first ascents for details. Also, if you have any further information on such ascents, please get in contact through the above address.

Gritstone – this precious rock

Climb the rock as it is. Do not be tempted to shape it to suit your inadequate skills or to gouge out protection placements where none exist, so leave your wire brush and chisel at home. Brushing with anything other than a toothbrush to remove excess chalk is rarely necessary. Even on new routes brushing should be with a nylon brush to remove lichen, moss and algae only (and only on crucial holds) and should never go so far as to expose pink new rock. Once the hard exterior layer is removed, the softer sandy interior erodes very rapidly. If you cannot do a route or problem in its existing state, go away and train harder or accept that you aren't good enough – yet! If new routeing please remember these ethics and in addition do not garden or remove vegetation.

Nick Dixon using unconventional methods to check out new route possibilities at Ramshaw. Photo: Allen Williams/Dixon collection.

Bouldering

This is the first definitive routes guide that has also tried to give definitive coverage to bouldering. The rise in popularity of this activity in recent years has, in some way, made this an obvious step. It also makes sense due to crossover between the two activities, as many people warm up or wind down on boulders, as well as the increasingly blurred distinction between bouldering, highball bouldering, short solos and routes on grit.

Compiling these problems has been quite a task. Traditionally, guides have recorded a select few – the bigger and the more famous. Allen William's OTE and Rockfax bouldering guides were a major new step in British climbing guides, and the first to document the major circuits in the area. This new guide covers all these circuits, and a good many more besides, and on top of that, all the problems dotted along crags and odd bits of rock throughout the entire county.

Despite pros and cons of various systems, V grades have been used here, and used along with traditional technical grades in order to ease in the system, and to help boulderers in the lower grades where the V system is less useful. These V grades have been applied to many traditional climbs, where they may seem more appropriate. Often, however, a highball boulder problem can feel bolder than many routes, but if it is a 'bouldering attitude' that is brought to these climbs, then it has seemed more appropriate to use a bouldering grade. In these highball problems, it is assumed that a mat and spotter are used (otherwise award yourself an E grade).

Many of the problems in this guide have been given names. These names are in no way an attempt to 'claim' these problems, just a way of identifying them. A few first ascents have been recorded, but in general, trying to get first ascent information for problems would seem like more trouble than it is worth, and in a way, not in keeping with the spirit of the sport. Due to the subjective nature of quality, stars have not been used for boulder problems.

A clear indication of how good an area is will be given in that area's introduction. As for individual problems, if it appeals, climb it.

The majority of the sections are self explanatory: if bouldering occurs among routes, it will be described there. If there is an obvious circuit, it will be described in a separate plan, located in the book near where it lies on the crag. To help boulderers locate problems amongst route sections, they have been highlighted in red. Also if, amongst text, the 'V' symbol occurs (Ⓥ), this indicates that there is some bouldering described in that section.

Bouldering mats

The growing use of pads for bouldering has many positive benefits, protecting both boulderers and the environment. As such, their use is a welcome trend. They are also commonly used to take the

sting out of bolder routes. This is entirely your choice, and in many ways a rational one, but remember the effect their use will have on the grade of a climb. It makes them easier.

Environmental considerations for boulderers

All climbing has an environmental impact. However, boulderers may wish to bear some special points in mind. In a session, a problem can be climbed many more times than a route. This leads to an erosion rate greater than that seen on longer climbs. Try to do all you can to minimise the erosion. Brushing is the most obvious issue. Wire brushes can easily remove the tough outer skin of the rock, leaving the soft unprotected rock beneath to wear away. If you must brush, use a soft, nylon-bristled brush. Always clean your feet before climbing, and climb well to avoid scratching about on the surface. Use as little chalk as possible. Never use Fontainebleau style resin or 'pof'. It ruins problems. Never ever attempt to alter the rock in any way. Don't apply ugly tick marks to the rock. Use a bouldering mat if possible. Try to visit different areas. Generally, always be a good ninja.

Where to go
A few hints for boulderers new to the area.

Classics of all grades
Roaches Upper and Lower Tiers, Newstones.

Highballs
The Cube, Oldridge Pinnacle, the Aiguillette (Hen Cloud), Doug-less Boulder (Lower Tier).

Escape from the heat
Ramshaw, Magical Bouldery Wood (Hen Cloud), Wright's Rock, Gentleman's Rock, Gib Torr.

When it rains
No guarantees here, but try Ramshaw Lower Tier and Night of Lust areas, Baldstones, Wright's Rock, Gentleman's Rock, Ousal Crag.

Escape from the crowds
Roaches Skyline (Doxey's Pool, Art Nouveau, Chasm and Very Far Boulders), Gib Torr, Fourth Cloud, Sharpcliffe, Back Forest, Gradbach Hill, Nth Cloud.

Easy stuff
Piece of Mind, Spring Boulders, Sharpcliffe, Dangerous Crocodile Bouldering, Gradbach Hill, Back Forest.

Hard stuff
Roaches Upper and Lower Tiers, Inertia Reel Area, Fourth Cloud, Magic Roundabout Boulders, Wright's Rock.

A special thanks to everyone
who helped to compile the bouldering sections
Percy Bishton, John H Bull, Justin Critchlow, Simon Davenport, Rupert Davies, Luisa Giles, Niall Grimes, Paul Higginson, Gus Hudgins, Julian Lines, Adam Long, Simon Nadin, Simon Panton, Richie Patterson, Mark Sharratt, Andi Turner, Sam Whittaker.

With pads, many bold routes can be enjoyed as highball boulder problems. Cecile Rittweger on The Gateless Gate, E3 6a, Oldridge Pinnacle (page 218). Photo: Niall Grimes.

Access and **conservation** notes

Our behaviour in the countryside is becoming more and more important, both for the continued survival of that countryside, and for our right to enjoy it. Please read these notes and act responsibly at all times.

Inclusion of a crag in this guide is not a guarantee of a right of access to it. That said, we are fortunate that the great majority of them are freely accessible with the co-operation of the landowner. In some cases, access is likely to be guaranteed when the Countryside and Rights of Way (CRoW) legislation is enacted in 2005. Even then, restrictions on climbing to protect cliff-nesting birds and flora will continue to apply, as at present. In any case, it goes without saying that failing to behave responsibly with regard to keeping to footpaths, not attempting to cross dry-stone walls, taking care not to damage stock-proof fencing and closing any gate you open, is hardly likely to improve any access arrangement. All it takes is a little consideration. In some cases, the access situation is sensitive; pay special attention to the notes in the relevant introductory section.

Moorland, landowners and access agreements

Many of the gritstone crags in this guide are owned by public organisations. That is not the same as saying that the public have an undisputed right of access. A balance has to be struck between access, land management, and conservation interests.

The Peak District National Park Authority

(PDNPA, Aldern House, Baslow Road, Bakewell, Derbyshire DE45 1AE, 01629 816200, aldern@peakdistrict-npa.gov.uk), owns most of the crags on the Roaches Estate and their wide management responsibility includes, in priority order, to:

- Conserve and enhance wildlife habitat.
- Conserve features of geological, geomorphological, and cultural interest.
- Protect and enhance the landscape.

- Provide public access, recreation and education as far as is compatible with the above.
- Meet the proper needs of agricultural graziers compatible with the above.
- Provide for, wherever possible, the social and economic needs of the local community.
- Manage with maximum financial efficiency.

The Staffordshire Wildlife Trust

(The Wolseley Centre, Wolseley Bridge, Stafford, ST17 0WT 01889 880100, www.staffs-wildlife.org.uk), owns Baldstones, Gib Torr, and moorland nearby, and their mission is to 'protect and enhance the wildlife and wild places of Staffordshire and to promote understanding, enjoyment and involvement in the natural world'.

Other crags in this guide belong to private landowners who, with a few notable, not to say notorious, exceptions, are quite supportive of public access but many of them also have responsibilities

The Big Man, John Dunne, hanging out on Round Table, E1 5a (page 49) at the Roaches. Photo: John Beatty.

and agreements covering wildlife protection. Climbers co-operation is therefore crucial to the continuing access we currently enjoy to the crags on the Staffordshire Moorlands and associated pasture land under voluntary agreements negotiated with the landowners by the BMC's full-time and voluntary access and conservation representatives. Our long-term interest as climbers and citizens is to continue this voluntary system of achieving a balance between responsible access, land management, and conservation. It is flexible and sensitive, and the relationships built up over time with most landowners are positive and supportive.

Access difficulties

Through much work, free access is granted to almost every crag in this guide. Please follow all instructions so as to keep that access for the future. If there are any special considerations, they will be mentioned at the start of each section. Also, please make regular visits to the BMC's Regional Access Database (RAD) at www.thebmc.co.uk, and click on the RAD link. Please notify the BMC if you have any access difficulties, via the RAD comments form, or phone the BMC office on 0870 0104878. If you have any other local access queries, try the website or the BMC office, and find out the contact details for the local BMC access rep. They are all climbers, and are on your side.

Moorland & access

The heather and bilberry moorland is invaluable at all times to ground-nesting birds such as grouse, curlew, lapwing, and animals such as stoat, hare, shrew, common lizards etc., whilst the rocky outcrops and grazed fields attract our friend the ring-ouzel. So please stick to public footpaths and other designated means of access to the crags listed in this guide and keep disturbance to a minimum. Moorland, which is an internationally important biodiversity habitat, has been removed at an alarming rate and the damage done to its plant and wildlife is only just beginning to be reversed. Both the Peak National Park and Staffordshire Wildlife Trust are vital protagonists in this process.

Dogs

Dogs are good company, but running loose over the moors they are bad news for wildlife. They will

Good boy, Jim. Photo: Paul Smith.

cause birds to abandon their nests and animals to flee and thus probably bring about the avoidable death of a season's young. You probably wouldn't even know it had happened. So if you really can't leave Rover behind at home, then make sure your best friend is under control and preferably tethered whilst you are climbing. Under CRoW legislation, new responsibilities will be placed on owners wishing to take dogs into open countryside.

Top-roping

If overdone this can cause difficulties for other climbers and damage to the rock. It is worth remembering that all routes are graded for ascents from the bottom up placing your own protection as you go. If you really do feel the need to top-rope then please:

- Give priority to anyone who wants to lead the route from the bottom up.
- Do not hog any area of rock for extended periods.
- Do not make continuous and repeated attempts at hard moves as this leads to rapid and unnecessary erosion of the holds, and they can't be replaced.

Sanitation

Another major environmental point to make is the one of sanitation. The sight of or proximity to rocks seems to excite peristalsis in some climbers with a consequent urgent need to find a secluded spot. The best advice is to 'Go before you go', i.e. before leaving home. If that fails, then please keep well away from the bouldering and climbing areas when leaving your mark and do not use or discard tissue as it takes weeks to disintegrate. Taking stones off walls to hide your contribution both damages the walls, which then have to be repaired at public, i.e. your, expense, and slows down the efforts of nature's scataphagous creatures who are keen to get stuck in to your waste offering. So help nature to help itself and leave it exposed. Sanitary towels, toilet paper and similar should be wrapped up and removed.

Litter

Finally, if you take a plastic bag with you, you can take home your litter and anyone else's that has been left around.

Guidance for groups

Groups can vary from large organised climbing parties under the control of instructors to small gangs of friends and even groups such as management trainees whose use of the crag is instrumental in achieving some purpose other than climbing. Many groups are well organised and controlled, and operate with sensitivity both for the needs of other climbers and for the crag environment. However, the following advice will be helpful in reducing some of the unintended (we hope!) consequences of group use of the crags and for giving guidance to sustainable practice for all. To lessen ground and rock erosion, disturbance to wildlife, and friction between users, try these ideas and spread the word:

- Encourage leading climbs instead of top-roping.
- If you need to top-rope then keep both the time you occupy any route and the number of ascents to a minimum. Avoid placing multiple top-ropes and do not leave set-ups in place when you are not actively using them.
- Keep group sizes small and under control, and in particular cut down movement over the ground at the base by your group.
- Ensure that rucksacks and gear as well as group members do not block footpaths and access.
- Move on frequently to new locations. If you occupy a route or area for a long time, for example, all morning, all afternoon, all day, all week, or regularly use the same routes and locations, you hasten erosion and deny access to others.
- Running up and down boulders can be great fun but it erodes the ground, deposits dirt on the rock, and teaches unsustainable practice. Try simple bouldering instead.
- Consider abseiling at 'purpose built' locations such as Tegg's Nose Quarry and Miller's Dale Viaduct. Abseiling for its own sake should only take place on artificial structures and not on natural crags.
- Take litter away and encourage the cleaning of areas on leaving.
- Keep noise down and discourage yelling, cheering, and applause. Find other and quieter ways to encourage group members.

Other useful information

Maps

The most useful map for the gritstone area is Ordnance Survey 1:25,000 Outdoor Leisure Sheet 24: The Peak District White Peak Area. For detailed exploration of the Churnet Valley, Ordnance Survey 1:25,000 Pathfinder Sheet 810 (SK 04/14): Ashbourne and the Churnet Valley will be found handy. Ordnance Survey 1:50,000 Landranger Sheet 118 covers the outlying areas of Bosley Cloud, Mow Cop and Heighley Castle.

Public transport

For the main gritstone areas, the nearest railway stations are Buxton and Macclesfield (for info, phone 08457 484950). There is a regular bus service, the X18, between Sheffield and Hanley, via Bakewell, Buxton and Leek. It goes every couple of hours and gives access to Ramshaw and Upper Hulme (gateway to the Roaches and Hen Cloud), although you may wish to ask the driver to drop you as close as possible to your destination (for info, phone

0870 6082608). It has to be admitted that many of the other areas in this guide are inconvenient to reach by public transport.

Parking

Always use the designated parking area for any crag. The main Roaches and Hen Cloud area has limited parking and during the summer months (usually from Easter until September) a Park & Ride scheme runs from Tittesworth Reservoir, Meerbrook. Follow signposts. A fine usually results from parking outside designated areas in this vicinity.

Food & drink

There is an almost omnipresent burger and ice cream van at the Roaches, and during the summer months the Roaches Tearoom opposite Hen Cloud is extremely civilised.

There are the usual chippies and similar in Leek and, for a curry, the Bolaka on Stockwell Street (the Macclesfield road) is definitely a worth a visit.

The Lazy Trout at Meerbrook is friendly, good value and has a fine garden with a view of what you are missing on the crag. The Olde Rock Inn in Upper Hulme is within easy walking distance of the Hen Cloud campsite. After a visit to Ramshaw or the Newstones area, the Traveller's Rest (near the Flash turn off the main A53 Leek-Buxton road) is highly recommended. The Ship Inn, Wincle, is handy for the Hanging Stone, has good beer and is recommended for a slightly more up-market meal. Leek is packed with pubs, but the Wilkes' Head on St Edward's Street is favoured for its beer (and has been the very tolerant host to many guidebook meetings!). Finally, the garage on the A53 at Blackshaw Moor is worth a try for newspapers (even climbing magazines) and sweeties.

Huts & camping

Don Whillans Memorial Hut, Rockhall Cottage, The Roaches. Owned by the BMC. Sleeps 12, mixed, in two rooms. Very good value. No dogs, smoking or camping. Contact the Booking Secretary: Michael Hunt, Vale Cottage, Foolow, Eyam, Hope Valley, S32 5QR (mike@cdmsconsultancy.co.uk, 01433 639368).

There are several convenient **Youth Hostels** in the area. Meerbrook: Old School House, Meerbrook (01538 300174); Gradbach Mill, Quarnford,

Buxton (01260 227625); Dimmingsdale, Little Ranger, Oakamoor (01538 702304). See www.YHA.org.uk.

There is a basic campsite below Hen Cloud. Contact Mr Day, The Holmestead, Upper Hulme, Leek (01538 300419). A more luxurious campsite may be found at the Camping and Caravanning Club, Blackshaw Grange, Blackshaw Moor (01538 300285).

For any other accommodation in the area, try the Tourist Information (*see contact below*)

Climbing supplies

Reaching New Heights, 1 Fountain Street, Leek (01538 373854) www.walkingclimbing.com

Mountain Fever, 25 Brunswick Street, Hanley, Stoke-on-Trent (01782 266137), www.mountainfever.co.uk

Jo Royle Outdoor, 6 Market Square, Buxton (01298 25824)

Climbing walls

The Stoke-on-Trent area seriously lacks a decent climbing wall. The nearest is:
Rope Race, Goyt Mill, Hibbert Lane, Marple, Stockport (0161 426 0226)

There is a small wall in Longnor but, although ideal for children, it isn't a serious venue for the hard core:
Upper Limits, Buxton Road, Longnor (01298 83149)

There is also a poor, decidedly old school, bouldering wall at:
Macclesfield Leisure Centre, Priory Lane, Macclesfield (01625 615602)

Wet weather entertainment

Alton Towers is the local centre of Babylonian excess and is conveniently adjacent to the lower Churnet crags. Ornithologists might try **Blackbrook Zoological Park** (Winkhill, on the Ashbourne road out of Leek, 01538 308293), whilst those with a bent for industrial archaeology might be interested in **Brindley's Mill**, Mill Street, Leek (weekends in the summer months only, 01538 483741).

Tittesworth Reservoir has a pleasant visitors' centre. When the weather is too poor to see **Jodrell Bank** from the crag it might be worth a visit (just off the A535, between Holmes Chapel and Chelford, 01477 571339). Those struggling to entertain small children should try the narrow gauge steam railway in **Rudyard** (01995 672280) which runs during summer weekends. Finally, **Poole's Cavern** is guaranteed weatherproof (Green Lane, Buxton, 01298 26978). **Tourist Information Office** is on the Market Square in Leek (01538 483741).

Mountain Rescue and First Aid

Dial 999 and ask for Police – Mountain Rescue. Briefly describe the nature of the incident and give the crag name and OS map reference as listed at the start of each crag section.

The Police will co-ordinate the Mountain Rescue team and, if appropriate, the county air ambulance that is available for evacuations from the crag. The local team is based in Buxton. Although **they should not be contacted directly for call-outs**, they are very happy to hear from anyone wishing to support their voluntary efforts:

Buxton Mountain Rescue Team,
8a Halsteads, Dove Holes, Buxton, Derbyshire
SK17 8BJ (01298 812232),
www.buxtonmrt.org.uk

Likewise, anyone wishing to support the County Air Ambulance might like to contact them at:
Staffordshire County Air Ambulance,
Appeals Headquarters, Burton Road, Dudley,
West Midlands DY1 3BB (01384 241133),
www.county-air-ambulance.com.

FIRST AID in case of ACCIDENT

1. **If spinal injuries** or **head injuries** are suspected **do not move the patient** without skilled help, except to maintain breathing and circulation.
2. **If breathing has stopped**, clear airways and commence **CPR** (cardio-pulmonary resuscitation). **Do not stop until expert opinion diagnoses death.**
3. **Stop bleeding** by applying direct pressure.
4. **Summon help.**

These are the basic principles of first aid. If you climb at all regularly, you should seriously consider taking a first aid course. Learning enough to save a life isn't at all difficult and one day you might be very glad that you (or someone else) did.

Geology

by Clare Bond

The geology in the Staffordshire area is dominated by the great escarpments of the Roaches, Ramshaw and the Clouds – this is also, unsurprisingly, the best area for climbing.

In the carboniferous period, approximately 345 Ma (million years ago), the White Peak was just a sea of warm clear waters. Then, either due to the up-lift of land in Scotland and Scandinavia or faulting enable rapid subsidence, deepening the warm tropical sea, the conditions changed. Sediments – grits and sands – from the land were washed into the sea and deposited, and over the years, settled and compacted into what we now know as gritstone. Sedimentary structures, cross-bedding, which can be seen on many of the climbing crags as diagonal layers within individual beds (layers of sediment) suggest that the sediment was mainly washed into the sea from the north – maybe from a granite in Scotland.

The grits are inter-bedded (or layered with) marine shales, muds and coal. If it weren't for the deposition of these inter-layers of shale and mud, we might have substantially larger gritstone outcrops! The classic Roaches scenery is dependent on these inter-layers, which are far 'softer' and therefore much more easily eroded than the gritstone. The erosion of the shale layers leaves the gritstone outcrops prominent on the landscape, forming 'edges'.

Individual layers or beds of gritstone often contain layers of different sized pebbles and grains. The pebbles have been transported in a high-energy flow, whilst the smaller grains require less energy to be transported. The pebbles are smooth and round, the result of abrasion during transportation. Individual pebbles are often the key to, and the crux of, many gritstone climbs. If you find yourself at the Roaches on Catastrophe International, whilst pulling on the pebbles think about how they got there and how rounded they are – or may be you should just concentrate on pulling!

Jason Pickles concentrating very hard on a great feature of Staffordshire geology, the Roaches Pebble, appearing here on A Fist Full of Crystals, E6 6b, (page 14). Photo: David Simmonite.

At the very end of the Carboniferous there was a period of compression that folded the rocks. The area of the Roaches, Ramshaw and the Clouds is part of a large syncline, a fold in the shape of a U, which trends north to south and plunges (is tilted) North. The core or centre of the fold contains coal deposits which lie on top of the layers of gritstone and shale. The structure is best seen from a distance with a pint in your hand at the Mermaid Inn. After several pints you may appreciate that the gritstone of the Roaches is in fact the same layer of rock that can be climbed on at Ramshaw – the layer is folded and outcrops on different limbs or sides of the fold.

Between the Permian and the Triassic (280–195 Ma), extensive erosion uncovered the limestone to the east. To the west a fault separates the Carboniferous sediments from those of the Triassic, but to the south-east the contact is an unconformity or erosion surface. In fact there are few Triassic rock outcrops and climbing is concentrated on those in the Churnet Valley. Here the Triassic sediments are thick beds of sandstone and conglomerate which are red in colour due to staining of iron oxides. The sediments are thought to have been deposited in shallow water lakes and seas, on the edge of vast deserts which covered most of the English Midlands. The conglomerates at Sharpcliffe Rocks, with pebbles as big as fists, show that local flooding did occur in the Triassic transporting quite large pebbles.

The rocks of Staffordshire have come along way from the Carboniferous tropical sea in which we started the story. When you're out on the moorland think that one day it may be back under the sea and future visitor to Staffordshire maybe dodging lava flows from volcanoes rather than bogs!

No route can sum up the brutal ecstasy of climbing on Ramshaw more than Ramshaw Crack itself, E4 6a (page 150). Here, guidebook writer Richie Patterson savours the wide joy of this mighty Joe Brown classic. Photo: David Simmonite.

History

by Niall Grimes

"Ramshaw Edge, a grotesque succession of ghoulish faces, bovine and porcine heads, and half-finished monsters springing from the parent rock. And beyond, where Hen Cloud extends its array of pinnacles, outlines that the camera may prove to be less than vertical or only slightly overhanging, but to the eye appear like curving horns, their points overweighted with threatening tons of rock. Then [the Roaches], another peak of strange shape that appears to be a loose accumulation of boulders of all sizes and the most extravagant forms, gnarled, rifted, fantastically weathered, and often perched in positions that seem to defy the laws of mechanics."

This flowery and doom-laden description of the three major Staffordshire crags comes from one of the area's first explorers, EA Baker, in his book *Moors, Crags and Caves of the High Peak*. Baker, originally from Derby, was a member of that great exploratory group of Peak District activists, the Kyndwr Club. Was it truly how the group saw this landscape, wayward and threatening, ready to pounce and devour at any time, or was it just a flight of Baker's fancy, combined with his prodigious poetic licence?

Perhaps a bit of both. The Kyndwr Club was formed in 1900, a collection of professional men who sought their adventures in the moorland around the Sheffield, Derby and Manchester areas. The key members were Baker, Sheffield's WJ Watson and the legendary JW 'Jimmy' Puttrell. This group, and Puttrell in particular had, since the late 1880s, roamed the entire district, adding rock climbs on every possible feature. The first entries of practically every crag's ascent list in the Peak bears Puttrell's name. However, it took the group a long time to ever venture Staffordshire's way, and when first they

did, they famously spent a day wandering lost in the mist in an attempt to find Lud's Church (a rumour of rock had been heard, mumble, mumble). When they eventually happened upon it, it was found to be disappointing. Perhaps this hapless day is where Baker's early visions came from.

The group did return, however. They explored Ramshaw Rocks, and ventured to Hen Cloud where Baker again gives an account of 'a tussle with gloves on' in the Pinnacles area. It is not sure which route this was, although it is more likely to have been **Chockstone Chimney** than Mindbridge. They also made a visit to the Roaches, where, despite a healthy fascination with Rock Hall, they managed to record the first route on this beautiful crag, **Raven Rock Gully**.

Some villagers were anxious to know if we had scaled this imposing crag [Raven Rock] which they evidently considered the finest climb about here, and were much disappointed to hear we had not attempted it. The rustic, being no climber himself, thinks nothing of impossibilities.
EA Baker

For many years the Roches have stood to the climber as an El Dorado, a glorious myth, whose wonders were known to exist, but were never explored due to their apparent difficulty, and it is only during the last few years that the rocks have been regularly visited.

Morley Wood, 1924

Yet, despite the obvious potential the area possessed, it appears they made few further visits to the county, perhaps setting in motion one of the overwhelming characteristics of Staffordshire climbing, that of its slightly forgotten nature. Time and again through its history it can be seen that, while it has never lagged behind in terms of quality nor difficulty, its light has often been eclipsed by events further east, or northwards in Yorkshire. Why this should happen is not obvious, but the result has been a relative quietness and 'localness' that is one of the most endearing traits that this fine area has to offer.

Little activity took place on the cliffs for over 10 years (Laycock and Thompson's notable Hen Cloud epic aside, as well as a few minor routes here and on the Roches) until 1913. In this year, a new breed of gritstone 'tigers' hit the scene. New techniques and attitudes were in evidence. Rock-climbing was generally no longer viewed as an 'exercise for the Alps'. Clothing and footwear was such as it was no longer so restrictive on movement. Woollen stockings and heavy nailed boots gave way to rubber-soled gym-shoes. The 'grab and pull' of earlier generations was gone in favour of more open climbing, relying more on friction and balance, techniques that were to influence the direction of British rock-climbing until the arrival of the brutality of the Rock and Ice. Most notably of these tigers was the powerful trio of Stanley Jeffcoat, Siegfried Herford and John Laycock. They 'discovered' the Upper Tier of the Roches, adding **Jeffcoat's Buttress** and **Chimney**, as well as Hen Cloud's classic **Great Chimney**. A testimony to their ability is Scafell's **Central Buttress**, Herford's mighty pioneering climb from 1914, recognised as the hardest lead in the country for some time. It has been argued that every major advance in British climbing has been instigated by climbers who have been trained on outcrops, and this example certainly supports that theory.

The final overhang of *Crack and Corner* was only overcome by the leader taking a shoulder. "The top must some day become an easy day for a lady, but at present it is no place for a gentleman."
Morley Wood

The bold and open climbing pioneered by this group was taken a stage further by climbers such as AS 'Fred' Pigott, Morley Wood and Lindlay Henshaw in the early '20s. **Bachelor's Buttress**, **Pedestal Route**, **Black and Tans**, **Crack and Corner**, **Left-Hand Route** – an ascent of any of these climbs, even with

The evening sun casts a magical glow on climbers enjoying Peter Harding's Valkyrie (page 18), as good today as it's ever been. Photo: Mark Crampton.

During WW2, genuine rubber tree rubber was in short supply so soles were made from rubber 'crumb' which gave poor friction and very poor wear. If one did find a pair of pre-war tennis shoes, their uppers were patched to keep them in service as long as possible: after a good day out on gritstone, one had to patch one's rubbers, or enlist the needle services of a willing girlfriend.
Peter Harding on the home front

today's equipment, will give an insight into what had been achieved by such climbers all those years ago, both in technical and psychological terms. However, the ultimate achievement of the era must still be Ivan Waller's mightily exposed **Bengal Buttress**. Waller was a dandy, fond of torturing passengers with excessive speed in his Alvis sports car. As revenge, one victim, Fred Pigott, led Waller to the Lower Tier and pointed the evil driver at an unclimbed slab. 'Waller', it is said, 'devoured the buttress very promptly.' So much for revenge. Even today this climb is renowned for its breakneck smearing and bold crux, and a real eye-opener to sticky-soled, pant-filling, leg-trembling leaders.

There followed, throughout the 1930s, another of Staffordshire's fallow periods. Little was added to any of the major or minor outcrops. It was a time of great depression in the cities, when the free time of unemployment and the depressing frustration of bleak cities forced a wave of working class men out into their local countryside for recreation. Here, the landed class saw 'escape' as 'invasion', and strict and sometimes aggressive keepering was applied in protection of what was seen as a threat. In some areas this fearsome protection was greater than others, and while some areas of the eastern Peak continued to provide climbs, one must presume that the landed class were more successful in their ruling in

This was the era during which the use of the rubber shoe began to pay good dividends, and along with this came the development of the shoulder belay which at first was considered to be so secure that it was not always practice for a climber to anchor himself to the rock.
AS Pigott talking about the 1920s.

Hawser ropes, Vibram soles and no runners. Colin Foord demonstrates climbing gear, 1960s style, on the direct start to Black and Tans (page 40).
Photo: Foord collection.

Staffordshire. This sad time was rounded off in the bleakest of fashions by the outbreak of the Second World War in 1939, and from then until its end in 1945, the country had little appetite for activities on rock.

The Karabiner Club led the way with exploration of the Skyline area in 1945, but the first big event of the post-war period came in the sweeping beauty of Peter Harding's **Valkyrie**. At the time, Harding, a wiry and quick-minded engineer, with a healthy faith in his own abilities, was acknowledged as among the finest climbers in the land, and raised standards significantly, not only in his local area, but in the mountains of North Wales. His climbs such as **Promontory Traverse** and **Demon Rib** at Black Rocks, and Cratcliffe's **Suicide Wall** were his big additions to grit; fierce, technical climbs up steep terrain. But he is equally remembered for routes such as **Valkyrie** and **Goliath's Groove** at Stanage, climbs which were not at the limits of the possible, but which bore such a touch of class that they would be destined to become the favourite classics of their grade.

In the aftermath of the horrors and privations of the War, there was a shift in the whole social structure of the country. While rationing persisted until the '50s, the post-war period was noted for its full employment, and a renewed sense of hope sweeping through the land. Better transport allowed easier access to the moors surrounding the great cities. Value was being placed on the outdoors. The traditional strictures that served to keep the lower classes 'in their place' were lessening, as evidenced by the election of a new Labour government. The Peak District National Park was decreed, guaranteeing access for all. These factors served to allow a new breed of climber onto centre stage in British climbing, and onto the Peak District in particular, and with it came new and refreshing attitudes that would go on to produce an advance in climbing standards the like of which has not been seen before or since.

The Valkyrie Club was already a strong group soon after it was formed in 1947, but when Joe Brown joined it soon after, it was set to make history. Characterised by a rough, working-class toughness, the group swept all before them. Uncredited routes from the 1951 guide, such as **Hedgehog Crack**, **Rainbow Crack** and **Central Climb Direct**, all hint towards a new type of route: steep long cracks, often reliant on jamming and devoid of the safety of ledges. Yet when Joe Brown led **Saul's Crack** on the Upper Tier in 1947, something new had begun. The route is a ferocious and technical jamming crack, overhanging and uncompromising, the start of a new breed of super-route.

Brown's next big addition was **Valkyrie Direct**. He jammed easily up to the left of the great flake, and disappeared round the corner to top out. Slim Sorrell was not in a seconding mood, so when a passer-by asked for a go, he was allowed to tie on. The passer-by followed with ease, even continuing up the nasty upper crack that Brown had avoided, and joined the leader on the summit. The young lad

Joe Brown

made the second ascent [of Sloth] with myself as
second when I was his gentleman's gentleman. When I
was out on the roof he tied off the rope to the belay,
and came down to watch me, giving me the shock of
my young life. When I asked if he was holding the rope
because of all the slack, up from the deck floated the
reply, "Of course I am."
Dennis Gray

Swinging free on the overhang of The Sloth (page 42),
one of the country's great HVS experiences.
Photo: Colin Foord.

was Don Whillans, and from this first meeting, the
two combined and formed the most dynamic and
fearsome partnership of theirs or any other day.

Many routes were to 'get the message' from these
two. **Matinee**, **Hen Cloud Eliminate**, **Delstree**, **Brown's
Crack**, **Don's Crack**, **Crack of Gloom**, **Sloth**: all,
arguably, the best lines on the best crags. From reading their accounts, you are left with the impression
that they just were not finding any of it difficult,
wandering up the routes with ease. The climbing
tends to be characterised by very technical and
gymnastic climbing, usually jamming, in a very
strenuous position. The age of the genteel balance
climb had gone, with Whillans' ferocious fist
swinging at its retreating back.

After this great time, which lasted well into the
1950s, there followed a lull in Staffordshire climbing. Perhaps the county was reeling from the
onslaught, or perhaps the great surge of development on the newly-fashionable limestone cliffs had
taken away the force. New route activity did take
place, along with a surge of discovery. The Churnet
valley yielded a great number of routes on its many
crags, and renewed interest was shown in Mow
Cop, Bosley Cloud and Gradbach Hill. But they were
not routes of any great stature or historic significance. Mike Simpkins' bold Roaches challenges
(**Wombat**, **Walleroo**, **Elegy**, and so on) kept the pot
simmering, of course, along with interesting additions elsewhere: **Chicken**, **Encouragement**, **The
Untouchable**, **Rubberneck** springing to mind. Still,
the '60s will not be seen as one of the great decades
of Staffordshire development.

But something new was in the air. Revolution,
floral shirts, Led Zeppelin guitar solos, drugs and
streaking. Denim shorts and EBs. The early years of
the 1970s marked the beginning of the great

Gritstone Renaissance sweeping Yorkshire, the
Eastern Edges and Staffordshire. The Roaches were,
once more, where it was at!

Looking at first ascents, one can see, from the
early '70s, a huge explosion in the numbers of new
routes being added in Staffordshire. The Roaches,
Hen Cloud, Ramshaw, as well as all the lesser crags,
were peppered with new climbs, many of them
pushing the technical standards of the day. The great
cracks had all been climbed by earlier generations,
but this one found the walls in between covered in
holds, and duly swarmed up them. These routes
may have sometimes lacked in stature or maybe
line, but that was less important. This was the era of
'the move'. Technical interest was prime, and this
was frequently combined with sizzling boldness as
sequences were often led away from the comfort of
cracks.

An almost obsessional level of interest was
shown by a good number of climbers. From the
east, the cream team of John Allen and Steve
Bancroft began their very fruitful raids, culminating
in their four big 'C' routes on Hen Cloud. Other
quality additions were found elsewhere at the
Roaches and Ramshaw. However, Staffordshire had

The present surge in development (1970s) was undoubtedly inspired by the achievements of Brown, Whillans, Crew and Boysen etc, the Rock and Ice era being *the* leap in climbing standards. Perhaps for the first time personalities were seen in a popular light. Be that as it may, we must not detract from their climbing achievements. Routes like the Mincer and Sloth had a distinct steepness about them – these were no longer the 'One-move-and-rest' of earlier climbs.
Pete Livesey

its own answer to the young Sheffield-based talents, in the shape of two curly haired rascals called the Woodwards.

Andrew and Jonny Woodward opened their account with the truly ground-breaking route, **Ascent of Man**. Not ground-breaking in terms of difficulty necessarily, but in style of climbing, for it was the first real pebble-puller to be added to the Roaches, a type of climbing for which that area of the crag would become renowned. From that point on, the two brothers, with Jonny becoming dominant, scorched the county's crags, reaping the yields of their prodigious talents. **The Undertaker**, **National Acrobat**, **The Joker**, **Patient Weaver**, all testify to their roving ability. However, it was at the Roaches where they really upped the bar.

On The Skyline, beauty and difficulty began to come together in near perfection. The year was 1977, and with **San Melas** the brothers realised that holds were a luxury, not a necessity. This was further proven with **Wings of Unreason**, with its ludicrous top move, and then **Track of the Cat**. This latter route was equal in quality to anything Bancroft and Allen were adding to the Eastern Edges. (A few years later Andrew matched this run with **Entropy's Jaw**, a route that completes a good Skyline tick-list of tough slab routes.)

The ultimate route, however, came on the Lower Tier, with Jonny's **Piece of Mind**. A route truly ahead of its time – totally holdless climbing on minimal smears in a position of utmost death, it was to wait almost 20 years for an on-sight ascent (although one hopeful did come dangerously close in 1986!). It was then rated E6 6c, and although not far off the mark today, this was seen as an extraordinary claim at the time, and attracted much criticism.

But then the Woodwards weren't above such criticisms. The era they were in, seems, more than most, to have been a particularly competitive one. With so many climbers with so much appetite, competition was fierce. The 1981 guide, following hot on the heels of this era, has a history section full of admonishments of greed and underhand tactics. The young brothers also were criticised for their heavy adoption of top-rope practice. This may have been slightly hypocritical, as this was, and had often been, a common tactic of the gritstone new-router. Perhaps it was just the level that they took this method to that in some way broke the subtle and unwritten rules of gamesmanship. They also attracted several cries of foul. Most notable was the **Traveller in Time/Jumbo** controversy on Ramshaw. Another was **Jack the Traverse** in the Churnet, claimed at E3 5b, but only repeated in very recent times. Many simply put these infractions down to youthful over-enthusiasm, and it must also be remembered that they were seen as young upstarts by the established community. Ultimately, Jonny's ascent of **Beau Geste** on Froggatt in 1982, acknowledged as the hardest route of the day, silenced all who had doubted his talent.

The pace continued all through the '70s and '80s, where one name is notable in first ascents. Gary Gibson, a local Stoke lad, is renowned throughout the British climbing scene for his near-manic obsession with new-routeing. He is, quite simply, a new route machine. Crags everywhere bear his name, but it was in Staffordshire that he acquired his taste. **Bad Joke**, **Fast Piping**, **Knossos**, **Shortcomings** and **Licence to Run** are just a few of the mountain of first ascents to his name.

Then in the early '80s, the climbing that was achieved in the '70s was taken to a new level, the result of a combination of training and incredible talent. This was the era of hard limestone sport

The hardest piece of climbing on the Lower Tier is the Woodward's Piece of Mind. Originally rated E6 6c by them, it is more in line with straight XS 5b. You have got to admire the Woodwards in a way. Often doing things for laughs and reaction, they have incurred the wrath of many a gritstone thug who took their showmanship and infamous overgrading to heart.
Dave Jones, Roaches and Hen Cloud, Crags, 1979

climbing, climbing walls and dieting. Luckily, it was also an era of very high unemployment, a 'dole culture' and spare time. Three cheers for Mrs. Thatcher! The outcome was that standards surged. Nick Dixon was prime amongst a group of Stoke residents. Fiercely strong, and with very high levels of drive and application, it wasn't long before he was to make his impact on the area's climbing.

The beautiful **A Fist Full of Crystals** began his bold campaign on the pebbly Lower Tier. In the same area, he went on to add **Pindles Numb**, and with **Catastrophe Internationale**, shifted pebble-pulling to a new technical level. However, it was with his route, **Doug**, that this technical level was combined with a high level of danger, to bring a new grade to Staffordshire. The area's first E8 (arriving at almost the same time as Dawes' **Gaia** and Dunne's **New Statesman**) employed all the tricks: reports of pillars of glue to hold ramshackle pebbles in place, and a group of hecklers below holding a 'fireman's blanket' to protect a fall – a fact that reflects Dixon's theatrical style more than his preservation instincts. It remained, however, an extremely bold outing, and one of the most important ascents in Staffordshire's history.

Simon Nadin may not be one of the first names known to climbers. He is, however, the very definition of British climbing talent. A lanky blond, quiet and with an almost unbelievable modesty about his own abilities, he first came on the scene in the '80s known as the Buxton Stick Man. Unusual, as his early climbing was mostly spent on the Buxton climbing wall developing his strength and technique; however, when he made it to the rock, he wasn't slow in applying these skills.

The rarefied grades of E6 and E7 were churned out thick and fast by the Stick Man: **Dangerous Crocodile Snogging**, **Never, Never Land**, **Master of Reality**, **B4XS**, **Barriers in Time**, **Art Nouveau**, **Painted Rumour**, **Paralogism**. The list of three-star hard routes with his name on them could go on for a long time. All show his ability to keep it together on big bold leads. Climbs such as **Thing on a Spring**, **Crystal Voyager**, **Who Needs Ready Brek?** and **Laguna Sunrise** all demonstrate, if it were needed, the level of technical ability he had. Added to this is a host of unclaimed and undocumented (and probably unrepeated) boulder problems scattered around, victim of Nadin's modesty and amnesia.

At the time

I was doing things like Paralogism and some of those other climbs at the Roaches, and I remember thinking that they weren't particularly hard routes really, and that I wasn't climbing that well. But then just after that I went to Europe and I won the World Championship and thought 'hmmmm…'.
Simon Nadin

What will be remembered, however, is by a long way the hardest and best set of additions in the history of Staffordshire climbing. Perhaps less known at the time than some of Dawes' creations around Sheffield, perhaps due to the isolation' of Staffordshire, or perhaps lacking Johnny's media-magnetic personality, Nadin's routes were the equal to what was being added anywhere in the country. Only, really, in the 1990s did many of his routes received repeats, (some are still unrepeated) and then rarely. Nadin was, without doubt, a tough buck.

Perhaps unsurprisingly, new route activity in the 1990s slowed down to an almost non-existent level when compared with what had taken place in the previous two decades. In the 'Hard Grit' resurgence of the mid-90s, methodical top-roping allowed many (but not that many) of the previous desperates to get repeats. A few harder routes were added to the area, a few of them landing in the E8 bracket. Seb Grieve, a Nottingham-based madman, who accounted for second ascents of many of Nadin's climbs, went on to add his own masterpiece, **Clippety Clop**, to the outrageous arête avoided by **Dangerous Crocodile**, using knees, denim and lunacy to great effect; Julian Lines smeared dangerously up (and very quickly back down again) the slab left of Piece of Mind, due to an **Obsession Fatale**; the talented teenager, Justin Critchlow levitated up Ramshaw's blankest arête, to produce the ridiculously technical, but survivable **Ultimate Sculpture**, and Mark Katz bouldered riskily up Hen Cloud's shortest and hardest climb, **The Young Pretender**.

But what that decade will be remembered for most will be the bouldering revolution. The popularity of this sub-sport exploded in these years, the result of the dominance of 'power' as a climbing medium, accessibility, user-friendliness, fun, sociability, 'newness' and fashion. Not that it was

Staffordshire

still has plenty of new routes to give up, and even if you can't find them yourself, most of them are mentioned in the text. However, below is a list of the most outstanding unclimbed lines left in the county. An ascent of any of these would be a great achievement, as they are all real Last Great Problems.

Go to it.

The Press Direct
Sustained, brutal slapping a long way above a perfect landing.

Ramshaw Crack Right-Hand
A gritstone route for the world's strongest sportclimber.

Sharpcliffe Arête Problem
The sit-down start lies far in the future.

Headless Horseman Arête
The ultimate Lower Tier challenge.
Has been top-roped.

Nth Cloud Problems
Three perfect projects, all V12 or harder.

The Hen Cloud Block
The arête right from Chameleon is featured, but they don't come much steeper.

That amazing boulder in the woods
It's out there somewhere.

Never stop exploring.

anything new. Brown and Whillans obviously tried their hands at it, leaving **Joe's Arête** and **Don's Crack** (although the Joe Brown Pad and the Whillans Toothbrush never caught on). From the '60s onwards, crags such as Baldstones and Newstones were developed by climbers such as Martin Boysen, perhaps the foremost technician of his time, Jerry Peel, Hugh Banner and Tony Barley. **Charlie's Overhang**, **Elephants Ear**, **Press Direct** and **Peel's Problem** are all good examples here. In the '70s, the short technical nature of the climbing broke down the barriers between what was considered bouldering and routes (**The Fin**, **Tierdrop**, **The Ultra-Direct**, **Mantis**). By the '80s, bouldering had achieved a status, with climbers such as Nadin, Allen Williams, Nick Dixon and Gary Cooper producing many of today's classic problems. **Finger of Fate**, **Inertia Reel**, **Crystal Voyager**, **The Cube** are just a few of those whose history is known.

Yet in the '90s, what we see are hordes of climbers who see bouldering, not as training for real routes, but as an end in itself. Paul Higginson, Justin Critchlow, Andi Turner, Mark Katz, Andy Brown and Dave Aucott among many others, were to scour the edges and boulders, and bring new levels of power to the sport. **Tit Grip**, **Epilogue**, **Boba Fett**, **Undercut Dyno**, **Simple Simon**, **Gibbering Wreck**, **Higginson's Arm** and **Grand Theft**, coupled with raids from Sheffield to produce **Inertia Reel Traverse**, **Mushin'** and **Ram Air**; all are top notch problems of the highest order, that go a long way to make Staffordshire every bit as good a bouldering venue as Stanage or Almscliff.

So, where are we now? In the early years of the third millennium, it is hard to see what there is left. This may have been said by older generations, but the impact of the last few years' exploration has left us with no sense of the impossible. The list of Last Great Problems is short, for both bouldering and routes. Perhaps the combination of power and skill will result in a rise in on-sighting standards, which currently lags behind cutting-edge first ascents by at least 20 years. There have been notable flashes and on-sights in the last few years, but these are very rare occurrences, far from the norm.

What is certain is that Staffordshire climbing will continue. People will still come, thrash, smear, pull, jam, layback, and top-out. People will still have beautiful days and great climbing on some of the greatest routes anywhere in this or any other land, enriched by its great history, immersed in its legends and great figures and epics. Staffordshire: there is no finer climbing area.

Go out and enjoy it, and may the Force be with you.

Great holds making up for great exposure on
the Neb Finish, VS 4b, the Roaches (page 41)
Photo: Niall Grimes.

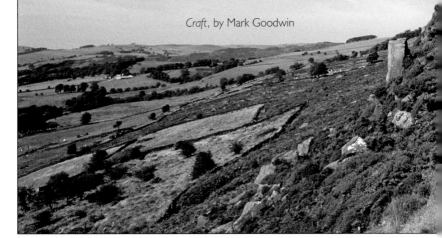

For the lover of solitude, the Clouds offer superb routes at all grades. Here, Stephen Coughlan climbs Smun, VS 4c (page 86). Photo: David Simmonite.

Pull

up on jugs of gritstone. Crimp
on folds of compressed sand. File
movement smooth in mind. Touch

rough quartz studs. Fashion
delicate pain in ornate thoughts. Jam
soft flesh fists tight in cracks. Sculpt
in the medium of wind-carved flakes and
overlaps. Balance

desires on sharp arêtes. Chisel
excess ages away as dust. Brush
now's stone powder to heart. Breathe

viscous patterns of smell. Varnish
this shape of flesh and grit with sweat. Then
abandon
the creation at its top. Give
the grit-hard and ego-soft art up. Jump.

Or coil
up the well furred rope. Shove
its complex coloured smile into
a worn rucksack. Walk

back home slowly. Feel
arrogant and vulnerable.

Craft, by Mark Goodwin

The Roaches

The Roaches

The Roaches

'Doubtless there will be the usual controversy over the grading of climbs and the Sloth in particular has been the subject of heated argument as to its standard. Hard Severe has been mentioned by some but more expert opinions seem to consider Very Severe appropriate.'

John Smith – A Climber's Guide to the Staffordshire Roaches and Hen Cloud Area, 1968

The Roaches

Character

A gothic cathedral of a crag; a place of pilgrimage for disciples of fist-jamming and pebble-pulling, a site of ritual observance for devout boulderers. The Roaches is steeped in a history that reaches from the pioneers of gritstone climbing, through the Golden Age of jamming, to state of the art test-pieces. It has enclosed misty cloisters and airy pinnacles and terrifying gargoyles; the sketchiest of nail-biting slabs, the most carnivorous of cracks and the wildest of roofs. This wealth of development and diversity of styles has resulted in classic routes over the full

spectrum of grades. Here the most accessible and enjoyable of VDiffs may be found within metres of the most uncompromising E8s. All this with water-colour pastoral views, and all within an hour's drive of the Potteries and Manchester.

The Roaches is a collection of areas, each a major crag in its own right. The left-hand side of the Lower Tier features a concentration of fierce, bold and pebbly slabs, as well as lots of bouldering. Truly an area for the connoisseur. To the right of the steps the buttresses appear even more gothic and imposing,

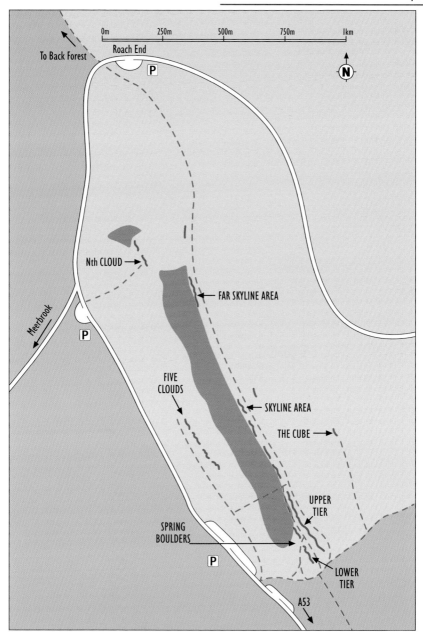

but are actually less compact and unforgiving than the left-hand section. Here is an excellent selection of routes of all grades, including some historic middle grade classics. All styles are catered for, with slabs and jamming cracks being especially well-represented, including some of the finest routes the area has to offer. Not only that, but a number of the routes are unusually long, providing exciting multi-pitch expeditions of a kind not often encountered on gritstone.

Above, the Upper Tier is more open and extrovert. Its centrepiece is the impressive sweep of the Great Slab, topped by the improbable roof of the Sloth, under which have stood generations of aspiring gritstoners, their palms damp with nervous anticipation. Here too are excellent routes of all grades, but with perhaps the pick of the easier routes. The Upper Tier has another time-honoured bouldering circuit, including some shiny 50-year-old classics dating from a time when this now all-pervasive genre was the preserve of the true eccentric.

Beyond the left end of Upper Tier, across a short, heathery gap, a series of buttresses known as the Skyline area extends along the ridge for a further mile. These delightful faces tend to be quieter than the always-popular more accessible areas. Here it is usually possible to have a buttress containing a few plum routes to oneself and even on the best -known classics queues are almost unknown. For the observant naturalist, in addition to the ubiquitous grouse, hares are numerous and common lizards can often be seen in sunny weather. However, only the most fortunate and sharp-eyed will see what is perhaps the most famous local wildlife. It is thought that the population of Roaches wallabies was, by 2002, reduced to only two individuals, unfortunately both female. Again, the climbing offers something for everyone, but the real speciality of the area is slab climbing, often bold, but always of superb quality.

Finally, the Clouds area offers another beautiful escape from the hordes on the main areas, with a series of buttresses stretching off below the Skyline, each with its own quirky character, offering again a top class selection of stiff walls and smeary slabs from the easiest grades up to solid extremes.

Access

The land is controlled by the Peak National Park Authority and there is generally open access to all climbing areas. However, access to areas of surrounding open moorland, especially the area between the Upper Tier and Skyline and the Five Clouds below them, is discouraged apart from public footpaths since they are designated quiet areas for wildlife, especially ground-nesting birds. This is relevant for access to the Cube, which should be approached via footpaths from the south-east (i.e. from the right-hand side of the Upper Tier), and not directly from the path to the Skyline. The other rule relates to bouldering on the Hard Very Far Skyline area. A local understanding has been arrived at that there should be no bouldering on the friable buttresses above the main path from Roach End. These rocks have flaky strata that are easily broken and worn leading to damage that is all too obvious to passers-by. There are plenty of much better areas, please keep off. Occasional local bird bans are imposed as necessary. These are clearly sign-posted and should obviously be scrupulously adhered to.

Parking & approach

For the main areas of the Roaches and Five Clouds, park in the lay-bys on the road below the crag. Parking outside the marked areas (including in front of the derelict cottage) will almost certainly result in a £30 fine. The police do not tolerate any partial blocking of the highway and local residents are reporting contraventions. Access is needed for locals and emergency vehicles at all times. Theft from vehicles at the Roaches and other isolated parking locations is currently undergoing a renaissance. Leave nothing on show. A seasonal Park & Ride scheme runs from Tittesworth Reservoir to the main gate up to the crag.

For The Very Far and Hard Very Far Skyline areas a quicker approach is to park at Roach End. Follow the lane along under the Five Clouds, through two gates (remember to close them behind you) to limited parking where the road bends round at the far end of the edge (also the parking place for Back Forest). A well-engineered path leads up the ridge to the trig point (10 minutes). From here, the Hard Very Far Skyline and bouldering areas are within 5 minutes easy downhill walk.

The Lower Tier

by Andi Turner

O.S. Ref. **SK006622**　　　　　　　　　　Altitude: **400m a.s.l.**

Fiercely classic climbing with top notch routes of all grades. The crag is made up of a run of smooth pebbledashed slabs on the left side, and a series of jutting prows on the main, right-hand side. The two are divided by a set of steps running to the Upper Tier.

Doug Moller, "Lord and King" of the Roaches.
Photo: Dave Bishop.

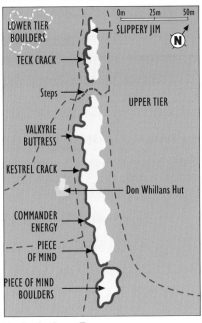

The Roaches Lower Tier

Conditions & aspect

The Lower Tier tends to be fairly sheltered, not being as high up the ridge, and with many trees nearby to break the wind. This shelter also makes some of the faces slow to dry and sometimes green, although, surprisingly, this green doesn't always effect the climbing. Faces south-west, getting sun from afternoon onwards.

Routes

Supreme. Everything from gutbustingly brutal cracks to sizzling slabs, and everything in-between, with 110 climbs, with every grade from Diff to E8.

Ⓥ Bouldering

Between three major circuits – the Spring Boulders, the Lower Tier Boulders, and Piece of Mind boulders, as well as problems on the left-hand end of the crag, the area has 200 problems, of every grade and every type.

Approach

A horrendous 5 minute march is needed from the main car-park.

The Left-Hand Section

The main path leads up through the larches towards the steps to the Upper Tier. To the left, above the popular bouldering circuit, stands an impressive set of buttresses, sometimes slabby above but always fiercely steep at their base. Here is the highest concentration of hard routes to be found at the Roaches. This, combined with the popularity of this area with boulderers, means that the lower sections of many of the routes here are frequently well-chalked: the upper sections less so! The climbing offers a satisfying balance of the strenuous and the tenuous, with more than a dash of the bold: on the pebbly slabs protection is usually conspicuous by its absence.

Descent: Use the steps.

About 20m beyond the left-hand end of the main wall is a small buttress in the woods consisting of a jumble of boulders, with a characteristic stunted tree growing at their base. This holds **Beware Coconuts** *(VS 4b, 1995), climbing the arête and squirming between branches to reach the top. Just to the left of the edge proper is a small cave with an obvious prow above, providing two short routes.* **Burrito Deluxe** *(E3 5c, 1979) is quite a serious little climb up the green left-hand wall of the prow from a grassy ledge.* **National Hero** *(E2 5c, 1978) climbs out of the right-hand side of the cave and up the right-hand side of the prow. The left-hand end of the first main buttress is marked by a vigorous holly tree, which conceals a secret way to the top for the thick-skinned.*

✪ Bouldering
Lots of time can be spent here inventing problems along the length of this wall.

❶ Snap, Crackle and Andy Popp
E1 5c   1987
7m Climb the left-hand end of the wall, just to the right of the holly. Full leathers may be required to avoid being fatally mauled!

❷ Apache Dawn E5 6c ★★   1993
8m From the middle of the pod, climb directly up on pebbles to a shallow divot and top out. Intimidating and intense.

❸ Catastrophe Internationale
E5 6b ★★   1985
8m Pure pebble climbing at an uncomfortable height. From the pod, choose your pebbles. The objective is a rounded boss on the right, just below the top followed by an entertaining pull over on trustworthy heather. The amazing thin slab just to the right has been climbed as far as the small shallow pocket just below the top. Any takers?

❹ Slippery Jim HVS 5a ★   1958
7m Climb the corner crack to its dirty conclusion. A classic, but often overgrown.

❺ Bareback Rider E4 6b ★★   1980
8m Ron Fawcett's favourite E3. Try to avoid being thrown from the technical and bouldery arête

before an awkward mantelshelf gains the sloping rib. Continue airily up the slab.

6 K.P. Nuts E6 7a   1989
8m A technical, nerve-racking and, so far, unrepeated Nadin test-piece. Climb the wall and make a technical rock-over to gain the slab above using the peanut-shaped pebbles. Compose yourself and float up the slab above to join Ascent of Man at the finish.

7 Ascent of Man E3 6a ★★★   1974
10m Welcome to pebble pulling. Make a hard move to reach a good break and then the fine flake above. Place wobbly runners and make a committing step left onto the pebbly ramp. Mantel onto the top as soon as you dare.

An independent right-hand start (V3), combined with a direct finish using the (from this side) even wobblier runners, is the very worthwhile **Ascent of Woman** (E3 6a).

V A number of satisfying boulder problems are also based around the Ascent of Man cave.

8 Days of Future Passed E3 6b ★   1974
9m The arête of the buttress has a powerful start (or jump) and a belly-flop finish with baffling rounded side-pulls in between.

9 The Aspirant E3 5c   1978
8m From the pedestal at the base of the left wall of the gully, make a surprisingly committing move to the obvious hold and then exit carefully onto the rib above.

The gully itself has been known to provide some entertainment in a hard winter, but is best avoided at all other times.

10 Ackit HVS 5b ★★   1958
15m The hanging corner. A strenuous start and then some tough laybacking lead to a welcome rest below the tricky final bulge above, which often fails to get the deft technique it deserves. A great leveller!

A desperate eliminate, **Just For Today** (E6 7a†, 1994), climbs the slab just to the right using runners in Ackit.

11 Barriers in Time E6 6b ★★★   1983
16m The impressive stepped arête marked a major breakthrough for its time and is still an unforgettable lead today. Climb the scalloped wall to the second break and protection. Proceed thoughtfully to the top via the rounded arête as the runners recede alarmingly. Traverse left into Ackit at the top.

12 Teck Crack HVS 5b ★★★   1958
26m Steep laybacking in an impressive situation; a Lower Tier classic. Start from the big ledge (best gained up the ramshackle gully below and right). Commit to the crack fully and it will succumb. Finish up the continuation crack to a historic bolt and seat belay.

The next routes tackle the short, but impressively bulging, lower wall to the right. Although originally claimed as routes, they are best seen as extended boulder problems. All are superb, offering powerful moves on sloping holds and all the usual Roaches brutality.

13 Inertia Reel Traverse V12 (7a)
Moffatt's awesome traverse is as hard as they come, and has had very few repeats

Lower Tier Boulders

Classic stuff, nestled among the larch trees below Teck Crack. A bit of everything at all grades. Good shelter and quick drying. Popular.

TECK BUTTRESS

SPRING BOULDERS

1 Easy Rib V0 (4b)

2 The Greener Traverse V3 (5c)
Traverse the finger-rail from left to right, with a bit of a lunge at the end. A **sitting start** off the poor crimps is V4 (6b), and going **straight up** from the first holds is V2 (5c).

3 Greener Mantel V2 (6a)
Move up off the crimps and mantel.

4 V4 (6b)
The arête from a sit start.

5 Heinous Mantel V7 (6c)

6 V3 (6a)
Move up using the flake and the arête.

7 V4 (6a)
Tenuous undercutting of the upper flake.

8 V3 (6a)
Tenuous uppercutting of the under flake.

9 V0 (5a)
From the big flake, go up and left along the edge.

10 Green Mantel V0− (4c)
Smear up the unbrushed slab.

11 Boss Slab V0 (5a)
The gentle slab past a boss. **Good sport** can be had jumping onto this one from the boulder behind and climbing no-handed.

12 V0+ (5a)
The thinner slab just left of the crack. Again, a good **no-hander**.

13 The Crack V0− (4a)

14 V1 (5a)
The thin slab 'twixt the crack and the chips. V2 **no-handed**.

15 Up Chips V0− (4a)

16 Arch V0− (5a)
Climb through the centre of the arch.

17 Arête on Left V0 (5a)

18 Pebble Tester
Squeeze your waist through the gap between the two boulders. If you can't do it, then don't go pulling on any pebbles, and don't trust RPs either.

19 Arête on Right V0 (5a)

20 V3 (6a)
The tallest part of the slab between the flake and the arête.

21 The Flake V0 (5a)
Or try it one-handed.

22 V5 (6b)
From the small flake, lip traverse right to easy ground.

㉓ Mantel V4 (6b)

㉔ Classic Arête
VO (5a)
Lots of good variants are available by omitting holds.

㉕ Stretch Left
V4 (6a)
From the arête, stretch left to the boss and mantel.

㉖ Undercut Dyno
V8 (6c)
Unleash a humungous Zebedee from the undercut to the top of 25.

㉗ Justin's Wall Project
From the undercut, go up the wall left of the dyno passing, but not necessarily using, the micro-crimps.

㉘ Stretch and Mantel
V5 (6b)
A beauty. Gaining the boss on the lip is the crux, but manteling out the top is a real test of confidence.

㉙ Flake Crack
VO (5a)

㉚ The Undercut Traverse
V4 (6a)
Traverse the undercut in either or both directions. While it's not very hard, you will almost certainly skid off it.

㉛ The Crack
VO− (4c)

㉜ Sketchy Wall
V3 (5c)
The wall between the two cracks is a little bit whoa, a little bit yayyyy.

㉝ Big Simple Flake
VO− (4a)
The flake crack is all too easy.

㉞ V2 (5c)
Climbing the rib, past the heathery ledge, is surprisingly tricky.

㉟ James' Slab
V8 (6c)
The steep slab directly above the first foot pocket.

㊱ Three Pocket Slab V3 (6a)
A committing step up at the top rounds off a memorable classic. Hard for the grade.

㊲ Arête on Right
V1 (5b)

㊳ Arête on Left
VO− (5a)

㊴ Short Slab
VO− (4c)

㊵ VO− (4a)
The left line on the slab.

㊶ VO− (4c)
The line to the right.

㊷ VO+ (5b)
Climb past the round feature.

㊸ VO− (4a)
The right-hand line.

Local hero Nick Dixon climbing his own Ant Lives, V6. Photo: Dixon collection.

⑭ Ant Lives V6 (6b)
The gruesome mantel (originally topping out to the right, adding a grade). The lower arête of Barriers in Time has been climbed on its right-hand side starting from Ant Lives, via a crazed series of slaps, **Sunday at Chapel** (E6 6c, 1988), using a side runner in Ackit.

Spring Boulders

A fairly classic circuit with a good mix of slabby pebble-pulling test-pieces as well as the usual Roaches brutality. It tends to be very boggy under some of the problems, in which case you may want to borrow a friend's bouldering mat. The slabs on Boulder C are a great place to learn to smear, while falling off the offwidth on Boulder F is a great place to learn to swim. Beware this area after dark, as the boulders have been known to wander off and 'graze', having crushed more than one slumbering boulderer in the past. They lie in the open field, just over the wall and the path from the Lower Tier boulders.

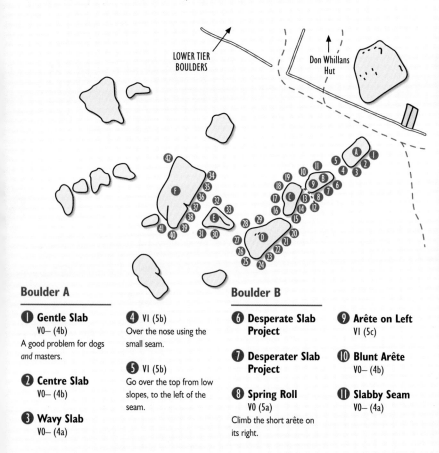

Boulder A

① Gentle Slab
VO— (4b)
A good problem for dogs *and* masters.

② Centre Slab
VO— (4b)

③ Wavy Slab
VO— (4a)

④ VI (5b)
Over the nose using the small seam.

⑤ VI (5b)
Go over the top from low slopes, to the left of the seam.

Boulder B

⑥ Desperate Slab Project

⑦ Desperater Slab Project

⑧ Spring Roll
VO (5a)
Climb the short arête on its right.

⑨ Arête on Left
VI (5c)

⑩ Blunt Arête
VO— (4b)

⑪ Slabby Seam
VO— (4a)

Boulder C

⑫ Bobarête
V7 (6b)
Skedaddle right to the arête and climb this. Worrying.

⑬ Boba Fett
V8 (6c)
Climb the tallest part of the slab on nothings. A smearing masterpiece. **Avoiding the arête** completely earns you a V9 (7a) tick.

⑭ Centre Slab
V7 (6c)
Climb the slab to the left on buttery smears.

⑮ Left Slab
V5 (6b)
The left side of the slab on pocks 'n' pebbles. A very thin time can be had traversing the invisible seam from left to right. *Boba's Traverse* V7 (6c).

⑯ Arête on Left
V0 (5a)

⑰ V0+ (5a)
Climb the flake and seam from a sit start.

⑱ VI (5b)
Step up the seam, no arête. With a sit-start on the right, this is V3 (6a).

⑲ Easy Wall
V0– (4a)

Boulder D

⑳ Blind Flake
VI (5c)

㉑ Scoops
V2 (5c)
Climb the top features to a featureless top. Climbers who have fallen into the incredible sponge below this route have reappeared in Peking.

㉒ Pebbles and Seam V2 (6a)

㉓ Pebbly Wall
V5 (6b)

㉔ Arête on Right
V3 (6a)

㉕ V0– (4b)
Arête and easy scoops.

㉖ V0– (4c)
Climb the wall from undercuts.

㉗ Runnel
V0– (4b)

㉘ V0 (5a)
Gain the hole on the slab from a good hold.

㉙ Chipped Slab
V0– (4a)
The **chipless slab** to the left is the same grade.

Boulder E

㉚ Slab to Summit
V0– (5a)

㉛ Arête
V0– (4b)

㉜ Mantel
V0– (4b)

㉝ A Nother Mantel
V0+ (5a)

Boulder F

㉞ Arête on Left
V6 (6b)

㉟ Skinned Rabbit
V4 (6b)
You will be. Hole, flake and topout. A **sit-start** makes it V6, mainly because of the weight of your wet pants.

㊱ The Grind
V6 (6b)
If you enjoyed the *Skinned Rabbit*…

㊲ Seconds Out
V2 (5b)
The offwidth will suit those with a strong work ethic.

㊳ V2 (5c)
The left arête of the crack.

㊴ VI (5b)
Ledge to slopey topout.

㊵ Impotence
V2 (5c)
The blunt nose direct.

㊶ Violence
V2 (5c)
Scurry up the beautiful scoop.

㊷ Ledgy Arête
V0– (4c)

The holes (on the side of **Boulder F**) were bored to take wooden poles to which guns were attached so as to fire a salute to the Princess of Teck on her famous visit. They missed and she later went on to marry the future King George V and become Queen of Britain.

Spring Boulders cont...

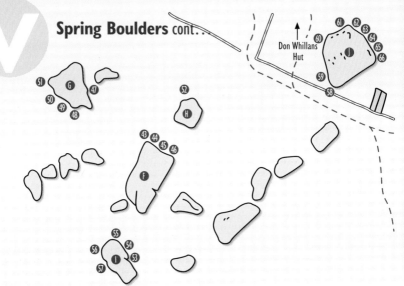

Don Whillans Hut

Boulder F cont.

43 Arête on Left
V3 (5c)

44 V5 (6b)
From the arête, pull out left into the scoop.
A **direct start** to this looks impossible, but then again, they said that about time travel.

45 Mr Nice
V4 (6b)
Hurdle the wall using a single chipped foothold.

46 Arête on Right
V5 (6b)

Boulder G

47 Easy Slab
V0– (4b)

48 Scoop and Ramp V0– (5a)

49 Heave Ho
V2 (6a)
Up on ledges.

50 The Lurch
V5 (6b)
Attain and ascend the hanging scoop with all guns blazing.

51 The Fly
V4 (6a)
The overhanging prow.
Starting low on the flake is V7 (6c). It has also been done without the big chipped foothold on the left at V8.

Boulder H

52 Critchlow's Choice VZZZZ
Lie down, take it easy. Maybe have a nap.

Boulder I

53 Friendly Ramp
V1 (5c)

54 V2 (6a)
To the hole and up.

55 Flakes
V0 (5b)

56 V2 (5c)
Move up from the left end of the pod.

57 V1 (5c)
Go up from the low hole. A good general piece of advice.

Boulder J

The Doug-less Boulder. Many of the problems here may require brushing first.

58 Project Nose

59 Scratchy Scoop
V3 (6a)

60 Green Rib
V0– (4b)

61 V3 (6a)
Steeply gain the horizontal chips. Swing right then lurch upwards for a vertical flake.

62 Slabby Arête
V0– (4b)

63 Sketchy Rib
V2 (5c)

The
Doug-
less
boulder

…used to be used by preachers to call the faithful to prayer. Steps were carved to allow non-climbing preachers access, and at the top is a hole cut in the rock where they would stick in a pole to steady themselves whilst they blew on a horn to call all the locals.

⑥④ The Rumour
V8 (6c)
The wall past the ripples may have been climbed by Simon Nadin. Haven't they all?

⑥⑤ Doug-less V4 (6a)
Climb the crack to the horizontal feature, and mantel it. Getting on for being a route.

⑥⑥ Particle Exchange
V6 (6b)
From the crack, step left on a brushed foothold and gain the arête.

⑮ Inertia Reel V8 (6c)
A Dawes classic starting just left of the vague nose. Undercut, bridge, palm and dyno. **Rupert's Sitdown**, V10 (7a), is all too obvious.

⑯ Teck Crack Direct V4 (6b)
Traverse the very sloping shelf then make desperate lunges to better holds by the blind crack. Up this to the terrace. **Thud V10 (6c)** is a unique low start. Pull on with hands in a low undercut and a round dish (feet on back wall), then swing up and gain the shelf of the direct with your feet. Do all you can to re-establish conventional mode and continue. Helmet advised.

⑰ Teck Crack Super-Direct V9 (6c)
Levitate up the cruel seam. Six-footers only need apply!

⑱ The Dignity of Labour V6(6b)
Step off the boulder and traverse left until dynamic moves up lead to an intimidating mantel using a square pebble. An adventurous landing may mean the original E3 is still deserved.

⑲ Skydivin' V5 (6b)
Jump from the boulder and gain the nose. Continue up this. **A Modest Proposal V6 (6b)**, gains the same finish by slapping out from the break below, via the left-hand prow. The roof crack has been climbed at E3 6a (V5), reputedly by Joe Brown.

⑳ Lightning Crack HVS 5b,4c ★   1958
1. 8m After a puzzling entry, layback the crack to reach a tree.
2. 12m Move up behind the tree and climb the triangular wall behind. Climb up to the sloping ledge and either finish direct or, better still, by a leftward rising pod.

㉑ Mushin' V10 (7a)
Ben Moon's brutal direct start to Pindles Numb; classic.

㉒ The Boozy Traverse V8 (6b)
From the holly, traverse left, finishing with a very pumpy sloping section. Continue up the overhanging prow for an extra grade.

㉓ Pindles Numb E4 6b   1984
11m Hand-traverse the handrail with increasing difficulty (V5), until it is possible to pull desperately into the groove above.

At the **time**...

...I'd done other respected routes, like **Crystal Grazer** and **Barriers** and **Piece of Mind** and I'd become aware that I was capable of something at the cutting edge, something that would break new ground in terms of both climbing difficulty and mind control. I particularly loved the area left of the steps and the scoop was compelling. With what was at the time, a lot of preparation, (2 days toproping) the ascent passed in an unconscious blur. I think this was my first real headpoint where I entered the zone of no thought.

Nick Dixon on the first ascent of Doug

㉔ Crystal Grazer E5 6a ★   1982

11m From the ramp, pull up left until standing on the lip of the overhang. Foot traverse left past a shallow groove until it is possible to move up and gain the obvious hold directly above the holly. Unprotected.

㉕ A Fist Full of Crystals E6 6b ★★★   1983

12m Brilliant, balancy and bold climbing on smears and pebbles. Start as for Crystal Grazer as far as the groove. Climb this and either step left onto a finishing foothold or continue direct. Surmounting the overhang to gain the groove directly is **Heredity** (E6 6c†, 1989).

㉖ Doug E8 6c ★   1986

12m Hard, blind and unprotected pebble-pulling up the shallow scoop at the right-hand side of the slab. Start as for the two previous routes but then climb immediately up the right-hand side of the front face of the buttress to finish up the hanging scoop.

㉗ Fred's Café VS 5a   1978

12m An unpleasantly green climb up the rightward-slanting crack at the right side of the buttress, finishing leftwards up flakes.

The Right-Hand Section

The first route starts immediately right of the steps. Descent for most of these climbs will be the main steps, although for routes beyond Hawkwing, skirting the Piece of Mind slab will be quicker.

㉘ Yong Arête HVD ★   1957–68

7m An interesting route climbing the blunt rib. Protection arrives too late for the leader, but may be appreciated by the second.

㉙ Poisonous Python E2 5b   1978

8m The innocent-looking curving cracks through the overlap give some surprisingly difficult climbing. A good variation pulls out right to the arête, once over the overlap, to finish up this.

㉚ Yong HVD ★   1957–68

9m The crack in the shallow corner is climbed on superb jams throughout, and is excellently protected. A perfect route for beginners.

When staying in the area, what finer base could you possibly have than the magical **Don Whillans Memorial Hut**, ancient and steeped in lore (and ghosts), grown into the rocks of the Lower Tier? This hut is available to rent by any members of the BMC at very reasonable rates, and is guaranteed to give extra-warm memories to any visit to the world's finest climbing area.

See introduction for booking details.

31 Something Better Change E2 5b 1978

9m The sadly chipped slab right of Yong is climbed direct. Good. An *en route* side-runner reduces the grade to HVS.

Across a gully to the right, at a slightly higher level, is a slim, angular buttress with a boulder bridge at its foot.

32 Wisecrack VS 4b 1957–68

8m The amusing slanting crack in the left-hand face of the buttress.

33 Hypothesis E1 5b ★★ 1963

10m The excellent cracked arête is technical, sustained and only just protectable.

34 Destination Earth E6 6b ★ 1984

12m An under-rated Nadin desperate. The centre of the front face is consistently hard, with a particularly testing crux at 7m. Originally led with a side-runner placed half-way up Hypothesis and called *Earthbound*. This method still gives a tough E4 6b.

The **Lower** Tier steps

and the pathway along the ridge were built in 1860, along what is possibly a Roman causeway. On August 23rd, 1872, the steps were used by the Duke and Duchess of Teck and Prince Francis to gain the upper tier for a picnic. A seat was carved into the rock for the Duchess, and railings put in place for safety.

Bengal Buttress

Down and to the right again is a bigger face with its undercut base and a twisting crack in its left side. It is often far more pleasant than its green appearance might suggest.

35 Cannonball Crack S 4a pre-1913

11m Slither up the crack in the left face, until a precarious move left onto a boulder allows the top to be gained.

36 Graffiti E1 5b 1978

15m Start at the base of the arête. Climb this until a move left gains a slim, slanting corner, which is climbed to the crack above and then to the top.

③⑦ Dorothy's Dilemma E1 5a ★★   1951
18m Climb the exposed arête in its entirety by a series of absorbing moves in a serious situation.

③⑧ Bengal Buttress HVS 4c ★★   1913–24
30m An inspired production from ancient times, being exposed, delicate and, even today, having dis-heartening protection. It takes a meandering, but logical line up the front face of the buttress. Move up to a grassy ledge, then go right up to a break, runners. Move up to gain an airy position on the right of the arête where a trying move leads to the top of Raven Rock Gully. Step left onto the face and go up the short crack.

③⑨ Schoolies E3 5c   1978
22m A bold direct line up the front of Bengal Buttress. An easier 5b alternative moves diagonally leftwards from the traverse to reach Dorothy's Dilemma.

Raven Rock

To the right, a fine tower stands proud from the crag, made even more impressive by the vast, sepulchral gully that frames it to the left. This beautiful and arresting buttress is home to some of the best climbs on the crag and is sometimes known as Valkyrie Buttress, after perhaps the most famous of these. It gives magnificent routes of all grades and although the climbs tend to be steeper than those found elsewhere in the area, by devious and inventive route-finding they usually manage to weave their wonderful ways upwards by guile rather than brute force. Usually, but not always… The first climbs lie in the recess to its left.

④⓪ Crack of Gloom E2 5b ★★   1958
23m A superb, dark and shadowy climb, with a character all its own, taking the mighty gloomy looming crack in the left wall of the recess. High moral fibre content required.

Steps (E5 6b ★, 2003) is a recent addition taking the leaning flake in the wall left of Crack of Gloom. Starting 2m left of this route, pull straight around the big roof, then climb past a small groove and

short crack to reach a good horizontal break. Step left to beneath a short left-facing corner. Climb the corner, then make an exciting traverse out along the lip of the big roof to gain the flake, which is fol-lowed to a wide shelf. (Protection is placed in the flake from below, but the position is strenuous and placements are blind.) Finish up the rib above, via the disappearing crack on its right side. An equally enjoyable, but less reach-dependent version travers-es out of Crack of Gloom on the good horizontal at 3m at E5 6a.

④① Raven Rock Gully Left-Hand VS 4b   1969
20m Ascend cracks and grooves in the left side of the gully, exiting through the skylight above.

④② Raven Rock Gully D ★   1901
20m A filthy climb, popular with deviants for over a century. An absolute must! Follow the flakes in the back of the gully until it is possible to squirm through the manhole above. The first route to be climbed at the Roaches, and the start of a great climbing tradition in the area.

④③ Sidewinder E5 5b, 6a †   1980
25m A wild route up the hanging arête above the overhang. Possibly unrepeated.
I. 7m From the foot of the crack in the right wall of the gully, hand-traverse right to climb the shallow groove in the blunt arête. Belay below the left side of the great overhang.
2. 18m Climb the left-hand side of the huge roof via the dubious protruding flake then make a long reach to gain a vertical flake on the wall. Finish up the arête. **Swinger** (VS 4c, 1968-73) is the crack in the right wall of Raven Rock Gully that can be used as a direct start to Via Dolorosa or as a route in its own right.

'The **finest VS** on grit...

…and therefore, by definition, the world' I tell them, laying on the hyperbole, 'quirky, intricate, dramatic….' They're indulging me because I'm so old; it's pretty well forty years since I did it and I have only the haziest of recollections, can't even remember who I was with, just have a sense of obscure and twisting line, devious little pitches, shadows, a slipping out on to the great slabbed prow of Valkyrie at some high-up point….

Jim Perrin on Via Dolorosa, Climber Magazine

🟦 Via Dolorosa
VS 4b, 4a, 4c ★★★   1913–24

33m A great historic climb, one of the very best of its grade in the area, which weaves a route up impressive terrain at a reasonable standard. Pitch 1 is very polished, and can feel like the crux. Start at the foot of the buttress left of a cave.

1. 8m Ascend a narrow polished slab (hard), then move up left through the polished holly tree to reach a ledge.

2. 10m Traverse left to the rib and follow a short crack, then a slab around to the left. Belay at a block by the arête.

3. 15m Climb boldly up right to a flake. Surmount this then move right round the arête and go up to the top just right of the arête. Sit down and enjoy the view.

🟦 Via Dolorosa Variations
S 4a ★★   traditional

28m By avoiding the polished corner (starting on the higher ledge on the right), and finishing left into Raven Rock Gully to avoid the last pitch, this superb climb can be enjoyed at a much lower standard.

Cold Bone Forgotten (E3 6b, 1988) is a problem over the lower roof left of Via Dolorosa with a side runner in the tree. Good fun in light showers.

🔽 A superb, long and powerful problem, **The Gutter**, starts in undercuts at the back of the cave at the foot of the buttress, coming out to slap up the angular arête up and left. V8 (6c).

🟦 Valkyrie Direct **HVS 5b** ★★   1951

25m A superb crack climb in this supreme setting, taking a steep direct line through the parent route. A good gritstone fight. Force a steep line straight up to the left side of the Valkyrie flake. From here, step slightly left, and finish up the obstinate crack to join Valkyrie.

🟦 Matinee **HVS 5a,5b** ★★★   1951

23m A magnificent, and very testing, exercise in jamming, this climb takes the huge, beautifully ugly crack, which splits the right-hand face of Raven Rock.

1. 15m Climb the sometimes green crack on glorious jams to a thread belay on the fine ledge (The Crevasse).

2. 8m Continue up the widening crack to the final bulge. Technicians will elegantly side-step this, but for mortals much humiliating floundering awaits.

Some **years** later...

...I went back to try to get some photos of the climb and was fortunate to find two young lads on the route. Meeting them at the top to congratulate them, I shyly mentioned that I had done the first ascent. At this they both went wide-eyed: the older one seized my hand, shook it vigorously and said: "You must be Joe Brown." Then, looking at me askance, he added: "But I always thought you were short and stocky with teeth like tombstones." Well, what else could I do but stay silent, try to look smaller, and give the toothiest smile I could muster?

Valkyrie pioneer, Peter Harding, on fame

❹❽ Valkyrie VS 4b, 4c ★★★   1946
38m Simply one of the best routes on gritstone – intricate, exposed and varied, and while it is *only* VS, it definitely climbs through HVS territory. The climbing demands an inventive approach, careful rope-work, and lateral thinking.
1. 15m Follow the corner then traverse left to a fine belay on the Crevasse. A nondescript pitch, also quite polished, the start of Pebbledash making for a much more sustained and interesting beginning.
2. 23m Climb up and over and down the huge flake until an awkward move left (all very thrilling) brings generally easier climbing up the forehead of the buttress.

Valkyrie Corner (HS 4b) *is the major corner taken in its entirety, and has a good big feel to it. The next routes all start from Valkyrie's Crevasse stance.*

Things **really** swung into action

at the beginning of 1979, in more ways than one. Rock Hall denizen, Dougie, came out of himself, producing an axe and scaring the shit out of three Oread Club members.

Not to be deterred, and on the same day, John Codling climbed the wall above Pebbledash, and called it Eugene's Axe. This was to be the first and last new route on the Lower Tier that year because of Dougie's insatiable appetite for climber's scalps!
Gary Gibson, Crags 20

❹❾ Northern Comfort E6 6c ★★   1996
10m Technical and slappy climbing up the overhanging wall, with a totally safe fall-out zone. From the crest of the flake on Valkyrie, climb diagonally leftwards to reach a rounded notch on the arête with difficulty (crux). Pull back right and follow the easier flake to the top.

❺⓿ Licence to Run E4 6a ★★★   1980
10m A superb fingery wall climb with some obscure moves. Protection is good but exhausting to place. From the stance, climb out right to, and up, a large layback flake until it is possible to break out right to another flake. Tricky moves up and right gain a finishing jug.

❺❶ Licence to Lust E4 6a ★   1987
10m Climb the wall to the right of Licence to Run to its second smaller flake. Step left and follow the thin crack-line to the top.

The Swan Wall

The steep wall to the right features perfect grit and a collection of routes generally marked by fierce fingery cranking, usually with a bit of heart-fluttering thrown in as well.

❺❷ Eugene's Axe E2 5c   1979
20m Climb the arête to the cracks above (very high side-runner at this grade). Use these to gain a ramp, and finish up this.

❺❸ Pebbledash HVS 5a, 4b ★   1969
1. 12m Climb the chimney and crack to a junction with the previous route. Scamper across the slab leftwards to the sanctuary of a belay ledge in the corner (or continue up Valkyrie).
2. 9m Climb the wide corner crack and escape through the tunnel or, better, climb the flake on the left to the top.

❺❹ Secrets of Dance E4 6a ★   1984
20m Fairly fierce. Follow Pebbledash to the crack above. From here, gain and follow the finger-ramp above. Finish via pockets and breaks. Not overly protected once out of the crack, but the climbing does ease, a little.

55 Against the Grain E6 7a ★★★   1985

20m A stunning fingery sequence above a relatively safe fall-out zone makes this a rare route at the grade. Easy ground leads to good cracks. From the cracks, step leftwards and make a desperate sequence of increasingly difficult moves on tiny edges diagonally leftwards to gain the sloping ramp on Secrets of Dance. Finish up this.

56 Thing on a Spring E6 7a ★★★   1986

20m One of Simon Nadin's most technical creations with some of the hardest climbing in Staffordshire. While not as sustained as the last route, it is ridiculously tenuous and the fall is not much fun, although probably unavoidable. From the cracks step right onto the ramp and foot traverse this to its end. Now compose yourself, and pop for the sloping break above. Thank your belayer, brush yourself down and try again. Once cracked, romp confidently to the top on much better holds.

On the **Swan Wall,**

at around 4m, is a carving supposed to represent a swan in flight; its age is unknown. The circular eye is obvious, but the eye of faith is needed to see the rest of the bird's body and wings. It was engraved when the ground was a lot higher.

57 The Swan E3 5c ★★★   1969

24m Manageable climbing in outrageous positions makes this a memorable lead. From the cracks (high runners), finger traverse out right. The footholds diminish as the handholds get bigger, culminating in a tough rockover to gain the rounded break. Follow the wide crack above to the top. It's probably wise (and usual) to consider what measures might be taken to curtail the massive potential swing.

The living end of grit technicality –
Andi Turner on Nadin's Against the Grain, E6 7a.
Photo: Turner collection.

58 Up The Swanee E4 5c ★ 1971

22m As for the Swan, but using the handholds for footholds across the traverse. Delicate.

59 The Mincer HVS 5b ★★★ 1951

20m Steep jamming with a tough reputation. Climb the crack (hard to start) through the stepped overhangs on jams, or, if you wish to avoid the point of the route, start direct. The overhang is the crux and will reduce all but the most adept to a flailing display of appalling technique. All that remains is the wide crack above.

60 Swan Bank E4 5c 1981

20m From The Mincer, make a move left to a flake and then go directly up to the wide crack above. Not well-protected, and involving the hard move up on The Swan.

Smear Test Slab

Thin smearing test-pieces mark out the climbing on this beautiful hanging slab, although the routes tend to be eliminates.

61 Smear Test E3 6a ★★ 1977

11m A good introduction to the harder slabs hereabouts. From the Mincer ledge, traverse horizontally rightwards to finish up the bottomless crack. An independent start can be made up left from the start of Pincer joining The Mincer at the overhang. This will still prove to be the crux for many!

62 Pincer VS 5a ★ 1957–68

20m A good bouldery start, but the top lacks direction. Follow the groove (crux) into Guano Gully. Ascend this until it is possible to step back left onto the slab to reach the bottomless crack.

Right: Sam Whittaker doing it the smart way.
The Mincer, HVS 5b. Photo: David Simmonite.

⑥ Bloodstone E5 6b ★★ 1983

19m A good eliminate, with some exposed slab climbing. Climb Pincer, or the bouldery bulge to the right, to the roof and good gear. Make a hard move over the overlap, the 'kicking bird' move, then blast directly up the slab. Runners are placed low in The Mincer, and in the upper crack. **Kicking Bird** (E4 6a ★, 1978) is another quality eliminate, although only differs from Bloodstone by avoiding the lower section of slab by climbing the crack on the left.

⑥ Bloodspeed E6 6b ★★ 1984

19m Probably the best line on this beautiful slab. From the ledge, smear up to the salvation of the crack (to find it isn't a crack). Climb this or the slab on its right. Very blank and insecure throughout.

⑥ Guano Gully HS 4b 1927

13m The gully to the right of Pincer, passing the boulder on its left.

⑥ Mousey's Mistake E2 5b 1978

15m Climb the gully passing the boulder on its right, then the slab on its left side. Bold and long undergraded.

In a way, **routes** like **Elegy** are easier to **solo**…

…because you know where you stand.
Although, there was that time in the 'seventies Phil Burke tried to solo it midweek. He got on the slab, got gripped, and just started screaming his head off, but, of course, there was nobody about. But then Dougie appeared at the top and looked over, and Burke was screaming, "Throw me a rope, quick!" Dougie disappeared, and when he came back, he tossed this loop of blue nylon rope down at Burke which tumbled down the slab and hit him – but Dougie hadn't tied it on to anything at the top, so the whole thing just snaked past Burke and fell to the ground, and so he just had to set off and shake his way to the top.
Ron Fawcett

Elegy Slab

Mousey's Mistake just brushes the edge of one of the classic slabs of gritstone. Its foot is guarded by an (almost) impassable overhang and so entry is by way of an awkward and character-building crack at its right-hand side, shared by the following three routes.

⑥ Elegy E2 5c ★★★ 1960

16m An absorbing route of the utmost quality, with a tough crux followed by a sizzling runout. With high gear in The Bulger pull left around the bulge (technical crux). Follow the flake left to its end then climb the slab above on smears and slopers (psycho crux). If you found this easy, then **A Little Peculiar** (E6 7b ★, 1993) climbs over the roof below to gain the flake direct. The crux features a one-armed footless mantelshelf onto the sloping lip, and may well be one of the hardest moves of its type in the world. Side-runners protect.

⑥ Clive Coolhead Realises the Excitement of Knowing You May Be the Author of Your Own Death is More Intense Than Orgasm E5 6b ★★ 1983

16m Start as for Elegy, but once round the bulge establish yourself over the flake (crux) and climb the right of the slab above. Takes longer to memorise the name than to do the route! Gear is placed in The Bulger and the Elegy flake.

69 The Bulger VS 4c ★ 1951
16m The crack climbed throughout. More difficult than would first appear and strangely rewarding.

The bouldery bulge and rib just right are **Dirty Wee Rouge** *(E3 6a†, 2003).*

70 Fledgling's Climb S 4a ★ 1927
13m A balancy route based on the left arête of the recess. Good footwork is required to start the wall, which is followed first left, then back right, to finish up the arête above. Good protection is sparse, and the route can be precarious when damp, so fledglings should beware.

71 Little Chimney Easy 1949–51
9m The little chimney in the left corner of the recess, surprisingly enough. Can provide a quick way down for the competent.

72 Battery Crack HS 4a 1968–73
10m The wide crack just right, with a tough exit out of the sentry box. Finish up the chimney.

73 Lucas Chimney S 1927
11m A good traditional thrutch up the wide chimney in the right corner, swinging desperately left to finish.

Kestrel Buttress

The attractive slim buttress to the right, and just above the roof of Rock Hall, with a powerful crack-line cleaving its centre.

74 Hawkwing E1 5b ★★ 1978
21m This weaves up the face giving reasonable, but sustained climbing, with protection that requires some care. Start just right of a chimney and follow a curving crack-line rightwards onto the front face to join the wide crack (Kestrel Crack). Climb this for 2m then traverse back left via the parallel slanting cracks to finish up the left arête.

75 Carrion E3 5c ★ 1980
19m A direct on Hawkwing. Climb over the triangular overhang right of Hawkwing, then continue straight up the centre of the buttress to finish up a short crack. **Poison Gift** (E3 6a, 1980) follows Carrion to the ledge, then hand-traverses a thinner, lower break out to the left arête to finish.

Fledgling's Climb, S (page 23). Photo: Niall Grimes.

The **natural** chamber,

now forming a sort of kitchen [to Rock Hall] has an interesting history. Before the cottage was built, it was lived in for nearly a century by a woman, Bess Bowyer, who was the daughter of a moss-trooper, 'Bowyer of the Rocks', once the terror of this neighbourhood. She herself was by no means a law abiding person, for the eccentricities of her dwelling place allowed her to shelter smugglers, deserters and other malefactors, and to outwit the authorities with success and impunity. A handsome girl, who passed as her daughter, was a still more romantic inmate of this weird habitation. She is said to have been heard often of a summer night singing in an unknown tongue among the crags. At last she was carried off by strange men, and the old crone was left disconsolate, afterwards being found dead in the cave she had lived in for so long.

E.A. Baker, Moors, Crags and Caves of the High Peak.

76 Kestrel Crack HS 4b ★★   1913–24
20m A great rounded gritstone climb, varied and well-positioned. Just right is an impressive groove. Climb this with stiff gymnastic moves (or a wedge and a squirm) to gain a ledge. (It is also possible to gain this point by coming in from the right.) The grand upper crack is made harder or easier depending on which way you face.

77 Headless Horseman E1 5b   1978
20m From the chockstone of Kestrel Crack, move out right to climb the striking arête on its left side. Poorly protected. **The Old Statesman** (HVS 5a, 1992) climbs a short flaky roof down and right.

78 Logical Progression E7 6c ★★   1998
18m An inventive solution to the challenge of the big blank wall. Make a desperate leftwards traverse of the lip to the obvious pockets (possible poor cam). Delicately rock up into these and finish more easily into Headless Horseman.

To the right of Logical Progression is a smooth wall which has so far only been breached by a 7a top

rope problem up the blunt nose and arête below the small triangular roof. Watch this space...

79 Flimney HVD   1957–68
18m Although somewhat overgrown, the necessary jungle bashing proves to be great fun. Climb a large flake left of the bushes and finish up the crack and corner behind.

80 The Death Knell E4 5c ★★★   1970
10m A bold route that deserves more attention. Climb the short arête, until a good hold can be attained in the crack. Using this, get established on the upper wall (crux), then continue more easily using either the crack or the arête. The original finish went up the heathery cracks on the left.

81 Rhodren HVS 5b ★★   1958
11m A great climb taking the stepped corner, with constricted undercutting making it a good warm-up for The Mincer.

To the right is a fallen flake forming an interesting arch, which marks the starts of the next two routes.

82 Flake Chimney D ★★   1949–51
14m A great adventurous little route. Layback the edge of the fallen flake, then 'walk the plank' into the corner on the right. The chimney leads to the top.

83 Straight Crack S 4a   1957–68
10m Bridge against the flake to start, then climb the crack just right of Rhodren.

Right of the arch is a buttress with an overhang at 3m.

84 Punch E4 6b   1957–68
14m At the left end of the overhang to the right, behind an ominous rhododendron is a short hanging groove, which is, unfortunately, often very green. Pull into this (crux) and climb the cracks above. Only for the gritstone thug.

85 Choka E1 6a ★★   1958
12m The large roof 3m right of Punch is overcome by gymnastic finger-jamming. Only the small detail of the offwidth above remains.

which reduces the grade to between HVS and E2 depending on how high you place it. The narrow slab just left has been climbed at E2 5c, using side-runners, and dubbed **Micro Storm**.

L - Nancy   8/3/04
8/8/04

⑨⓪ Prow Cracks D ★ *S - Zoe* 1957–68

10m Ascend using both cracks and a variety of technique. If you can't jam, you'll need to bridge and if you can't bridge, then learn to smear. A good first lead. Either of the cracks can be climbed independently, the left at VD, the right at HVD. Both are good exercises.

⑨① Commander Energy E2 5c ★★★ 1975

12m A route of tremendous exposure up the 'out there' arête. Climb the rounded right arête of the slab to the triangular roof. Pull over this on a good flake (spike runner) and layback dramatically up the flying arête above. The arête has also been climbed on the left, gained by a massive span from Prow Cracks; **Voila 3** (E4 6a†, 1989). Alarming.

⑨② Sumo Cellulite E4 6a ★ 1989

12m For the same exposure, only without the holds, climb the upper slab to the right of Commander Energy's flying arête. From below the roof, teeter right up the curving crack, before a precarious step up gains a thin hold, then continue direct.

⑨③ Rocking Stone Gully VD traditional

8m The chunky corner to the right lives up to its name. Elegant semi-layback moves avoid the half-way grovel.

L - Nancy   3/8/04
S - Zoe

⑨④ Captain Lethargy VD traditional

8m Climb the well-formed crack right of the corner. Finish on the left.

⑨⑤ Sifta's Quid HS 4c ★★ 1968

9m An entertaining climb, with an entertaining history. Climb to the ledge. Now either climb up over the bulge, or for much more fun, squeeze through the tunnel by the huge boulder under the roof. The scene of much amusing thrutching, most of it 'on the spot'. A classic Roaches rite of passage. The roof just to the left is breached by **Dougie Returns Home** (E1 5b†, 1992), having started directly up the slab.

⑧⑥ Circuit Breaker E3 6a 1980

10m From the crack, move immediately left to the arête and pull over the bulge. Place protection then climb the flake in the arête above to a pull over onto the slab.

⑧⑦ Hunky Dory E3 5c ★★★ 1975

10m A steep Roaches classic that requires a bit of effort. Climb the snaking crack until it is possible to break out right onto the resting ledge. Continue up the bold wall to an easier-than-it-looks finish. It is also possible to finish left at the top of the crack by means of a less bold 6a mantel. **Fluorescent Stripper** (E3 6a, 1985), continues artificially up and rightwards from the resting ledge.

⑧⑧ Prow Corner VD ★ 1957–68

12m The main corner is a good climb. Climb the tall crack and finish up the spectacular 'flying' crack. A good variation is to stick to the twin cracks on the right (HVD 4a ★) with a well-protected crux. All classic stuff.

⑧⑨ Chalkstorm E3 5c ★ 1977

10m A bold route requiring some concentration. Climb the centre of the slab on sloping holds and rockovers. Traditionally climbed with a side-runner,

Piece of Mind Slab

The main buttresses of the Lower Tier conclude with another famous slab, this one home to some of the boldest friction climbing on grit. Its routes are all excellent, serious and committing solos. The left edge of the slab has been climbed on its right-hand side at E3 6a.

96 Obsession Fatale E7 6b ★   1992
IIm The unprotected centre of the slab is climbed direct to its utterly blank and unforgiving crux at the very top. Regularly head-pointed but on-sight attempts have ended in North Staffordshire A&E on more than one occasion.

97 Piece of Mind E6 6b ★★★   1977
IIm The blunt central arête is a very serious proposition demanding the cleanest of technique and the coolest of heads. Balance up via scoops until a precarious step right can be made onto a faith in friction foothold and so the top. One of the first routes of its type on gritstone, well ahead of its time. A direct finish has also been climbed at a similar grade, **The Emergency Exit**.

Staffordshire was always a very important area for me.

I wasn't putting up the hardest routes there, but while I was doing my own first ascents around Sheffield, I would regularly go over to test myself against other peoples' routes, kind of like a gauge if you like, by which to measure myself, my own performance, my own routes. I remember one day doing *Bloodspeed*, *Script for a Tear*, *A Fist Full of Crystals*, *Barriers*, all E6s, all on-sight, then trying to finish off with *Piece of Mind*. I slipped off the last move and bounced all the way down the slab, then ran through the boulders, until my shoe lace caught on a tree root and stopped me. The lace probably saved my life.
Johnny Dawes

A new route, **Final Destination** (E8 6c, 2003), climbs the steep slab, starting as for the next route and finishing just right of Piece of Mind. As per usual on this slab, it is utterly serious.

Piece of Mind Bouldering

A very quiet circuit with masses of problems. They mostly tend to be short and, while there is good variety, many tend to be of the 'rollover' type, although there's a good selection of slabs and arêtes, as well as a few oddments. It gets the sun from first thing to last. Generally clean, but with the lack of traffic, some of the surfaces can be a bit biscuity.

PIECE OF MIND

❶ **Arête on Left**
V1 (5c)

❷ **Arête on Right**
V1 (5c)

❸ **Open Bum Cleft**
V3 (6a)

❹ **Sketchy Arête**
V2 (5c)

❺ **Adventurous Arête** V3 (5c)

❻ **Gentle Slab**
V0– (4a)

❼ **Mantel and Pocket** V0– (4a)

❽ V2 (5c)
Climb the arête on the right. A **sit-start** is V3 (6a).

❾ V3 (6a)
The steep narrow wall.

❿ V2 (5c)
Pad up the vague arête.

⓫ **Arête on Left**
V2 (5b)

⓬ **Arête on Right**
V2 (5c)
The **sit-start** is V4 (6a).

⓭ **Weird Little 5c**
V2 (6a)
The rounded arête of the boulder opposite 12.

⓮ **Chips Ahoy**
V2 (5b)
Sail directly up the slab from the first chip.

⓯ **Left and Up**
V0– (4b)

⓰ **The Stretch**
V3 (6a)
Gain the useless seam and use it.

⓱ V0– (5a)
Straight up from ramp.

⓲ **The Potty**
V0– (4a)
Pull into the scoop.

⓳ **Croissant Groove**
V2 (5c)

⑳ Scab V2 (5c)

Up the feisty crack from a sitting start.

㉑ Buster V5 (6b)

From the jams at the bottom of Scab, reach up and right to a blind flake. Move up and left and top out. Avoid the crack apart for the hands to start.

㉒ Jackpot V4 (6a)

Start as for Buster, but continue along the lip to make a rollover at the end. The **rollover** move alone is a sweet V0 (5a).

㉓ V0− (4a)

The little arête above a cutaway. A tough time can be had pulling **over the bulge** just right from a sitting start, V6 (6b).

㉔ V0− (4b)

Up the lazy wall.

㉕ Easy Arête
V0− (4b)

㉖ Slab and Crack
V0− (4c)

㉗ V1 (5c)

From the crack, rock leftwards.

㉘ Wildy's Right
V3 (6a)

The sharp arête on its right.

㉙ Wildy's Arête
V2 (6a)

The arête on its left. The sit-start is V5 (6b).

㉚ Easy Crack
V0− (4a)

㉛ V5 (6b)

Sticky wall on slopers.

㉜ Flake and Arête
V2 (5c)

A hard **sit-start** goes at V7 (6b). Or start from the flakes and **smear right** to the top of 31, scary V2 (5c). An **unclimbed project** goes left from the flake, along the lip, to mantel out above the rectangular chip on the wall below. Combined with the sit start, this would give a good tough problem.

㉝ Off Work V2 (5c)

Surrender you swine!

㉞ Left Off V3 (5c)

The left arête of the offwidth leads to a sketchy topout.

㉟ Twisted Crack
V4 (6b)

The wide crack can be climbed on its left or right sides, or directly by deviants.

㊱ Grewsome
V4 (6a)

Over the gruesome bulge.

㊲ The Jams V2 (5c)

㊳ V1 (5b)

The hanging arête of the slab.

㊴ V1 (5b)

The slab on round flakes.

㊵ V1 (5a)

Smear leftwards up the groove.

㊶ The Blob V1 (5b)

Up the arête to the blob.

㊷ Crinkles Wall
V5 (6b)

㊸ S Arête

The arête is unclimbed.

㊹ V1 (5b)

A quaint little slab.

㊺ Annie's Egg
V5 (6a)

Jump across the gap to gain the hanging scoop, and don't fall off.
Worth E4.

㊻ Radical Runnel
V2 (5c)

㊼ Justin's Arête Project

㊽ Little Mantel
V0 (5a)

㊾ Holly Mantel
V0+ (5b)

㊿ Flake and Groove
V0− (4a)

The land above the Abbey of Dieulacres (right of the Roaches) was known not only as 'Roches' but as 'Land of the Rush'; for frequently an angry rush of wind would come tearing down the slope from the 'Windygates' beside Hern's Cloud, as demons tried again to claim the body of the nobleman who had founded the Abbey.

The monks now called *Bel* (the supreme god of light) *Beelzebub* and *Baal-Zebul*, the 'lord of the flies'. In more recent times there are still reports of people being knocked down by 'the rush'.

Gordon Stainforth, The Peak, Past and Present.

The upper arête of Commander Energy is a thrilling
finale to one of the Lower Tier's best E2s (page 26).
Jim Graham climbing. Photo: Alex Messenger.

Ron Fawcett on The Thin Air, E5 6a. Photo: John Beatty.

98 The Thin Air E5 6a ★★★ 1980
9m Quality climbing on the right-hand side of the slab, above a serious landing. Starting in a scoop on the left, climb rightwards to a distinctive ripple whence an airy rockover gains the rounded and easily-fluffable top.

Lower Tier Girdle Traverses

The Golden Age of Girdle Traversing appears to have passed. In case it again becomes fashionable, the descriptions of three of the genre are included in all their original splendour.

99 The Girdle Traverse HVS 5a 1960
80m A wandering line but pleasant nonetheless. From almost the top of Bengal Buttress, traverse the chockstone and continue to join Valkyrie at the lip. Reverse this to the stance in the crevasse, then move right to the corner. Go up a short way, and move right across the great wall via high-level breaks. Descend into The Mincer and continue by a line almost at the top of the crag into The Bulger to finish.

100 The Underpass E1 5b 1963
50m A variant on the Girdle Traverse. From the end of the traverse on Bengal Buttress, reverse the crux of Crack of Gloom into the gully and pass rightwards beneath the chockstone into Raven Rock Gully. Continue the traverse round under the great overhang to meet Valkyrie Direct. Awkward moves gain Matinee which is followed almost to the top. Take the right-hand branch of the crack to finish.

101 The Super Girdle E4 5c, 6a, 5c ★★ 1980
45m Perhaps a hybrid, but still marvellous horizontal movement on the best of gritstone slabs.
1. 22m Follow The Swan, but continue at the same level to join The Mincer.
2. 11m Traverse Smear Test, place gear, then continue slightly downwards into Guano Gully by sustained tiptoeing.
3. 12m Move out again onto the Elegy slab, and traverse boldly across the slab horizontally to meet and finish up The Bulger. It is advised to step down and arrange protection in the flake of Elegy at halfway.

The Upper Tier

by Chris 'Gus' Hudgins

O.S. Ref. **SK005624**   Altitude: **425m a.s.l.**

The biggest, most classic and most popular section of the Roaches. The routes here offer a height and big feel rarely available on any other grit crag, and are well situated high up on the exposed ridge. The central sections are all very clean, and sometimes polished. Smaller sections to the left and right are a little quieter. One of the most impressive aspects is the stature of climbs from even the lowest grades, and for people operating up to HVS, some of the most memorable days out on grit are on offer here.

Conditions & aspect
Very exposed and quick drying apart from some climbs on the left-hand section that are sheltered by trees. Faces south-west and gets sun afternoon and evening.

Routes
Awesome, over 100 routes, with mighty cracks, corners and overhangs from Diff to E7. Everything you could ever want.

☑ Bouldering
Just as good, with 120 problems. The classic Upper Tier boulders, combined with problems on the crag, the Cellar and Attic and the Cube will keep you amused for a while. All styles and difficulties.

Parking & approach
The Roaches parking. Approach is under 10 minutes.

The Upper Tier is usually approached from the steps through the Lower Tier, in which case the first area encountered is the right-hand end of the Great Slab area, easily recognised by the spectacular capping overhang of The Sloth and the boulders comprising the venerable Upper Tier circuit. Descriptions start at the left end of the crag, 100m away.

Left-Hand Section

The Upper Tier starts in a rather unspectacular fashion on the far left, among the larch trees. Its left-hand side is defined by a worn track leading to the top of the escarpment. The buttresses to the left again are part of the Skyline, which stretches off into the distance. The first climbs lie on the small slab a few feet above the level of the main path.

L - Nancy 7/8/04

❶ Rooster D5 - Zoe   1957–68
7m Climb directly up sloping holds from the top of the leaning blocks to the ledge and tackle the jamming crack above.

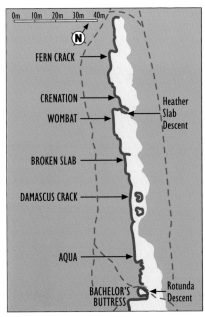

The Roaches Upper Tier

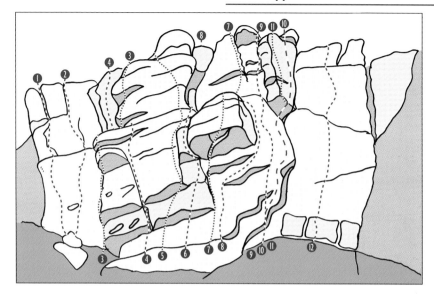

❷ Chicken Run S 4a   1949–51
12m From the top of the blocks, gain the long pocket then climb up on worrying polished rock. From the right side of the large ledge, and gear, move left taking care with more polished holds to the top.

❸ Freak Out E1 5b   1971
15m From below the arête, use pockets to reach a break. Continue around the bulge and climb up to gain the sloping ledge. Finish up the rounded arête above.

❹ Fern Crack HVD 4b ★★   1931
18m A good climb, which can be tackled in two pitches. A very steep (desperate) start allows a crack and flake to be gained. Make use of both of these to ascend to a thread and move left onto a ledge. A mantelshelf onto the next ledge remains before a possible belay is reached. Shuffle, or walk (depending on how comfortable you feel) leftwards all the way round the corner, to follow sloping holds up the right wall of the recess. Bring lots of slings.

❺ Demon Wall HS 4b   1945
15m Sensible rope work will enable the route to be climbed as a single pitch. Climb up to the left-hand

end of an overhang and make a steep and committing pull into a sandy corner, leading to a large ledge. From here, tricky moves on polished holds lead up the wall to the left of the chimney. **Heartbleed** (HVS 5b, 1979) pulls over the roof to the left to the ledge, followed by a direct finish.

❻ Perverted Staircase VS 5a   1958
12m Well named. The steep crack leading to the left-hand side of the overhang provides an uphill struggle. Obscene entertainment.

❼ Simpkins' Overhang E4 5c ★★   1979
14m A route that stresses both arms and the mind in equal measure. Climb steeply to the flake in the roof. Hand-traverse this with your feet on the wall for as long as you can (but not long enough!), before cutting loose, and then desperately trying to re-establish contact with something. Finally, pull over with your heart racing. The **Fantasy Finish** is a possible final pitch up the thin runnel at the back of the sandy ledge, at E3 5c†.

❽ Inverted Staircase D ★★   1931
21m A friendly wander up the groove on the right-hand side of the overhang, beginning below and

left at the lowest point. The groove leads to a huge party ledge on the left and a belay. From here the remaining squeeze through the small gap between the boulders provides a fun finale!

⑨ The Tower of Bizarre Delights
E3 5c ★   1978

16m This route follows the overhanging grooved tower and short crack above the corner of Inverted Staircase by intense and serious moves, until the short crack is reached.

⑩ Crenation E1 5a ★   1978

17m To the right is a triangular wall. Climb the rounded arête below this wall to a bulge. Move right from here round the corner to climb the triangular wall on hidden holds.

⑪ The Sublime E2 5b ★   1979

16m As for Crenation to the bulge. Burst over this, then power up the hanging arête.

⑫ Heather Slab HVD 3c   1949–51

14m The recessed slab to the right is climbed centrally and directly. The short wide crack is avoided just to its left. The right arête of the slab gives a worthwhile Severe. The gully to the right gives a Moderate, finishing left, while the right fork is the Heather Slab descent.

West's Wallaby Area

To the right lies an area of dramatic overhanging territory, set in tree enclosed surroundings. The wooded nature of this area affords shelter in windy conditions, the price being some dampness after wet weather. The following routes either tackle, or avoid, the impressive overhang at 5m.
Descent: The easiest descent is to skirt round to the left (facing in) of the crag, or use the Heather Slab descent.

⑬ Capitol Climb HS 4a   1954

14m A miniature mountain route. Climb the short corner near the left-hand side of the buttress. Step right between the roofs to gain the protruding nose, crux. Move round this to follow the crack on its right then the slab above.

Group use

The use of crags by large instructed groups is now a feature on the cliffs. However, these groups can sometimes monopolise routes and areas. It is good practice for the leaders of these groups to be sensitive to the needs and wishes of other users, particularly if another team is seeking to do a climb in a more traditional style.

Such ascents don't tend to take very long, and such courtesy will always foster good relationships.

⑭ Wombat E2 5b ★★★   1960

20m A rapid approach will pay dividends on this, the hard classic of the area. Attain the break below the roof. Good protection is available here, and in the flake early on, but is more dubious further out. Climb to the lip, and pull round on reasonable holds to the wide crack and easy slab above. A traditional runner in the adjacent tree is unnecessary, hard to arrange and well… cheating! **Wrong Way Round** (E2 5b,1979) is a dirty route avoiding the roof on the left.

⑮ Live Bait E4 5c   1981

20m To the right is a tiny flake on the wall. With difficulty, climb past this to reach the break. Move right to the hanging block, then explode leftwards across the roof at its widest point. An alarming reach then gains easier ground.

⑯ Walleroo E2 5c ★★   1960

20m More inverted pleasure. Neatly layback the crack to the great block. From the right-hand side of this block, difficult, fingery moves lead leftwards through the bulge into a faint groove; blind. Finish easily up the slabs above.

⑰ West's Wallaby VS 4c ★★   1960

23m A good climb that negotiates steep terrain at a modest standard. Climb to the block, then swing dramatically all the way to the gully. Move up and left from here to finish on slabby rock. A very good **Direct Finish** (5a) tackles the obvious steep challenge above the traverse, and is more satisfying, being much more in character with the rest of the route.

⓲ Between the Lines E4 6a   1986
20m Climb the thin crack and the arête on its right hand-side to the block. Move off the block to climb directly up the wall.

⓳ Late Night Final HVD   1951–57
20m Squirm, curse, and grunt up the overhanging chimney, and continue up the stony gully.

Maud's Garden Area

Right of the overhanging terrain of the Wombat section, the rock once again turns gentle and inviting, with a series of recessing slabs. There is a wealth of climbing here for the lower grade climber, and the routes are never busy. Climbs also tend to be well-protected, and all in all, it makes a great place for beginners to hone their skills.

Descent: Skirt the crag in either direction, or use the gully by Heather Slab.

⓴ The Valve E4 5c ★   1978
15m A bold route following the tower that looms over the gully on the right. Start on the left side of the arête, left of Beckermet Slab. Gain the ledge, then pull up the short overhanging wall just right of the arête to the base of the tower. Move right across the curving rampline then break out left to finish up the arête.

㉑ Beckermet Slab VD ★   1945
15m From the foot of the gully, bridge out to gain the horizontal break on the left wall. Swing onto this with difficulty, then move left to the arête. Gain a ledge above and finish up the slabby arête.

㉒ Maud's Garden VD ★★   1945
21m A tricky start that has been bold for nearly 60 years (which didn't prevent inexcusable recent attempts to manufacture nut placements) and a thrilling finale, with interesting climbing in between.
1. 12m Follow the well-trodden path up the centre of the slab with interest and as much technique as you can muster. This leads to a crack and protection. Press on to the sandy alcove and a belay.

2. **9m** Wriggle up the chimney and, at its top, step out left onto the wall, where good holds lead into more and more exposed territory and the top. The overhang direct is 5c. The right side of the slab is **Lybstep** (VS 4b, 1978).

㉓ Contrary Mary VS 4b ★   1951–57
15m A tricky pull over the low overhang gains easier ground among a sea of heather. This leads to a break above where the angle changes (not for the better!) and a bold finish up the headwall.

㉔ Coldfinger VS 4b   1978
15m Climb the arête, stepping out right above the overhangs at the top.

㉕ Reset Portion of Galley 37 HS 4a   1958
12m Ascend the corner until forced awkwardly right below the roof. Finish up the crack.

㉖ Broken Slab HS 4b   1945
12m A bold start leads to easier climbing with spaced protection. Ascend the wall direct, then bear right to reach a crack. A difficult move starts the crack, which is then followed to the top. Alternatively, a groove to the right of the slab can be taken to a direct finish, VS 4b.

㉗ Dawn Piper HVS 5b ★   1978
7m A worthwhile problem up the sharp arête, followed by easier climbing. **Skallagrigg** (HVS 5b, 1997) is the steep wall on the left. It is clean and technical in its lower half, although the crack must be avoided at the grade.

㉘ Runner Route S 4a ★   1955
11m From the corner, pad delicately rightwards across the slab. Mantelshelf onto the break (good runner), then move left to the holly and continue up the crack behind it. **Jog**, (HVS 5b, 1996) climbs just left of Runner Route to the hanging slab. Climb this slab, artificially avoiding the left edge.

㉙ Ging E1 5c   1996
11m Climb the slab, heading for the 'headwall'. From there, layaway off the right edge to reach the horizontal break and so to the top, with a runner in the crack on the left

㉚ Damascus Crack HS 4a ★★   1955
12m The polished crack provides excellent protection and good climbing. After reaching the ledge, follow slightly suspect flaky rock up the buttress above. A finish up the short crack in the tower up and left is VS 4b, making a superb exposed finish.

The list below is suggested with the novice leader in mind. Those emerging from the climbing walls, uncertain where to begin, might find it useful as an introduction to the outcrop's easier climbs and a stepping stone to its fine portfolio of challenging Severes… steps that are well worth observing in the process of fully learning key skills (most notably route finding, runner placement and belaying) before embarking on harder things.

Lower Tier

Raven Rock Gully looks uninviting but develops into quite a challenging slot with the crux (very safe) as the final move. Good fun at night with a headtorch and also in wet conditions when it gives a real speleological struggle; *Prow Corner* – straightforward crack work amidst impressive rock scenery.

Upper Tier

Left-Hand Route – steep entertaining jug pulling on a minor buttress. *Right Route* – well-protected and straightforward but in a fine position. Not hard for the grade. Don't miss out the final pitch; *Pedestal Route* – a journey amidst spectacular rock scenery. With the overhang of *Technical Slab* forming the dramatic exit this must be considered the top of its grade … an exciting outing; *Black Velvet* – tough for its grade and replete with challenging but well-protected moves. Tails off at the finish which is more of a relief than a defect; *Jeffcoat's Chimney* – a big line up an impressive cliff. The final pitch offers great excitement and is often avoided. Another good headtorcher. *Beckermet Slab* or *Maud's Garden* – rather unprepossessing climbs that provide useful training at a steady standard. *Inverted Staircase* – an excellent test-piece at the grade amidst fine rock prows, technically harder than the more exposed *Right Route*.

Skyline

Lighthouse – Short but entertaining; *Perched Block Arête* – interesting climbing amidst problems of a far higher standard; *Karabiner Chimney* – a poor man's *Central Buttress of Scafell* complete with its imitation *Great Flake*.

Twelve fine climbs in the lower grades on the Roaches

Jill Whittaker reaches the belay ledge on Maud's Garden, VD (page 35). Photo: Alex Messenger.

③ Third Degree Burn E2 5b ★   1978
9m Unprotected climbing in as direct a line as possible up the wall.

③ Libra HVS 4c ★   1957–68
14m The technical crack-line becomes increasingly tricky near the top. From here, the route wanders left and up a small tower on some awesome pockets.

The Central Massif

The next section is a little steeper, but again, routes are marred a little by heather.

Descent: Go right (facing in) to the Rotunda descent.

③ Joe Public HS 4a   1978
18m Just round right from the arête, start up a groove, or the wall just right (4b), or the wall just right again (4c) to gain the break. Take the best rock from here to finish up an enjoyable steep crack. **A Day at the Seaside** (VS 4b, 1982) is a poor route taking the centre of the wall and slab to the left, finishing over a small triangular roof, while **The Attempted Moustache** (VS 4c, 2000) is a counter line to that, gaining the ledge from the left using a pleasant rib, then finishing via heather and a short crack.

③ Lone Ascent VS 4c   1951–57
18m Right again, just out of reach, is a good, but often green hold in the middle of a good, but often green wall. This is gained by delicate moves, a long reach, or a hoofing big jump. Move up and right in a rather intimidating position up the often green wall to the left of a crack, to a final wide, often green crack. Good if you like green things.

③ Little Perforations E2 6a   1985
15m Climb the vague scoop in the wall just right. Technical and reachy moves constitute the crux above a faint horizontal break. Finish easily straight up.

③ Central Massif HD   1945
15m Climb to a large protruding flake on the right, then go direct in the same line to the top. Better and

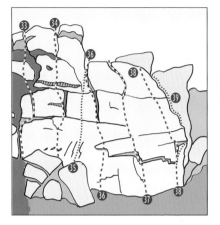

easier than it looks. **Wipers** (VS 4b, 1978) takes a strict direct line up the wall 2m left and finishes up the right arête of the upper wall.

③ Aqua VS 4b ★★   1954
12m One of the better routes in the area. The obvious crack-line through the roof yields easily to finesse. The rest is often covered in an assortment of vegetation but is luckily a lot simpler.

③ Quickbrew E2 5c ★   1981
12m Stiff! A massive jug in the hanging right arête enables protection to be placed before a cunning move or a desperate pull round the roof on brick edges. **Public Enemy Number One** (HVS 5a, 1979) takes a parallel line 1m left.

③ Tealeaf Crack S 4a ★   1957–68
12m Climb up to the square overhang. Move around this on the right to a crack. A difficult move up and a step left gain the pleasant arête above.

Cornflake (M, 1957–68) is the chimney up and right, which manages to avoid all vegetation to give some good climbing. **A Short Trip to a Transylvanian Brain Surgery** (S, 1978) is a pleasant route which climbs the front face of the buttress. A steep move near the top is fortunately well-protected.

Rotunda Descent: The best descent in this area is to come down the stepped rocky ramp to the left of the Rotunda, the next feature. This breaks into two branches, both of which are reasonable.

40 Rotunda Buttress VS 4c   1945

18m Start at a wide crack left of the gully. Follow this for 3m before moving up and left with some concern to a ledge. Ascend rightwards, then left to another ledge below an arête. The steep final wall provides the punch.

41 Rotunda Gully M   4000BC

15m A bit of a non-climb. Climbing the crack in the left-hand face is a better option as an alternative finish at HVD, making the outing almost worthwhile.

Black and Tans Area

The Upper Tier starts to flex its muscles from here on, giving lots of high quality, long climbs. The first couple of buttresses lie to the left of the towering smoothness of Great Slab, and give a good range of high quality lower grade climbs, with a few desperates thrown in for good measure.

Descent: Walk down to the left of Rotunda Buttress.

42 Bachelor's Buttress VS 4b ★   1922

18m This ancient classic offers delicate mantelshelving in exposed situations. Climb the slab to the gully. Traverse the hanging slab up and right, past a nut placement. Summon your courage, then move up to a short crack and the top. A direct finish (VS 4c), goes directly up from the middle of the traverse.

43 Gypfast E4 5c ★★   1979

18m The underside of the roof gives a very exciting ride. Follow the great roof rightwards, to its widest point, on flakes that are better than they look (protection in the lip of Saul's Crack, and Bachelor's Buttress). A direct start up the centre of the slab is 5c.

44 Something Biblical E2 6a ★   1987

18m Climb the slab to the roof. Using the protection offered by Saul's Crack, but not the holds, pull through the roof. Finish up the wall above.

The Upper Tier: Right-Hand Section

45 Saul's Crack HVS 5a ★★★   1947

18m The Master's first addition to the Roaches; perfectly protected, but it makes you work for it. Amble up the crack to a niche and make an easier-for-the-short move (at last!) to pass this. The corner above requires proficient jamming to ensure you have enough puff left for the final intimidating roof. Keep going, the holds are there.

46 Humdinger E1 5b ★   1969

18m Follow the wall to a tiered overhang, and a jug on the lip. From here, a tormenting move gains (or doesn't) the obvious yet distant hold above.

47 Jeffcoat's Chimney VD ★★   1913

24m A historic classic of considerable character, one of the Upper Tier's first climbs.

I. 18m The slippery chimney is followed past a cave to an accommodating belay ledge. Going right at 3m and regaining the chimney where the wall steepens is Diff.

2. 6m From the left hand edge of the ledge, move right by a long step and go up to the overlap. Move left from here to an easy finish.

48 Jeffcoat's Chimney Variations
HS 4a, 4c ★   **traditional**

I. 18m The unprotected left wall of the chimney is followed boldly to the cave. Gain the left arête and climb this and the left wall above to the ledge.
2. 6m Boulder up the wall from the right to escape left.

49 Jeffcoat's Buttress   HS 4c, 4a ★★★   1913
A tremendous route, with consistently difficult, varied and enjoyable climbing.
I. 18m A technical fingery start (avoidable) leads to better holds and an easier corner. Follow this, then perform an impressive but straightforward traverse right above the roof to a belay beneath two cracks.
2. 9m Follow the cracks above the belay to finish.

50 Hanging Around   HVS 5b   1978
24m Climb the bulging wall, then continue direct to reach the large cracked roof. Move strenuously right beneath the roof until technical moves gain the crack above.

51 Ruby Tuesday   E2 5b, 4b, 5b ★★   1971
30m A big undertaking involving both bold and plain hard climbing.
I. 12m Climb directly up to the overhang. Powerful moves over this lead to a niche. From here, delicate climbing on small holds leads rightwards to the belay.
2. 6m Move easily left and up to the next belay.
3. 12m Follow cracks, then forsake these for a bold traverse to gain and climb an overhanging arête and chimney. An alternative (should you for some strange reason want something harder and more committing) bisects the traverse midway by pulling directly through the roof and to the top, at E4 6a.

52 Black and Tans   S 4a, 3c ★★★   1922
30m A fantastic climb, classic in every sense, with a technical crux on the lower corners, and a psychological crux on the upper slab.
I. 12m Climb a shallow corner to a ledge (a runner hereabouts will be appreciated by the second), then shuffle left to belay in the next corner.

2. 18m Climb the corner above and follow a good break left onto the nose. Continue directly by means of exposed mantelshelves and good pockets.

53 Black and Tans Variations
HVS 5a ★   traditional

26m Climb the wall directly to the first corner, then tackle the wall above the ledge to cross the upper overhang just left of Black Velvet.

54 Black Velvet   HVD 4a ★★   1957–68
27m Classy climbing taking a good direct line up some impressive terrain. Climb to the first hanging corner, as for Black and Tans. Pull steeply up the cracked wall above, and continue to pass the roof on the right.

55 Diamond Wednesday   HVS 5a ★   1978
26m A good, well-protected, if slightly artificial, climb. From the holly, follow the slim groove and crack to a small triangular roof. An awkward move round this leads to slabby breaks above.

The Great Slab

To the right lies a towering bastion of top quality grit, giving routes up to 30m in height, where soaring slabs are punctuated by small ledges and unlikely overhangs. All the routes here have a big feel about them, with lots of splendid multi-pitch adventures, superb crack-lines and some of the most spectacular roof climbs to be had anywhere. Unsurprisingly, this quality has led to great popularity which, over 90 years of sport, has left a few of the routes quite polished, so beware. High and exposed, it catches the wind but dries quickly.

Descent: The best descent is to walk right (facing out), and come down past the Rotunda.

56 Hollybush Crack   S 4a ★★★   traditional
26m The major crack-line is a fine big pitch. Bridge the chimney, avoiding getting bitten by the holly, and step into the wide crack. Follow this, with good holds and protection, all the way. This climb was previously described as finishing, somewhat illogically, up what is now The Neb Finish.

57 The Neb Finish   VS 4b ★★   1957–68
25m Reasonable though rousing climbing, crossing the hanging sidewall. Once over the overhang on Hollybush Crack, arrange a high runner. Step down again, and traverse rightwards on pockets, feet just above the lip, further and further away from that runner, to a finish near the arête. (Previously the finish of Hollybush Crack.)

The following 2 routes meet Hollybush Crack at the big overhang.

58 Technical Slab   HS 4a ★★   1945
23m A brilliant exposed route, high in the grade due to its technicality and seriousness. Ascend the slab, with delicate stretches between well-spaced holds, and distant protection, to the roof. From here, the Neb Finish makes for a three star combination (although be careful with the ropework).

59 Pedestal Route   HVD 4a,3c ★★★   1922
27m Engrossing for the grade and a good day out.
I. 12m Climb by any means to the large ledge at 4m. From the centre of this, layback either side of the flake to a dainty mantel onto the pedestal, and belay.
2. 15m Shuffle leftwards and use the break awkwardly to gain a standing position. Continue left into the corner, before moving over a small roof by bridging the gap. Finish steadily up the corner.

(**Hint:** A cleverly placed nut at the small roof will avoid the feeling that you are pulling your belayer up the route as well as yourself!)

60 Gillted   E5 6a† ★   1979
30m The first of the big climbs crossing the Great Roof. From the corner on the left, follow the obvious handrail running rightwards to its end. Swing blindly round under the very lip of the overhang to reach the cave (large sling runner). Exit up and right via a pocket. This finish is desperate, and may be unrepeated, the only known repeat went up the arête on the left. Previously given E4, it is possibly harder than Painted Rumour.

61 Painted Rumour   E6 6a ★★★   1985
26m This mighty route attacks the gigantic overhang at its widest, wildest point by some strenuous

and scary yarding. Stuff in some gear before climbing out to the cave where a spike runner and a leg hook rest can be taken. Peel and eat a banana, then pull leftwards out of the cave and move up the headwall on sharp rugosities (crux) to finish.

⑥ The Sloth   HVS 5a ★★★   1953

24m Superb, intimidating and steeped in legend – a route to bring out the Whillans in you. Climb to The Pedestal. Move up to the 'cheeseblock' (sling runner), and launch out across the juggy flakes to the lip and wide crack above. Protection is available on the way but have you the strength to place it?

⑥ Loculus Lie   E5 6a ★★   1983

28m One word: exposure. From the lip of The Sloth, make a breathtaking traverse leftwards in the middle of nowhere. Excitement builds to near-unbearable levels until the cave is gained by a blind reach. Finish as for Painted Rumour. The original line reached left from the cheeseblock onto suspect flakes before moving back to the lip of The Sloth. This is rarely climbed and the route is just as superb without.

⑥ New Fi'nial   E6 6b† ★★   1985

28m The meat of this route is a powerful rightwards traverse from The Sloth, in a mega 'out there' position along the very lip of the roof. Sloping holds, heel-hooks, and a cool, cool head are pressed into service to pass the crucial short crack 5m along before heading for the top.

⑥ Central Route   VS 4b ★★   1949–51

15m Serious climbing on small, and rather shiny, holds. Follow the slab directly, then traverse under the overhang to the belay ledge of Right Route. High in the grade, and remember the second when placing gear.

⑥ 99% of Gargoyles Look Like Bob Todd
E5 6b ★   1986

24m An obscure classic with some hard and bold climbing. Arrange protection in a suspicious collection of brittle breaks and flakes above Central Route. Pull desperately into the groove and continue with care.

⑥ Right Route   VD ★★   1922

24m Morley Wood's early addition is one of the most popular routes on the crag, although novices may be unnerved by some of the frictionless footholds.

1. 15m Follow a line of pockets to the roof (take care not to jam protection). Make nervous moves left and then up more easily to the large ledge.

2. 9m Balance leftwards over the void to reach the crack which leads to the top. Initially precarious, the climbing soon eases.

In January 1953, **Don Whillans...**

...the 'Villain', was staying with Joe Brown in the barn below the Roaches.

"Hey, how about having a go at the big overhang?" Joe Brown said suddenly.

"What now? In this?" The snow was drifting down quite thickly.

"Why not. It'll be dry under the overhang," he said.

A mob followed the two to the cliff, where Whillans won the toss for the lead. From the stance below the overhang, he jammed outwards along the roof.

"By this time I was committed. I jammed my way along the crack until only the heel of my foot remained on the flake. I reached out over the lip of the overhang for a hold above it and my foot came off the flake. I was hanging free from the tip of the overhang. I quickly pulled up, jammed a foot in the crack, and pulled over the overhang. I was up. Easy if you use your loaf."

from Don Whillans: **Portrait of a Mountaineer**

68 Right Route Right VS 4b ★ 1957–68
15m As for Right Route to the roof. Thrutch over this to gain the corner and the top. **Kelly's Connection** (HVS 5a, 1957-68) takes a strenuous traverse line from the roof to the large pocket on Kelly's Direct.

69 Laughing all the way to the Blank
E4 6a 1993
14m Follow Kelly's Direct to the ledge and then move directly up the groove above to the large vegetated break. Pull out confidently onto the scary headwall and proceed thoughtfully to the top.

70 Kelly's Direct E1 5b ★ 1968–73
15m Climb the thin crack to a ledge. Taking some care to place protection here, move precariously up, right and out to reach a thin flake before making an impressive lunge to a large pocket. Take further pockets from here in a direct line to the top.

71 Kelly's Shelf S 4a ★ 1924–49
17m Using excellent handholds, make an elegant step or graceless flop (delete as appropriate) onto the shelf, then caterpillar along it to a finish up a crack. An alternative finish over the bulge to gain pockets is HS 4a.

V Kelly's Pockets
The flat wall below Kelly's Shelf is covered in an assortment of pockets, lending themselves to an infinite number of problems and variations. Traversing from below Paralogism to join these can be done at up to V6 (6b).

72 Paralogism E7 6c ★★★ 1987
15m Awesome! This Nadin masterpiece is widely acclaimed as one of grit's hardest roofs, featuring blind slappy bouldering in a position of great danger. Starting at the right arête, make committing moves to gain the hanging coffin. A blind slap gains small holds on the left, before crossing the roof leftwards on better holds. From the lip, move right to a careful finish. Has been soloed on-sight.

The scooped overhang to the left, one of the last gaps on the Upper Tier, has been top-roped at 7a, but still awaits the lead.

73 Antithesis E5 6c ★★ 1980
15m An overlooked technical masterpiece. From the ledge up right, desperate, intricate moves lead leftwards to an outstanding position on the nose and a direct finish. A cheeky runner high in Bed of Nails protects a swooping winger, not forgetting to keep your feet high!

74 Bed of Nails E2 5b ★ 1978
12m From the gully above the ledge, traverse the break leftwards to the base of the wide slanting crack. Climb this awkwardly to a niche before finishing easily up the left arête.

75 Easy Gully Wall VD 4a 1957–68
21m Bold, technical climbing leads to a sandy ledge. Trend rightwards to a short layback crack and a bulge. Move up and traverse left below the overhang to finish up a wide crack.

76 Jelly Roll VS 4b, 4b ★ 1957–68
23m Another good route that reaches the whole height of the crag.
l. 8m Climb the thin crack to belay on the block. Strenuous.

The Upper Tier Boulders

The ultra-classic Roaches circuit. Hard rock, hard problems and good landings combined with shelter and quick drying make this the most popular of the Roaches areas.

Boulder A

① Juggy Groove
VI (5b)

② The Nose V5 (6b)
Start from the low beak. The **standup** version is V4 (6a).

③ Vague Arête VI
(5c)

④ Right Groove
V2 (6a)
The low start to the narrow groove is V6 (6c).

⑤ Left Groove
V4 (6b)
Classic. **Eliminating** the chipped foothold is V5, and the **sit-start** is a tough project.

⑥ Higginson's Arm
V9 (6c)
An eliminate lip traverse starting under Left Groove and finishing up The Nose. Ask a local for full details.

⑦ One Inch Punch
A bendy project up the centre of the wall. Hold-wise, if you can see it, it's not in.

⑧ Flakes and Chips
V0+ (5b)
Without the chips it is V4 (6b) A **sit-start** is V4 (6b).

⑨ Easy Groove
V0− (4c)

⑩ Arête on Left
VI (5b)

⑪ Seams Polished
V2 (5b)

⑫ Slippery Groove
V0 (5b)

Boulder B

⑬ V4 (6b)
Climb the nose from a hanging start.

⑭ Broken Wing
V7 (6b)
From the start of 13, traverse left to finish up 15.

⑮ VI (5b)
Up the wall past the breaks.

⑯ VI (5c)
Traverse right past two diagonal breaks to finish up the far arête.

Boulder C

⓱ Jug Up VI (5b)
Go up on bumper holds from the low jug.

⓲ Glued Up V2 (5c)
From the glued flake, climb the wall to the finish of 17. **Dynoing** between the two is a hard V8 (6c).

⓳ V6 (6c)
Hoist up to the top from the sloping finger rail.

⓴ VI (5c)
From the sidepull flake to the top.

㉑ Nadin's Traverse V7 (6c)
Not 'im again! From the start of 17, traverse right and finish up 20.
Or, keep going and finish with Staircase at V8, or (you're getting tired now) keep traversing, with hands just below the top and finish with Cooper's Traverse, at a V9–.

㉒ Staircase VI (5b)
The chunky flake from a sit-start.

㉓ Mantel VI (5c)

㉔ Cooper's Traverse V3 (5c)
Monkey along the lip to easy ground. V5 **footless**.

㉕ V4 (6b)
Sit-start and over the bulge.

Boulder D

㉖ Joe's Portholes V0– (4b)
Gain the top from the big hole. A **sit-start** is VI (5c). A desperate eliminate, **Mean Ol' B'stard** V8 (6c), starts in the low hole and sidepull to the right, snatches the micro-gaston right of the porthole, and finishes off left.

Apocalypse Now dynos from bottom to top at a lanky V7 (6c).

㉗ V2 (5c)
An eliminate using thin flakes.

㉘ V7 (6c)
A harder eliminate avoids the better flakes on the right.

㉙ Joe's Arête V3 (6a)
Doff your cap to the old master by climbing the polished arête. The cleanest of technique (and boots) is needed to unlock the key, but once done, it all falls into place. Variations possible, including one handed ascents. Traversing to the arête from the porthole of 26 is V3 (6a).

㉚ Big 'Oles V0– (4c)

Boulder E

㉛ Don's Crack V0+ (5b)
Climbing **between the crack and the right arête** is V4 (6a).

㉜ Don's Arête V0– (4b)

Boulder F

㉝ Easy Mantel V0– (4b)

㉞ V2 (5c)
Start from a hanging crouch and mantel through the scoop.

㉟ Arête on Right VI (5c)

㊱ Arête on Left VI (5b)

㊲ Crimpy Wall V0 (5b)

Boulder G

㊳ V0– (4c)
Move up and right.

㊴ V0– (4c)
Climb up and over the nose.

Boulder H

㊵ Short Arête V2 (5c)
Sit-starts vary from V3 to V6 depending on what you use.

㊶ The Boss V5 (6b)
Over the lip using the boss. Careful with those shins, now.

㊷ Knees Up V3 (5c)
The rising finger traverse to the top of 41. A tricky **sit-start** using the pinches and undercuts is V6 (6b).

㊸ V4 (6a)
From the round hold, rock directly up and left.

㊹ Grand Theft VI0 (6c)
The classic lip traverse from the left arête to finish up 41. Could still go all the way.

㊺ Left Arête V0 (5b)

One of the many new desperates that have been added to the classic Roaches bouldering circuit. Andi Turner on Grand Theft, V10 (page 45). Photo: Niall Grimes.

High Quality **Bouldering**

🅥 If you like your bouldering spiced up with a bit of height, there are a few venues you might like to visit. **The Cube** and the **Doug-less Boulde**r on the Roaches, **The Aiguille** on Hen Cloud and **Oldridge Pinnacle** in the Churnet all hold routes that have been traditionally seen as bold solos or badly protected leads. However, with their flat landings and the advent of modern pads, these can be best enjoyed as highball bouldering, and all provide tough cranking, with that extra bit of challenge thrown in for extra reward.

2. 15m Boldly follow the wall to a spectacular hanging groove. Follow this to finish as for Crack and Corner.

⑦ Magic Child HVS 5a   1978
7m Gain holds leading right to the large pocket. Hand-traverse the ledge above leftwards before moving up, and right again to finish.

⑱ Ped X-ing E3 5c   1997
11m Climb directly to the break and gain much-needed protection. From here move up and search desperately for adequate holds among a selection of appalling slopers.

⑲ Roscoe's Wall HVS 5b ★★   1955
11m Impressive but amenable once the bouldery start is solved. A stiff pull above a somewhat worrying landing gains the niche in the centre of the pink wall. Swing right and up on fantastic holds and wish that there were more. Round Table makes a superb continuation pitch for the unsatisfied.

⑳ Crack and Corner S 4c, –, 4a ★★   1922
35m A classic long expedition with a desperate start and a thrilling finish, where you should spare a thought for the original pioneers with tweeds, plimsolls, and no belays.

Climbers high on Crack and Corner, S (page 47).
Photo: Dave Garnett.

I. 12m Jam, layback and swear your way into the undercut crack, which will take more gear than you can possibly put in.

2. 8m Wander left along the ledge to a belay.

3. 15m Pockets above lead to a large ledge on the left. The corner then leads to a superb finale: the roof. Layaway off the crack, get your feet high on the wall, and streeetch for a hidden jug!

Alternatively, **Bud Love (E4 6a ★, 1996)** moves left along the parallel cracks on the third pitch to an even more imposing view of the overhang. From here, a flake is used to surmount this (hopefully) rapidly.

81 Babbacombe Lee E1 5b ★   1978

11m A broken line, but giving good exposure. Boulder up the left hand end of the undercut wall, and follow a short crack to a contorted rest and a bold, reachy finale over the nose.

✪ Babbacombe Bouldering

A few problems lie on the undercut wall. **Babbacombe Start V1 (5b)** is the start of the route, as far as the ledge. A gnarly **sit-start** to this is V7 (6c). The steep blank wall to the right has a vague fingerhold at its centre. **Go Left V7 (6c)** hangs this then moves up and left on minimal holds, and **Go Right V6 (6b)** starts the same but rocks up right for a sharp sidepull. **Hanging Start V5 (6b)**, hangs the finger-jug on the lip further right, then swings footless for hopeful holds diagonally right.

82 Destination Venus HVS 5b   1979

24m A traverse of the lower wall from right to left. From the ledge on Babbacombe Lee, move into Crack and Corner. Step down before making difficult moves left into the niche on Roscoe's Wall. Traverse left passing the large pocket into Jelly Roll.

83 Hangman's Crack S 4a   1949

11m An interesting climb. The right-hand side of the wall leads to a large black roof flake. Step left to attack the wide crack. Difficult to protect.

The next two routes start from the ledge above the lower buttress, and take imposing lines up the steep rock above.

84 Trebia E4 6a †   1981

10m Difficult moves up the undercut rib lead to a niche below the final roof. Take this direct at a shallow hole.

85 Round Table E1 5a ★★   1974

11m A route of surprisingly low grade taking the impressive crack and finishing at the highest point of the buttress. Steep and committing moves lead into the wide crack. Swing right across the bulge to an easy finish.

Blushing Buttress

Down and right is a fine compact buttress, with good steep routes based on strong crack-lines and friendly flakes. The rock is excellent, and it is a good escape from the hordes on Great Slab.

86 Scarlet Wall HS 4b   1949

11m Crank up the crack on the left of the buttress and move right to a large ledge. Move up carefully to a thread runner and precarious exit. The slab just left provides a bold HS 4a variant.

87 War Wound HVS 5c   1978

11m A difficult but very contrived start leads past a break to a large ledge. From the left edge of this, climb the bold, slabby arête.

88 Left-Hand Route HVD 4a ★   1924

13m Good climbing, steep at the start then delicate further up. Layback the hanging flake past the left-hand end of a roof, then trend delicately ever upwards.

89 Right-Hand Route S 4b ★★   1924

13m An elegant line, steep and clean. A hard layback start on shiny footholds (avoidable on the right) leads to a ledge. From here tackle the easier than it looks roof crack above.

90 Aperitif HS 4b   1968–73

25m A rising traverse of the buttress from left to right. Start low in a cave to the left of Scarlet Wall. Traverse right along the lip to the crack of Scarlet Wall, then hand-traverse into Left-Hand Route.

Cellar and Attic Bouldering

This is the small area above Blushing Buttress. The problems give some good entertainment. More problems exist around the back, but the quality of the rock is such that it is hard to see the bouldering being worth the erosion.

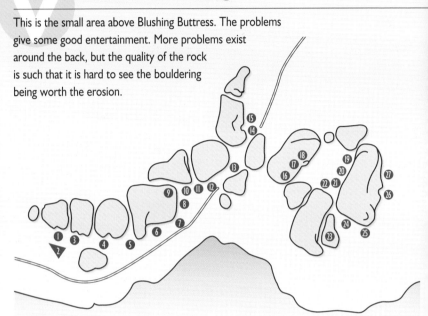

❶ Sitdown Crack
V1 (5b)

❷ V4 (6b)
From holds near the top of Sitdown Crack, traverse left to easy ground.

❸ Roof Problem
V1 (5a)

❹ The Squirm
V0+ (5a)
Climb the thin crack, then squirm through the jaws above.

❺ The Finger
V1 (5b)
Climb the arête then move left up the finger.

❻ Little Wall
V0 (5b)

❼ V0− (4b)
Surmount the bulge above the crack.

❽ V1 (5b)
Gain the flake on the wall.

❾ Arête V2 (6a)
Layback the awkward arête.

❿ Sexy Steve
V3 (6a)
Snatchy crimping up the wall left of the crack. It can be **dynoed** from the lower crimps at V7 (6c).

⓫ Scrack V0− (4b)

⓬ Reachy Wall
V2 (6a)

⓭ V0+ (5a)
Move directly up the wall from the runnel. **Handy Traverse.** A good warm up traverse is possible from problem 6 to 13 at V1 (5b). Pleasant.

⓮ Arête V0− (4b)

⓯ Risky Runnel
V1 (5b)
A lovely problem following the open runnel to a harrowing top-out.

⓰ Fingery Slab 1
V1 (5b)

⓱ Fingery Slab 2
V1 (5c)

⓲ Easy Groove
V0− (4a)

⑲ V0– (4c)

⑳ **Tiny Groove**
V0– (4b)

㉑ **Right Slab**
V0– (4a)

㉒ **Cellar Dwella**
V8 (6c)
A one move wonder using sidepulls to gain the top.

㉓ **The Gates**
V4 (6a)
The thin slab on the leaning boulder.

㉔ **Crinkly Wall**
V2 (5c)

㉕ V4 (6b)
Surmounting the bulging arête is remarkably similar to giving birth. Only harder.

㉖ **The Downpipe**
V5 (6b)
Somehow try to ascend the angry pipeline on the front of the boulder.

㉗ **Pipe Entry**
V7 (6b)
From a sitting start on a blind flake, pull up to the lip. From here, go left to the pipe's lip and up. Alternatively, **crank up and right** to mantel using the thin flake. Spoiled for choice?

Follow this for a few moves until it is possible to reach the ledge on Right-Hand Route. Swing right strenuously to reach the gully, then continue right across the next buttress.

(91) Gully Wall VS 4b — 1957–68
9m The large flakes lead steeply upwards to an awkward move left to gain the nose of Right-Hand Route. The wall to the right is **Grilled Fingers** (HVS 4c, 1979), finishing direct with long reaches.

(92) The Rib M — 1957–68
8m The right-hand rib of the gully, and started by coming in from the gully.

(93) Rib Wall VD — 1957–68
8m Climb the front wall of the buttress in a good position passing a niche and a large ledge in as direct a line as possible. The direct start left of the niche is a strenuous 5b.

(94) Sparkle VS 4b — 1978
8m Step off a block and use a variety of flakes and pockets to ascend, then traverse off leftwards. The direct finish is 4c.

V The Cellar and the Attic Bouldering
Situated above Blushing Buttress is a good bouldering area. *See the topo opposite.*

Calcutta Buttress

The next pert little buttress is again home to a clutch of fine steep routes on good rock, as well as some obscure but good bouldering, and like the last buttress, tends to be fairly quiet.

🟡 Sign of the Times E1 5c   1979
6m A hard move on the arête leads to a break and good runners, before a small flake leads to a **belly-flop** climax.

🟡 Calcutta Crack S 4b ★★   1949–51
6m An awkward start, especially for the short, leads to steep satisfying climbing on ideal jams.

🟡 Mistral E2 6a ★   1987
6m A fierce boulder problem start leads to a short wall and bomber gear in a large break. From here tackle the small prow on small but improving holds.

🟡 Calcutta Buttress VS 5b ★   1957–68
11m Hard pulls up and then left gain a mantelshelf requiring great balance or a long reach. Continue right to a niche, then escape back left.

🟡 Genetix E3 6a   1979
11m Pull up to the suspicious flakes in the roof (now very brittle) and make an unprotected haul over to finish up the right side of the arête on green slopers.

🟡 Stop… Carry on! HVS 5a   2001
8m The hanging scoop on the left wall is unprotected. An awkward start leads leftwards onto a ledge, whence the scoop is climbed rightwards.

🟡 Calcutta Crab Dance HS 4c ★★   2002
29m A right to left traverse taking in some hearty terrain. From the first moves of the previous route, continue leftwards with either protection or jugs, but never both. Follow the line around the nose to Calcutta Crack (possible belay), then finish more easily.

🟡 Between the Tiles HVS 5a   1979
25m A left to right girdle of the buttress at half height with an awkward section below the central prow and a tricky finish rightwards up the scoop.

🟡 Pepper VS 5a   1957–68
7m Ten metres right of Calcutta Buttress is another buttress. Climb the overhung front face to a ledge, then move left to finish up a crack.

🟡 Garlic HVS 5a   1979
7m From a short corner to the left move up before swinging right onto the ledge of Pepper. From here tackle the overhang on its right-hand side. **Dazed and Confused** (E3 6a, 2002) is essentially a direct start to this. Starting on the left of the buttress, under the roof, slap up the wall to finish as for Garlic.

🟡 Too Drunk V7 (6c)
Right of Pepper Buttress is a large boulder with a very overhanging front face. This is the central line on the overhang, from a sitting start, pulling onto the upper face on sloping pockets.

🟡 Drunk Enough V6 (6b)
The right arête, from a sitting start.

Behind these problems, more buttresses stretch off for 30m. On the last of these, a flat wall faces off towards Hen Cloud, with a few obscure routes to please the connoisseur. The left arête is **Shelty** *(HVS 5c, 1987).*

CALCUTTA PROBLEMS

A relatively unvisited set of problems at the bottom of this pert little buttress. They tend to be fierce and fingery numbers, mainly pulling over overhangs of one form or another.

① Bombay Overhang
VI (5b)
Round the bulging nose on good holds. Add an extra grade for traversing in from the right.

② Calcutta Crimp
V4 (6b)
Starting from a long fingerhold over the roof (or the jug below, harder and better), rock upwards towards the upper break.

③ Dirtnap
V8 (6c)
Start as for Sleeping with the Flowers. Scratch desperately leftwards to finish at the top of the nose.

④ Sign Start
V2 (5c)
Some powerful locking-off leads up the arête to a good break. **Sleeping with the Flowers** V5 (6b), is a sitting start to this coming from the back of the roof. Don't use the block on the right.

⑤ Mistral Start
V3 (6a)
Crinkle over the roof on crisp crimps. V4 from a low start.

⑥ Limbless Limbo Dancer V6 (6b)
Odder than a wallaby. From a low start, scurry up the vague rib.

⑦ Dish Grab
V5 (6b)
Start low in the break, then hoist up and right for the positive dish.

⑧ Calcutta Rib
VI (5c)
The chirpy rib at the right of the buttress.

⑨ Calcutta Traverse V3 (6a)
Traverse the shelf from right to left, pulling into Calcutta Crack at the end. **The Black Hole Start** V7 (6c), yields more bottom scraping by joining this from the crack on the right, on cruel crimps.

⑩ Ou est le Spit? E5 6a ★   1986
5m A reclusive classic up the centre of the face, above a threatening boulder. Use some suspect sandy holds to reach the small grooved feature. Make use of this to move up to a better than it used-to-be hold (due to wire brushing; no more please) over the sloping top and use this to top out. Impressively dangerous, given its length. Just right, **Wolfman of the KGB** (E3 6b, 1987) is an extended boulder problem starting up the left-leaning ramp.

Ⓥ Fifteen metres in front of this is a boulder with a couple of problems. **The prow** facing Hen Cloud, starting low in the crack, is V3 (6a), and the sweet **finger crack** on the front is V0 (5a).

Finally, with no connection to the Upper Tier at all, see overleaf for the Cube.

The Cube

Also known as Window Buttress and Back End Boulders, this small collection of blocks can be found 250m immediately behind the first buttress on the Skyline containing The Pugilist. First developed by Nick Dixon and Simon Whalley in 1986 as micro-routes (some can be led), their length, landing and climbing style lend them to be seen more as high (and not so high) bouldering, especially with a pad and spotter. Tackled this way, it is a superb venue, with a beautiful lonely setting overlooking wild moorland. Lots of sun, but quite exposed. **Access** is slightly sensitive, due to the natural value placed on the quiet surrounding moor by naturalists, so be discreet and approach from the right, not directly from the Skyline. At the right side of the Upper Tier, take the track running back from the crag, past old poles and 100m after a small stream, a vague sheep trod runs off this on the left, leading to the Cube. Takes under 10 minutes from the Upper Tier.

❶ Cube Traverse
V4 (6b)
Traverse the three faces, with hands at the level of the mid-height break. Scenic.

❷ Flakes VI (5b)

❸ Cube Crack
Vdiff (4a)

❹ Period Drama
V2 (5c)
Traverse rightwards round the arête, and when the break fades, move up on edges by interesting moves. Can be led at E1.

❺ Jump V4 (6b)
The square arête demands a dynamic approach. The **sit-start** is V7 (6c), and the blank wall to the right will eventually go at about V11.

❻ The Cube V5 (6b)
A highball classic, with fingery wall climbing above a perfect landing. E3 as a route. The **direct start** up the scoop is V9 (6c).

❼ The Pube V3 (6a)
Start as for the Cube, but continue up the arête on the left. Short and curly. The **sit start** is V9 (6c).

❽ Right Pube
V4 (6a)
The arête on the right.

❾ Back Crack
VI (5b)
The crack and mantel. V2 (6a) for the **sitting start**.

❿ Cave Exit V7 (6b)
Surmount the lip from the back of the grungy cave. Thuggy.

⓫ K2 V0– (3c)

⓬ V0 (5a)
The slab from the slot. Avoid the ridge for as long as possible.

⓭ Summit Slab
VI (5b)
Thin smearing past the porthole.

⓮ Notch Slab
V0+ (5a)
Another delicate passage.

⓯ 2K V0– (3b)
Remember, in mountaineering, you're not up 'till you're down.

The Skyline Area

by Chris 'Gus' Hudgins

O.S. Ref. **SK002634** | Altitude: **480m a.s.l.**

The Skyline is effectively a continuation of the Upper Tier, although it offers a stark contrast to the situation offered by the rest of the Roaches. As opposed to the often bustling, sometimes noisy and crowded atmosphere which occurs on the lower and upper tiers, it is not uncommon to find peace and solitude among the short but perfectly formed buttresses, as well as awesome views. The lack of visitors, however, is definitely not an indication of the quality of climbing, and make no mistake about it, some of the best routes on gritstone at all grades can be found here. One only has to look.

Conditions & aspect

The crag itself consists of a number of bays of rock, rather than one continuous outcrop. These separate buttresses can offer surprising shelter from the wind due to the proximity of trees, but are otherwise very open to all other weather. When the sun does grace the rock, however, some of the best days climbing are on offer. Faces south-west, getting sun afternoon and evening.

Routes

Over 140, from the easiest to quite hard. Good for slabs. Sometimes overgrown, but this will be indicated in the text. Check out some of the esoteric spots.

Ⓥ Bouldering

Superb, over 70 problems, with 2 major circuits, as well as a lot of smaller charming esoteric collections. These can all be taken in on one classy day.

Parking & approach

Park as for the Roaches or at Roach End, depending on where you are and where you are going. For getting between buttresses, it is usually best to return to the top path. Individual approach times given throughout the text and are, **a)** from the Upper Tier, (remember to add 10 minutes to get here), and **b)**, from Roach End.

The climbs are described from **right** to **left**.

The first three routes are located on a seemingly insignificant, but attractive, little buttress just left of the ascent path. It is characterised by very pink rock at its base, and an overhang on the right, below a cracked arête.

❶ The Pugilist HVS 5c ★ 1957–68

7m A steep crack and groove give a punishing prelude to good hidden holds above the overhang which allow the arête and crack to be climbed. A poor route, **Stomach Punch (VD 4b, 2002)**, climbs up the right wall of the buttress.

❷ In Passing E2 5c 1976

8m The crack to the left provides another (reachy) fight to the death. Cower below the overhang before stepping left and pulling onto the slab above. Probably yet to receive a stylish ascent.

❸ Southpaw S 4b 1957–68

7m If the plant life is successfully avoided, the crack-line just left gives a good warm up. Just left again is a short-lived 4a problem.

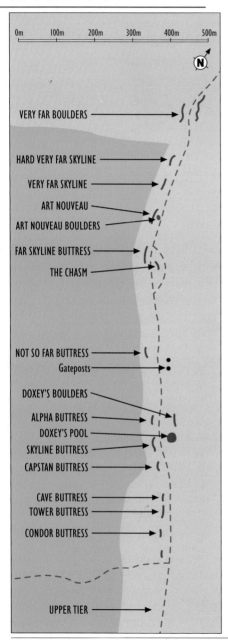

0m 100m 200m 300m 400m 500m

N

VERY FAR BOULDERS

HARD VERY FAR SKYLINE

VERY FAR SKYLINE

ART NOUVEAU

ART NOUVEAU BOULDERS

FAR SKYLINE BUTTRESS

THE CHASM

NOT SO FAR BUTTRESS

Gateposts

DOXEY'S BOULDERS

ALPHA BUTTRESS

DOXEY'S POOL

SKYLINE BUTTRESS

CAPSTAN BUTTRESS

CAVE BUTTRESS

TOWER BUTTRESS

CONDOR BUTTRESS

UPPER TIER

Condor Buttress

This lies 100m to the left and is named after the classic challenge hereabouts.
Approach from the clifftop path: a) 5 minutes, b) 25 minutes.

❹ Lung Cancer S 4a   1977
7m Starting just right of a block, climb left under a roof. Move up, then go back right below another overlap using a crucial jam to contort through an awkward move. Moving right from the start of Lung Cancer and gaining the undercut arête via a good hold on the lip of the overhang is **Breathless** (HS 4a, 2003).

❺ Chicane VD   1978
7m This is the clean, blunt arête. Step straight off the block (or, better, start up the crack just right at 4a) and pass to the left of a small roof. Finish past a shallow but useful pocket. **Chicanery** (HVD, 2003) is the direct start up the crack just left.

L - Nancy 7/8/04
S - Zoe

❻ False Chicane VD   2003
7m Start at the small block a few metres left of the arête, to finish diagonally right up the slab. The line previously labelled as Chicane.

L - Nancy 7/8/04
S - Zoe

❼ Navy Cut VD   1957–68
7m Climb the niche to the left to a chimney above. Either wedge yourself in and battle to make vertical progress or, for the claustrophobic, move slightly right and apply a somewhat more open approach.

❽ Bruno Flake VS 4b ★   1957–68
7m The corner leads to steep, awkward, and sometimes powerful climbing through the roof/flake crack (large gear useful). Tough, but a good trophy.

❾ Wheeze HVS 4c ★★   1976
8m Climb the initial arête to a break and runners, then use both balance and reach to move onto the upper arête and into an impressive position. Not an easy climb to protect.

⑩ Tobacco Road VS 4c ★ 1957–68
8m Take a direct line up the wall. Although independent, the climbing is spookily similar to Wheeze, if less finely positioned.

⑪ Toxic Socks HVS 5b 1996
8m Another, rather claustrophobic, direct line just left.

L - Nancy
S - Zoe 7/8/04

⑫ Time to be Had VD 1978
8m Just right of the easy corner is a cracked wall.

⑬ Licensed to Fill HVS 4c 2002
8m From 3m up the easy corner, move left onto the steep side-wall to a long, sloping pocket. From here take a strict line up the centre of the wall. Protection arrives a little late.

⑭ Nosepicker HVS 5b ★ 1975
8m Move delicately up to the overhang and, for once, take the easy way out avoiding it to the left by pleasantly delicate moves. The direct is **Johnny Pooh Poohed** (E2 6a, 1996), taken by altogether steeper moves. Hardcore!

⑮ Condor Chimney VD ★ 1957–68
8m Although the deep chimney just left gives the impression of offering a deadly struggle, a confident approach transforms it into a pleasant bridging exercise.

⑯ Cracked Arête HVD 1951–57
15m A pleasant two-tier route with some good smearing practice. Starting from a lower level, opposite the large boulder, climb the polished but still appealing arête, followed by the slab and flake crack above the ledge. Useful for developing those essential multi-pitch skills.

⑰ A.M. Anaesthetic VS 4c 1978
8m The precarious blunt arête. Testing climbing.

⑱ Condor Slab VS 4b ★★ 1957–68
12m The top-notch VS of the buttress. A bold and very rewarding route requiring some faith in your ability. Start up a short crack and make tenuous moves up and left to the obvious hole, whence a trying move leads upwards to a ledge. Step right and finish centrally.

⑲ Chicane Destination VS 4c 1978
40m A rightwards horizontal outing beginning at the hole of the previous route. Your destination; Chicane!

Ⓥ Little Skyline Face
A little 5m high face lies 30m below the crag at this point, with a cutaway in its left arête. **Left Arête** features awkward laybacking, V4 (6a). **Centre Slab** is a tough classic, V5 (6b) climbing past very shallow pockets, all at a bit of a height. **Right Arête** is V1 (5c).

Trio Buttress

The height of the crag now begins to increase and really gives an impression of what it has to offer. From now on the buttresses offer more continuous rock and have an excellent and concentrated selection of low-grade routes. Some of them have long runouts, so a cool head is often needed, while the longer routes on Tower Buttress will bring a smile to the face of jaded mountaineers. Approach: a) 3 minutes, b) 25 minutes.

20 Ralph's Mantelshelves HVD 4a   1951–57

8m From the bottom right-hand end of the buttress, trend up and left by a series of ledges. The top one, in particular, is a full-on belly-flopper. A fine variation makes the hard start then continues up the right-hand wall of the buttress on surprising holds (**Ralph's Direct**, HVD 4a, 2002).

21 Lighthouse VD ★   1951–57

10m After a tricky start, follow a beckoning line of shallow grooves in the centre of the buttress from toe to top.

22 Substance VS 4c   1978

8m The left arête, climbed on its steep left-hand side, is tricky and quite intense.

The next four routes are based on, in and around the gloomy recess to the left: **Trio Chimney** (VD, 1951–57) is the short but enjoyable chimney in the right-hand corner. Start inside the cleft and remember to exit before it closes off. **Recess Wall and Arête** (HVS 4c, 2002) smears up the centre of the recess then the sharp arête above and left. **Square Chimney** (M, 1951–57) is the chimney in the left-hand corner, with a well-protected crux at the top. **Left Twin Crack** (HS 4a, 1951–57) begins 2m up Square Chimney, then follows a groove and crack to the left. Entertaining while it lasts.

The following climbs, just left again, offer direct and varied climbing of a more optimistic and open nature.

23 Shortcomings E1 5c ★★   1978

10m The attractive wall and beckoning flake provide a superb challenge. However, the route is well-named: the lower section is tricky and both making and protecting the crucial move to the flake are very height-dependent.

Rassp! (E2 5c, 1995) follows Shortcomings to the break then moves rightwards to finish up the wall. The climbing and rock are good, but it lacks the stature of its neighbours.

24 Safety Net E1 5b ★★★   1975

10m The blunt rib beneath an even grander roof is gained via a powerful, undercut, boulder problem start. A thought-provoking but well-protected move gains the roof. From here layback your way to glory!

29 Topaz E2 5b ★★ 1979
10m Just to the left, a rib leads straightforwardly enough to the roof. The crack above provides good holds leading rapidly up to the ramp and a suddenly rather exciting position. Fortunately, good protection in the crack and a safe fall-out zone provide the confidence needed to handle it. Usually.

25 Pebbles on a Wessex Beach E3 6a 1982
10m Ascend the centre of the short wall just to the left to the roof. With a runner in Safety Net, make a huuuge reach for the much wider and more flared flake crack above and left and storm up it.

30 Strain Station E4 5c† 1981
12m A worrying proposition, climbing the roof and blunt arête to the left. It is gained direct or from the right. Difficult, and possibly unrepeated.

26 Paul's Puffer E4 6b 1989
7m Follow the crack just left directly up and over the roof, finishing up the wide crack above. This may also be reached more traditionally by an awkward traverse from the grim recess on the left (**Hank's Horror**, E1 5b, 1963).

31 Rowan Tree Traverse VD 1951–57
15m From 5m up Topaz, ascend a long way leftwards to gain a ledge and a final layback crack.

Central Traverse (HS 4a, 1951–57), is a good problem that traverses this buttress, from Letter Box Gully to Square Chimney, using the half-height break.

32 Middleton's Motion VS 4b ★ 1957–68
10m A character-building lead with a wild finish. Bisect the previous route at a small cave to finish via an obstinate crack.

27 Letter Box Gully M 1951–57
10m The slabs leading up to the huge jammed block couldn't be easier. From here, grovel your way through the gap under the block. Not for the big boned. The short crack on the right gives a VD with an awkward finish.

33 Spectrum VS 4c 1977
8m Quite a technical route, which gains the finish of Rowan Tree Traverse via a faint groove.

28 Letter Box Cracks VS 4c 1957–68
7m Choose either of the cracks beside the jammed block above the gully, or maybe both.

34 Bad Sneakers E2 5c ★ 1977
8m The beckoning slab to the left requires balance, bottle and actually quite good sneakers. Purists will

Going to Extremes

One of the biggest barriers in climbing, is breaking into **Extreme** climbing. The magical E1 can seem off-putting. As a help, here are some routes of HVS that should prepare a leader for all the skills needed to climb E1, and then some good E1s to get started on.

Hint: Some climbers may find the E1s easier than the HVSs, so don't be put off.

HVS

- **Delstree**, a steep and pumpy test in jamming;
- **Mantis**, good arête laybacking, an essential technique for harder grit;
- **Boysen's Delight**, as technical as they come, with perfect pro;
- **The Crippler**, get used to that brutality fella me lad;
- **Bengal Buttress**, bold and holdless, a feature of Extreme.

E1

- **Sneeze**, friendly, sweet and brisk;
- **Encouragement**, 2 pitches, spread the load;
- **Slowhand**, with a short bold section;
- **Safety Net**, a good fair climb;
- **Wild Thing**, a beautifully obscure test of boulder and bold.

climb direct up the middle (E3 5c), pragmatists will trend slightly left (and the floundering will veer rapidly to the arête).

㉟ Spare Rib HS 4a ★   1977
8m The rib left of the gully, started from its base on its left-hand side, gives technical climbing requiring a bold (not bald) head to reach and leave the mid-height protection. An awkward scrambling descent is possible just to the right of this route.

㊱ The Black Pig VS 4c ★★   1957–68
8m Use the chimney to make initial vertical progress (the pedantic direct start is 5c) but forsake this as soon as possible in favour of the thin, right-wards-slanting crack. The VS climber's London Wall, but not as well protected!

㊲ Ogden Recess VD   1957–68
8m Follow the chimney in its entirety. Good fun.

㊳ Ogden Arête HS 4b ★★   1957–68
8m The left side of the clean-cut arête has a steep, technical and rather blind start and an airy finish.

㊴ Ogden HD   1951–57
10m The well-trodden path up the crack gives good practice for the harder lines in the area. **Cold Man's Finger** (E1 5b, 1992) is a direct up the wrinkled slab to the left.

Left of Ogden is a vegetated but easy scrambling descent.

㊵ Oversight VD   1968–73
10m A good climb at the grade. The left arête of the stony gully, without sticking to any particular side. **Wad Man Slang** (S 4a, 2000) is a disappointing crack just to the right.

㊶ Bad Poynt D   1968
7m Start 3m to the left at a perched block and climb up it to a slab and crack.

Tower Buttress

This is the tall jutting buttress to the left.

㊷ Thrug VS 4c ★★   1957–68
10m The steep crack splitting the right wall has escaped from Ramshaw. It gives a perfect test of jamming and definitely has a macho air about it.

㊸ Shrug E2 5b   1998
8m Climb the right arête of the first small pillar. From the top of the pillar climb directly up the wall passing two flakes, the second larger than the first.

44 Perched Block Arête VD 4a ★   1951–57
15m A powerful line following the arête, climbed largely on its right, from its lowest point to the top block from where it becomes necessary to either gain a final chimney on the left or press straight on (VS 4b). Another alternative is to move right in search of a fine layback flake (a finish that holds both unexpected surprises and exposure, HVS 4c). Both of these variant starts can be begun up the chimney left of the original start.

45 Tower Chimney D ★   1945
18m The flaky frontal chimney of the tower is a long, traditional treat. Starting up the right-hand groove is equally good. The bold may prefer to wander left along the top ledge to tackle the nose of the buttress at S.

46 Tower Face E1 5b ★★   1977
15m A classic hard route. The flaky crack leads to a slanting break and crucial protection. The awkward short crack leads to a bold stretch to sloping holds. Finish directly up another flaky groove. Excellent, but not to be underestimated.

47 Tower Eliminate HVS 5b ★   1963
15m Around the arête to the left, a steep disjointed crack-line leads to a niche. From here, either finish up another crack or, better, move right onto the arête. Strangely gratifying.

48 Sorcerer's Apprentice VS 4c   1978
10m The wall on the left leads to sloping ledges and a crack.

Cave Buttress

About 25m left is the first of the connoisseur buttresses on the Skyline. The lack of traffic hereabouts is not justified and such route names as 'Cave Crack' and 'Cave Arête' ought to be irresistible! Approach: a) 5 minutes, b) 25 minutes.

49 Joiner HVD 4a   1951–57
9m An impressively clean, technical arête, taking the little groove on the right at the top. Quite bold. Even more so if finished direct.

50 Connector VS 5b   1978
9m The flake in the wall to the left gives an excellent boulder problem start. The upper part is less impressive.

51 King Swing VS 5b   1978
7m Start at the right-hand edge of the cave. After placing a sensible high runner, swing immediately round the arête to the right. Steep pulls gain the excellent finishing slab.

52 Cave Crack HVS 5a ★   1957–68
6m Essential practice for all contemplating The Sloth. Climb to and up the major feature. Two alternative and rather artificial starts are available; the left arête of the initial groove (5c), or the **Mousetrap Start**, which traverses in from the left (5b).

53 Stephen HVS 5a ★   1957–68
7m Short but brutal. Climb the carnivorous crack and overhanging groove springing from the left

Grit slabs come in all shapes and sizes,

and are sprinkled with holds that vary from jug-like breaks through ripples and pebbles to mere shadows where faith rather than friction holds sway. The confident can wander at will on a slab, creating their own lines, slashes of colour on a compliant canvas; abstract lines of sinuous movement or arrow straight, but tilted to the limit and stripped of holds.

Barry Hobbs, On The Edge

edge of the cave. **Automatix** (E2 5b, 1981) starts just right and follows flakes rightwards to the finish of Cave Crack.

54 Cave Arête HVD 4a ★ 1951–57
14m Another really good route. Starting from the lowest point of the buttress, follow the arête to a ledge. Take to the slab on the left for a while, before finishing, in a good position, back on the arête itself. A direct finish is possible at 4a. **Cave Buttress** (VD, 1951–57) gains the ledge from a short corner, then goes left to finish up a crack. Poor.

Battle through the jungle for 65m leftwards, or just walk pleasantly over the top, to reach a little buttress containing:

55 Capstan's Corner D 1951–57
8m The pleasant right edge of the buttress. The slot and left side of the wall is another possibility at the same standard.

56 Mistaken Identity S 4a 1951–57
10m To the left is a greasy groove with a slab to its left. Climb the slab then tackle the roof on either side.

57 Sally James VS 4c 1979
10m The left arête of the buttress, 10m further on. As pert as ever.

Skyline Buttress

A further 50m left is the most impressive face that the Skyline area has to offer. It has a good selection of long classics, guaranteed not to disappoint, but unfortunately a few routes that are now too overgrown to be enjoyable. It is best approached from above, descending steeply either side of the buttress. Approach: a) 10 minutes, b) 20 minutes.

58 Slips E3 6b ★ 1982
8m The undercut right arête of the buttress is begun from the slab below. Hard-as-nails moves are needed to reach the sloping crack further left, the upper arête, and the sanctuary of Slab and Arête. The Strapadictomy of western grit!

59 Skytrain E2 5b ★ 1977
10m The leftwards-leaning crack provides a pleasantly technical outing leading onto Slab and Arête. The original continues rather artificially up the slab to a bold finish, but the final section of Slab and Arête gives a fine E1 overall.

60 Slab and Arête HS 4a ★★★ 1945
18m A classic route that builds to a crescendo at the top of the exposed right arête. At this grade, avoid the now-polished and desperate start up the pock-eted slab by moving in from the left. Traverse the half-height break all the way to a memorable finish up the right edge of the buttress.

61 Acid Drop E4 5c ★★★ 1973
15m A gem that could have escaped from Bosigran. Climb above the traverse of Slab and Arête (which provides the impressively distant runners) to the exquisite arching overlap. From here make the famously height-dependent move to gain a good hold (6b for proficient shorties, and E5) to thank-God gear under the roof, which provides a baffling but enjoyable contrast.

Right: Never too young. Kate Garnett enjoying Cave Arête, (HVD), with Roger High belaying. Photo: Dave Garnett.

62 Drop Acid E4 6a† ★   1987
15m Follow a series of thin flakes up the slab just left of the arching overlap of Acid Drop to reach the roof. Pull over and finish direct. A side-runner in Abstract protects.

63 Karabiner Cracks M   1945
12m The cracks and chimney to the left. Finishing over the roof and up the crack just right is also a good exercise (**Abstract**, HVS 5a, 1957–68). Yet more adventure can be had by continuing the traverse all the way under the roof to the finish of Slab and Arête (**Poodle Vindaloo**, E2 5c, 1982).

64 Karabiner Slab VS 4c   1957–68
12m The central line on the slab left of the crack. Quite bold and high in the grade.

65 Karabiner Chimney VD ★   1945
12m The chimney on the left is pleasant right to the very end.

66 Enigma Variation E1 5a ★★   1976
10m A bold but well-behaved route. Balance across to the lovely right arête and follow it by straightforward moves in a bold position to a useful knobble and a gear placement a little too far round the arête for comfort. Move up and then break out left onto the slab.

67 Mantelshelf Slab VS 4a ★   1947
10m A character-building slab climb. The central line up the slab involves a technical mantelshelf and

continues into bolder and bolder (though easier and easier) territory.

68 Bilberry Traverse VS 4a   1945
35m A mid-height traverse from the gully bounding the buttress on the right to Mantelshelf Slab. Traverse left to the arête and reverse Slab and Arête to reach Karabiner Chimney. Precariously cross Enigma Variation (crux, runner above) to the ledge of Mantelshelf Slab. Finish up this.

69 Come Girl VS 4c   1968–73
13m The blocky rib, 5m left of Mantelshelf Slab, finishing at a crack. Increasingly bold and currently rather dirty. **Go Girl** (HVD, 1968–73), allegedly climbs the very vegetated cracks 2m left leading to the finish of Come Girl, while **Lost Girl** (HVS 5a, 1999) starts as for Go Girl and cuts a swathe left to reach a pleasant undercut slab. Place protection on the left of the slab, then move across rightwards and tackle the bulge above by use of a flake.

The Pinnacle

This is an elegant pillar slightly lower and to the left.

70 Pinnacle Arête VS 4c ★   1945
6m The right arête of The Pinnacle is a real beauty with one particularly perplexing, and not well-protected, move. **Pinnacle Slab** (HVD, 1951-57) is the undistinguished slab up and to the right, finishing at the top of the main edge.

There is reportedly 'some trivial fun to be had on the slab and thin crack just to the left' (**Split Personality**, E1 5b, 1979). However, if done at all directly, the steep slab is very much harder than this.

71 Pinnacle Crack D   1949–51
7m The wide crack bounding the left side of The Pinnacle's front face.

Alpha Buttress

Yet another fine buttress packed with quality lines lies 30m left. While the crag is not very tall, the routes here definitely pack a punch. Best approached from above.
Approach: a) **10 minutes,** b) **20 minutes.**

72 Looking for Today HVS 5b   1976
7m Struggle up the blind crack and bulge to reach the useful thin flake and easy ground.

73 Right-Hand Route S 4a ★   1951–57
12m Climb the crack and chimney until a traverse left leads to the right-most of two flakes in the upper wall. Continuously interesting.

74 Definitive Gaze E1 5c   1979
10m Starting immediately left, balance up into a scoop and make a tricky exit on the left. Finish direct avoiding the tempting flakes of neighbouring routes. Leaving the scoop on the right and finishing directly is **Wicked Wind** (E3 5c, 1989).

75 Wallaby Wall S 4a   1951–57
10m An awkward start leads to an excellent series of moves up the wall to a ledge and then across to the left-hand of the two upper flakes.

76 39th Step E2 6a   1979
8m The shallow groove and slab 3m to the left, trending slightly rightwards and with a runner in the crack on the left.

77 Sennapod Crack VD   2002
8m Hurry up the crack just right of the easy corner. It goes with less of a struggle than you might have been expecting.

78 Sennapod D   1978
7m The corner on the left.

79 Bounty Killer VS 5a   1996
7m Climb the flaky cracks in the side-wall of the next buttress, right of the arête.

Just left is an impressive slab divided at around half-height by a wide break. This provides welcome holds but scant protection for its routes.

80 Mantis HVS 5b ★★   1974
8m The clean arête is begun on its right by steep, technical laybacking above a gnarly landing. Protection arrives unhelpfully late and the upper arête, taken on its left, is more straightforward. Starting the route by laybacking the arête on the left is a good alternative. E1 5c.

Doxey's Pool

A really classy venue, sat high on the Roaches ridge, with great views over
miles of farmland towards the Cheshire plains in front, and wild lonely moorland behind.
The climbing is good, powerful and rounded. Landings are perfect, although sometimes
are boggy at the left side. The skin on the rock is thin, so treat it with respect, especially
where brushing is concerned.

❶ V5 (6b)
Up the bulging arête at the
back to the roof. Traverse
right. If you top out, then
report yourself to the local
police right away.

❷ Left Cheek VI (5a)
Climb the left arête of the
crack.

**❸ Soggy Bottom
Crack** V4 (5b)
Overcome all odds and
jam out from the back of
the crack.

❹ V5 (6b)
From a rounded hold by
the crack, swing right to
the front face and move
up. The **jumping start** is
V3.

**❺ Staffordshire
Flyer** V4 (6a)
A Doxey's classic, crimping
left to the steep arête.

❻ The Arête V5 (6b)
Starting low from
undercuts is V7.

❼ Drowning Pool
V7 (6c)
Start from a rounded hold
down and right and
somehow gain the blind
flakeline above. From a
standup it is V4.

**❽ Another Nadin
Traverse** V10 (7a)
Holy moly, who the hell is
this Nadin anyway? From
the low start of 6, traverse
the lip to finish up 7.

❾ Groovy Crack
V0 (5b)

❿ Chipped Wall
V0– (4b)

⓫ Thin Flake VI (5b)

⓬ VI (5b)
From the thin flake,
delicately traverse the
buttress to finish up 6.

⓭ V0– (4b)
Climb the slanting crack
then up the wall.

⓮ V5 (6b)
Up the sloping sidewall
past a pocket.

⓯ Arête on Left
V4 (6b)

⓰ Arête on Right
V2 (5b)
Use the flake. **Avoiding
the flake** gives a V5
problem.

⓱ Blind Flake
V2 (5c)
Climb without using the
arête. The flake can be
climbed using the arête,
but this becomes similar to
climbing the arête with the
flake.

⓲ V6 (6b)
Squirm up and right to a
small pocket on the slab.

⓳ V5 (6b)
Step up, then inch left to
the same pocket.

EA Baker and the Kyndwr Club
were walking the Skyline one hot summer day
and happened upon Doxey's Pool. "The very
picture of coolness. We could not resist."
Two dived in and struck out for the middle.
"Out there the bottom was spongy, and
seemed to be covered with an oozy
accumulation of decayed peat, which,
on being stirred up, discharged a violent odour,
as if some noisome explosion had gone off."
Moors, Crags and Caves, 1903

⑳ V3 (6a)
Climb the feature
rightwards to the top.

㉑ Little Flake
V3 (6a)
Thugging into this from
jams and undercuts is
V5.

㉒ Bulging Arête
V2 (5c)
Start on undercuts for
an eye-popping V5.

㉓ V0– (4c)
Jam the nice crack then
continue up the arête.

㉔ Easy Arête
V0– (4a)

㉕ Pancake
V0 (5a)

㉖ Li'l Crack
V0– (4a)
The arête to the right is
similarly pleasant.

A 30 foot high weed-covered monster
was reported as raising slowly from the
depths of the murky pool and pointing a
finger at a female picnicker in the 1920s.

Doxey's Pool
is a **phenomenon**

because it has no water coming in to it,
it is on top of a hill, yet it never dries up.
It is said the pool is bottomless, and it
links up to the Blakemere several miles
away by subterranean passages.

These pools are inhabited by a mermaid,
one of the few inland mermaids in the
country. The pool is named after Doxey,
daughter of Bess of Rock Hall, who was
renowned for her singing, which was
said to be foreign and melancholy.
She was taken away one night by men
who were sheltering in the caves, was
raped and then drowned in the pool.

㉛ Hallow to our Men E4 6b ★   1981
4m In the bottom centre of the slab, a shallow
scoop provides the starting point for desperate
climbing on the smallest of edges. Unfortunately,
independence is lost at the break but continuing up
San Melas gives a very sustained outing.

㉜ San Melas E3 5c ★★   1977
8m Pebble-pulling up the lower slab, slightly to the
left, gains the break. Place protection, take a deep
breath, and commit yourself to a series of high steps
and rockovers, with very little in the way of handholds. Pleasant balancy exercise for gritstone divas,
but nail-ripping desperation for thugs.

㉝ Days Gone By S 4b   1978
7m The right-hand of three close parallel cracks.
Quite hard if done strictly, but suffers from its inter-
fering easier neighbour.

⑧④ Breakfast Problem VD ★   1951–57
7m The merging twin cracks to the left provide tons of protection, and good climbing as well. A popular first lead.

⑧⑤ Formative Years E3 6a   1982
7m The cute slab to the left looks temptingly escapable. Oddly, it is an altogether different story when high up above the unfriendly landing!

⑧⑥ Alpha Arête S 4a   1957–68
7m The blocky left arête of the green corner. Sweet but bold.

⑧⑦ Alpha D   1951–57
7m The small groove on the left. Hard work but well-protected.

⑧⑧ Devotoed VS 5a ★   1979
7m The ridiculously stubborn crack leads to an equally silly sloping finish on the left wall of Alpha.

⑧⑨ Rodeo E1 6a   1993
7m The blunt overhanging rib 2m left is ascended using a skin-ripping jam and leads to a mantelshelf directly above to finish.

⑨⓪ Melaleucion VS 5a ★   1976
7m Steep climbing over the bulges on the front face. A tough gem.

⑨① Omega S 4a   1957–68
7m Start just left and make a hard pull over a bulge to find yourself faced with a belly-flop on the right.

⑨② Bone Idol VS 4c ★   1977
33m Yet another routine buttress traverse, but what a buttress to traverse! Start at Omega and finish on Right-Hand Route. Fun.

Thirty metres left of Alpha Buttress is a large broken and vegetated buttress. This has no routes but the weird pinnacles on the top tier and the slabs just left give some good low grade problems. The left-most slab is particularly good.

Not So Far Skyline Buttress

About 100m beyond Alpha Buttress, twin stone gateposts will be found by the top path. Just beyond these, a faint path leads down under the trees and right (facing out) along to a small but steep buttress with a central green overhang at its base. The top of the buttress is marked by a large castellated boulder by the path.

At the right end are some good short problems on a small three-tiered buttress with a large embedded flake providing a convenient mounting block but a horrible landing. The worthwhile rib just right of the buttress is HD 4a. **Three Tier Buttress** (VS 4b, 2003) itself starts off the flake and pulls up to a crack on the right. Alternatively, the tempting flake just left may be laybacked boldly over the mantrap beneath at about 4c.

About 5m left is an attractive bouldery overhang with a huge jug that begs to be dangled from (**Monstrous Angel**, HS 4b, 2003). The poor corner left again with a dirty escape left round the overlaps is about Severe. In the centre of the crag is a big, rather dirty, roof about 2m above the ledge, currently guarded by a turf cornice. To its left a scruffy VD takes the short chimney and hanging garden finish.

The highest part of the buttress is just about big enough for a couple of slightly more substantial routes.

⑨③ Not So Fast VS 5a   2003
7m Start at the sculpted slab left of the big roof, below twin cracks through a small overhang. Pull through to a good break and then wobble up the awkward rounded finish.

⑨④ Not So Steep VD   2003
7m Five metres left, a juggy prow leads steeply to a wide crack.

From the ledge above, the deceptively short but ungradable offwidth provides an excellent comedy finish to either route. The left arête of the buttress gives a good climb on good holds (**Not Much Further**, VD, 2003).

Chasm Boulders

These boulders are to be found along the path in the region of Far Skyline Buttress, a couple of hundred metres beyond Doxey's Pool. They are slightly obscure, but are found in a spot just after the main track divides, in-between the two paths. It is a nice little clutch of short problems, although the surface can be a little crunchy. An interesting venue, one of the few areas in the Roaches where the rock will actually spot you. However, while it is also likely to encourage you and console you, it is unlikely to share the driving.

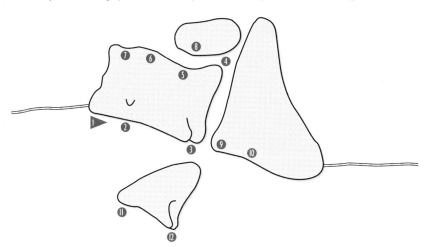

❶ Chasm Crinkle Project
Traverse the lip from slopers on the left, along the beautiful crinkly feature, to the arête.

❷ Gritstone Pimple V4 (6a)
Pull over, aiming for the spot. Scary.

❸ Ramp V0 (5a)
Climb the ramp to the arête. The topout is escaped to the right. If you do the top direct, award yourself a medal.

❹ Acne Arête
V6 (6c)
A tasty morsel up the hanging arête. If you are pumped, then lean back. The **sit-start** is V7 (6c), using a round hold and a heel-hook on the left, although you'll need to tuck your knees in to avoid resting on the side wall on the left, especially if someone is watching.

❺ Squeezer's Spots
V5 (6b)
From a sit-start.

❻ Spotter's Pop
V4 (6b)
Sit-start on crimps.

❼ Pussin' Boots
V5 (6b)
Start sitting, with feet on the back flakes.

❽ Spotter's Slop
V6 (6b)
Climb from the sloper to the top. Can be **dynoed** at V7 (6c).

❾ Mantel
V1 (5b)

❿ Harder Mantel
V3 (6a)
Totally holdless, unfortunately.

⓫ V0 (5a)
Climb past the round feature on the wall to the arête.

⓬ Triptych Groove
V7 (6b)
The groove and arête are climbed from a sit start. A real thuggy, technical classic.

Rugged individualists seeking an unusual adventure will make straight for the next routes. Approximately 150m beyond the stone gateposts, an overhanging prow of a boulder, engraved 'TH' will be found on the left of the path. Reconnaissance directly downhill for about 30m may locate the top of a wide slab below an active badger sett. Native guides may be hired in Leek.

95 Don't Go Down to the Woods Today
VS 4b ★   1989

8m Or if you do, be sure to tell your mum where you're off to. Neat moves lead up the middle of the surprisingly clean slab to an overlap and a step left to the gap in the cornice. No protection or, indeed, belay (an extra rope may be needed) but great fun.

Thirty metres left, at the same level, is another buttress with a small cave.

96 Deep in Mystery   E1 5b   1989
7m Pull over the overhang left of the cave and climb the pocketed slab to an unnerving mantelshelf.

Far Skyline Buttress

After this point the edge deteriorates into randomly spaced pieces of grit on the hillside, with little of worth for 350m or so. Just beyond the Chasm Boulders, the flat top of the crag can be found. An awkward descent reaches a steep buttress characterised by a roof at 2m height in its centre. The first route on the buttress is 5m right of this roof. Due to the proximity of trees and the lack of traffic, the starts of some of the routes can be somewhat vegetated. Despite the bushwhacking, the upper sections of most of the routes manage to justify the struggle. Approach: a) 15 minutes, b) 15 minutes.

97 The Black Ram   S 4a   1970
11m The crack and square cut groove 4m left of a small, leftwards slanting chimney has several green inhabitants. Fortunately there are steep cracks in good rock above.

98 Black Ram Arête   VS 4c   1970
11m Start 3m left, by making a heroic mantelshelf onto a tiny ledge 1m off the ground. Step right to reach and climb a thin crack, which demands neat footwork. All this leads to a vegetated ledge below the final attractive arête. Uncomfortably close to the previous route on more than one occasion.

99 Dangler   VS 4b   1970
11m From the same small ledge on Black Ram Arête, head directly up the almost non-existent crack on surprising holds to one of the more obvious runner placements in the area. After powering over the bulge, the hairline cracks in the slab above provide a satisfying prelude to topping out.

100 The Chimney   VS 4a   1969
11m A powerful start involving muscular laybacking, or rubber limbs, enables the chimney right of the roof to be climbed. Currently rather choked with heather.

101 Entente Cordiale   E3 6a ★   1981
12m After a dynamic start directly over the central roof, step left and climb the left arête by an engaging sequence of moves. From the wide break, smear boldly up the centre of the upper slab. A little wandering but with some memorable climbing and puzzling protection.

102 Honky Tonk   HS 4b ★★   1969
12m Thrash up the deep, V-shaped cleft immediately left of the roof. Stretch tenuously right onto the lip of the overhang. Pausing only to savour the improbable exposure, head right for the arête which gives pleasant climbing before the top. **Steeplechase Crack** (VD, 1970) is the dirty, vegetated crack that cuts through a square niche just left, although the flora may be bypassed entertainingly on the right.

103 Dazzler   S 4a ★   1970
8m The twin, thin cracks residing in another shallow niche provide another tricky start. Fortunately, sideways jug pulling, good protection and sinker jams await. **Mudhopper** (VD, 1970) is the grassy left-slanting groove on the left.

⑩④ Slither HS 4b   1970
8m Climb the attractive slab and deceptive hanging groove 3m left of Mudhopper.

⑩⑤ Steeplechaser D ★   1970
8m Climb an open corner to an overhang, which is hurdled on the left.

⑩⑥ Tree Grooves VD   1970
7m Climb the groove round the corner, or the slab to its left, to a second, easier, groove.

⑩⑦ Tree Corner D   1970
7m The corner and overhang behind the dead tree.

⑩⑧ Chronicle VS 5b   1979
7m The overlap and slab just right of the end of the crag.

⑩⑨ Flutterbye Grooves S 4a   1969
7m From the left-hand end of the crag gain wispy cracks from the left or, better and harder, direct. Follow the cracks.

⑩⑩ Microcosm D   1979
7m A groove on the left moving right onto the front of the buttress at the top.

⑪⑪ The Girdle Traverse S 4a   1970
30m A traverse of variable line which rarely exceeds 4m above the ground.

The **Very Far Skyline** Area

The buttresses from this point onwards contain some of the finest routes in the area. While many are the preserve of the more experienced climber, there are several gems open to all comers. Approach: a) 15 minutes, b) 15 minutes.

*One hundred metres left of the end of Skyline Buttress, three large rectangular boulders just off the path on the left, the end of the first conspicuously split, provide a waymark for locating the first of the routes. These are the **Art Nouveau Boulders** (see topo.) The square face below, almost completely hidden from above, contains Art Nouveau. For a little*

relaxation, there is always **Transcendental Medication** *(D, 2001) on the slabby arête some 20m to its right.*

⑪② Pop Art HVS 5a   1989
7m An eye-catching inverted miniature of its up-market neighbour, unfortunately a little too close to the edge of the canvas. From the middle of the steep slab, step up right to stretch for a good hold near the arête. From here good holds lead straight to the top. Bold and smart moves, although easily escapable.

Coma Sutra (HS 4b, 2001) is the pocketed slab and scoop 5m left.

⑪③ Art Nouveau see page 72

Very Far Skyline Buttress

The final two buttresses are both similar, undercut at their base, above which perfectly formed slabs and grooves give sublime climbing. The first, and slightly smaller of the two, is 100m left of Art Nouveau.

⑪④ Mild Thing D   1977
7m From the propped flake on the right of the buttress, climb the unsatisfying cracks above. Worth it for the name alone.

⑪⑤ Script for a Tear E6 6c   1985
7m From the same starting point, step left onto the lip of the undercut slab and smear desperately upwards. This is made a much better route by smearing in along the lip from Wild Thing.

⑪⑥ Wild Thing E1 5c ★★   1977
7m There are no such things as reach problems, just strength problems. From the large jug pocket to the left at head height, reach a distant edge by technical mastery and hydraulic arm strength, or a bunk up, and attain a standing position.

The groove that follows provides perfect delicate movement, while the confident can choose which pockets to eliminate.

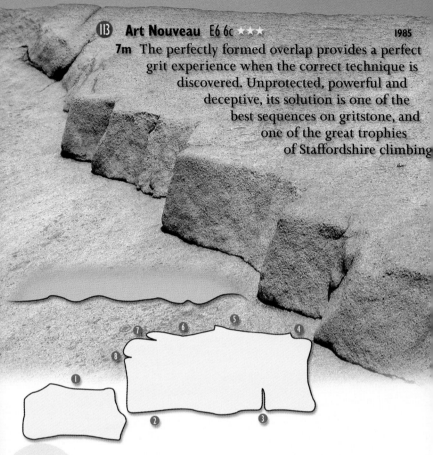

113 **Art Nouveau** E6 6c ★★★ 1985

7m The perfectly formed overlap provides a perfect grit experience when the correct technique is discovered. Unprotected, powerful and deceptive, its solution is one of the best sequences on gritstone, and one of the great trophies of Staffordshire climbing

Art Nouveau Boulders

Ah, Skyline grit. Is there anything finer?
A limited number of good problems on very clean rock. A worthwhile venue on a longer circuit. Two classic projects exist, but, as the man said, you can fall but you better not bounce! They are set on the crag side of the path right above Art Nouveau.

1 Mono Slab
V0– (4c)

2 Sidepull Wall
V8 (6c)

3 Crack V0– (4b)

4 Flaky Romp
V0 (5a)

5 Project
The wall left of the groove.
Spotter advised.

6 Project
Open V groove. 1 hold. 2 spotters.

7 Juggy Flakeline
V0+ (5a)

8 Crack and Arête
V3 (5c)

⑰ Entropy's Jaw E5 6b ★★★   1982

7m From the standing position on the previous route, step delicately right to climb the thin seam by even thinner smearing, thumb sprags, and, with luck, brilliant footwork. Essentially unprotected; there is an RP placement near the top but protection is unlikely to be placed on the lead. A barely independent start can be made just right as an exercise in strenuous pedantry.

⑱ Triple Point E1 5c ★   1982

7m After the gut-wrenching crux of Wild Thing yet again, step through onto the left arête and follow it by some great moves. A super combination. A direct start is possible up the left side of the arête at 6b.

⑲ The Calf Path E2 6b   1991

12m From the propped flake of Mild Thing, traverse left above the lip, finishing up Triple Point. Really just an excuse to climb more perfect rock.

⑳ Mr Decisive HVS 5b   1989

7m Five metres to the left is a jutting flake. The slabby arête is climbed on its left-hand side.

㉑ Curvature VS 4b   1979

6m About 30m left is an arête on a large boulder. Climb the arête on its left. Still unaccountably obscure. **Very Connoisseurish** (E2 6a, 1970s) is the arête on the boulder slightly further left again and **The Parrot and the Balaclava** (HS 4b, 1989) takes the undercut slabby wall just to its right.

By bluffs where boughs were bare they passed,

Climbed by cliffs where the cold clung:

Under the high clouds, ugly mists

Merged damply with the moors and

melted on the mountains;

Each hill had a hat,

a huge mantle of mist.

*A comely knight, Sir Gawain, passes through
Staffordshire in the 14th century, from Sir Gawain
and the Green Knight, by Brian Stone*

Jams O'Donnell on Prelude to Space, HVS 4c.
Photo: Jams O'Donnell.

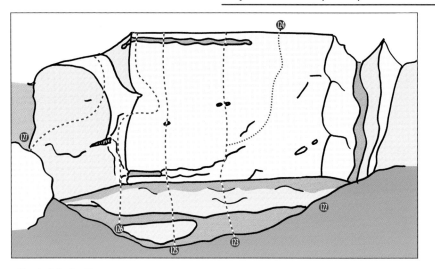

Gus' **Slab** Exams

The Roaches has long been seen as the capital of gritstone smearing, and rightly so. However, the holdless, and sometimes bold, nature of this style of climbing can sometimes terrify the uninitiated. For this reason, here's a little curriculum of slab test-pieces to help you along your way. Do 6 of them, and you are competent. Nine, and you are sticky. Do all 12, and you will never need another hold ever again.

Maud's Garden, VD – a pleasant introduction with a bold start; **Slab and Arête**, HS – a longer route to test you. But can you handle the exposure? **Technical Slab**, HS – flexibility always comes in handy on slabs. The holds are there, but how will you reach them? **Condor Slab**, VS – a good taster of the type of cerebral control needed to progress up the list; **Mantelshelf Slab**, VS – another example of the steadiness required for a runout; **Prelude to Space**, HVS – now you really are the proud owner of a cool head; **Hawkwing**, E1 – it's all coming together nicely now; **Elegy**, E2 – a tricky combination of faith in friction and a long runout to test your determination; **San Melas**, E3 – time to test that flexibility we talked about; **Wings of Unreason**, E4 – your slab skills will get you into an interesting position, but do you trust them enough to smear your way up. I'd just jump! **Counterstroke of Equity**, E5 – may require the ability to see footholds where others can't; **Obsession Fatale**, E7 – oh no! It's all gone wrong, you've gone mad!

Hard Very Far Skyline Buttress

Forty metres on lies the centrepiece of the area. The rock on the fine slab is perfectly featured and provides a great choice of holds and means of ascent. The obvious line linking the two pockets in the centre of the slab just calls out to be climbed, and it is reassuringly easy to see that the top of the slab is a good, positive hold should you need to "lay one on" for the top as a last resort – something that may be worth bearing in mind. Approach: a) 15 mins, b) 15 mins.

⑫ **Prelude to Space** HVS 4c ★★ 1977

10m A sample of the quality on offer hereabouts, at a more reasonable price. The right edge of the slab is unprotected and technical for the grade, involving excellent balancy moves in an interesting position.

⑬ **Wings of Unreason** E4 6b ★★★ 1977

11m Brilliant, and appropriately named, taking the centre of the beautiful slab direct via unusual pockets. The powerful, undercut start probably constitutes the technical crux although the excitement undoubtedly lies

Sometimes everything's perfect. Mark Sharratt scorching up Counterstroke of Equity in dream conditions. Photo: Ben Tye.

above, involving an experience not available on any other route!

The next two routes traditionally used protection in Wings and, whilst eliminates, they offer scintillating thin slab climbing that more than makes up for any lack of line. Both now go completely independent of Wings, and are harder and better for it.

Counterstroke of Equity E5 6c ★ 1985

11m After making the starting moves of Wings, and placing protection, move back down, and then right on a thin horizontal seam. From here, smear fiercely and directly up the slab to the right to a worrying top move, or a monster pendulum. For lovers of terror, **Counterstroke Direct**, E7 6c, climbs over the roof to gain the upper section directly, where you will sizzle like a fried egg, having avoided all holds and protection in Wings.

Nature Trail E5 6b ★★ 1985

11m To the left, a strenuous direct start through the roof leads onto the slab and protection in the pockets of the next route. From a standing position in these, smear directly to the top of the crag. Originally done with protection in Wings, easing the grade.

Track of the Cat E5 6a ★★★ 1977

12m One of the best routes at the Roaches, and for many people one the best on grit, is based on the flying left arête of the slab. From around the corner slightly to the left, powerful moves lead into a groove and small protection. Careful climbing rightwards from here leads to a pull round onto the slab and twin pockets. The immaculate arête above culminates in a truly exhilarating final move, with the gear a distant memory.

A great way to see this slab at a more reasonable grade is **Enchanted Forest** (E2 5c★★, 2003), which starts up Track of the Cat, traverses the slab with hands in pockets, then down slightly to gain and finish up Prelude to Space.

Willow Farm E4 6a ★★ 1977

10m To the left again the buttress is terminated by a neat little slab capped by a sloping gangway. Gain the right edge of this slab from the left and move up on tiny edges. A long reach over the top of the gangway may find a good hold, but some frantic yet precise footwork is required to reach easy ground. Worth three stars on any other buttress!

Very Far Boulders

Another classic set of boulders, good solid Skyline rock. The problems are seldom powerful, being more smeary and technical. Lower grade boulderers will find a lot to go at here.

The rocks above here have attracted climbers in the past. You are politely requested not to climb on these as they are friable and are eroding badly. Also, some of the area close by is sensitive for the protection of endangered species (wildlife, not human).

1 V0 (5b)
The left arête of the small chasm behind the main boulders.

2 Thin Seam
V0 (5b)
The thin seam right of the arête.

3 Green Jam Crack V0– (4c)
Right again, in the chasm.

4 Rounded Arête
V0– (4b)

5 Open Groove
V2 (5c)
Smear and palm up the sweet groove.

6 Two Pocket Slab
V2 (5c)
Climb past two small pockets to reach a short crack directly. Technical, demanding good footwork.

7 Lazy Trout
V2 (6a)
Climb the tallest part of the slab to reach a deep pocket.

8 VI (5c)
Go up just left of the arête to reach the upper arête.

9 V2 (6a)
Clamp your wicked way up the steep arête, full on. A very tasty **sit-start** goes from the slot underneath, V7 (6b).

10 Crack V0– (4a)

11 VI (5b)
From the wide crack, pull left to deep pockets, and follow these over the bulge. Exciting, but positive.

12 V2 (6a)
Up the right side of the arête. Sitting starters can do a **sit-start**, V6 (6b)

13 Off-Fingers Crack V2 (5c)

14 Pinkies to Perkies V0– (4b)
Hell of a nice!

15 V0– (4a)
Pad up the delicate slab.

16 VI (5c)
From beneath the arête, pull left and get established on the slab.

17 Inner Tube
V4 (6a)
Sit-start. From hands in the big round hole, lurch upwards to the top.

18 Short Arête
V0– (5a)

Very Far Boulders cont...

⑲ Wall and Rib
V0– (4c)

⑳ Left Crack
V0– (4c)

㉑ Right Crack
V0– (4b)

㉒ Easy Ramp
V0– (4a)

㉓ Flight Exam
V0+ (5b)

A peach. Climb the slab using the pocket for hands, feet and everything else. Essential practise for Wings of Unreason.

㉔ V1 (5b)

From the pocket, smear right and up, avoiding the top with your hands.

㉕ V5 (6b)

Technical and fingery climbing up the vague arête.

㉖ V4 (6a)

The right arête of the wall.

The Five Clouds

by Andi Turner

O.S. Ref. **SK001625** | Altitude: **375m a.s.l.**

*"Cloud Nine can also be climbed direct at 5c/6a...
Surely the most important addition to gritstone in the last five years!"*

Sarcastic response written in the *Chutney Valley Recorder* new routes book in Hanley.

The Five Clouds are the string of outcrops punctuating the subsidiary ridge below the Skyline area of the Roaches, clearly visible from the road leading to Roach End. These are little gems of crags that rank with the best to be found on the Skyline (from where it is clear that there are seven clouds, not five!). The grit is fine-grained, compact and sound, and formed into cracks, pockets, edges and scoops simply designed for climbing. The lines tend to be confident, straightforward challenges, often either steep forceful crack-lines or bald friction slabs. There is also a wealth of bouldering and a fine collection of micro-routes providing superb soloing for the competent. The setting gives the crags a delightfully peaceful and isolated ambience, heightened by almost guaranteed solitude, making the area feel a hundred miles from the hectic Roaches nearby.

Conditions & aspect

Very clean, compact rock. Quick-drying and relatively sheltered; climbing is possible all year round. Faces south-west, getting sun from midday till sunset.

Routes

Only about 50, but with a high proportion of multi-starred classics including arguably the Peak's finest HVS.

Ⓥ Bouldering

Limited but superb. Some excellent mini-routes, and bouldering around the crag, including a couple of the area's hardest, and a classic free-standing boulder below the Fourth Cloud.

Parking & approach

Park as for the Roaches. Inside the gate, turn immediately left along a quarry track. Where the track turns uphill into the quarry and towards the Upper Tier, follow a smaller track, past a National Park sign, straight on towards the First Cloud (10 minutes). To approach from the Upper Tier, follow a well-worn path from its northern end down into the quarry to join the lower track (10 minutes). Please do not take short-cuts from the road: the drystone walls are daunting and precarious, and their demolition is guaranteed to sour access agreements.

Access

Occasional bird restrictions will be clearly signposted. Observe these restrictions. Generally, although nominally in the designated 'quiet area' exclusion zone, there have been no problems as long as the proper approach is used. Please respect the privacy of the nearby cottages and the atmosphere of the place by keeping the noise down.

The climbs are described as one normally approaches from the Roaches lay-by, i.e. from **right** to **left**.

The First Cloud

Just past the small quarry the first Cloud is encountered up on the hillside – a large block with a cave at its base. There is some good slab climbing on this, and several routes have been done. However, in keeping with tradition, these routes continue to be un-named, un-graded, and un-recorded, so that it is still possible to have a true on-sight, not to say pioneering, experience.

The Second Cloud

The next cloud is 70m to the left, and consists of two buttresses separated by a grass slipway. The first buttress is split by a central dog-leg fissure, Communist Crack.

frisky V2 (5c), the crux being avoiding the wall on the right. Another sweetie goes up left from the pocket to a **slim flake**, then crank for the rail above, V2 (6a).

❷ Communist Crack VS 5a ★   pre-1968
8m You know you want to. Easy for the confident but surprisingly steep and awkward to protect for the floundering.

❸ The Outdoor Pursuits Cooperative
E1 5a   1998
8m The wall 3m left of Communist Crack is short but committing, with a grisly landing. From the boulders gain the narrow ledge and move up on small holds to the U-shaped crack, and on to the top.

Ten metres to the left, across a grassy slipway, a fine sharp arête springs up.

❹ Finger of Fate E2 6a ★★   1983
7m The perfect arête, climbed on its left, is a supreme test of barndoor laybacking. The situations are exciting, although difficulties decrease with height. ❼ Highball V4. **KGB** (HVS 4c, 1977) avoids the crux on the right. A desperate companion, **Nadin's Secret Finger**, V9 (7a), swings onto the left edge of the finger at a very poor hold with the aim of reaching the diagonal break at the top of the above route.

❺ Yankee Jam VS 5a   1973–80
8m The widening crack protruding from the smelly cave just left.

❶ Marxist Undertones VS 6a ★   1973–80
8m A delightful solo with a desperate low crux. From a deep pocket, dyno to the sloping ledge and mantel it. Continue up the arête on rugosities to the top. The VS climber's Parthian Shot. ❼ The first move is a superb boulder-problem in its own right (V2). Climbing the undercut **right arête** direct is a

Allen Williams on the highly technical
Finger of Fate, E2 6a.
Photo: Niall Grimes.

All around lay **the elements**

of a familiar landscape, each rendered special by the light that fell across them. Ahead, holding me transfixed, the sun fell down upon the earth, split, its contents spilling out. It appeared to me as though solid particles were raining down on distant streets and lying abundantly in fields. It was a place to which one could actually go, perhaps just ten miles away, across the plains of Cheshire.
Andy Popp,
At the End of an Evening Climbing in Staffordshire.

6 Lenin VD   *TR·Nancy 8/8/04*   *TR·Zoe*   pre-1968
8m Pleasant climbing up the crack just to the left again. *They looked scarey!*

7 Legends of Lost Leaders E3 5c ★   1980
8m A bold proposition starting up the centre of the slab by an awkward mantel and a committing reachy finish up the right hand arête. The unconvinced can escape leftwards along the ledge.

8 Stalin VD   *TR·Nancy 8/8/04*   *TR·Zoe*   pre-1968
8m The crack to the left.

9 Jimmy Carter HVD   1973–80
6m Climb the amiable rippled wall on flakes and protrusions.

The Third Cloud

The largest and finest of the clouds, with an imposing sheer face and a clutch of excellent routes spread across a range of grades. Indeed, all the routes are worth doing, with the notable exception of the first one.

10 Pointless Arête VS 4b   1977
6m Well it is really, as you can escape at almost any point.

11 The Big Flake VD   pre-1968
7m Wriggle, wiggle and writhe up the chimney. Superb. Laybacking the flake is a pointless E3 5b†, **Geordie Girl** (1990s).

12 The Little Flake HVS 5a   pre-1968
8m Overcome the small overhang with a ferocious pull.

13 Tim Benzadrino E3 5c   1979
7m The fat wall is spattered with tempting holds, but is positioned above a less than inspiring landing. Do you feel lucky?

14 The Bender VS 4b ★   1968–73
7m Thin curving cracks, almost in the gully, left of the two flakes.

⑮ Icarus Allsorts E4 6a ★★   1977

15m A wonderful name for a wonderful climb, based on the rounded right arête of the buttress. Purists will start by pulling through the roof of the cave to gain the top of the jutting block. From here step back across left to gain a flake and get onto the slab above the roof, and follow this to the ledge at the base of the wide corner crack. Step left and climb the arête in an exhilarating position, taking care not to fall off, as the gear leaves something to be desired. Taking the right arête of the wide corner crack gives **Waxwing** (E1 5a, 1979).

⑯ Flower Power Arête E2 5c ★   1968

15m From the rib left of the windy cave, climb to a small ledge. Balance up into the rounded flaky scoop, make a long move to a layback flake and follow it to the ledge above. Jam yourself in the tight chimney and squirm to the top.

⑰ Crabbie's Crack VS 4c ★★★   1950s

15m Crack climbing of the utmost quality, at the upper limit of the grade. Climb the perfect jamming crack, to arrive, exhausted, on a ledge. Finish up a little crack or, for an excellent delicate contrast, climb up and right to finish up the arête – the **Flaky Wall Finish** (HVS 4c★★★).

⑱ Crabbie's Crack Left-Hand

HVS 4c ★★   1968

16m A fine alternative to the crack follows flakes leftwards to easier ground. **Bakewell Tart** (E2 5c, 1991) forms a direct start to this route by climbing the arête on the left with the aid of some thin flakes.

To the left, at the foot of the main wall, a small round cave is usually full of unidentifiable charred remains and sheep poo. Endless eliminates and traverses can be invented on this low-level buttress to warm up or to hone one's technique for some of the more taxing routes on the buttress.

⑲ Laguna Sunrise E4 6c ★   1984

15m A desperate variation start to the next route. Clamber easily just right of the strange cave to stand in a break. Move up onto a flake, then scamper, scrape and slip up left to the central jug. A technical masterpiece ahead of its time. Side-runners are used but groundsweepers are still customary!

⑳ Appaloosa Sunset E3 5c ★★★   1977

16m An exquisite solution to the 'blank' slab. Climb the crack (Rubberneck) or the arête just right and, at 3m, launch rightwards along the diagonal line of holds, until a series of delicate and precise rockovers leads towards a jug. This is hard to gain and even harder to leave! Wander to the top past an obscure circular flake. Gear is placed high in Rubberneck at this grade otherwise award yourself a hard E4. The traverse can be gained direct at 6b from undercuts left of the cave; **The Eclipsed Peach Start** (1983), a worthy variation. Some great climbing can be had by **Walking on Sunshine** (E3 6b★, 1993). This forsakes Rubberneck, and foot-traverses the Appaloosa hand-holds until an awkward move gains the jug. Continue into Crabbie's to finish.

㉑ Rubberneck HVS 5a ★★★   1967

15m An exemplary route, sustained, technical and well-protected; the classic of the crag. Rubberhips may be a more appropriate name. Start at the base of the scoop, dislocate your femur from your pelvis, and move up to the crack above (crux), where superb runners can be placed. Swarm up the crack and finish up the slab above, elated.

Top **Style** Points

An effort has been made in the first ascents list to record style improvements for ascents of the harder routes in the county, say, E6 and above, routes which have only previously been done with inspection from a top-rope. These records are very incomplete, and all further information would be welcome. The top performances have been on *Paralogism*, *Doug*, *Obsession Fatale* and *One Chromosome's Missing* (and on one of these, the hero didn't even make it to the top). Next to that, *Black Eyed Dog*, *A Fist Full of Crystals*, *Piece of Mind*, *Bloodspeed*, *Barriers in Time*, *Painted Rumour*, *Script for a Tear* and *National Acrobat* have all 'had the treatment'.

See **The Roaches First Ascents** *on page 92 for details, and be careful out there.*

Perfect jams make up for the wild situations on Crabbie's Crack. VS 4c (page 83). Sam Whittaker climbing.
Photo: David Simmonite.

㉒ Cloudbusting E4 6b ★ 1986

8m A real boulder problem in the sky. Start as for Rubberneck then climb the sickle-shaped flakes on the left to their termination. Sketch rapidly leftwards across the slab, mantel up and clutch at the grass. Run down to the ground and do it all over again. Protection is placed in Rubberneck at this grade.

㉓ Persistence V3 (6a)

The sweet and appropriately named problem based on the little flake.

㉔ Who Needs Ready Brek? V10 (7a)

Persistence won't be enough to get you up this one; fingers of steel and outstanding technique are also required. Bounce out right from Persistence to the thin crack-line and glide to a reasonable hold 4m right. Levitate up to the next holds, where enlightenment is achieved. Old school E4 for those with nuts and a rope.

㉕ Elastic Arm HVS 5b ★ pre-1968

5m Gain the wide crack from the left, then stretch, contort and squabble with this mighty fissure. Knee-pads advised.

㉖ Sands of Time E4 6a ★ 1993

5m A sustained and scary route up the hour-glass-shaped wall to the left. Follow the blunt nose to the good hold in the middle of the wall. Pull up and leftwards to finish. Side-runners are of limited comfort.

㉗ Tip Toe HVS 4c 1993

5m The left side of the hour-glass is defined by a slabby scoop. Climb the slab using the arête and go directly over the bulge above. Easily escapable.

㉘ Squash Balls VD 2001

5m The impressively smooth and tight chimney. A classic of its ilk.

㉙ Glass Back VD pre-1968

5m The steep crack above the left end of the terrace.

㉚ Blue Bandanna E1 5b ★ 1978

20m A pleasant girdle covering much good rock. From the block at the base of Icarus Allsorts traverse left over the cave and into Crabbie's Crack. Continue to the Left-Hand Variant and across to Appaloosa Sunset. Nip across the hollow flakes to the refuge of Rubberneck. Finish up this, or prolong the expedition up the slab to the left.

The Fourth Cloud

The next buttress is slightly smaller but every bit as sweet. Again, it offers fine technical climbs on the best of rock. Mostly, the landings are superb and therefore ideal for a picnic or for falling off onto.

㉛ Roman Nose E2 5b 1977

7m Bold and hairy. Step off the block and climb middle of the slab on little bendy flakes to the top. Protection is minimal, and the holds might snap off.

㉜ Roman Candle HVS 5b 2002

7m Much more sensibly, why not stride left off the block and pull into the well-protected thin crack?

㉝ Chockstone Corner D pre-1968

6m Every crag needs one! L- Nancy 8/9/04 S- Zoe

㉞ Mantelshelf Route D ★ pre-1968

8m Rock up and up to the top via the ledges.

㉟ Mirror, Mirror E4 6b ★★ 1979

10m Definitive Five Clouds quality, with tough technical climbing throughout. Climb the sharp iron-rich rugosities to the sloping break (nuts up and right). Skip left into the undercut arch and gain the thin crack. Finish more easily.

㊱ Boysen's Delight HVS 5c ★ 1968

9m A satisfying climb, ascending the groove in the perfect wall to a steep exit onto the ledge. Getting into the groove is pleasantly tricky and the protection is guaranteed to make you smile. Finish up the crack above. Ⓥ The scoop to the left gives a fine problem. **Milky Buttons**, V8 (6c).

37 Private Display EI 5b ★   1970
9m An intimidating route; tough with obscure, absorbing moves. Start on the rock on the left and climb the vague rib and thin crack above.

38 The Shining Path E6 6c†   1997
9m The slab on the left is climbed by extremely thin smearing. Pull over the small roof to a horizontal break (small cams), and continue up the bald slab above directly. Hard, but painfully contrived. The left edge of the slab is **Winter in Combat** (EI 5c, 1985).

39 Right Block Crack S   pre-1968
9m The right-hand twin. The unclimbed roof to the left again has a nasty landing, but a few tempting holds.

40 Left Block Crack S   pre-1968
5m And the left-hand twin.

41 Smun VS 4c ★   pre-1968
9m Climb the crack, bypassing the overhang on the left, and continuing up the corner above to a demeaning finish onto the grassy ledge.

42 Stranglehold EI 5b   1979
10m Gain the upper crack of Smun steeply from the left via an undercut and a layback.

43 The Boston Strangler E2 5b   1991
11m Follow Stranglehold until just below its junction with Smun. Swing left on to the rib, then move up and leftwards to finish around a block.

44 Meander VD ★ *L - Nancy 8/8/04* *S - Zoe* pre-1968
8m A pleasant route starting up the slab on its right-hand side, then move leftwards on the upper slab to the top. If only it were longer!

45 Meander Variation EI 5b   1977
9m Start up Meander and then gain the centre of the short steep wall by means of the hold in the centre of the wall. Bold.

46 Wander VD   pre-1968
5m The crack to the left. **V** The left arête gives a V0 (5b) problem; **Static**.

V Fourth Cloud Bouldering

A boulder beyond and below the main crag gives a couple of the best problems in the area. Many other eliminates are possible and worthwhile.

47 The Hanging Slab V7 (6c)
Rock desperately up onto the slab, through the undercut scooped face, then gibber directly upwards. Mega. The **Full Lip Traverse**, V8 (6c), starts as for this, then drapes rightwards to finish up the right arête.

48 The Hard Arête V7 (6b)

The frustratingly slopey right arête of the flat, downhill face. The **sit-start** to this problem, from down and right, is a mighty V11 (7a).

49 Left Arête V2 (5c)

The easier arête on the left of the flat face, using flakes on the front.

Ⓥ The capped slab on the hillside higher up and left provides some superb smearing practice. The classic is the right side of the slab, **Holdless Slab**, V2 (6a). Smearing left along the lip and up the **left arête** is V2 (6a), while the **left arête direct** is V3 (6a). The **tower** a bit left gives a V2 (5c) problem if the front face is stuck to.

The Fifth Cloud

The last of the Five Clouds, 100m left again, provides a small but fitting finale.

50 Foxy Lady MVS 4c   1977

7m The crack in the steep left face of the buttress, exiting right onto the front face.

51 Fifth Cloud Eliminate HVS 5a ★   1969

9m From just left of the leaning arête, swing up right to the ledge. Move across the slab to gain a shallow finishing scoop. This can be reached directly by the heathery crack below at the same grade.

52 Cloud Nine E2 5b ★   1977

10m Definitely requires cumulative nimbleness. From the ledge on the arête, move up and then make a committing reach/slap for a good little edge, just below the bigger ledge. Finish with ease.

53 Always Dreaming E4 6b   1993

6m Climb the hanging right-hand arête of the buttress. Start on the right then swing left to climb the slabby arête. **Ⓥ** Staying on the right is V2 (5c).

Ⓥ Fifth Cloud Bouldering

The **direct start** to Cloud Nine gives a shin-scraping V2 (6a). The brutally overhanging arête on the back of the block is an unclimbed highball.

From here, the next rock is the Nth Cloud. In many ways a continuation of the Five Clouds, but a crag with its own personality. However, to approach, do not continue walking from the Fifth Cloud. Instead, return to the main parking and follow the approach instructions below. Delicate negotiations with landowners has secured access to this beautiful crag as long as the correct approach is used.

The best gritstone climbing in **Derbyshire** actually **lies** in **Staffordshire.**

Paul Nunn, Mountain Magazine

Sam Whittaker makes the final technical moves to reach the strange hollow flake on Appaloosa Sunset. E3 5c from where bold but easier climbing leads to the summit. Five Clouds climbing at its best. (page 83).
Photo: David Simmonite.

The Nth Cloud

by David Garnett

O.S. Ref. **SK998636** | Altitude: **425m a.s.l.**

This is the attractive outcrop, conspicuous from the road leading up from Meerbrook. It is the logical conclusion to the Five Clouds chain of buttresses, but situated about 1km further along the ridge. Nth Cloud is rarely visited and small, with only a handful of routes. Yet here is a real little gem of a crag, with one of the finest single slabs of gritstone in the area (an extravagant claim given the competition) and top-class bouldering. The rock is sound, clean (despite the lack of traffic), peerlessly rough and beautifully textured with a variety of ripples, scoops and pockets. All this gives some delightful slab and crack climbing in what feels almost like a mountain crag in its solitude and outlook.

Conditions & aspect

The buttresses face south-west and the fine open slabs dry quickly, giving good climbing all year round. In blustery weather the crag can feel quite exposed, but even a hint of afternoon sun more than makes up for it.

Routes

Amongst barely a dozen routes are some real classics, including one of the boldest in the Peak and the superb Pillar of Judgement, worth the price of admission on its own. However, there is also easily enough in this splendid area to provide a quality day's climbing for an adventurous VS team.

Ⓥ Bouldering

The short clean walls to the left of the main buttress offer excellent bouldering, some of it very hard indeed.

Approaches & access

The road under the Roaches and Five Clouds leads round to Roach End meeting the lane rising steeply from Meerbrook at an acute-angled junction. Approaching from the Roaches, about 50m before this junction is an angled gate on the right with stone gate-posts, whence a track leads almost directly to the crag. There is space for two or three cars on the verge opposite the gate. However, please take care not to obstruct the gateway. Access to the crag is sensitive and this, more convenient approach has been recently negotiated. Please don't give the farmer any reason to regret his co-operation.

From the road, some clean flat walls can be seen 150m to the left of the main crag. The first routes are to be found amongst the boulders in the trees, at a slightly lower level. The most obvious feature among the large boulders is a wide corner crack.

❶ Josephina E4 5c   1998

6m Just left of the corner, an undercut start leads rightwards to a small ledge on the nose. Finish to the left on a slab and arête. Unprotected with a horrible landing.

❷ Gromit HVS 5a   1997

8m The obvious corner crack. Good thrutchy jamming leads to a tricky exit.

❸ Gromit Arête V2 (5c)

An exciting problem up the arête to the right, starting on the left-hand side. The **sit-start** is V7 (6c).

Swivel Finger Wall

The clean walls above the trees contain some beautiful boulder problems, made from perfect grit and with perfect landings. There are lines here that will eventually provide some of the best and hardest problems around.

4 The Flakes V4 (6a)
The flakes at the left end of the wall are sustained and high above a sketchy landing. A good problem.

The thin flake and roof just right is a desperate project. Right again, sidepull flakes leading to a rounded top have been tried by some of Britain's best, but has still not gone. Worthy.

5 Swivel Finger V3 (6a)
Excellent laybacking up the classic arête, with a tricky start and an awkward finish. A supreme problem. The **sit-start** is V5. **The Thrutch** is a full-bodied classic up the chasm right of Swivel Finger, V0 (4c). Another top-drawer project is up the very fingery flake right of The Thrutch.

The next routes are on the left-hand buttress of the main crag.

6 Shaun's Other End VS 4c   1997
12m Climb the flake to the ledge. Continue up the square face above on its left edge.

7 Grenadier VD ★   1960s
12m Climb into the obvious sentry box just right and exit to the ledge. Finish up the wide crack.

8 Happiness from Outer Space S   2002
12m The right arête, via pleasant pockets and a good break. Nice.

9 Slanting Crack S   1960s
12m The awkward wide crack just around the corner to the right.

10 Mayhem VS 5a   1968
12m The even more awkward right-hand crack leading to an overhang. Move left and struggle on.

11 Green Chimney VD   1960s
11m The eponymous feature just right again, finishing round the chockstone.

V An angular boulder perched above the crag has a couple of steep problems, The **Leaky Traverse** V2 (5c) starts on the left beneath the little roof then traverses up past a couple of steps to finish on the shelf. **Manteling leftwards** through the steps in the lip is V1 (5c).

The buttress to the right gives a number of extended boulder problems.

12 Inexplicably Anonymous S   1960s
5m The obvious crack gives good jamming.

13 Totally Unprecedented HVS 5a   1985
7m The left arête of the open corner, started on the left and finishing slightly to the right. Alternatively, start by climbing the left face of the corner directly. The corner itself is VD, but often dirty.

⑭ Crystal Voyager E4 7a ★★   1984
6m Very technical climbing, slightly too high to be a boulder problem, up the right wall of the corner. Reach the faint flake and continue on poor pockets. Tricky. ❷ **Highball** V8.

⑮ Spankasaurus Does Chicago V3 (6a)
The arête to the right is a good highball boulder problem.

⑯ Dreadful V0 (5b)
The edge of the buttress to a jug.

The Main Face

The main attraction is undoubtedly the superb main slab.

⑰ Little Crack VS 5a ★   1968
6m The brilliant finger crack at the left end of the main buttress. If only it were longer.

⑱ Rowan Tree Crack S   1968
9m The crack with the useful tree is now barely climbable.

⑲ Ageing Adolescents E6 6c   1984
10m The slab to the right via shallow pockets. Normally climbed with a runner in the tree at E4.

⑳ Plumb-Line VS 4c   1968
12m The right-hand crack. Again, currently rather vegetated.

㉑ Judge Dread E6 6b ★★   1986
15m Bold and transparently thin climbing up the unforgiving main sweep of the buttress. Climb the pockety rib past a hole (wedged nuts) to the ledge. From its centre, gain an incut at the base of a diagonal seam (RPs), and climb this to the top.

Judge Jules (E8 7a, 2003) is a last minute addition to this slab, and perhaps the hardest lead in the guide. Gain the ledge as for Judge Dread. From its left-hand side, step up and left to gain a mono. Very thin climbing leads directly to the top of the slab.

㉒ Pillar of Judgement E4 5c ★★★   1975
15m Elegant and bold, with its crux high on the perfect right arête of the slab. Climb the pocketed crack, then step right and balance confidently up to reach the wide finishing crack. Remember to take something big enough to take advantage of it. The lower arête may be climbed direct at 6a.

㉓ The Perp E2 5b   2002
25m Side-steps Judgement only to cross Judge Dread. An entertaining girdle, starting from the ledge behind the holly (on Barbecue Corners). Step awkwardly round the arête, hand-traverse the ledge and step delicately into Plumb-Line. Traverse pockets to Rowan Tree Crack. Climb this for a few feet until a foot-traverse into Little Crack can be made. Finish up this. Careful ropework aids the getaway.

㉔ Barbecue Corners HVD ★   1960s
18m Climb the corner to the right of the pillar. Masochists may wish to belay in the holly.

John H Bull on Nth Cloud. Photo: Dave Garnett.

㉕ The Pinnacle Start and Shaun's End
HVS 5a ★ 1960s
18m Two variations on the last route combine to make an interesting and independent way up the cliff. Climb boldly up the front face of the pinnacle. Jump to the ledge in Barbecue Corners and then gain the scooped ledge in the right wall. Either continue rightwards along it or, better, climb the short awkward crack above.

㉖ Metaphysical Scoop E4 6b ★ 1987
9m Short but cerebral. Climb Barbecue Corners to reach the pocketed scoop on the right. Puzzling and committing moves up and right gain the line of large pockets. Finish philosophically via mantelshelves.

The Roaches First Ascents

1901	**Raven Rock Gully**	1927	**Fledgling's Climb**
	Members of the Kyndwyr Club	1927	**Lucas Chimney**
pre-1913	**Cannonball Crack**	1931	**Inverted Staircase, Fern Crack** A S Pigott
1913	**Jeffcoat's Chimney, Jeffcoat's Buttress**	1939	**Calcutta Crack** A S Pigott
	Stanley Jeffcoat	1945	**Karabiner Chimney,**
1922	**Bachelor's Buttress, Black and Tans**		**Pinnacle Arête, Bilberry Traverse**
	A S 'Fred' Pigott		R Desmond-Stevens, G Stoneley
	Pedestal Route Left-Hand, Pedestal Route	1945	**Karabiner Crack, Tower Chimney**
	Right-Hand, Right Route, Crack and		(originally Chimney Direct)
	Corner Morley Wood		A Simpson, R Desmond-Stevens
	'On Crack and Corner the leader took a shoulder	1945	**Slab and Arête, Central Massif**
	from his second who was securely tied on to the		(originally Slab Route)
	block and it looked impossible without this.'		G Stoneley, R Desmond-Stevens
	Rucksack Club Journal	1945	**Demon Wall, Beckermet Slab, Maud's**
1913–24	**Via Dolorosa, Kestrel Crack,**		**Garden, Broken Slab, Rotunda Buttress,**
	Upper Tier Girdle		**Technical Slab** A Bowden Black
1913–24	**Bengal Buttress** Ivan Waller	1946 Oct 6	**Valkyrie** Peter Harding, A Bowden Black
1924	**Left-Hand Route, Right-Hand Route**	1947	**Mantelshelf Slab** Karabiner Club members
	Lindlay Henshaw	1947	**Saul's Crack** Joe Brown
1927	**Guano Gully** Originally named as	1949	**Hangman's Crack, Scarlet Wall,**
	Dodo's Dilemma but misplaced in the 1957		G W S Pigott, C Topping
	guidebook, this route has kept the former name.	1924–49	**Kelly's Shelf, Flake Chimney** Harry Kelly

1951	**Dorothy's Dilemma** Joe Brown, Merrick 'Slim' Sorrell, Dorothy Sorrell
1951	**Valkyrie Direct, Matinee, The Mincer, The Bulger** Joe Brown, Don Whillans *Matinee was called after the audience who sat on the boulders and watched the pioneering of Brown and Whillans on their through leads. The Mincer was named for obvious reasons.*
1949–51	**Little Chimney, Lucas Chimney, Flake Chimney, Calcutta Crack, Central Route, Heather Slab, Chicken Run, High Crossing, Pinnacle Crack**
1953 Jan	**The Sloth** Don Whillans, Joe Brown
1954	**Aqua** Joe Brown, Don Whillans
1954	**Capitol Climb** R Handley, Nat Allen
early-1950s	**Crabbie's Crack** Bob Downes, Miss Nea Morin *The Flaky Wall Finish added by Colin Foord in 1968.*
1955 May 25	**Damascus Crack** G W S Pigott, W H Craster
1955	**Roscoe's Wall** Don Roscoe
1955	**Runner Route** Nat Allen, D Campbell
1951–57	**Wallaby Wall, Alpha, Breakfast Problem, Mistaken Identity, Cave Arête, Joiner, Ogden, Ralph's Mantelshelves, Cracked Arête, Right-Hand Crack, Pinnacle Slab, Capstan's Corner, Rowan Tree Traverse, Square Chimney, Late Night Final, Central Traverse, Lighthouse, Trio Chimney, Left Twin Crack, Letterbox Gully, Perched Block Arête, Cave Buttress, Pinnacle Slab** John and Tony Vereker, Graham Martin and some members from North Stafford Mountaineering Club
1951–57	**Lone Ascent, Contrary Mary**
1958	**Crack of Gloom** Joe Brown, Don Whillans *'Brown and Whillans forced the dark and strenuous Crack of Gloom and stories were whispered of a couple of points of aid.'* **1981 Guidebook.**
1958	**Teck Crack, Choka** (I pt.)**, Rhodren** Joe Brown *Rhodren was later attributed a point of aid which was certainly not in evidence in earlier descriptions. The first free ascent of Choka is unknown but was certainly achieved soon after the 1973 guidebook.*
1958	**Ackit** (right-hand finish)**, Slippery Jim** Don Whillans *Ackit Direct Finish climbed by the Barley brothers on May 1, 1967.*
1958	**Reset Portion of Galley 37, Perverted Staircase** Geoff Sutton *The former route was*

named after a printer's error that appeared in the 1957 guidebook.

1958	**Lightning Crack** Don Whillans, Joe Brown
1960	**The Girdle Traverse** Alan Parker, Paul Nunn, Bob Brayshaw
1960	**West's Wallaby** Graham West *The Direct finish added by Mike Simpkins in the same year.*
1960	**Walleroo, Wombat, Elegy** (I pt.) Mike Simpkins *Elegy was climbed free by John Yates in 1969.*
1963 Sep	**The Underpass, Hank's Horror** Dave Salt, Colin Foord
1963 Sep	**Hypothesis, Tower Eliminate** Colin Foord, Dave Salt
1967 May 1	**Rubberneck** Robin Barley, Tony Barley
pre-1968	**Communist Crack** Hugh Banner
pre-1968	**Lenin, Stalin, The Big Flake, The Little Flake, Elastic Arm, Glass Back, Chockstone Crack, Mantelshelf Route, Right Block Crack, Left Block Crack, Smun, Meander, Wander** *All of these routes appeared uncredited in the 1968 guidebook.*
1968	**Sifta's Quid** John Amies *The result of a bet by Dave Salt who claimed that everything that could be done, had been done. Amies never received the pound.*
1968	**Bad Poynt** Ray Baddley, Terry Pointon
1957–68	**Yong Arête, Yong, Wisecrack, Pincer, Flimney, Straight Crack, Punch** (I pt.)**, Prow Corner, Prow Cracks, Pepper, Calcutta Buttress, Rib Wall, The Rib, Gully Wall, Jelly Roll, Easy Gully Wall, Kelly's Connection, Right Route Right, The Neb Finish, Black Velvet, Cornflake, Tealeaf Crack, Libra, Rooster, The Pugilist, Southpaw, Navy Cut, Bruno Flake, Tobacco Road, Condor Chimney, Condor Slab, Letter Box Cracks, Middleton's Motion, The Black Pig, Ogden Recess, Ogden Arête, Thrug, Cave Crack, Stephen, Abstract, Karabiner Slab, Alpha Arête, Omega** *The first free ascent of Punch was made in 1978 by Jonny Woodward (solo).*
1968	**Crabbie's Crack Left-Hand** John Yates (solo)
1968 Nov	**Plumb-Line, Little Crack, Rowan Tree Crack** John Yates, Colin Foord
1968 Nov	**Mayhem** Colin Foord, John Yates

1968	**Boysen's Delight, Flower Power Arête**
	Martin Boysen *The latter named after the rather*
	floral T-shirt worn by the first ascensionist.
1969	**Fifth Cloud Eliminate** John Yates
1969 Jul	**Humdinger** Mick Guilliard
1969 Oct 12	**The Swan (1 pt.)** John Gosling, Mike
	Simpkins *The aid was a peg! FFA Ron Fawcett*
	and Geoff Birtles, 1977.
1969	**Raven Rock Gully Left-Hand, Pebbledash**
	Dave Salt
1969	**The Chimney, Honky Tonk,**
	Flutterbye Grooves Colin Foord
1960s	**Barbecue Corners, The Pinnacle Start,**
	Grenadier, Green Chimney, Slanting Crack
	North Staffordshire Mountaineering Club
	members *Shaun's End added in 2002 by Phil*
	Hitchings and Richard Taylor.
1970 Apr	**The Black Ram, Black Ram Arête, Dangler,**
	Steeplechase Crack, Dazzler, Mudhopper,
	Slither, Steeplechaser, Tree Grooves,
	Tree Corner, The Girdle Traverse of
	Far Skyline Steve Dale, Brian Dale
1970	**The Death Knell, Private Display**
	John Yates, Colin Foord *Originally Death Knell*
	finished up dirty cracks just left. The direct finish was
	added by Jonny and Andrew Woodward in
	1977. Private Display was named from the leader's
	split trouser seams.
1971 Apr	**Up the Swanee** John Yates
1971 Jun 22	**Ruby Tuesday** Mick Guilliard, John Yates
1971	**Freak Out** Steve Dale, Brian Dale
1973 Jun	**Acid Drop** Jerry Peel, Tony Barley *Named*
	by Jonny Woodward in 1979, believing it to be a
	first ascent. Peel's name, Skytrain, along with the first
	ascent claim, was mistakenly transposed to a route
	further right. The names are being kept to avoid
	confusion.
1968–73	**Swinger, Aperitif, Kelly's Direct, Waistline,**
	Oversight, Go Girl, Come Girl, Battery
	Crack, The Bender
1974	**Ascent of Man, Days of Future Passed,**
	Mantis Andrew Woodward,
	Jonny Woodward
1974 Aug 17	**Round Table** John Allen, Nick Colton,
	Steve Bancroft
1975 Mar 2	**Safety Net** John Allen, Steve Bancroft, Tom
	Proctor
1975	**Nosepicker** Jonny Woodward (solo)

1975	**Pillar of Judgement, Commander Energy**
	John Allen, Mark Stokes
	The former named and top-roped by Colin Foord in
	November 1968.
1975	**Hunky Dory** Gabriel Regan and party
1976	**Melaleucion** Steve Dale, Barry Marsden
	Named after the black and white family cat.
1976	**In Passing, Wheeze, Looking for Today**
	Jonny Woodward
1976 Sep	**Enigma Variation** Andrew Woodward,
	Jonny Woodward
1977	**Mild Thing, San Melas, Wild Thing,**
	Prelude to Space Andrew Woodward,
	Jonny Woodward *The latter two routes*
	were reputedly climbed in spring 1974 by
	John Allen and Steve Bancroft.
1977	**Foxy Lady, Bad Sneakers** Dave Jones
	Bad Sneakers was named after Simpson who had
	been attempting to steal all of Jones' lines.
1977	**Wings of Unreason, Track of the Cat, Bone**
	Idol, Spectrum, Spare Rib, Lung Cancer,
	Cloud Nine Jonny Woodward,
	Andrew Woodward *Wings claimed to be the*
	hardest route in the world (at HXS/E6 6c) due to
	the extensive amount of top-roping required before
	the ascent.
	'Magnifying glass for aid'.
1977	**Appaloosa Sunset, Roman Nose**
	Dave Jones, Ian Johnson, John Gilbert
	On the former, a home-made protection device, for
	the hole at half-height, was measured for the ascent
	well in advance.
1977	**Chalkstorm, KGB, Pointless Arête**
	Ian 'Hotshot' Johnson, Dave Jones
1977 Oct 15	**Piece of Mind** Jonny Woodward,
	Andrew Woodward *Dawes fell off the last move,*
	on-sight, in 1986, and somehow survived. Flashed by
	Kevin Thaw in 1997, after watching top-ropers, and
	ground-up by Pete Robins in 2001. Pete also took the
	fall from the top move, but dusted himself off, and got
	back on again. The direct finish added in a panic by
	Niall Grimes in 1996: "More an emergency exit than
	a direct finish."
1977	**Icarus Allsorts, Tower Face** Al Simpson,
	Dave Jones *The initial section of Icarus Allsorts*
	had been climbed earlier in the year by Dave Jones
	and John Gilbert.
1977	**Meander Variation, Willow Farm**
	Chris Hamper

1977	**Smear Test** Gabriel Regan and party
1977	**Skytrain** *Wrongly credited to Jerry Peel and Tony Barley. Their name, Skytrain, actually referred to their previously uncredited first ascent of what has become known as Acid Drop.*
1978	**Diamond Wednesday, Wipers, Short Trip etc, Something Better Change, Sparkle, War Wound, Shortcomings, Substance, Poisonous Python, Crenation, Coldfinger, Hanging Around, Fred's Café, Chicane Destination, Chicane, A.M. Anaesthetic, The Aspirant, Time to be Had, Sennapod, Days Gone By, Bed of Nails, National Hero, Graffiti, The Valve, Third Degree Burn** Gary Gibson, either solo, or with Ian Johnson, Nick Longland, Dave Jones, John Perry, Mark 'Ralph' Hewitt, Derek Beetlestone or Fred Cook
1978	**The Tower of Bizarre Delights, Joe Public, Babbacombe Lee, Mousey's Mistake, Sorcerer's Apprentice, Blue Bandanna** Dave Jones, either alone, or with Bob Cope, Tony Bristlin, Ian Johnston or Al Simpson
1978 Apr 6	**Schoolies** Phil Burke, Gary Gibson *Later climbed direct by John Codling*
1978 Apr	**Dawn Piper** John Codling (solo)
1978 May	**Lybstep** John Dodd
1978 May	**Kicking Bird** Al Simpson, Dave Jones (AL), Nick Longland, Tony Bristlin *Strung together over two evenings. Where Jones failed on the first pitch Simpson used his knees. Most repeat ascensionists follow suit!*
1978 Oct 14	**Headless Horseman** Jonny Woodward
1978	**Hawkwing** Al Simpson, Dave Jones
1979	**Heartbleed, Destination Venus, Curvature, Between the Tiles, Definitive Gaze, Split Personality, The Sublime, Stranglehold, Topaz, 39th Step, Genetix, Public Enemy Number One, Wrong Way Round, Chronicle, Microcosm, Inspiration Point** Gary Gibson, either unseconded, or with Dave Jones, Ian Barker, John Perry or Phil Wilson
1979	**Gypfast, Garlic** Phil Gibson
1979	**Gillted, Simpkins' Overhang** Phil Burke, unseconded, or with George Cooper *Gillted named after Burke's ex-girlfriend. Only known repeat by Dave Aucott, although he went up the arête left of Painted Rumour, the original finish being desperate.*

Possibly the hardest of the three roof routes. Mike Simpkins had top-roped the overhang over a decade earlier.

1979	**Eugene's Axe, Waxwing** John Codling, Andy Fox, Dave Jones *Eugene's Axe named in honour of Rock Hall Cottage denizen Doug Moller who had erected a fence around The Lower Tier and fended off all-comers with an axe. Lower section first climbed by Dave Wiggin in 1978.*
1979	**Mirror, Mirror** Andrew Woodward (solo)
1979	**Grilled Fingers, Burrito Deluxe, The Fantasy Finish, Tim Benzadrino, Sign of the Times** Dave Jones, either unseconded or with John Codling or Gary Gibson
1979	**Sally James** Nick Longland (solo)
1973–80	**Marxist Undertones, Yankee Jam, Jimmy Carter**
1980	**Legends of Lost Leaders, Carrion, The Thin Air, Circuit Breaker, Poison Gift, Licence to Run** (1 pt.) Gary Gibson, either unseconded, or with Derek Beetlestone or Fred Crook *A controversial hanging rope was used on The Thin Air. Licence to Run was given a joke grade of E2 5c, which it retained. FFA by Pete O'Donovan and Gary Cooper in the same month.*
1980 Sep	**Antithesis** Jonny Woodward *Climbed in marked contrast to his previous first ascents, Woodward reluctantly took over the lead after Gibson had shown the sequence to everyone but failed to complete the lead.*
1980	**The Super Girdle** John Codling, Dave Jones
1980	**Sidewinder** Phil Burke, Bob Toogood *The first pitch was climbed by Gary Gibson in 1979.*
1980	**Bareback Rider** Dave Jones
1981	**Trebia, Live Bait, Hallow to Our Men, Automatix, Strain Station, Entente Cordiale, Swan Bank** Gary Gibson, either solo, or with Derek Beetlestone, Mark Hewitt or Hazel Carnes, the future Mrs Gibson
1981	**Quickbrew** Fred Crook, Ian Barker
1982	**Pebbles on a Wessex Beach, Slips** Gary Gibson
1982 Apr	**Entropy's Jaw** Andrew Woodward (solo)
1982 Jul	**Formative Years** Howard Tingle (solo)

| 1982 | **Triple Point, Poodle Vindaloo**   Jonny Woodward *The direct start to Triple Point was added in 1983 by Nick Dixon.* |

1982 **Triple Point, Poodle Vindaloo**   Jonny Woodward *The direct start to Triple Point was added in 1983 by Nick Dixon.*

1982 **Crystal Grazer**   Phil Burke

1982 **A Day at the Seaside**
Fred Crook, Ken Crook

1983 **Loculus Lie, Bloodstone, Finger of Fate**
Simon Nadin, Richard Davies *An early start was made on Loculus Lie to avoid sweaty hands and to study for exams the following day.*

1983 Sep 25 **A Fist Full of Crystals**   Nick Dixon *Climbed in mistake for Crystal Grazer. Named from a top-rope ascent by Jonny Woodward who commented: 'Undoubtedly the hardest piece of climbing on the Roaches. It has three desperate moves involving an unlikely toe-jam move, a weird high sort of bridge and an all out crystal move. There are no runners and a fall would land you painfully in a holly tree. It will take me quite a time to pluck up the courage to lead it!' Climbed on-sight by Andy Popp and Johnny Dawes in 1985/86.*

1983 Oct 20 **Barriers in Time**   Simon Nadin *Climbed ground-up, with falls, by Allen Williams, headpointed by Nick Dixon, and flashed by Tony Ryan, all within a few months of the first ascent.*

1983 **Clive Coolhead etc**
Nick Dixon, Steve Lowe

1983 **The Eclipsed Peach**   Allen Williams

1984 **Destination Earth, Crystal Voyager, Secrets of Dance, Laguna Sunrise**   Simon Nadin *Destination Earth originally led with a side-runner by Phil Burke as Earthbound. Possible 2nd ascent by Sam Whittaker, 3rd Chris Hudgins, 2002. Crystal Voyager repeated by Andi Turner, 2003.*

1984 **Ageing Adolescents, Pindles Numb**
Nick Dixon *The former was led with a deviation into Rowan Tree Crack for holds and protection. Simon Nadin climbed without the crack for holds, but used the side-runners. Done without side-runners by Julian Lines in October 2003. The name of the latter refers to the effects of a fall into the holly tree.*

1984 Sep 25 **Bloodspeed**   Simon Nadin *Climbed on-sight by Johnny Dawes in 1986 and Kevin Thaw 1992.*

1985 Jan **Winter in Combat**   Richard Davies (solo)

1985 **Against the Grain, Script for a Tear**
Simon Nadin *Second ascent of the former by Justin Critchlow, 3rd by Andi Turner, 1990s. The latter climbed on-sight by Johnny Dawes in 1986.*

1985 Apr 23 **Totally Unprecedented**
Gary Gibson (solo)

1985 Jul 13 **New Fi'nial**   Simon Nadin, Richard Davies, Gary Cooper *Unrepeated?*

1985 **Catastrophe Internationale, Fluorescent Stripper**   Nick Dixon, solo, or with Andi Lovatt *The former climbed on a BMC international meet.*

1985 Oct 13 **Painted Rumour**   Simon Nadin, Martin Veale *A loose flake was glued back to the roof! Climbed on-sight by Dave Thomas in 1998 and Ben Bransby in 1999.*

1985 Nov **Nature Trail, Art Nouveau**   Simon Nadin *Art Nouveau on-sighted by Adam Long in 2001, and climbed ground up by Pete Robins in 2002.*

1985 Dec 27 **Counterstroke of Equity**   Richard Davies *Stolen whilst Simon Nadin was sampling his first (and last!) taste of Scottish winter climbing. Direct start by Julian Lines, 2003.*

1985 **Little Perforations**
Gary Cooper, Fred Crook

1986 Feb **Ou Est Le Spit?**   Nick Dixon, Simon Nadin *Originally E6, holds being improved by wire-brushing.*

1986 Apr **Judge Dread**   Nick Dixon, Simon Whalley *Top-roped first, and using a pre-placed runner complete with long extension to, essentially, top-rope the crux. The first proper ascent by Mark Sharratt in 2002, solo.*

1986 Apr **Doug**   Nick Dixon *Only soloed after some optimistically glued pebbles had been pulled off during a top-roped ascent. A very major route. Second ascent by Justin Critchlow, aged 16!, 3rd by Julian Lines. Flashed on impulse by Nik Jennings in 2000, having seen a friend headpoint it, and having previously headpointed A Fist Full of Crystals. It remains, however, a supreme achievement.*

1986 Jun 12 **Thing on a Spring**   Simon Nadin *Success after numerous failures, most ending in airborne retreat. Second ascent by Kevin Thaw, late '80s, and still a coveted prize, with currently only 4 known repeats.*

1986 **99% of Gargoyles Look Like Bob Todd, Cloudbusting**   Simon Nadin

1986 **Between the Lines**
Gary Cooper, Fred Crook

1987 Feb 17 **Paralogism**   Simon Nadin *One of the hardest roof climbs in Britain? 2nd ascent, Seb Grieve 1997. Soloed, virtually on-sight* and totally on impulse, by Ben Heason in 2003, without mats or spotters. "I'd seen Seb Grieve do it on a video and thought, if he can do it, so can I."

1987 Feb 17 **Metaphysical Scoop**
Andy Popp, Steve Lowe, Gwion Hughes

1987 **Licence to Lust, Drop Acid, Shelty, Wolfman of the KGB, Dolly Mix, Mix**   John Allen and party

1987 **Something Biblical, Mistral**
Gary Cooper, Fred Crook

1987 **Snap, Crackle and Andy Popp**
Fred Crook, Gary Cooper

1988 Feb **Sunday at Chapel**   Nick Dixon, Allen Williams, G Cole, I Dunn, C Dunn Unrepeated?

1988 May **Cold Bone Forgotten**   P Mitchell, P Evans

1989 **K.P. Nuts, Heredity**   Simon Nadin
Some of the nuts have been eaten since the first ascent. Both unrepeated?

1989 **Paul's Puffer**   Paul Mitchell A direct start was also rumoured at 5c in the 1981 guide.

1989 Apr 1 **Mr Decisive**   Tim Twentyman (solo)

1989 Apr 14 **Don't Go Down to the Woods Today, Deep in Mystery, The Wicked Wind**
Julian Lines (solo)

1989 May 18 **The Parrot and the Balaclava, Pop Art**
Simon Alsop

1989 Jul 15 **Voila 3, Sumo Cellulite**   John Allen

1991 Jan **The Boston Strangler**
Tom Nonis, Geoff Hornby, Suzi Sammut

1991 Jul **Bakewell Tart**
John Hudson, Keith Phizacklea

1991 **The Calf Path**   Julian Lines

1992 **Cold Man's Finger, Dougie Returns Home, The Old Statesman**
Justin Critchlow, Tez Richardson

1992 Jul **Obsession Fatale**   Julian Lines
Lines took a ground fall from high on the route prior to the first ascent, having already done the same on an E8 and an E7 in the area. Second ascent Sam Whittaker, 1998. Kevin Thaw also fell off the last moves in 2002, on an amazing on-sight attempt. "I just looked down at it from above, saw the holds, and thought, Yeah, that'll work." Even considering the fall, this was still one of the best bits of on-sight climbing yet in Staffordshire.

1993 **Sands of Time, Tip Toe**
Richard Pickford, Sara Cummins

1993 **Apache Dawn, Rodeo, Walking on Sunshine, Always Dreaming**   Julian Lines
Apache flashed on-sight by James Ibbertson in 2003.

1993 **Laughing all the way to the Blank**
Gary Cooper, Fred Crook

1993 **A Little Peculiar**   Paul Higginson Higginson had to train his already bumpy body specifically for the crux. Unrepeated?

1994 Aug **Just For Today**   Paul Clarke Unrepeated?

1995 **Rassp**   Richard Taylor, Kirsti Hicky

1995 Oct **Beware Coconuts**   Phil Hitchings

1996 **Toxic Socks, Bounty Killer, Johnny Pooh Poohed**   Mark Katz

1996 **Jog, Ging**   Graham Cole, Nige Bilby, Kenny Atherton

1996 **Northern Comfort**   Niall Grimes, Alan Millar Unrepeated?

1996 **Bud Love**   Justin Critchlow, M Bowyer

1997 **Ped X-ing**   Gary Cooper, Fred Crook

1997 **Gromit, Shaun's Other End**   Phil Hitchins, Richard Taylor

1997 **Skallagrigg**
Graham Cole, Kenny Atherton

1997 **Shining Path**   Mark Katz

1998 **Shrug**   Dave Bishop, John White

1998 **Logical Progression**   Sam Whittaker
A difficult climb that still avoids the main challenge hereabouts. Repeated by Mike Lea, 2000.

1998 **Josephina**   Richard Taylor

1998 **The Outdoor Pursuits Cooperative**
Pete Buswell, Roger Austin

1999 **Lost Girl**   Steve Clark, Lynn Robinson

1990s **Geordie Girl**
Geoff Hornby, Alex Sammutt

2000 **Wad Man Slang, The Attempted Moustache**   John H Bull, unseconded, or with Karen Dalkin

2001 **Squash Balls**
Dave Garnett, Kate Garnett (aged 5)

2001 **Stop…Carry On**   Mark Sharratt

2001 **Transcendental Medication, Coma Sutra**
John H Bull

2002 **Licensed to Fill**   Chris Hudgins

2002 **Dazed and Confused**   Mark Sharratt, Justin Critchlow

2002	**Roman Candle, Happiness from Outer Space, The Perp** John H Bull, Dave Garnett
2002	**Calcutta Crab Dance, Recess Wall and Arête, Stomach Punch** Steve Clark, Lynn Robinson
2003 Jun 11	**Not So Fast** Dave Garnett, John H Bull
2003 Jun 11	**Not So Steep** Ged O'Sullivan, John H Bull
2003 Jun 11	**Monstrous Angel** John H Bull, Ged O'Sullivan
2003 Jun 11	**Not Much Further** John H Bull
2003 Jun 14	**Breathless, False Chicane, Chicanery, Three Tier Buttress** Steve Clark,

Lynn Robinson. *A buttress apparently ignored since the dawn of time receives two independent visits in less than a week!*

2003 Aug 25	**Steps** Neil Foster, Clare Reading, Dave Simmonite *A special thanks to long-time Roaches Devotee, Fred Crook. Direct start added in September.*
2003	**Dirty Wee Rouge** Iain McKenzie
2003 Oct	**Final Destination** Ben Heason
2003 Oct	**Judge Jules** Julian Lines, Justin Critchlow *A last minute addition to the guide provided what is probably the hardest lead in the area. Several 'full length' falls were taken onto hopeful gear before the route finally fell to Lines.*

ⓥ Roaches Bouldering First Ascents

Only in recent years have first ascents on boulder problems been recorded in any way, and previously to that, only the most famous problems had any known origins. Below is a list of the first recorded ascents for problems where such information is known. Many of these will be wrong, as they may well have been done before by someone else.

These someone elses will include Jimmy Puttrell, Morley Wood, Lindlay Henshaw, Joe Brown, Don Whillans, Dennis Gray, Nat Allen, Mike Simpkins, Dave Salt, Colin Foord, the Barleys, John Yates, the Woodwards, John Allen, Steve Bancroft, Nick Longland, Dave Jones, Martin Boysen, Phil Burke, Simon Nadin, Nick Dixon, Allen Williams, Andy Popp, Justin Critchlow and Paul Higginson.

A Modest Proposal Tom O'Rourke, 2002.
Acne Arête Andi Turner, 2001.
Acne Arête Sit-Start Justin Critchlow, 2001.
Annie's Egg Nick Dixon, 1990s.
Ant Lives Nick Dixon, April, 1987.
Apocalypse Now Mark Sharratt.
Boba Fett Simon Nadin
Boozy Traverse Simon Panton,1994.
Cellar Dwella Justin Critchlow.
The Cube Nick Dixon, Allen Williams, Simon Oaker, Simon Whalley, March, 1986.
Dignity of Labour Nick Dixon, 1983.
Dirtnap Simon Willson.
Don's Crack Don Whillans.
Dreadful Dave Banks, 1989.
Drunk Enough Simon Panton, 1994.
Grand Theft Justin Critchlow, 2003.
The Gutter Aussie Andy.
Higginson's Arm Justin Critchlow, 2000.
Inertia Reel Johnny Dawes, March, 1986.
Inertia Reel Traverse Jerry Moffatt, 1998.
Joe's Arête Joe Brown.
Jump Simon Whalley, March, 1986.
Limbless Limbo Dancer Paul Higginson, 1999.
Mean Ol' B'stard, Milky Buttons Justin Critchlow.

Mistral Start Gary Cooper, 1987.
Mr Nice Justin Critchlow.
Mushin' Ben Moon, 1996.
Nadin's Secret Finger Simon Nadin, 1985.
Open Bum Cleft Johnny Dawes.
Particle Exchange Mark Katz, September, 1996.
Period Drama John Bull, 2000.
Pipe Entry Andi Turner, 2003.
The Pube John Bull, 2000.
Pussin Boots The Leek Lads, 2001.
Rupert's Sitdown Rupert Davies.
Skydivin' Justin Critchlow, Paul Higginson, 1999.
Sleeping with the Flowers Justin Critchlow, Andi Turner, 2001.
Spankasaurus Does Chicago Nik Jennings, 2000.
Spotter's Dyno Justin Critchlow, Andi Turner, 2001.
Spotter's Pop The Leek Lads, 2001.
Squeezer's Spots Andi Turner, 2001.
Swivel Finger Simon Whalley, Nick Dixon, 1986
Teck Crack Super-Direct Paul Higginson, 1990s.
Thud Paul Higginson, 1997.
Too Drunk Simon Panton, 1994.
Triptych Groove Andi Turner, Justin Critchlow, 2001.
Undercut Dyno Richard Williams, 1998.
Who Needs Ready Brek? Simon Nadin, April 1986

Rupert Davies on his own sitdown start to Inertia Reel V10 (7a) (page 13). Photo: Jon Barton.

Dave Garnett on Second's Advance, HVS 5a (page 120). Photo: Niall Grimes.

Hen Cloud

Now my Brother lays upon the Rocks

He could be dead, He could be not, He could be You

He's Chameleon, Comedian, Corinthian and Caricature

The Bewlay Brothers, by David Bowie

Hen Cloud

by Niall Grimes

O.S. Ref. **SK008617**	Altitude: **400m a.s.l.**

Hen Cloud

The massive gritstone fortress of Hen Cloud is without doubt one of the most noble and majestic crags in the whole of the Peak District. Proudly guarding the summit of a steep hillside, its impending walls rise abruptly from the escarpment, and to those unused to the crag, project the forbidding impression of a grim fortification. On closer acquaintance, the crag will indeed be found to be steep; however, it is far from impregnable. Get to grips with the climbs here and you will tend to find good holds and generally sound protection, making them welcoming, while still retaining a formidable level of challenge.

Challenge and reward come in equal measures, of course, and the satisfaction gained from an ascent of one of Hen Cloud's fine routes is not to be matched

anywhere on grit. The climbs here have traditionally been considered hard for their grade. This may well be true if one arrives at the crag unfit; the steepness then can seem unforgiving. However, for the climber with a bit of get up and go, the climbs will be found to be peerless challenges. Fierce but honest, bold without being dangerous. And in many ways, once a climber has climbed a route of their grade on Hen Cloud, they can fairly claim themselves to be a master of that grade.

Conditions & aspect

With its elevation and aspect, Hen Cloud is a superb crag to visit when the sun shines and, especially on summer evenings, is a great place to watch the sun set. In colder, and especially windy weather its exposed position can be keenly felt and sometimes, in the wetter months, parts of the crag become

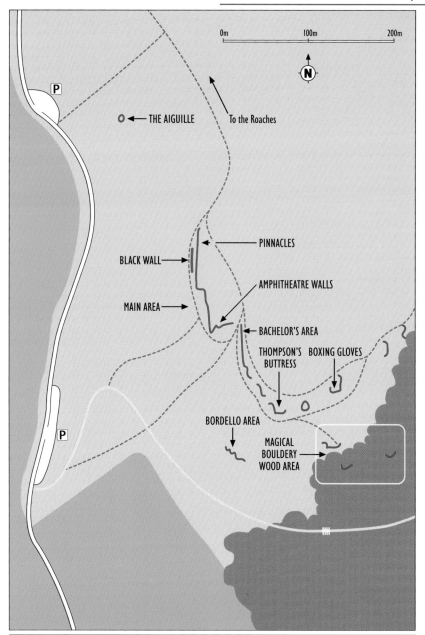

green. However, this often appears much worse than it actually is, and the crag has an unfair reputation for being lichenous. Black Wall does take a lot of drainage and can be very slow to dry after prolonged rain.

Faces
Generally west and south-west.

Sunshine
Plenty of south faces getting early sun, and for most of the day. Main faces come into the sun early afternoon, and remain in it until sunset.

Routes
Superb, with 170 routes. Generally long, steep cracks and faces. High quality, but a limited number of easy routes. Mid and higher grades are very well served with some of the best routes in the area.

Ⓥ Bouldering
Limited, although The Aiguille does provide some top-class highball problems, and the Magical Bouldery Wood has some interesting problems in a supreme setting, with good shelter from sunshine and strong winds. In total, 30 problems.

Parking & approach
Parking is available in the lay-bys on the road below the crag, but beware the restrictions on parking on the verges, which are periodically ruthlessly enforced. A seasonal Park and Ride scheme runs from Tittesworth Reservoir. From the gate on the road, walk along the unmetalled lane that runs under the crag. A track leads to the Central Area from the first bend, or a little further on, a larger one runs up to the middle of the crag. Both are steep warm ups (5–10 minutes). For the Bordello area, the Bottom Buttresses, the Lower Buttress and Biscuit Buttress areas, follow the unmetalled lane below the crag. The Bordello area comprises a group of small crags about 50m up from the track and 100m before the woods. For the others, walk as far as the cattle grid in the woods, where a track leads up left to the first rocks almost immediately. Finally, a track leads across from the right end of the Roaches (10 minutes), giving handy access to The Aiguille and the left side of the crag.

The **Bawd Stone**

is an isolated stone, found just north of the path between the Roaches and Hen Cloud. It is balanced atop a sharp edge of rock and two pointed stones, leaving a void beneath it which is full of water. The stone is renowned for its healing properties, and the sick used to be brought to it to be cured. This 'cure' involved crawling through the 18 inch muddy gap beneath the stone in an attempt to knock the devils off your back!

The stone used to be painted white each May Day (Beltane), a day when locals would roll large cakes down the hill into the 'Custard Field' below. This tradition was a remnant of the ancient tradition of rolling burning barrels of tar down the slope in honour of the supreme god of light, Bel. Bel was later christianised into Ba'al Zebul, the Lord of the Seat, or the perversion, Beelzebub, the Lord of the Flies.

Recently, cup and ring markings (carved indentations and rings) have been discovered on the stone, the first to be found in Staffordshire, suggesting the stone was of interest to prehistoric man.

Food & accommodation
See the main introduction. The Roaches Tea Room opposite the crag provides famous breakfasts, but is closed in the depths of winter.

Access
The Peak National Park wish to encourage ring ouzels back to the traditional nest-site under Hen Cloud. It will post notices on site asking climbers and walkers to voluntarily avoid the area between March and July. The BMC does not recognise precautionary restrictions and leaves it to individuals whether they wish to comply or not. If the birds do not nest the voluntary notices will be removed as soon as this is determined, usually mid-April. If the birds do nest, however, the BMC and the Peak National Park will agree any minimum necessary restrictions and these will be posted on site with a covering BMC Logo and will also be recorded on the BMC Access web-site.

The Aiguille

The first climbs lie on an attractive pinnacle close to the road, and slightly left of the main crag. The lines are in that murky area between routes and highball boulder problems. They are probably best enjoyed with pads and a spotter. Whichever way you care to climb them, they are magnificent.

❶ Starlight Left V4 (6b)
Superb moves lead up the narrow face, using both arêtes, to the break. Step right to join Starlight and Storm, or jump off.

❷ Starlight and Storm E3 6b ★★   1986
7m An exquisite micro-route. Boulder up the right side of the arête to the break, from where further inventive climbing gains the summit. ♥ **Highball** V6.

❸ Simon's Slab V7 (6c)
Scratch desperately up the centre of the slab past the pocket.

❹ The Aiguillette HS 4c ★   1913–27
6m The right arête, via a well-protected but gung-ho high step near the top. At this grade step off the boulder to start. Starting from the ground gives a few more excellent moves at about 5c.

The Pinnacles

The first area of crag proper is characterised by a distinctive row of pinnacles at its centre. The rock on some of the areas can be sometimes a bit scratchy and the routes a little shorter than on the main sections, but they are great routes nonetheless. It can also serve as a good introduction to the crag, as the area lacks the intimidation of the bigger sections.

♥ The first rock of any consequence is a flat clean wall known as **Zoom Wall**. This contains three problems, the left and right sides being 4c and the centre being 5a (all V0-).

❺ Nutted by Reality E1 6b ★   1978
7m The rippled wall 10m right, directly up its centre. Few will manage the start first go (V4), but every effort needs to be made to flash the easier, but rounded and unprotected, finish. This is where the nutting may occur.

A poor route, **Slipstreams** (HVS 5a, 1979), climbs the twin cracks on the right of the dirty wall 8m right. Other lines are possible. **Little Pinnacle Climb** (VD, 1968–73) is the grotty corner-line to the right.

The next routes all begin off a grass ledge starting a few metres above the path.

❻ November Cracks S 4a   1927
12m Climb the cracks on the front face of the first pinnacle to a leftwards exit on to the ledge, then corner crack behind.

❼ Bulwark E1 5a ★   1957
12m Exposed situations combined with thoughtful protection and some rather soft and sandy holds make for a memorable lead. Start on the right wall of the tower, and tiptoe out to the arête, whereupon a tricky move gains a scratchy ledge. Delicate climbing now leads up to an awkward finish on good flutes.

❽ Slowhand E1 5a ★★   1978
11m Bulwark's smarter brother which follows the scoop just right. From the recess near the gully, pull

Tom Briggs grasping his way to the top of Slowhand, E1 5a (page 105). Photo: Niall Grimes.

out left and move up to a deep flake crack. The blind flake above is used to gain the airy summit.

*The gully to the right is a handy but awkward descent (***Chockstone Chimney***, M, 1947–51).*

⑨ Mindbridge E7 6c   1984
11m The steep right wall of the gully features an inverted coffin-shaped shadow, the substance of this climb. Boulder up the wall to a break, and possible protection, and a chance to wish your friends good-bye. From here, the way ahead is dark and lonely…

⑩ Master of Reality E6 6c ★★★   1983
11m A contender for the best E6 in the county; a stunning route with consistently fine climbing, it is based on the unique dinosaur's spine of grit running up the front of the second pinnacle. Work up the lower wall on positive features and marginal pro. At the break, place good medium nuts and cams, take a deep breath, and let rip with everything you've got, aiming for the next break. Inspirational.

⑪ Master of Puppets E6 6b† ★   2003
11m The arête to the right by reachy moves above a nasty back-breaking block.

*The notch (called ***The Notch***) between the second and third towers can be gained by a crack (5a), or a ramp to the right (5b).*

⑫ Chicken E1 5b ★★   1960s
12m A really good route with plenty of variety. Follow the steep crack that cleaves the buttress to a break. Swing right to a ledge, then back left up an unnerving scoop to the top. Two variations exist: **Pullet** (E1 5b, 1978), climbing the lower right arête, and **Chicken Direct** (E4 6b, 1981), which climbs the left arête above the first crack, but these both lack the charm of the original.

⑬ Piston Groove VS 5a   1957–68
11m A technical start allows major fun to be had in the tight V groove.

⑭ Man oh Man E4 6a ★   1999
9m Climb the crack in the wall right of the groove. Good climbing in restricted situations.

⑮ The Mandrake E5 6a ★   1979
10m From Victory (and a runner level with the overlap), make a powerful hand-traverse leftwards to the brittle flake on the arête and finish boldly up this. Beware the fatal scream should you pull anything out. The direct start awaits a suitor.

⑯ Mandrill E5 6b†   2000
10m Knuckle down to the wall on the right, pulling over the overlap at the good hold on The Mandrake to a very thin crack (small wires and micro-cams), then direct to the top.

⓱ Victory VS 4b   1957–68
9m The winning crack to the right; nice climbing. The thin crack just right is **Short 'n Sharp** (E1 5c, 1978). Escapable.

⓲ Green Corner S   1957–68
8m The corner is green. And usually slimy too.

The next routes start from the grassy ledge to the right.

⓳ Blood Blisters E4 6b   1981
9m A gnarly overly-hard route which gains the upper arête of the wall. Boulder up the wall below the crack and small pro. Go left to the arête and scratch frantically to a biodegradable finish.
Ⓥ Blood Blisters Direct is a V3 (6b) problem up the lower arête.

⓴ Electric Chair E2 5c ★   1978
9m The line of least resistance. Climb the right edge of the wall to a ledge, then traverse left to a crack and the first protection. From here, good moves lead up and right into a final scoop. Bold.

㉑ Bad Joke E4 5c ★★   1979
8m I *say*, I *say*, I *say*… from the ledge on Electric Chair, continue up the wall via long and satisfying cranks. Totally unprotected, but the moves are obvious and never nasty. Low in the grade.

㉒ Gallows E2 5b ★   1978
8m Bold and tricky. Climb the hanging arête on its left to a disappointing break. Swing quickly right and gain the summit using a pocket. The route can be climbed all the way on the right, slightly easier, or continued on the left to the top (**The Trap Door Finish**, E4 5c†)

㉓ Recess Chimney VD   1957–68
7m Climb the chimney, and take either exit to the top.

㉔ Black Eyed Dog E6 6b ★   1987
8m The rounded arête right of the chimney, and gained from the ledge, leads with greater and greater difficulty to a rounded finish. Unprotected.

On **Hen Cloud** can be found the **pick** of the **climbing.**

It is as shapely and defined a summit as any 3,000ft *sgurr* in the western highlands. We will tackle the most prominent of this handsome set of teeth as a first trial of what the Staffordshire sgurr can offer in the way of problems. It is not a considerable climb– quite the reverse– yet not too easy. Let us call it a tussle with gloves on. For if, as is likely, the stony giant knocks you backwards, there is a thick pad of heather to fall back on, with deep cushions of peat below.
EA Baker

㉕ The Sorcerer E3 6a ★   1978
8m The wicked crack on the front has a bouldery start, then a continually technical and rounded battle all the way to the top. A very good climb.

㉖ High Tensile Crack HVS 5b ★★   1962
8m The little corner crack just right has a strenuous start on stiff technical hand jams, but soon relents. The wall just right sports another two unclimbed crack-lines. These are easy in their upper sections, but are guarded by starts that, while heavily featured, would be desperate. The runnel of the left crack is particularly attractive.

㉗ Chockstone Crack M   1947–51
11m A deep and meaningful experience up the rocky cleft. The grassy rampline just to its left is an awkward access route.

Black Wall

The obvious flat black wall at the lower level is home to a number of fingery crack climbs. The rock here is of a different nature to the rock elsewhere, with slightly lower friction. Unfortunately it seeps badly, but when dry, the routes offer excellent climbing.

㉘ Buster the Cat HVS 5b   1979
8m The slim crack and groove.

Brown and Whillans day out

Undoubtedly the greatest partnership on British rock, these two dominated new route activity from the late 1940s right into the late 50s. Their legacy is some of the best lines anywhere, mostly around the VS to E1 range. Anyone who feels they are competent at these standards may wish to try their luck repeating all their routes in a day.

They are, starting at Ramshaw: *Don's Crack*, *Prostration*, *Brown's Crack*, *The Crank*, *Masochism*, *Great Zawn*;
Hen Cloud: *Bachelor's Climb* (left-hand finish), *Bachelor's Left-Hand*, *Hen Cloud Eliminate*, *Second's Retreat*, *Slimline*, *Reunion Crack*, *Delstree*, *Main Crack, En Rappel*.
Roaches: *Choka*, *Rhodren*, *The Bulger*, *The Mincer*, *Matinee*, *Valkyrie Direct*, *Crack of Gloom*, *Dorothy's Dilemma*, *Teck Crack*, *Ackit*, *Lightning Crack*, *Slippery Jim*, *The Sloth*, *Saul's Crack*, *Aqua*.

In a spirit of generosity, **Ramshaw Crack** can be avoided, but feel free to try it.

🕘 Pug VS 4c   1968–73
8m The main crack at the left gains a hanging garden.

Two short problems exist on the black wall to the right, both leading to a poor break below incipient cracks. Neither of these cracks has been climbed.

🕥 A Flabby Crack E6 6c† ★   1992
10m A line of hopeless seams and nothing finger-pockets is followed to a desperate final move.

🕛 The Stone Loach E5 6b ★★   1981
10m A very good climb combining a powerful and technical first half with something altogether different in the second. Cracks lead upwards with difficulty and good protection, to the wide break. Now the fun begins. The prehistoric gash above your head is longer than it looks.

🕝 Anthrax E4 6a ★★   1975
20m A varied battle up two very different sizes of crack. The thin bit; a bouldery start leads to nice holds and protection. The crack above is steep and tough to the very end. Now the thick bit; at the break, banish all thoughts of sandwiches, and stomach-traverse left and climb the tough upper gash of The Stone Loach.

🕞 The Lum HVS 4c   1957–68
10m A despicable skirmish up the unaccommodating chimney line.

🕟 Bantam Crack VS 4c ★   1957–68
10m Fine jamming up the varied hand crack. Less pleasant when the top is dirty, although a prior inspection and cleaning is easy.

Delstree Area

The crag now starts to reach its characteristic form, with big, strenuous crack-lines on sound rock. Steepness gives a continually challenging feel to the routes, although they also tend to be well-protected, and superb. The first few routes start on a grassy terrace reached by scrambling up from the right.

Descent is via the easy path in the centre of the crag.

🕠 The Better End E3 6a ★★   1962
11m At the left end of the terrace, a forceful crack climbs a leaning wall. Ascend said crack to a slopey ledge. With protection placed, set sail on the butch leaning layback – somewhat alarming – which leads to the surface. Excellent. The tempting scoop to the left is unclimbed.

🕡 The Raid E4 6a ★   1978
13m A good route with a bouldery start and a fine headwall. Climb the angular scoop in the arête (with the spotter well lashed down) until a pull left gains a crack and a ledge. Small wires protect the cracked upper wall, although the confident will find this straightforward.

37 En Rappel HVS 4c ★★ 1927

12m A couple of exposed mantels lead into a ramp-line. Follow this to a good ledge. From here, pull out left onto the crest of the crag, and over onto the heather above. The original finish traversed right from the good ledge to gain a wide finishing crack (known as **Blizzard Buttress**). Less direct, but providing more adventure.

38 Caesarian E4 6b ★★★ 1978

12m The centre of the steep wall is brilliant; top of the range, in every sense, with just about every move being 5c or more. Boulder up past vertical flakes to reach slanting breaks and good gear. An almighty move from here gains the next break, and a still tricky finishing crack. One of the big 3 E4s on the crag.

39 Main Crack VS 5a ★★ 1957–61

12m Men have disappeared for days in this fissure. Some have never returned. The big crack is mean to start, but then relents with fine jamming. However, dimensions once again turn nasty near the top, and knees may be called for. A must for the hairy trousered adventurer. **Pointless but Pumpy** (E1 5b, 2002), traverses the obvious horizontal crack leftwards out of this route to gain ledges on En Rappel.

A pedestal atop **Delstree**

is the home to some ancient Runic markings in the form of two stick men (one may be Simon Nadin) and a circle with a snake coming through it possibly representing healing properties. Other engraving includes much graffiti, including many Polish names dating from wartime. There have also been a hell of a lot of 'Daz's in the area.

40 Delstree HVS 5a ★★★ 1957–61

20m The superbly positioned corner perched on the front of the face is a real gritstone classic. Start under an awkward overhang. Negotiate this, surprisingly gymnastic, then move delicately left to the base of the shallow corner. Jamming ecstasy follows to a balding finish. 5a every magnificent step of the way.

41 Levitation E5 6a ★ 1979

20m The steep arête. From the foot of Reunion Crack, climb a thin crack in the wall, then the wall above heading for the arête. A difficult crux high above the runners makes this hard for the grade, so beware. E3 with high side runners.

Hen Cloud has a well-earned reputation for steep crack climbing, much of it the legacy of the Rock and Ice era. Here, Craig Harwood muscles up Joe Brown's Reunion Crack, VS 5a. Photo: Niall Grimes.

㊷ Reunion Crack
VS 5a ★★   1957–61
20m The overhanging corner/ flake is impending and strenuous; however, the gear is plentiful, and the holds are as friendly as can be. It is gained by surmounting the overhang as for Delstree, then following the ramp rightwards to the base of the corner. A brisk crux follows.

43 The Pinch E1 5c   1978
20m From a long way up the easy gully (**Slab Way,** **M**), climb the arête of the black tower to the left. The last move (crux) is pointlessly easy for the tall, and easily impossible for the short. The grade is meaningless.

44 Fat Old Sun E3 5a, 6a ★   1974
40m A traverse of the buttress gives constant exposure and covers much fine rock.
1. 11m Climb the Bitter End to the ledge, then traverse right to the scoop of En Rappel.
2. 26m Step down, then stretch along the rounded break, passing the base of Caesarian's crack, to a hiding place in Main Crack. Move up, then forcefully tackle the disappearing undercut to a less good hiding place in Delstree. Step up again before airy moves gain the big jug on Levitation, leading to the top.

Central Area

The biggest section of rock on Hen Cloud is the complex fortress of the Central Area. Numerous corners and ledges break this section up, although the climbing in between the ledges tends to be forceful. The main features of the area are the dominating corner system taken by Central Climb, and The Terrace, a lush grass covered ledge, accessible only by climbing, bisecting this climb at half height. The rock, apart from some sections towards the left, is good and clean, although some of the more classic climbs on the right are now a little polished. **Descent** for these climbs is down the path in the centre of the crag.

The first routes climb a dark left-facing wall above the grassy terrace gained by going down or up Slab Way, the broken gully line right of Reunion Crack.

45 Qantas E1 5b   1978
8m Climb the thin groove on the left of the wall to a good nut, then swing right to the next groove to finish. Sweet.

46 Press On Regardless E2 5b   1978
10m From the break on Qantas, traverse right to the arête, gaining an amount of exposure as you go. A tricky move up the left side of the arête leads to steadily easing climbing. Bold.

Down and right is a promising-looking flat wall containing several climbs that don't really live up to expectations.

47 The Ape E1 5b   1962
11m Climb the wide crack till it is possible to monkey rightwards along a horizontal break, then finish.

48 The Monkey in your Soul E3 5c   1978
15m Climb the thin, steep, well-protected crack in the centre of the wall to its termination. From here, traverse right to the poor finish of Broken Arrow. The finish lacks direction and the direct finish lacks holds, although a tough leftwards variation would be possible.

49 Broken Arrow E1 5b   1978
11m Climb hollow flakes at the right of the wall until difficulty and unpleasantness force one round right. Pull left again onto the face to finish.

50 Roof Climb VS 4b, 3b ★   1947–51
30m A route that takes an easy line amid some imposing territory.
1. 20m The square-cut corner is followed, first on the right, then the left, where some back and footing leads to The Terrace.
2. 10m Climb the easy gully right of the arête, or much better, do Final Crack (Route 54).

51 The Long and the Short E1 5b, 5b ★   1960s
25m A technical first pitch is followed by a frantic thrash on the second.
1. 15m The elegant groove is bridged romantically to the terrace. This pitch alone gives a quality HVS.
2. 10m Casting all thoughts of elegance adrift, submit to the wide crack bounding the steep wall. Escape right onto the face at half-height, and finish up an open groove.

52 Anaconda E4 6a, 6b ★   1976
25m Generally good climbing, but spoiled by the odd scruffy interlude.
1. 15m Climb the tight right-angled groove, very reasonably, to a green overhang. Pull strenuously

round left to gain gear and good holds, and move up to a flake. An apocalyptic top-out now follows.

2. 10m On the steep wall above The Terrace, stand on a ledge, and make a desperate move to a poor finger-jam. Traverse more easily left to a black flake to finish. A much better idea is **Anaconda Variation**, E3 5c★★, which follows pitch 1 of the original route to the flake over the roof, then traverses right to the superb finishing moves of Borstal Breakout.

🔵 **Borstal Breakout** E4 6a, 6b ★★★   1978
33m The sublime first pitch features meaty bouldering in safe situations.

1. 23m Attack the steep hand-jamming crack above the grassy ledge, and climb this to a little roof. Above, the crack peters out. Move up and execute a superb and very testing sequence on big open holds to gain salvation.

2. 10m Start as for Anaconda, but continue direct to easy ground. An unbalanced pitch.

🔵 **Final Crack** HS 4b ★★   1947–51
10m Magnificent jamming on perfect rock. Starting on The Terrace (gained from Roof Route or Central

Climb), take the obvious crack right of the flat wall with the final bulge providing the crux.

🔵 **Central Climb Direct**
  VS 4c, 4b, 4a ★★   1947–51
25m A series of variations on the original makes for another good, long expedition.

1. 8m The sinuous fissure below the fine arête is a classic example of the gritstone udge.

2. 11m Climb the middle pitch of the parent route, or the exposed flakes to the right.

3. 11m The noble groove just to the left is followed to the summit.

🔵 **B4XS** E7 6b ★★★   1986
10m Crikey! An all-out lead of the highest order up the dominating rounded arête. Thin, smeary and serious, only the luckiest of leaders will miss the crippling ledge in the event of a fall. Begin on the first ledge of Central Climb, gain the arête, and follow it, using holds and flutings on the right side.

Nadin's central challenge to Hen Cloud,
with delicate arête climbing in an outrageous
situation. Mark Sharratt shows what it takes
to climb B4XS, E7 6b (page 113).
Photo: David Simmonite.

I did **B4XS**

when Jean Minh Trihn-Thieu came to visit over from France. He had slept on my doorstep and when we found him in the morning he was wrecked but we put him in the car and took him straight to Hen Cloud with Dave Jones the Aussie. We roped B4, then all three of us led it, me, Dave and then Jean. Jean was a bit wobbly and shaky and wanted to go down again, but we shouted at him and made him go up again. The onlookers couldn't believe their eyes. No ascent for 10 years then 3 in one day.
Seb Grieve

57 Hens Dropping E1 6a   **2002**
8m A filler-in pitch best used as a harder start to the following route. Climb the black flake right of Central Climb Direct to a wide break. Stand up here with some difficulty and continue direct to the ledge of Central Climb.

58 Standing Tall E2 4c, 5b   **1979**
31m A mopping-up exercise with some nice climbing, starting between Central Climb Direct and its parent at an obvious square niche.
I. 15m Pull out of the niche directly and climb the bulging rounded rib above to a ledge. Continue up, right of the corner, on positive flakes.

This crack **repulsed** a **good number** of **pioneers**

before being climbed by John Laycock in 1909. Unfortunately his second, AR Thompson, was unable to follow it as 'he was handicapped by a congenital disability that made all climbing a matter of heroic endeavour'! Laycock continued but became benighted and was rescued several hours later by a sturdy chauffeur. He later confessed: 'Not everyone has been benighted on gritstone and, though one ought to be ashamed of a want of prudence, the episode is delightful to me in retrospect; gritstone has its romance no less than granite.'
Paul Nunn on Central Climb

2. 16m A bold rambling pitch. From 3m up the corner, hand-traverse the ramp right to Encouragement and so to the ledge. Move up and left on good, but spaced, holds before stepping back right and exiting carefully past a loose block.

59 Central Climb VS 4c, 4b, 4a ★★★   **1909**
32m A route with a superb line and flawless historical pedigree, although the lower sections are beginning to age. The belays are all magnificent. Start at the well-worn shallow corner just to the right.
I. 10m Climb the cantankerous crack to a ledge.
2. 11m An awkward corner (excellent thread) leads to a second ledge. Thrill seekers can avoid this by a bold 4b traverse right to the ledge on positive finger-holds. Steep cracks above lead to The Terrace.
3. 11m Go directly up the well-used cracks above, or veer rightwards at half-height (slightly easier). Prudent climbers will carry either a headtorch or a chauffeur.

60 Encouragement E1 5b, 5b ★★★   **1960s**
30m A beautiful and balanced climb, with a thoughtful first pitch, and a steep second pitch where the less time spent thinking the better.
I. 15m Gain the square-cut hanging groove. Follow this with sustained bridging and a cunning swing left near the top to a handsome belay ledge.
2. 15m The obvious crack above succumbs to a satisfying series of hand and finger jams. This pitch is steep and testing, but protection is perfect. Finish up the ridge.

61 Jean the Bean E5 6b† ★   **1997**
15m A fine bold climb up the short unprotected arête to the right of Encouragement's first pitch. Very high in the grade.

62 K2 S 4a, 4b ★★   **1927**
30m A great expedition, demanding on the arms.
I. 12m The next major corner leads steeply to a ledge.
2. 18m Above the stance, follow the steep Y-shaped crack. This is more technical than any obscure Himalayan namesake, and more slippy. Above, an easier groove leads to the summit ridge.

One of the best additions to Hen Cloud in
the 1970s. Jon Read committed on the bouldery
crux of Borstal Breakout. E4 6a (page 113).
Photo: Niall Grimes.

Hen Cloud was once the site of a **private zoo**

when animals were moved from London and Chester for their safety during the war. The animals eventually escaped, and began breeding in the area. Bennett's wallabies were once common, as was a roaming yak. The yak was last seen heading for Buxton! On top of Hen Cloud are some old metal pegs – the remnants of a large aviary where the zoo's birds were kept.

⑥ **7 of 9** VS 5a   2002
30m An escapable eliminate but with some good moves. From the base of the K2 corner, climb a steep crack to the rib. Continue steeply up the left side of the rib then follow a short crack to rejoin K2.

⑥ **The Arête** HVD 4a ★★★   pre-1913
30m Follow the exposed stepped ridge all the way to the summit of the mountain, with a exposed but positive step at half height for the crux. Better than anything in the Alps.

Amphitheatre Walls

Right of The Arête, the walls and routes taper up to the central path. All the climbs benefit from morning sunshine. The first of these lies on the left wall of the big gully.

⑥ **Arête Wall** VS 4c ★   1957–68
18m The first steep hand crack on the gully wall is very strenuous going on perfect jams. From a block move right and go up. A poor man's Crack of Gloom.

⑥ **Easy Come** HS 4b   1978
12m A thin crack 4m right again is steep and stiff. Finish diagonally rightwards via a slab onto The Arête.

⑥ **Easy Gully** M   1913–27
35m The moderately easy gully.

⑥ **Songs of Praise** E2 5c   1971
12m Undercut and layback the wild flake on the upper wall of the gully. A very awkward move is needed to escape right to easy ground and finish.

⑥ **Loose Fingers** E2 5c   1980
9m The crack just downhill is consistently awkward and often dirty.

⑦ **Prayers, Poems and Promises**
E1 5b ★   1978
11m Just right again, gain a ledge on the arête. Using a hole on the arête and the crack to the left (small pro useful), climb up the rib to a rightwards exit and an easy finish.

⑦ **Modern** S 4b ★★   1947–51
18m A super climb that heaves its way up the chunky flakeline on the front of the face. While steep, generous holds give the climb a friendly aspect. From a stance, climb the tough right-hand of two steep cracks on the vertical wall.

Ⓥ A good fingery boulder problem climbs the clean wall above the flat rock ledge on the front of the buttress, V2 (6a). This was originally the start of **Flexure Line**, which carried on up the buttress with little direction.

⑦ **Ancient** VD ★   1947–51
18m A good climb with a fine finish. Gain the niche on the right of the buttress, then pull out left and follow a line just left of the arête to a ledge and possible belay. Follow the steep, left-hand crack-line above.

Jon Read leaving protection a long, long way behind on the first ascent of The Driven Bow, E7 6c (page 117). Photo: Niall Grimes.

On **wet winter** days,

the wind howls round the upper turrets where the vertical fissures cut through the summit, and thin mists frequently cling to the rocks. In the evening sun, Hen Cloud is rosy, a split pyramid, formed almost entirely of sand-hued rough gritstone. The pebbled grit holds the lichen which invades the bloody wounds of jamming scars and colonising them, delaying recovery to the next weekend, or beyond.

Paul Nunn, Classic Rock

73 Even Smaller Buttress HVS 5a   1985
6m A delightful solo which ascends the steep arête on sidepulls. Like this? You'll love Solid Geometry.

74 Small Buttress HVS 5a ★★   1979
6m Monkey up the front of the little buttress. Even smaller than Even Smaller Buttress. The arête on the little buttress just right is **Andrei's Route** (HVS 5a, 2002), but is artificial.

75 Bitching HVS 5a ★★   1978
7m The crack in the left wall of Bow Buttress. The crux is the start but the rest has a certain urgency.

76 The Driven Bow E7 6c ★   2002
8m A thrilling sequence, a long, long way above the safety net. Climb the short crack, and fiddle in some pro at its apex. From here, fingery cranking leads upwards past an alarming slap and a desperate pull onto the top.

77 Bow Buttress S 4a ★   1924
8m A little climb, but strenuous. Climb the rising right-trending line, which intersects the arête, as far as the wide crack. Move up this then finish up left under the capstone.

78 Solid Geometry E1 5b ★★   1980
8m The fine square-cut arête has little protection. Exciting but positive, and difficulties are short-lived.

Bachelor's Area

To the right of the descent path lies one of the finest walls on gritstone. The bulging wedge-shaped wall is home to many strong lines, and many required the strengths of the Brown/ Whillans and Allen/Bancroft teams to subdue them. In many ways, it is the routes on this wall that give Hen Cloud its reputation, a reputation based on hard-fought struggles of the highest quality up steep, soaring crack-lines. It is worth noting that belays are very hard to find on the first few routes, and full-length ropes will be useful for going far back in search of placements.

V A few sweet boulder problems lie at the left end of the wall. **Right Ramp**, V0 (5a), is the right-trending rampline. Just right is **Left Vein**, V0 (5a), and right again is **Right Vein**, V1 (5c).

⑦ Stokesline E2 6b 1977
6m A problem start leads to the easier crack. The wall 2m to the right is climbed by **This Poison** (E3 6b, 1981) a good problem up the wall using a pebble.

⑧ Slimline E1 5b 1957–61
9m The crack to the right, with most of the activity centred around the widest section.

⑧ Peter and the Wolf E6 6b ★ 1990
10m Classy bouldering at an uncomfortable height. Using a good pocket, gain the half-height break. From here, good pinching and undercutting brings better holds to hand, and a sprint to the top. As usual, protection only arrives after the climbing has eased off.

⑧ Fast Piping E4 6b ★ 1981
11m A stiff wall climb with hard moves leading away from good gear. Gain the short crack, then make desperate moves up and left to get established in the next crack. Uneasy moves then gain the brittle flake. The wider upper crack is not easy, but is followed with well-protected relief.

⑧ Hedgehog Crack VS 4b ★★ 1947–51
11m The obvious steep crack, with superb jamming leading to a slightly wide finish.

⑧ Comedian E3 6a ★★★ 1976
12m A superb route with tough, technical moves. Climb the crack till stiff moves lead right to a horizontal break. Nibble back left to the crack, which is followed on helpful jams to an entertaining groove through the final bulge. Cams are useful, especially the larger sizes.

⑧ Frayed Nerve E5 6a† ★ 1981
12m Good delicate climbing with an entertaining fall potential. Climb the steep groove left of the big crack, then some chunky horizontals, to a deep break. Place some large cams here, and commit to the less steep wall above, exiting via the little rounded groove. Sporty.

⑧ Second's Retreat HVS 4c ★ 1952
15m The steep V groove heaves and bulges, and provides good climbers with a thrilling series of deep, wide challenges. Again, lots of big cams can ease the passage, and the growth in the crack is not the problem it would appear.

⑧ Second's Advance HVS 5a ★ 1962
15m Climb a thin crack and the narrow groove above to a jug below a steepening. Above this, a grossly overhanging hand-crack leads beefily to a slabby ledge below a scoop. Traverse left to the chimney crack to finish. The direct finish, up the green scoop, is tough sustained 5c with no more protection, making the route a nasty E2.

⑧ Corinthian E3 5c ★★★ 1976
17m A fine steep crack climb, where the holds and protection are never quite as good as they would appear. Climb to the base of a faint bulging crack containing a rusty peg. From here, grapple up the rounded, pumpy crack. Testing, but still the easiest of Bancroft and Allen's 'C' routes.

⑧ Hen Cloud Eliminate HVS 5b ★★★ 1957–61
18m One of the best routes of this grade in the Peak. The discontinuous cracks give gruelling jamming, but the finish, struggling into the groove where the rock lies back, gives the crux. Prudent mountaineers will carry no fewer than two large cams for this section: altogether now, 'I bet Joe Brown didn't have them'.

⑨ Cool Fool E6 6b ★ 1981
20m The steep arête features hard insecure climbing in a thoroughly terrifying situation. Begin up a shallow groove until a ledge, where protection can be placed behind a boulder. Go left, and climb the bold arête, until a crack on the right (Rib Crack) is reached with great relief, and gear. Move left again and continue to a rounded top.

⑨ Rib Chimney S 4b ★★ pre-1913
20m This soaring and confident line gives one of the best chimney outings in the Peak, with a particularly technical bridging section in the middle. **Rib Crack** (VS 4c, 1962), is the enjoyable crack in the upper left wall.

㊲ Caricature E5 6a ★★★ 1976

22m John Allen's western masterpiece, and one of the best E5s on grit. It is also one of the most challenging, taking a tortuous and sustained line up the upper wall right of Rib Chimney. From a ledge well up that route, place a high runner, and make a difficult traverse right, using small holes for the hands, to the front face. Gear. Tough moves lead into a scoop, followed by continually demanding moves right to the very top.

㊳ Chiaroscuro E6 6b† 1985

24m An eliminate line seeking out some fine areas of rock. From the top of the first crack of Bachelor's Left-Hand, undercut left and balance up the rib as far as Caricature. This section alone would make a very good direct start to Caricature, at E6. Move right, and having placed a side-runner in the big crack to the right, gibber up the bulging slab, trending slightly left. Very hard. Beware!

㊴ Bachelor's Left-Hand HVS 5b ★★★ 1957–61

25m A majestic climb, continually steep and challenging, and as good as anything on grit. It takes a sweeping line up the right side of the wall, starting

Hen Cloud HVS

Hen Cloud has been traditionally seen as being stiffly graded, and this nowhere more than in the HVS grade. Routes are steep, and need a fight to get up. Because of this, upgrading has been suggested. On the other hand, maybe they are just hard for the grade – 'proper HVS'. Whatever your opinion, the three big classics, and subject of most debate, *Delstree*, the *Eliminate* and *Bachelor's*, have been left as HVS. However, if you are successful on them, you are probably ready for most E1s.

from below a prominent crack. Gain this crack with difficulty. At its terminus, make a powerful swing right to a horizontal flake crack then move up to the rounded ramp above. From here, the major crack to the right is taken, which, while still steep, is less taxing than what has gone before.

㊵ Parallel Lines E6 6c 1985

25m The smooth wall to the right is taken, using a ridiculous series of hopeless non-holds, up and into a shallow groove and a respite. Possibly unrepeated; the first ascent used runners in the initial crack of Bachelor's Left-Hand, which is more a badly placed top-rope than a side-runner. It remains, however, desperate.

96 Bachelor's Climb VS 4c ★★★ 1947
27m A carnival of jamming up the butch crack leads to a possible stance on The Pulpit. Escape up Great Chimney (the original way), but miles better is to traverse left and finish up Bachelor's Left-Hand, in which case this is the crux and the route becomes hard for VS.

97 Space Probe E4 6a, 6a ★★ 1979
1. 12m Step right to the arête, and follow this till a committing reach gains a break. Go round right, and balance up to the ledge.
2. 8m The **Helter Skelter** Finish. A single tricky move up the arête above gains good holds leading left to an easy finishing groove.

98 Great Chimney S 4a ★★★ 1913
18m An excellent climb of the old type. Any combination of the corner cracks can be used although starting in the left one and transferring to the right at Pulpit height is the most obvious.

99 Rainbow Crack VS 5a ★★ 1947–51
18m The confident flake crack on the wall right of Great Chimney. Gain a ledge at half-height by either of the two starts. Both are strenuous and slightly awkward, although the superb jamming of the upper half makes it all worthwhile.

100 Arêtenophobia E6 6b ★ 1996
16m The arête left of Chameleon. Traverse right to place a runner in the flake at the overhang, then back left to climb the bold arête.

101 Chameleon E4 6a ★★★ 1977
12m The handsome line on the steep wall is everything E4 should be. Climb to the overhang, then make an exacting traverse left to a deep flake in the roof. Determined pulls from here gain the upper flake, which still needs a bit of huff and puff. Magnificent.

102 Sauria E5 6a ★ 1986
10m The right arête. Unfortunately runners are quite low and the climbing higher up is sustained and slappy.

103 Left Twin Crack HS 4b ★ 1957–68
9m The left of the, er, twin cracks. Short-lived, but fine laybacking or jamming after a problem start.

104 Right Twin Crack VS 4c 1957–68
9m The right crack has a spectacular finish.

The next route starts 18m right of the start of Rainbow Crack.

105 Flour Wall E2 6b 2002
8m Boulder desperately up the wall left of the arête to the crack. The finish, to the left of the crack, is harder than it looks.

106 Dead Banana Slab HVS 5c 2002
7m Start below the arête and boulder up to gain the obvious good hold on its right above the bulge. Step right, and ascend the slab via pockets.

Below and 15m to the right, a small buttress emerges with an obvious chimney.

107 Just Thirteen VS 5a ★ 1995
5m Layback and jam the frisky flake up and left from the chimney. Fun.

108 Footpath Chimney VD pre-1913
18m Climb the chimney with an awkward bulge to a possible belay. Scramble over blocks and finish up an arête.

Above here the crag recesses back and up for 20m.

109 Desperado E5 6b 1993
8m Climb the steep clean slab and wall at the back of the recess.

V Below and right of the last route is a small slab with two problems on it. The **left arête** is **V0–** (4c) and **the wall** just right is **V0** (5b). Opposite these problems is a huge and grossly overhanging arête. This awesome and heavily scalloped feature has been investigated by some of the strongest climbers in the area, and maybe top-roped once. However, it remains without doubt Hen Cloud's 'Last Great Problem'. The upper right arête of this block contains **Wavelength** (E1 5c, 1990).

Thompson's Buttress

About 20m further on, the path drops down a little just before the next set of rocks.

⑩ Thompson's Buttress Route One
S 4a ★   pre-1913

15m The first corner crack is climbed, then the steep fissure above and right. Good moves, if a little broken.

⑪ Thompson's Buttress Route Two
VD   pre-1913

15m Just right, a set of giant stairs is climbed to the ledge. Climb the wide crack above.

⑫ Tree Chimney HVD   pre-1913
15m The obvious chimney, passing a steepening on the right. **Tunnel Vision** (HVS 5a, 1979), climbs the face to the right, somewhat artificially.

The Inaccessible Pinnacle

Right again, across a broad grassy gully, is a rounded buttress with a little pillar laid against its front face.
Descent is slightly tricky. Either reverse the short back face, awkward, or go down the slab and make a little leap across the chasm.

⑬ Cold Sweat E1 5b ★   1979
8m Nice climbing up the wall left of the arête, trending towards the arête to finish. Bold.

⑭ Pinnacle Face VS 4b ★   1947–51
12m Climb up the slabby crack formed by the little pillar to its summit. Step left, and follow the absorbing slab on little ripples, with protection finally arriving just below the top. A more recent route, **Face Value** (HVS 5a, 1978), having started up the front of the pillar, climbs the slabby wall just right of Pinnacle Face.

⑮ Pinnacle Rib HVS 5a ★   1957–68
11m Brilliant obscure movements, the essence of gritstone. Gain the top of the pillar by its right-hand crack. From here, all sorts of moves are needed to scurry up and right, then on to the summit. **Delusion** (HS 4b, 1979), is a poor route up the V groove to the right.

The Boxing Gloves

Forty-five metres to the right is a triple buttress of boxing glove type formations. Despite the forms and shapes of these rocks, they manage not to offer much bouldering. However, they have some worthwhile routes.

⑯ Shoe Shine Shuffle HVS 5b   1979
8m A strenuous crack on the left wall of the first glove. Swing right onto a projection and scuffle to the top.

⑰ Diagonal Route VD   1957–68
12m The dog-legged slanting crack.

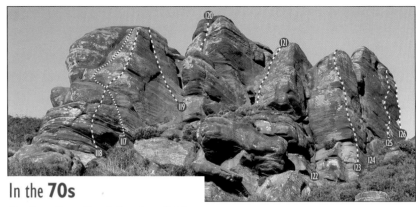

In the **70s**

Con Carey, Jimmy Campbell, and myself did a new route on Hen Cloud called **Heart of Gold**. We gave it the grade of Mild Extreme, 5c. (It was just around the time when E grades were starting to be introduced.) Steve Bancroft was producing his, what was to become a sort of Bible at the time, *Recent Developments*.

When it came out he had given Heart of Gold a grade of HVS 5b. I asked him if he'd done the route to check the grade since we'd all found it quite hard and thought this was a little harsh. He said he hadn't repeated it but he'd given it the 5b grade as he considered that it wasn't possible for us to climb 5c.

At that time, Bancroft 5c (as used in his little guide) was renowned for being really testing, and not given away easily.

Nick Colton

⑱ Triumph of the Good City HVS 5a   1979
11m Just round to the right is a small cave. Juggy bouldering over the roof leads to a ledge. Continue up the arête above.

⑲ Jellyfish E4 5c   1979
8m The rampline on the fluorescent green left wall of the gully.

⑳ Pete's Back Side HVS 5a ★   1979
7m Very peculiar moves are needed to ascend the runnel above the ledge on the next boxing glove.

㉑ Central Tower VD   1968–73
8m The slabby face just to the right. Unprotected.

㉒ The Nutcracker S 4a   pre-1913
8m An historic struggle up the crack to the right.

㉓ Heart of Gold E2 5c ★★   1976
10m The arête is a little gem, well worth seeking out. Climb directly to a useful hole. Wobble into a standing position in this, then proceed thoughtfully to the top. Sustained and varied.

㉔ The Deceiver VS 4b   pre-1913
8m The short, but fierce, crack just to the right of the arête.

㉕ Touch E4 6c ★   1985
7m A ferocious boulder problem, V7, leads up the wall to an unhelpful break, where desperate measures are called for.

㉖ Scrabble E3 6a ★   1993
7m The arête right of Touch has tricky climbing at an uncomfortable height.

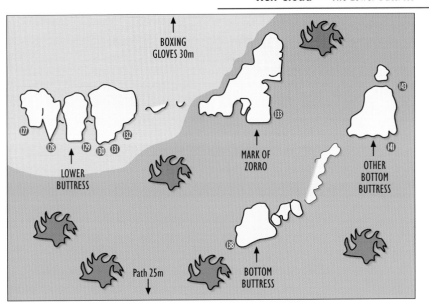

The Lower Buttress

Fifty metres in front of The Boxing Gloves, and at a lower level, another little row of outcrops is located at the upper edge of the woods. The area is clearly visible from the drive below, directly above the left edge of the woods, and can most conveniently be approached from below (turn uphill at the cattle grid). The rock is of high quality, and all the routes are worth doing. The area is also worth a visit because of its setting, sitting above beautiful beech and larch trees; its ambience is very different from that of the main crag, and it would be an excellent spot for a picnic, or for young lovers to go in search of privacy.

At the left end of the buttresses is a gully bridged by a large leaning block. Some 15m below is a prominent Scots pine. The first route takes the slabby arête that forms the right wall of the gully.

⑫ Boysen's Arête E2 6a ★ 1990s

7m The perfect little bouldery arête, above a nasty drop.

⑫ The Young Pretender E8 6c ★★ 1998

6m The stunningly beautiful boulder problem arête, thrusting like the bow of a ship, just to the right. Although short, its difficulty is of the highest order and the landing is not very good.

To the right, separated from each other and their neighbouring buttresses by a series of broad gullies, are two arêtes.

⑫ Hal's Ridge VD 1962

11m A slightly disappointing climb up the fine ridge.

The name **Hen Cloud** has several possible sources. One was *Hern's Cloud*. Hern the Hunter was the ancient god of The Chase, and this was his domain. Hern was horned like a stag, reminiscent of the peak's double horns.

The alternative is that it comes from the ancient Briton word for 'boundary', as the peak was once the boundary between different realms.

Cloud is also thought to come from the old English word for 'high up'.

⑧⓪ Short Man's Misery HVS 5a   1976
9m The more substantial steep arête, followed on its left-hand side, has some fine open moves. Oddly, with its long reaches, the climbing favours the tall.

⑧① Crispin's Crack HVS 5a ★   1962
11m A very good test of jamming skills. Climb the short hand crack left of the oak tree, until a ferocious move gains a little slab. Finish up the sweet scoop.

⑧② Duck Soup HVS 4c ★   1978
9m Open climbing; easy moves but with little protection. Start right of the oak tree, and follow a sharp ramp to join, and finish up, Crispin's Crack.

*Some 10m right of Duck Soup some slightly greener blocks nestle closer to the trees. The first substantial one has a chimney and a slim arête on its left (**Boboon**, VD, 2002). Just right, the small overhang and bulge above give **Mark of Zorro** (VS 5a, 2002). The arête just to the left is VS 5a if a very eliminate approach is used. Around the corner, the right face has a striking serpentine crack springing from a horizontal break at 3m and a large triangular flake to its right.*

⑧③ Mick's Metaphor E1 5c ★   1990s
9m The sinuous crack starting off a block on the right is short but technical. The frictionless little wall above the ledge provides an excellent comedy top-out (6a).

Ⓥ The wider crack to the right gives a good V0− (4c) jamming test, finishing at the dirty slab. A leftwards **traverse** from its base, is V2 (5c). A good project would be to **pull left** from Mick's Metaphor onto the bulging arête and finish via flakes. However, a very horny tree awaits to do you some damage if you were to fall off this the wrong way. On the buttress just right, **Probably Boysen's Arête** is the beautiful cracked arête, with bold 6a/b climbing.

The Bordello Area

Back down at a low level, this is the next area encountered on walking along the track. The first (once quarried) buttress has a silver birch to its left and a big flat boulder below.

⑧④ Bordello E3 5c ★   2003
10m Starting at a drilled thread, climb the arête to a good foothold. Trend left (hidden hold), passing a short crack to finish. Unprotected and harder than it looks.

⑧⑤ Border Skirmish E1 5b   2003
10m Starting on a ledge below a scoop to the right of Bordello, hand-traverse a slanting borehole rightwards. Step onto a ledge on the right arête of the buttress, and climb the face direct past a sloping ledge. Artificial, but unprotected with a bad landing.

The second, larger buttress is 20m right and is split by a wide crack, on whose left is a face with a ledge at 4m.

⑧⑥ Sedition and Alchemy E3 6a ★   2003
12m Based on the arête to the left of the wide crack. A groove leads to a good ledge on the right (crucial Rock 1/2 above). Step left and up to reach breaks (crux – harder for shorties), and continue up the arête on good holds.

⑧⑦ Fire Down Below VS 4c   2003
12m The unforgiving wide crack can be jammed or laybacked but needs big cams at this grade.

Trouble at t'Mill (HS 4b, 2003), is right of the wide crack. Start at a steep little arête (V2 on its right side) to gain a big ledge. Climb grooves and ledges above. Escapable. Ⓥ **Appocaliss** V3 (6b), is the isolated arête some 10m further right.

Magical Bouldery Wood

The copse further right has some boulders and larger buttresses scattered amongst the trees. This is a beautiful location, especially on autumn evenings when slanting rays of sunlight and the whispering of the beech trees lend the area a sense of Tolkienesque magic. The area has a number of interesting routes and good bouldering, as well as a number of unclimbed projects. However, while most are good, their greatest reward comes from their special setting; sit down on a rock, take it all in.

The Bottom Buttresses

The first of these lies directly below Mick's Metaphor.

⑬⑧ Mad Lines E1 5b   1997

5m The prominently pocketed, rounded left arête, climbed direct, is reachy, balancy, much harder than it looks… and unprotected.

⑬⑨ Spacepube VD   1997

5m The ramp to the right is also poorly protected, but more amenable. For the disappointed a 6c direct start is possible!

⑭⓪ Pluto's Ring E1 5c   1991

5m The steep and technical right arête is climbed via a good flake and some committing reaches to and from the unforgiving rounded break. The gear is too far up to be placed comfortably and too far down for comfort! May the Force be with you.

The second Bottom Buttress is a few metres round to the right. On its left is an eponymous bulge split by a thin crack.

⑭① Bewhiskered Behemoth E2 5c   2003

11m Climb up to the bulge and apply yourself to the crack using spaced hidden pockets to reach a gruelling jam-cum-mantelshelf finish.

⑭② Sanitarium E5 6a   2003

9m Starting at the impressive, wide crack on the right, scamper up to the ledge and place protection before moving right and tackling the fearsome gritty bulge above. A side-runner in the flake of the following route seems sensible. **Ⓥ** A **direct start** up the lower wall to the ledge is V7 (6c).

⑭③ Jetez le Pantalon E2 5b   1990

9m Climb direct to the prominent flake/spike just right and thence to the top.

Ⓥ In front of this route is a rounded boulder. Start sitting using the **crack and right arête**. Struggle up to a rounded break, and gain erection from here, V7 (6b). Another 50m right is a small bouldering outcrop, consisting of short arêtes. The **leftmost arête** is a very technical V6 (6b), with few useful holds. The

The **Advanced Beginner**

The routes on Hen Cloud and Ramshaw err towards a higher general standard of climbing, but there are still some fine easier classics worth seeking out. The following routes are good climbs for beginners to tackle, but generally require a bit more competence than beginners' routes on the Roaches.

Hen Cloud

- **Central Climb** 3 pitches, each of which offers challenge, particularly the second which gives a tough struggle;
- **K2** a fine open climb with very interesting, but well-protected, technical moves;
- **The Arête** airy and scenic, with sketchy protection (where it counts) lending it a serious feel particularly in less than perfect conditions;
- **Modern** tucked away but surprisingly challenging on close acquaintance;
- **Rib Chimney** a poor name for a fine feature which is architecturally interesting and offers crack climbing with a serious feel;
- **Great Chimney** very good, particularly if the left-hand finish is taken;
- **Thompson's Buttress, Route One** for a few moves this generates a big climb feel, if you enjoy this and Great Chimney add *Route 1* on *Ben Nevis's Carn Dearg* to your sports plan.

Ramshaw

- **Phallic Crack** mixing it at an easy standard in apparently big country;
- **Boomerang** also has a big feel, particularly in overcoming the initial moves, but succumbs easily, though elegantly, thereafter;
- **Magic Roundabout** delicate slab work. Good conditions are essential, but then it is a delight.

slabby wall on the boulder just right is V0– (5a). The **arête to the right** is V6 (6b), and the **bulge and slab** at the right side is V4 (6b), providing lots of scratching, and V5 (6b) if the right arête is avoided.

About 50m along and right from the Bottom Buttress, above the trees and within sight of the Heart of Gold area of the upper crags, is a narrow buttress with a chimney on the left. **Last View** (VD, 1979), is the small face left of the chimney, while down and right, at the toe of the buttress, is a clean little ramp. Climb up this, past a little hole to a ledge. Move left and finish up right of the chimney. This is **The Weirdy** (VD, 1968-73).

Biscuit Buttress

A further 50 metres on is the last of the rocks. By now, the rock has deteriorated quite a bit, but it is still a fine spot for those looking for solitude.

The climbs include **High Energy Plan** (HVS 5a, 1979) which climbs over the first roof encountered; **Shortbread** (HVS 5a, 1969), climbing a groove 3m to the right and finishing to the left; **Shortcake** (E1 5b, 1976), a rightward finish to the previous route; **Gingerbread** (HS 4a, 1976), the face to the right; **Ginger Biscuit** (VS 4b, 1976), the arête right again.

Hen Cloud First Ascents

1909	**Central Climb** John Laycock, AR Thompson *A direct finish was added in 1927. An eventful and historic first ascent.*		1952 May	**Bachelor's Climb** (Left-hand finish), **Second's Retreat** Joe Brown and party *The first addition by one of Hen Cloud's, and everywhere else's, major figures.*

1909   **Central Climb**   John Laycock, AR Thompson   *A direct finish was added in 1927. An eventful and historic first ascent.*

pre-1913   **The Arête, Rib Chimney, Footpath Chimney, Thompson's Buttress Routes, Tree Chimney, The Nutcracker, The Deceiver**   *The latter two routes were known as Hall Cracks 'A' and 'B' respectively. 'Exceedingly destructive to the climber's well-cut tweeds.' All recorded in the Rucksack Club Journal in 1913, the first guide to Hen Cloud.*

1913   **Great Chimney**   Siegfried Herford, Stanley Jeffcoat   *A powerful team. Herford went on to add, in 1914, Scafell's Central Buttress, one of the country's most celebrated climbs.*

1924   **Bow Buttress**

1913–27   **The Aiguillette, Easy Gully, Final Crack**

1927   **November Cracks, K2, En Rappel**   Arthur Burns   *En Rappel was known as Blizzard Buttress until an ascent by Joe Brown.*

1947   **Bachelor's Climb**

1947–51   **Hedgehog Crack, Rainbow Crack, Chockstone Crack, Chockstone Chimney, Roof Climb, Central Climb Direct, Final Crack, Modern, Ancient, Pinnacle Face**   *'Hedgehog Crack is beset with thorny problems, all of which can be solved if the hands can be persuaded*

to stay jammed.'   **1951 guidebook.**

1952 May   **Bachelor's Climb** (Left-hand finish), **Second's Retreat**   Joe Brown and party   *The first addition by one of Hen Cloud's, and everywhere else's, major figures.*

1957   **Bulwark**   Clive Shaw   *Marked the formation of the North Staffordshire Mountaineering Club.*

1957–61   **Main Crack, Delstree, Reunion Crack, Slimline, Hen Cloud Eliminate**   Joe Brown

1957–61   **Bachelor's Left-Hand**   Don Whillans

early-1960s   **Encouragement, The Long and the Short, Chicken**   Tony Nicholls

1962   **Second's Advance, Hal's Ridge, Crispin's Crack, Rib Crack**   Bob Hassall

1962   **High Tensile Crack**   Colin Foord

1962   **The Ape**   Pete Ruddle

1962   **The Better End** (1 pt.)   Dave Salt   *Originally named The Bitter End. Climbed free in 1975 by John Allen and Steve Bancroft, and renamed from a spelling mistake in* Crags Magazine.

1957–68   **Piston Groove, Victory, Green Corner, The Lum, Bantam Crack, Arête Wall, Left Twin Crack, Right Twin Crack, Pinnacle Rib, Diagonal Route, Recess Chimney**   *All of these routes appeared uncredited in the 1968 guidebook.*

1969 May	**Shortbread** John Yates
1971 Apr	**Songs of Praise** John Yates
1968–73	**Little Pinnacle Climb, The Notch, Pug, Central Tower, The Weirdy**
1974 Aug 18	**Fat Old Sun** (1 pt.) John Allen, Steve Bancroft (AL) *Climbed free in 1978 by Steve Bancroft and Dave Humphries (AL).*
1975 Jul 27	**Anthrax** Steve Bancroft, John Allen (AL)
1976 Feb 26	**Comedian** Steve Bancroft, John Allen *The first of the really great routes to be added by the Sheffield raiders. Started on the right where Frayed Nerve now starts. The described start was climbed by Dave Jones in 1980.*
1976 Jun 20	**Heart of Gold, Short Man's Misery, Shortcake, Gingerbread, Ginger Biscuit** Nick Colton, Con Carey, Jim Campbell, (various leads), John Tout
1976	**Corinthian** Steve Bancroft, John Allen
1976	**Caricature** John Allen, Steve Bancroft *'Allen stepped over the threshold of the possible to produce Caricature, after several airborne retreats.'*
1976	**Anaconda** John Gosling
1977 Jul 16	**Chameleon** Steve Bancroft, Nicky Stokes, Al Manson
1977	**Stokesline** Mark Stokes
1978 Apr 2	**Slowhand** Dave Jones, Roger Bennion, Gary Gibson
1978 Apr 2	**Electric Chair, Nutted by Reality, Pullet, Gallows** Jim Moran, Simon Horrox, (various leads), Geoff Milburn, Dave Jones, Roger Bennion
1978 Apr 2	**Face Value** Gary Gibson (solo)
1978 Apr 5	**Short 'n' Sharp** Dave Jones, Ian 'Hots' Johnson, Gary Gibson *Climbed by Simon Horrox as the cheekily named Apology, knowing that Jones had failed to lead it previously. However Horrox did not know that Jones had returned three days earlier to lead it.*
1978 Apr 16	**Easy Come** Al Evans, Geoff Milburn
1978 Apr 17	**Borstal Breakout** Jim Moran, Al Evans, Simon Horrox *A day off work was needed as the route had been cleaned but not completed on the Sunday. Top-roped first by Simon Horrox on April 4. It was erroneously assumed for some time that Jim Moran et al had completed both pitches. The second pitch was actually climbed by Dave Jones with a nut for aid in 1978. The route in its described form remained unclimbed until after the production of the*

1981 guidebook which had described a free ascent! It had certainly been led clean by 1983 but who actually made the first complete free ascent will probably remain a bone of contention.

1978 Apr	**The Monkey in Your Soul, Prayers, Poems and Promises** Al Simpson, with John Holt or Dave Jones
1978 Apr	**Duck Soup** Al Evans
1978 May 17	**Bitching** Gary Gibson, Kons Nowak
1978 May 17	**The Pinch, Broken Arrow** John Holt, Dave Jones, (various leads)
1978 May	**The Raid, The Sorcerer** Jim Moran, Al Evans
1978 May	**Qantas, Press on Regardless, Zoom Wall** Dave Jones, Al Simpson
1978 Jun	**Caesarian** Martin Berzins, Bob Berzins *This was with a deviation to the left, avoiding the main difficulties. Climbed direct by Jonny Woodward in September 1980.*
1979 Feb 25	**Space Probe** Jonny Woodward, Ian Maisey *The second pitch, Helter Skelter, had been climbed in 1977 by Steve Bancroft and Al Manson.*
1979 May 29	**The Mandrake** Jonny Woodward *'I placed runners in Victory, level with the overhang, but these are probably unnecessary since when a hold broke off from the flake I hit the deck despite the runners.' Possibly unrepeated until an ascent from Jon Read in 2003.*
1979	**Cold Sweat, High Energy Plan, Jellyfish, Bad Joke, Small Buttress, Triumph of the Good City, Last View** Gary Gibson, solo, or with Phil Gibson or Ian Barker
1979 Jun 10	**Shoe Shine Shuffle** Phil Gibson, Gary Gibson
1979 Jul	**Levitation** Phil Burke *Climbed with very high side runners, which were eliminated by Simon Nadin in 2001.*
1979	**Slipstreams, Buster the Cat, Standing Tall, Tunnel Vision, Delusion, Pete's Back-Side** Dave Jones *All climbed during guidebook work.*
1980 Sep 14	**Loose Fingers** Gary Gibson (solo)
1980 Jun	**Solid Geometry** Dave Jones (solo)
1981 Jun 28	**Blood Blisters** Gary Gibson
1981 Jul	**Fast Piping, Flexure Line, This Poison** Gary Gibson, with Jon Walker or solo *The upper crack of Fast Piping had been climbed previously as a variation to Hedgehog Crack.*

Staffordshire Grit

1981 Aug **Chicken Direct, Cool Fool, The Stone Loach, Frayed Nerve** Gary Gibson *A good month! The lower arête of Cool Fool had been climbed as Charisma by Nick Postlethwaite in 1980. James Pearson probably did the second ascent in 2003, without the runner in the lower boulder. On The Stone Loach, a long sling was clipped into a wire in the pod to protect the crux moves which had been practised extensively on an abseil rope.*

1983 Sep 22 **Master of Reality** Simon Nadin *The lower front face was climbed a few days later.*

1984 Sep 26 **Mindbridge** Simon Nadin (solo) *Protection exists, but Nadin decided to solo the line to provide the concentration necessary for success. Unrepeated.*

1985 Apr 18 **Chiaroscuro, Even Smaller Buttress** Gary Gibson *Chairoscuro is an undergraded dark horse at E5 6a originally. Unrepeated.*

1985 Jul 31 **Touch** Simon Nadin

1985 Aug 3 **Parallel Lines** Simon Nadin *While attempting to eliminate side-runners in the 1990s, Dan Honeyman fell and smashed up a wrist. Unrepeated?*

1986 May 16 **Starlight and Storm** John Allen, Martin Veale

1986 Jun 6 **B4XS** Simon Nadin *Second, third and fourth ascents all came in one day from Seb Grieve, Jean Minh Trihn-Thieu and Dave Jones, 1996.*

1986 Oct 10 **Sauria** Martin Boysen *Unrepeated?*

1987 May 6 **Black Eyed Dog** Andy Popp *Misnamed as Dog Eye Rib in the previous edition. Climbed on-sight by Sam Whittaker in 1996.*

1990 Mar 16 **Peter and the Wolf** Andy Popp *Unrepeated?*

1990 Mar 16 **Wavelength** Graham Cole, John Hattersley

1990 **Jetez le Pantalon** Colin Cheetham, John Perry, Rob Barnett

1992 Feb 25 **A Flabby Crack** Neil Travers

1993 **Scrabble** Justin Critchlow

1993 **Desperado** Mark Katz

1995 **Just Thirteen** Mark Katz

1996 Feb **Arêtenophobia** Seb Grieve *Needing the extra impetus to succeed on the bold lead, Grieve had no option but to don one of his wife's dresses for the ascent. The underwear was his own. Grieve recalls climbing the arête on the steep and featureless left side. However, Neil Bentley recalls that "…He climbed it on the right, I'm sure, I was there. Seb never remembers that sort of stuff." Second ascent followed immediately by 'Aussie' Dave Jones.*

1997 **Jean the Bean** Justin Critchlow

1998 Jan **The Young Pretender** Mark Katz *Unrepeated?*

1999 **Man oh Man** Simon Nadin

1990s **Boysen's Arête, Probably Boysen's Arête, Mick's Metaphor** Martin Boysen *Claimed by Boysen long after the event, considering them insignificant at the time. Variously reclimbed and reclaimed over the years.*

2000 **Mandrill** Andy Cave, Martin Veale, Rab Carrington, Martin Boysen, Tom Leppert

2002 **Hens Dropping** Niall Grimes, Richard Harland

2002 **Mark of Zorro, Boboon** Andi Turner

2002 Feb **Dead Banana Slab** John Cox

2002 Feb **Andrei's Route** Andrei Kosenko

2002 Feb **Flour Wall** Andrei Kosenko, Bob Smith (both led)

2002 Sep 13 **7 of 9** Graham Cole and Alison Trinder *Originally started further right.*

2002 Oct 19 **The Driven Bow** Jon Read

2003 **Master of Puppets** Mark Sharratt, Andi Turner

2003 Mar 12 **Sanitarium** Mark Sharratt, Martin Dearden

2003 Mar 13 **Bewhiskered Behemoth** John Perry, Andi Turner

2003 Jun 22 **Trouble at t'Mill, Bordello, Sedition and Alchemy, Border Skirmish** John H Bull (solo) *The first route climbed after a week marked by redundancies at work. On Sedition and Alchemy, a sling was clipped into the crucial runner during a solo ascent.*

2003 Jul 5 **Fire Down Below** Jon Read, Dave Garnett and John H Bull

Ⓥ Hen Cloud Bouldering First Ascents

Appocaliss Justin Critchlow.

Blood Blisters Direct Start Justin Critchlow 1994.

Simon's Slab Simon Nadin 2000.

A climber about to commit to the crux of Rib Chimney, S (Page 120), a deep journey into the heart of Hen Cloud. Photo: Niall Grimes.

Ronan Browner on Masochism, HVS 5b for some, E7 7b for others, (page 141). Photo: Niall Grimes.

Ramshaw Rocks

3

"Arrive there on a warm summer evening, fighting fit and determined, preferably with a few preliminary bouts under your belt, crash the jams in, move quickly, and the climbs submit.

"Arrive on a bad day, and it is a different story; the rock will maul you and you will retire, bloodied, to lick your wounds."

Martin Boysen

Ramshaw Rocks

by Richard Patterson

O.S. Ref. **SK0I9622** | Altitude: **4I0m a.s.l.**

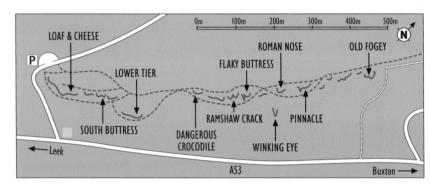

Ramshaw Rocks, though forming part of the triumvirate of larger gritstone crags in this area, has a character and atmosphere all its own. As its name suggests, it is more a series of buttresses than a continuous edge in the classic gritstone style. Viewed from the road below, the rocks present a Gothic nightmare: vast jutting fins and prows of rock, mainly overhanging, split by many wide, steep cracks and fissures. The plane of the rocks, combined with the brutal weathering, has accentuated the roughness of the larger grained grit, leaving a coarse, pebbly and, in places, less compact skin. This fragile surface has led many to be wary on first acquaintance and, in truth, it does seem strange to those used to the finer grit of the Eastern Edges. At Ramshaw, perseverance has its reward and, in general, the grain adds to the adventurous feel rather than detracts from the climbing – however, this statement may seem less convincing the further one is from protection! Conversely, the side walls and backs of these steep jagged buttresses contain many less extrovert but equally intense gritstone experiences. Testpieces abound, but equally there is scope for the beginner to hone their movements on more moderately angled grit. As the locals who walk

dogs and kids up the paths and over the dykes and shelves on this shallow side will testify, it can be great fun to explore, scramble and simply enjoy fathoming a way up, down and around!

The climbs at Ramshaw favour those with technique (the cracks), confidence (the slabs), and sheer bloody-mindedness (the weird offwidths). Even more than at most gritstone crags, the effort expended and satisfaction gained are certainly at odds with the length of the routes. These attributes, combined with Ramshaw's odd aesthetics and its relative unpopularity, provide a gritstone experience which a climber of any grade is unlikely to forget, whether later basking in the glow of success, or ruefully licking their (often bloody) wounds.

Conditions & aspect

Running roughly north-east to south-west, Ramshaw is undoubtedly at its best on a sunny morning, and an alpine start on a fine summer's day will reveal a truly delightful aspect denied to the lazy. Sitting proudly atop the ridge, the crag unsurprisingly catches the wind. On the credit side this means that the main buttress fronts will dry quickly in most circumstances, and the crag can provide

The routes at Ramshaw

reflect the various stages of its development well. The fifties and early sixties left behind both classic easier cracks and strange wide fissures, whilst the late sixties and early seventies saw the addition of more open friction climbs. As both rubber and protection advanced, at the turn of the eighties, more audacious climbs became possible, limiting the more recent additions to the more improbable and outrageous walls and arêtes.

a welcome escape from the heat on warm summer afternoons. This exposure can, however, make for an (extremely) cold day out in winter. Improvements in pollution control are credited with a re-greening of the grit and although the faces are in the main clean, the gullies and north-facing side-walls can remain damp, dank and slow-drying. Faces mostly south-east. Plenty of sun until the afternoon. There is also some rock facing south remaining in the sun for most of the day.

Routes
Superb. Over 150 routes. All grades well catered for. Lots of pebbly slabs, steep walls and ferocious cracks.

Ⓥ Bouldering
Very good. Over 40 problems, mostly never before documented. A few circuits exist, along with plenty of problems at the base of the routes. Lots of pebbly slabs and arêtes and brutal slappy test-pieces.

Parking & approach
Ramshaw Rocks overlook the A53 Buxton to Leek road, about 8 miles from Buxton and 4 miles from Leek. The crag itself is best reached via the un-named

lane found at the southern (Leek) end of the crag. This is followed to limited parking at the back of the crag. Parking on the A53 is not recommended as it is a fast, busy road, though there are a couple of spaces opposite the bottom of the lane. Be especially careful not to block farm access or the road itself. From the parking area, the approach is obvious, and takes between 30 seconds and ten minutes.

Food & accommodation
See main introduction. Also the Traveller's Rest pub, 3 miles towards Buxton for food and beer.

Access
The main crag is owned by Harper Crewe Estates and there are generally no access problems. Exceptions are a) the Winking Eye section, which has been vandalised in the past. Climbers have been asked to avoid the routes on this unique gritstone formation to preserve it in its present state, and b)

The Lady Stone, which is on private land; at present the owners are against climbers using it and once again, therefore, this section should be avoided.

The first climbing is not found on the actual edge itself, but on a small lone pinnacle south of the lane, about a 150m hike through the heather. There are several recorded routes and possibly room for some minor eliminates, making it worth a visit for the dedicated. **East Face** *(M, pre-1973) climbs the very small slab facing the lane, while* **After Eight** *(S, 1979) takes the short wall just left of the south-east arête to finish up the arête.* **Southern Crack** *(VD, pre-1973) is a much better bet than either of these, taking the obvious wide fissure in the centre of the south face to finish on the crenellated top. Other routes and some boulder problems have been claimed here, but their stature is slight and they are best left to be periodically rediscovered by the adventurous.*

The Main Crag

The main edge starts 35m east of the lane at a flat-topped block with a second large block perched on top; together these are known as The Loaf and Cheese. The first proper route climbs the left side of the steep front face.

❶ Assembled Techniques E4 6a ★   1986
8m A good climb that tackles the front face of the Loaf and Cheese block via some awkward climbing. Move up to an obvious hand-jam slot and either go

straight up onto the ledge then right onto the Cheese, or right to the scooped hole and a committing rightward finish.

❷ Loaf and Cheese VS 4c ★   pre-1973
11m Difficult but thankfully short-lived moves up the rather crumbly crack lead to a ledge. A further ledge is gained by a mantel, and from here the pinnacle can be climbed at the front or the back to give a pleasant finish.

❸ Dream Fighter E3 6a ★   1984
8m A worrying finish on a less than sympathetic surface gives this route its character. Gain the crack, followed by a committing pull onto the slab above. Good.

❹ Green Crack VS 5b ★   1972
8m Despite appearances, a superb route epitomising the Ramshaw experience in miniature. Climb the green groove into the wide crack, where difficulties force a welcome, but almost certainly ungracious exit onto the slab above. *Crack School no. 5.*

❺ National Acrobat *see right*

❻ Traveller in Time E4 6a ★★★   1977
11m A less difficult but equally fine climb. Climb the steep groove until a stretch left gains a smaller flake. Plenty of small but dubious protection here makes the subsequent mantel and shuffle left, to an always ungainly top-out, an exciting experience.

5 National Acrobat

E(for Effort)6 6c ★★★   1978

9m The obvious hanging crack held out against repeat ascents for over twenty years, giving an indication of the talent and determination required for success. The crux section, leaving the crack and getting established in the hanging groove above, provides one of the meanest sections of climbing on grit.

Crack School no. 12

Patch Hammond succeeds on the first ground-up ascent of the Ramshaw test-piece National Acrobat, E6 6c. Photo: Adam Long.

CRACK School

Richie Patterson

My personal opinion is that the modern climber is somewhat under-skilled in the area of crack climbing, so in a spirit of generosity(?) I have set a task which when completed will (maybe) enable even the indoor addict to face that prime stopper of gritstone climbing – the crack.

Within the text I have selected a tick list of Ramshaw's best crack climbs that should enable any climber that completes them to hold their head high and proud in any pub in the land. Hopefully this mastery will lead them to espouse the virtues of the bloodied hand, (fist, elbow, and knee?) and to continue to pass on the grand gritstone tradition, which Johnny Dawes so presciently called

"THE best forgotten art"

The CRACKER'S Dozen

1. **Phallic Crack HVD**
   Spectacular climbing on a big buttress.
2. **Great Scene Baby S**
   Short and stiff to hone the technique.
3. **Tricouni Crack HS**
   Not quite hard as nails.
4. **The Crank VS**
   Now you're really learning. A jammer's milestone.
5. **Green Crack VS**
   An awkward change of angle.
6. **Great Zawn HVS**
   Wide, ballsy and committing.
7. **Brown's Crack E1**
   Very short, but just plain hard.
8. **Foord's Folly E2**
   Thin hand technique can but help.
9. **Imposition E2**
   Another difficult change of angle.
10. **The Undertaker E3**
    Short lived but perplexing.
11. **Ramshaw Crack E4**
    Hands to fists to arm-bar. Testing.
12. **National Acrobat E6**
    The path to true mastery.

Neil Bentley attending Crack School. Ramshaw Crack.
Photo: Seb Grieve.

7 Body Pop E4 6b ★★   1984

11m More commitment required! From the top of the groove, the right arête is gained adventurously. Luckily, as height is gained, the climbing eases enough to keep you moving in the right direction. Usually.

8 Wall and Groove VD   pre-1973

9m The crack is often green, but much better than it looks. Starting from beneath the prow (or direct), move up to gain the chimney proper which is surprisingly tough.

9 The Arête S   pre-1973

9m A steep route which takes the obvious tongue-like flakes to gain a ledge.

10 Louie Groove E1 5b ★   1968

8m The square-cut groove is easy at the bottom but more intimidating as height is gained, and has seen a few wobblers. Sneaky gear for those who look.

11 Leeds Slab HS 4a   1980

8m Ascend the centre of the cutaway on 'chippers' to finish up the notched rib.

12 Leeds Crack D   pre-1973

6m The short crack right of the slab gives good introductory jamming. The short blunt arête to the right is a pleasant HVS 5b.

13 Honest Jonny D   1976

5m The short little groove just right of the rib.

Fifteen metres right and higher up is a blunt-nosed pinnacle with a thin crooked crack on its front face. It can be

climbed by going up the wall on the left at 6b: **Take Her Under**.

14 The Undertaker E3 6a ★   1973

6m A mini National Acrobat, and like that route, only a fierce approach (or a very long reach) aids progress as the initially co-operative crack turns unhelpful a frustrating distance below the next good holds. *Crack School no. 10.*

The wall to the right features a couple of short solos: **Pink Flake**, *4c, takes the obvious booming flake in the wall to the right, gained from the right; it is 5a to gain the flake direct;* **Mantel**, *4c, is shorter and features a fun move onto the rounded shelf farther right then straight up.*

15 Overdrive E3 5c   1977

7m Something of a gripper, with anxiety rising with height. Ten metres right of The Undertaker is a small triangular roof/buttress. Using good but creaky holds, gain the lip of the roof and mantel boldly up to finish on a selection of gritty slopers. The two cracks underneath this have also been climbed as **Twin Cracks** (D, pre-1973), and **Double Chin** (VD, 1973–81), both of which finish up the wider broken groove above.

16 Prowler HVS 4c   1973–81

6m Take the very friable roof to the right at its widest point and finish up the secondary prow.

Right again is a buttress with a prominent recessed crack to its left. The two short grooves to the left of this crack have been claimed and, though worthwhile exercises, are hardly routes. Both go at about 4c.

Donie O'Sullivan giving his all on The Great Zawn, HVS 5a, one of the wider tests in the Ramshaw Crack School. Photo: Niall Grimes

"The **Traveller**

on the once-important coach road from Buxton sees glowering above him, on Ramshaw Edge, a grotesque succession of ghoulish faces, bovine and porcine heads, and half finished monsters springing from the parent rock. And beyond, where Hen Cloud extends its array of pinnacles, he sees still more impossible shapes set in stone, outlines that only the camera may prove less than vertical or only slightly overhanging, but to the eye appear like curving horns, their points overweighted with threatening tons of rock."

EA Baker
Moors, Crags and Caves of the High Peak

⑱ Broken Groove D ★   pre-1973
8m The striking feature provides a good, easy route with a big feel. The arête just right, **Broken Groove Arête** (D, pre-1973), is also worthwhile.

⑲ Gully Arête E1 5c   1986
6m The slight arête, climbed strictly on the right, is harder than it looks. The upper arête is a lot easier.

⑳ Wellingtons VD ★   pre-1973
8m The wide crack to the right of the gully invites a 'get-stuck-in' approach. Big boots may help. Good fun.

⑰ The Great Zawn HVS 5a ★★   1950–65
8m The next feature is the striking wide crack, which just screams to be climbed! Initially wide and tricky, a good hold at mid-height provides welcome relief; then it gets tough again. Large cam recommended though a wobbly chockstone also provides some relief. *Crack School no. 6.*

㉑ Masochism HVS 5b ★★   1950–65
9m Aptly named. The disconcertingly steep hand-to-fist crack leads with venom to a large ledge. The second bulge is less savage but with 'chockstone et al' it still maintains interest to the end. Good fun and obviously undergraded but what the hell, it's traditional!

As **so often** happens in the **Alps,**

discussion turned to grit. Joe [Brown] was extolling the hidden delights of Ramshaw and inevitably we dwelled on the great challenge of the crag; the huge hanging crack splitting the largest buttress. It had not been done. The next time I saw him he suppressed a creasing smile; "Oh, by the way, that crack…". A chockstone had miraculously inserted itself in the depths of the crack; it had proved useful! It was perhaps Joe's last great gritstone route – a fitting finale.

Martin Boysen

Moving round and up, under the prominent (unclimbed) bulge/arête is a raised, sheltered bay containing a number of excellent routes.

㉒ Trivial Traverse HVS 5a   1977

6m Traverse the sidewall using the horizontal break. Can be finished either by going up when a large foothold is reached or by carrying on to the arête, which is pleasantly ascended on flutings.

㉓ T'rival Traverse E3 6a ★   1987

6m This delicate and tenuous climb provides a test of nerve and skill in the art of friction climbing. From the ledge, follow the holdless ramp to the sanctuary of a small flake, then make a scary high step to reach the break. Finish direct. Gear is put in the break up and right at this grade: how far along determines how scared you get. **Rock Trivia** (E2 6c, 1987) climbs through the right side of the traverse.

㉔ Sneeze E1 5b ★★   1979

8m The incipient crack is gained from the left and, though protectable, seems best savoured without the encumbrance of a rope. A fine climb. Rumours exist of a direct start, somewhere in the V9 region.

㉕ The Crank VS 5a ★★   1950–65

8m Some real Joe Brown jamming, and delightful with it. Climb the crack on sinkers until a step right forces a bit of thought and leads to a wider finish. *Crack School no. 4.*

㉖ Ultimate Sculpture E8 7a ★★★   1994

8m The incredible blank arête provides the sternest challenge at Ramshaw. Climb it using faith, friction, and immense talent. Very minimalist!

South Buttress

The next buttress is the most substantial on the whole edge and sports a number of fine routes. It is particularly good for its easy routes, which cover impressive terrain at a moderate standard. It is bounded on its left edge by a chimney.

㉗ Chockstone Chimney VD   pre-1973

8m The chimney quickly gives in after a short spar with the obvious chockstone.

㉘ Maximum Hype E4 5c   1987

10m Starting at the end of Chockstone Chimney, this route boldly tackles the left wall of the buttress. Gain a short blind flake and move up and slightly left with difficulty to gain a more centrally placed good hold. Another good hold follows as well as some protection and an easier finish back out to the arête. Gritty.

㉙ Gumshoe E2 5c ★★★   1977

14m One of the best routes at Ramshaw, with a disconcertingly obscure crux. Start up the shallow green groove to arrange some rather disappointing protection. Move up left to better holds and a more reasonable finish. High in the grade. A bold indirect finish, **Wine Gums** (E4 6a, 1985), makes a difficult stretch up and right after the crux to gain reasonable but gritty holds. Finish direct or slightly right.

㉚ Tally Not HVS 5c ★   1972

14m Follow the lower corner up and right. Make a difficult move out left to the second corner, which still needs all your attention for a couple of moves until the climbing eases. Cleaner than it looks.

㉛ Battle of the Bulge VS 4b ★★   pre-1973

9m A superb little crack climb. Not half as tricky as the name implies, and while it doesn't require a tiny waist, a beer belly won't help either!

③ The Cannon VS 4c ★   pre-1973

13m A difficult start up the friable flakes provides a shot in the arms on this exciting climb. Move up and right to gain the easier groove. Pass the 'cannon', and step right to a direct finish.

③ Torture E4 5c   1981

12m Move up on sandy slopers with poor gear to a committing pull into balance and an easier finish. Not often done and only a little more attractive than its name suggests.

③ Whilly's Whopper VS 4c   1979

12m Follow the wider crack until a step left can be made into a short hanging groove. Finish direct via a grapple with the, shall we say, prominent feature?

③ Phallic Crack HVD ★★   pre-1973

12m Wide at the bottom, thrutchy at the top, with fine climbing in between. Follow the crack, wrestling the large knob on the way, to finish up the obvious groove. Very good sport. *Crack School no. 1.*

③ Alcatraz E1 5b ★★   1968

12m Just round the corner is a short slab capped by an overhang with a crack running through it. Initial tricky moves lead to a wider crack, which is followed

more reasonably. Though a little green at the start this route gives good climbing.

③ Juan Cur E5 6a†   1991

12m Follow the wall and arête right of Alcatraz as far as possible, until a step left can be made to join the final 3m of that route. A tied-off piece of wood was used in the 'handrail' to protect the first ascent. 1" × 2" × 12" if you really want to know!

③ The Untouchable E1 5b ★★   1968

11m Just right of the arête, a finely positioned crackline snakes up the buttress edge. Gained from the right, the thinner lower section of the route is hardest; the wider upper section, once gained, is testing but with more solid climbing. Pumpy and very good.

③ Corner Crack S 4a   pre-1973

8m The crack to the right is short but sweet.

④ The Rippler HVS 5b   pre-1973

8m The route to the right provides intricate and fingery climbing. Starting round to the right of the previous route, use ripples to reach a better rail at mid-height. Finish slightly right on very good edges. Bold. A direct start can be made at a fragile 6a

coming in from nearer the left arête. **Cold Wind** (E2 5c, 1984) follows the right arête.

❖ *Below and right is a small blank face with a couple of problems and potential only for Spiderman.* **Midge** V2 (6a) *takes the bulge and twin cracks at the left-hand end and* **Cleg** V0– (5a) *the hanging groove at the right-hand end.*

The Lower Tier

After South Buttress, the crag opens out with a large gap to the next obvious buttresses. However, at a lower level, approximately 50m down and right, is a short but very steep buttress, a mini crag in its own right, and home to a number of superb routes and some classic all-weather bouldering.

41 Crab Walk Direct V2 (5c)

A short steep crack. **Sensible Shoes** V1 (5b) crosses the roof left of the hanging crack. Traversing right under the roof is the **Smoothment Traverse**, V3 (6a), while climbing the **roof direct** is V6 (6b).

42 Sketching Wildly E6 6c ★ 1994

11m The tiered roofs provide a stiff battle. Climb to the first roof, place a couple of (poor) cams and

Ramshaw Rocks

boasts an enviable selection of cracks and fissures in a myriad of widths, lengths and grades and as may be gathered from the introduction it is, in modern parlance, a somewhat 'old-school' venue. Because of this it is also a crag where the 'classic' climbers' fallback of technique may well outweigh all the indoor training in the world.

make very difficult moves rightwards to better gear and more hard moves on slopers over the final roof. ❖ The start of this can be done as a V1 (5b) problem in its own right, **Overlap**.

43 Crab Walk S 4a ★ pre-1973

20m A good long climb covering interesting terrain. Start near the centre of the buttress and climb up left via good holds to gain a ramp line which is followed leftwards to finish up a short crack.

44 Brown's Crack E1 5c ★★ 1950–65

14m A gem from the old master. Gain some giant holds below the obvious crack, breathe deep, then fight, fist and furkle your way up the unhelpful crack. Short and just plain hard. An eliminate, **Outflanked** (E1 5c), places gear in the crack then moves out to climb the short green groove left of the crack with one hard move. *Crack School no. 7.*

Certainly it is a crag to **confront,**

for the only way to avoid it is to keep driving. It has all the subtlety of a prize fighter defiantly sticking his chin out. As with all gritstone, the climbing needs a positive, dynamic approach – total commitment to the moves. It is not enough to think you can make a move – you must be certain of it.

Ramshaw Rocks, by Martin Boysen.

45 Prostration HVS 5a ★★ 1950–65

14m A good climb. Follow the short crack to the roof, somehow gain the ledge, realise you're stuck, struggle upright (crux), and scuttle up the secondary crack. Not to be taken lying down!

46 Tit Grip V10 (6c)

Using two tiny holds below Prostration, dyno for the top. Doing a rounded mantel at the top of this is an old problem, **Roll Off** V2 (5b). A desperate **sloping traverse** is also possible here, starting low below the start of Brown's Crack, and slapping right along the lip to come back down to good holds at the start of Colly Wobble **V8 (6c)**. (The Hem Line traverse avoids this section by going slightly higher here.)

47 Colly Wobble E4 6b ★★ 1987

11m The short hanging wall, marked by four holes, the remnants of an old plaque (which said "**No climbing on these rocks**"), provides an unusual and technical outing. Gain the holes and somehow utilise them to make a long stretch for the ledge above. Luckily a half-sized Tri-cam in one of the holes makes it all a little more amenable.

48 Don's Crack HVS 5b ★★ 1950–65

11m Notably difficult for the pint-sized climber, the steep crack provides another test of crack technique. Follow the initial crack to a hole (birds' nest *de rigueur*); from here, a long reach or some funky jamming provides access to the upper crack, which eases towards the top.

49 Tierdrop E5 6b ★★★ 1980

8m Although its original stature has been diminished by the use of pads, this is as fine a highball as can be found anywhere. Reach the obvious vein, either direct or from the right, both crimpy. Using determination, finger strength and burl, get to a chipped runnel on the lip. From here, crimps two feet away tantalise... but can you commit? **V** V7 in new money. **Sam's Left Hand** is a slightly harder variant, reaching left from the runnel to a sloping slot leading to the top.

50 Tier's End VS 5a 1979

8m A stiff pull round the overhang leads to a good crack. Move left and finish up a shallow groove. **V** A good V0.

51 Abdomen S 4b 1968–73

34m A girdle of the Lower Tier. Using gut instinct follow the central break under the roof, gained from grassy ledges at the left-hand end, to finish above Colly Wobble.

52 Hem Line V6 (6b)

Left-to-right or right-to-left, this long low-level traverse provides very pumpy sport. The crux section under Colly Wobble and Tierdrop is a good test of slopey grit technique. Generally dry and a good warm up on Ramshaw's colder days.

Further right is a number of small buttress/boulders containing a selection of problems. All have been claimed; none is harder than 5c, but they are in the main slight entertainment. The original edge is the next destination with two prominent buttresses appearing, the first containing not a lot while the second is host to a very prominent flying fin and a couple of grit's finer and wilder exploits.

53 The Comedian VS 4b pre-1973

9m The left-hand buttress has less scope than at first appears. Climb the front face to below the roof and three possible exits. Left is easy at 4a, straight up is an exciting 5b, and the original right is an amusing 4c crawl, to finish one metre right of the arête. The undercut rib and hanging scoop left of this is **Paul's Rib** (E5 6c, 1994).

54 Camelian Crack VD ★ pre-1973

6m The crack on the next buttress is short and sweet. The slab left of the crack is **Pat is Parched** (E1 5b, 1994) but is rather small, myopic and seems impossible at the grade without using either the arête or the crack.

I did ***Dangerous Crocodile*** sometime at the end of Summer, so was pretty hot. I remember I got stopped by a copper on the way out for overtaking in a dangerous place and he scolded me for my stupidity. I don't think he appreciated it. Later that day I soloed the route with no-one at the crag. To give myself some help I talked to myself. It worked very well. That's how all the mad talking and screaming started!

At the top I was so relieved I took off my shirt, and for some reason, didn't stop until I was stood there completely naked.

Seb Grieve

(55) Dangerous Crocodile Snogging
E7 6c ★★★ **1986**

12m **The next square buttress has a remarkable flying fin on its left-hand side; this route picks its way delicately across the sidewall covering some unlikely ground. From below the left arête, steeply gain the wide break, and the rounded hold above, at the base of the arête. From here, struggle into a standing position on the left of the arête. Make one (hard) move up and stretch left for an elusive small flake in the middle of the wall. Matching here allows a breather (though no way out) while the final moves up are uneasily insecure. Easy for 6c.**

More a cayman's kiss than the real thing, **Blockbuster** (E5 6b, 2001) is a shorter (though reachy), more direct Crocodile but with some difficult climbing nonetheless. Place gear high in Camelian Crack and move up and right to the flake of Crocodile, to finish grimly as above.

Dangerous Crocodile Snogging

Dangerous Crocodile Bouldering

The first circuit lies in the area around **Dangerous Crocodile Snogging**. There isn't masses in the area, but most are good quality, and the landings are good. The rock in some areas is a bit scratchy, so tread softly after wet weather.

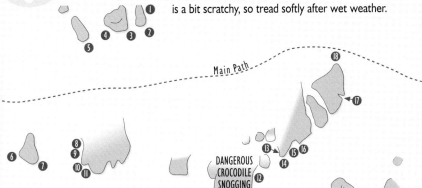

❶ V1 (5c)
Flakes to the top.

❷ V0 (5a)
The easy arête.

❸ V1 (5b)
The slabby arête.

❹ V0− (4a)
Meander up the rampline.

❺ V0 (5a)
Pull over the roof.

❻ V0+ (5b)
An easy flake leads to a floppy topout.

❼ Little Prow
V6 (6b)
Start on the shelf and climb the desperate rounded arête.

❽ The Scoop
V1 (5c)
Swing up into the scoop and mantel gloriously onto the summit.

❾ The Lurch
V4 (6b)
Lurch for slopers and power directly upwards on treacherous holds.

❿ Ossie's Bulge
V3 (6a)
From a good slot, mantel upwards then scamper left to finish. So good, in fact, you'll want to do it again. This time, go **straight up** at V4 (6b).

⓫ Ram Air V8 (6c)
A modern classic with a sustained rounded sequence up the arête. Hard for the grade, and be careful with that landing.

⓬ Elastic Wall
V6 (6b)
Lurch upwards from the crimpy sidepull.

⓭ Arête on Left
V1 (5c)

⓮ Arête on Right
V1 (5c)

⓯ 5c Wall V3 (6a)
The crimpy little wall, on crimps.

⓰ Baby Groove
V0− (4a)

⓱ Hanging Crack
V0− (4c)

⓲ Classic Mantel
V1 (5c)
A tricky mantel at the point of the block.

⓳ Johnny's Groove
V8[2] (6c)
The groovy seam is entered by dynamic high-speed double bridging techniques (see *Best Forgotten Art*). Far out.

⓴ Crocodile Slot
V3 (5c)
An exacting struggle up the wide slot, requiring full body awareness.

㉑ Right Slot
V2 (5b)
More 'bouldering' Ramshaw style, up the tall offwidth near the arête.

In a way, I find belaying more terrifying than leading. I remember Seb doing the first ascent of *Clippety Clop*. He'd top-roped it alright, but when he went to solo it, he just started shouting at himself. It was mad.

"I am Jerry Moffatt. I am Jerry Moffatt. I'm on top-rope…"

constantly. Then on the crux, he took his feet off and screamed "Nooooooo…", and I just thought, this is it. He's off. But it was all part of the plan.

Andy Popp

Oh no! Julian Lines about to lose all points of contact while attempting the second ascent of *Clippety Clop* (E7 6c). Photo: Paul Higginson.

56 Clippety Clop, Clippety Clop, Clippety Clop E7 6c ★★★ 1991

12m One of the great lines on grit: the immaculate and ludicrous arête bypassed by Dangerous Crocodile is taken in its entirety. Start as for Crocodile, then rock onto the ramp on the right of the arête. Grapple and stretch to good holds on the arête, and ride this to a layback finish. A Friend 6 and a plank combined in the break seem, by consensus, to have reduced the grade from its original E8!

57 Elastic Limit E3 6b ★   1974
9m The crack in the centre of the buttress seems a lot nearer than it actually is. A difficult and dangerous stretch from below occasionally sees success; if so, swing up and right to gain a ledge then finish direct. Spotters strongly recommended.

58 Creep, Leap, Creep, Creep E4 6b   2001
6m The blunt arête left of Wriggler climbed on its right-hand side with gear at two-thirds height. Apparently can be done dynamically from the break.

59 Wriggler HS 4a   pre-1973
6m Severely wide but very short lived. Fun, despite everything.

60 Arête and Crack VD   pre-1973
13m Climb the short blunt arête left of the cave and move up to a crack, which is followed to a wide exit left.

61 Handrail E2 5c ★★   1977
12m As the crack of the previous route peters out step up and place gear in the prow on the right, then boldly swing round the arête to follow the obvious traverse line. With feet and mind pedalling simultaneously carry on fearlessly to an exit up the wider crack. Very good but high in the grade.

62 Handrail Direct E4 6a ★   1984
9m Go up the easy groove to stand below a blank scoop. Climb this on smears and pebbles to join the original before the swing right. Okay as long as you don't fall. The vague green streak to the right is

Cedez le Passage (E6 6b†, 2000), which joins the previous climb when holds run out. Utterly pointless and totally terrifying.

63 Assegai VS 5a ★   pre-1973
11m Uncomfortable on the sharp end! The knobbly, sharp, gritty corner is harder than it looks, especially moving onto the slab.

64 Bowrosin VS 4c ★   1969
12m A good, though broken, route. Climb the slab to where a step across leads to a crack which is followed with a hard move as the angle changes.

65 English Towns E3 5c ★   1979
12m Takes the impressive shield of rock. Go direct up the steep wall left of centre to a break where a scary mantel up and right leads to a more positive stance. Follow the easier angled slab to the top. The grade is for an ascent without side runners in Bowrosin. Good.

66 Spanish Fly E2 5c   1992
12m A counter to English Towns. The wall left of Boomerang is climbed to the wide break. Move left until a mantel from here allows the slabby nose to be climbed.

67 Boomerang VD ★★★   pre-1973
12m The wide crack is a great gritstone feature, and makes for a superb and well-protected climb. Finish left or via a short steep crack on the skyline (better but harder). A great first lead, although it feels exposed at the top.

68 Wick Slip E5 6b ★   1987

12m A dream come true for the pebble cognoscenti. Having rounded the first bulge of Boomerang, place some gear up and left and step out onto the gripping arête. Place a good cam in the obvious slot and step out right to finish.

69 Monty E4 6b   1990s

12m The slab below is followed on pebbles to a horizontal crack and some gear. Traverse right and finish up the blunt arête. At this grade a step is made into The Watercourse for contemplation before the arête is climbed.

70 The Watercourse HS 4a   1969

15m The wide groove/scoop has a tricky start. Follow this to a second groove and traverse left to finish up a cracked nose. **Up Your Slip** (E2 6a, 2001) is an extended problem over the short roof right of the finish of The Watercourse.

71 Dan's Dare VS 4c   1969

9m Up and right is a green and awkward flaky groove just right of a short chimney. Climb this.

Arthur Scargill's Hairpiece is Missing, (5b, 1984) is a better name than a route and follows the right-hand side of the small prow to the right. The prow direct would also be a good problem.

72 Gully Wall HVS 5a   pre-1973

9m Starting from a pedestal right of Dan's Dare, follow a short groove up to a wide crack then a small ledge, with a tricky move to leave this and gain the wide break.

Ramshaw Buttress

The large steep buttress to the right is the epitome of Ramshaw. As well as looking as mean as hell it provides, amongst others, two of the most stunning routes on grit, albeit with distinctly different characters.

73 Little Nasty E1 5b, 5a   1968–73

14m The crack is pretty grim for 3m but then relents to give pleasant climbing to a ledge and belay. From here the thin groove in the middle of the top of the side wall of the buttress is aimed for, to provide a reasonable finish.

74 Electric Savage E3 5c, 5b ★   1978

14m Though again not as fierce as its name implies, this route takes in some steep and exciting ground. After the initial moves of Little Nasty, a thin traverse right out of the crack gains a crack leading to the large ledge (belay). From here, climb the 'roof-like' crack on the left edge of the buttress. Finish direct.

75 Ramshaw Crack E4 6a ★★★   1964

7m The strangely beguiling and ridiculously steep crack starting from the centre of the ledge moves from hand to fist to arm-bar width all within twenty feet. Climb it. One of grit's great cracks and still an intimidating lead even after all these years. *Crack School no. 11.*

The thin crack and arête right of Ramshaw Crack have been top-roped at F8c. However, while the crack will take protection, clipping it, never mind placing it, is virtually impossible, so for the moment, it remains Ramshaw's dream project.

76 Four Purists VS 5a ★   pre-1973

7m Back at the lower level, this is the next obvious crack right of Electric Savage. Steeper, wider and more difficult than it first appears, the short crack to the ledge is very worthwhile. Can be finished up the second pitch of Little Nasty.

77 Never Never Land E7 6b ★★★   1986

12m The sublimely subtle wall to the right succumbs to a more contemplative approach. Follow and place high gear in Four Purists, then make difficult moves to leave this and hook the obvious flake in the middle of the wall. Tinker here for poor gear and without getting lost (boys) follow the line of small crimps and scoops direct to a mother of a finish. Easier if you don't panic!

78 Green Corner S 4a   pre-1973

6m Climb the slabby groove 5m right until it steepens to require more pull to get up the short crack.

The main path heads down from here but right of the gully the crag continues up past several very short cracks known as the Zig-Zag cracks, giving some good sport in the 3c to 4c range. Past these is a mini-ledge, and a much more impressive buttress bounded on its right by a wide crack.

79 Rollercoaster E6 6c† ★   1990
10m Climb directly up the blunt left arête of the buttress to gain protection in the horizontal break on the right. Finish desperately up the horrendously sloping slanting break, to an equally sloping top out. Hard and scary.

80 Boom Bip E7 6c ★★   2002
8m An audacious route which crosses rather than climbs some very unlikely territory. Climb directly up to the centre of the large overhang, to the large jugs and gear. From here, screw your courage to the sticking place and attempt the full body dyno direct to the top of the crag. Must be seen to be believed!

81 Imposition E2 5c ★★   pre-1973
8m The crack on the right always seems just too wide and provides a difficult exercise. The bulge at ten feet is perhaps the main sticking point, but once round that, continue gingerly, jamming or laybacking, up the offwidth finish. Very good. *Crack School no. 9.*

82 Iron Horse Crack D   pre-1973
6m The tiny jamming crack next right.

83 Scooped Surprise E3 6a   1984
6m A two move wonder, which uses pebbles and the short blind crack just right of Iron Horse Crack to pull into the shallow scoop. Finish direct. Bold.

84 Tricouni Crack HS 4a ★   pre-1973
6m The next crack is a pleasant exercise for fat fingers or thin hands. *Crack School no. 3.*

85 Rubber Crack VS 4c ★   1973
6m To the right again is a short crack and corner.

86 Darkness S   pre-1973
9m Lengthened by starting up the slab below Rubber Crack, this route takes the curved crack on the right to a ledge, then immediately up the first crack encountered.

*Below here, on the main path, is a block with a small roof, bounded by small grassy grooves on either side, giving two Diffs, **Army Route** and **Dusk** (both pre-1973). Both finish via a grassy section then clamber up the scrappy jumbled mass of blocks and chimneys above. More exploration can be had amongst these around this grade. A good problem, **Scout In Situ** (5a, 1987) pulls round the roof of the small prow and another, **Antlers Hall** (5b, 1994) climbs the sharp arête up and right of Dusk.*

Flaky Buttress

Thirty metres to the right is a tall, jagged buttress. The gully to the left of the main wall has been claimed as Flaky Gully (D, pre-1973), but is short, green and totally without merit.

87 Flaky Wall Direct VS 4b ★   pre-1973
14m A good solid climb. Just to the left of the prow is a green streak which is followed on good holds to reach a ledge. Step left then go straight up past some large spikes into a groove that certainly maintains interest to an airy perch.

Gritstone crags are smaller,

less mountainous, less natural in line, and more littered and abused than any other climbing area in the world. Yet it is on grit that it nearly always started; that everyone was at some time euphoric about it, and it has always been a place that climbing people regard as important; gritstone is theirs more than any other place on earth.

Pete Livesey

88 Flaky Wall Indirect VS 4c ★   pre-1973
16m Follow Flaky Wall Direct to the ledge, move up and right via some flakes and move round the corner. The finish up the front face is the most difficult section. A very worthwhile **Super Direct** (E1 5b★, 1996) joins the top of this by climbing the left side of the steep arête.

89 Cracked Gully D   pre-1973
14m The wide blocky groove to the right is a good introductory route. The arête to the right has been claimed as **Cracked Arête** but hardly seems independent (VD, pre-1973).

90 Arête Wall D   pre-1973
9m Take the V-shaped groove for 4m then finish up a slightly steeper flaky crack.

Magic Roundabout Buttress

The slabby buttress right again. The starts of many of these routes make good boulder problems, and many other independent problems exist on the back of this buttress and on the attractive boulders to the right. See bouldering topo.

91 Crystal Tipps E1 5c ★   1976
7m Climb the wall about 1m right of the left arête of the buttress making a committing move to gain the obvious layback flake and grass above. Good fun.

92 The Ultra Direct E2 6b ★   1984
7m About 3m in from the arête is a jug at head height. Using this and the thin seam above, make a

hard mantel to get established on the slab. Finish direct and still with interest. Neat!

93 Magic Roundabout Super Direct
E1 5c ★   1975
7m The next flake in the bulge about 1.5m to the right is climbed to gain the slab above. Carry on to finish between the normal route and The Delectable Deviation. Hard at the start and committing at the top.

94 Magic Roundabout Direct HVS 4c ★ pre-1973
7m Take the final (thank God) shallow groove, crux, to the break. Trend right and aim for the luminous slot directly above the start of Magic Roundabout.

95 Magic Roundabout S 4a ★   pre-1973
7m A fine delicate route. Start at the small broken niche on the right of the buttress. Follow the lowest break to finish at a black flake.

96 The Delectable Deviation VS 4c   pre-1973
9m Start 2m to the right and walk along the higher break. Somehow not as good as the others. **Perched Flake**, a Diff, finds any way up the short flake to the right to finish up the blunt arête.

Behind the buttress, past a short arête, is a slabby wall containing the next route.

97 Force Nine E4 6c ★★   1985
9m Good bouldering at an even better height. To the right, the pebbly wall/scoop is climbed with difficulty, aiming for a thin flake at 4m. A gnarly move here should gain a standing position and the top.

Hidden below Magic Roundabout buttress is a small outcrop with some worthwhile climbs.

98 Port Crack S   pre-1973
8m Start by bridging from below or from the slab on the left.

99 Time Out E2 5c ★★   1979
9m The central crack. Moving right to a subsidiary upper crack provides the crux.

⑩ Starboard Crack EI 5b ★   pre-1973
9m Vile but fun: the right-hand crack is like jamming porcupines.

Roman Nose Buttress

This is home to more steep Ramshaw challenges.

⑩ Big Richard VS 4c ★   pre-1973
10m The first routes start under a prominent spike at 3m. Gain the spike – either direct, strenuous, or via the ramp to the right, technical. The chimney above is most difficult to enter; exit to a ledge and finish up the wall/groove on the right.

⑩ The Proboscid EI 5b   1980
10m Do the start of Big Richard, then layback the exposed and serious nose above.

⑩ The Crippler HVS 5a ★★★   1969
10m Starting further right again is another route to inspire. Climb from the back until forced left, and make difficult moves to gain a groove. Getting stood at the top of this is also entertaining, from where a slabby finish can be made. A more direct approach can be made by climbing steeply though a bulge to join the original; 5b. A good problem, **Wheel of Misfortune** (E2 6a, 2002), can be had up the hanging prow just right, avoiding the block on the right.

Winking Eye Buttress

Fifty metres past the boulders is Roman Nose Buttress. At a lower level and set forward of these blocks is a pointed outcrop.

Due to serious damage caused to this unique feature, please avoid this buttress. Routes are included purely for completeness:

- **Owl'ole**, D, is just right of the pinnacle;
- **Middle Route**, S, the crack to the right;
- **The Shoulder**, HVD, the corner left of the face;
- **South Cheek**, HS, goes up to the eye, steps on the nose and mantelshelves onto the forehead;
- **North Cheek**, VD, climbs the slab and corner on the right until a traverse left leads to the eye and the manoeuvres of South Cheek;
- **Collar Bone**, D, the slab to the right of the corner;
- **The Veil**, S, traverses the buttress at half-height.

All routes climbed pre-1973.

⑩ Escape HVS 5b   1977
8m As height is gained the difficulties increase on the wall to the left of the large chimney. Very green but still fun.

⑩ Mantrap HVD   pre-1973
8m The chimney itself yields to less of a struggle than first appears.

Magic Roundabout Boulders

A good circuit with two distinct styles of climbing: delicate pebble pulling and steep rounded slapping. The delicate problems are set on the front of the main buttress and are the starts of routes. Continue to the top for double ticks. They can be green after wet weather. The steeper problems are mainly on a herd of fine boulders just to the right. They are clean and quick drying.

❸ Super Direct Start V2 (5c)

Over the bulge again, using the thin left facing flake, as far as the break. (E1 to the top.)

❹ Roundabout Direct V0– (4c)

The narrow groove as far as the break.

❶ Crystal Tipps
V2 (5c)

From the first jug in from the arête, pull over the bulge and move up to the flake. (E1 to the top.)

❷ Ultra Direct Start V4 (6b)

From the second jug, pull over the bulge and head for the break. (E2 to the top.)

❺ Magic Arête
V2 (5c)

The arête on its right.

❻ Be Calmed
V3 (6a)   1986

From the arête, pull out right into a scoop and mantel it.

❼ Calmed Left-Hand V7 (6c)

A variation on the last problem gains the scoop from the right, slapping left with difficulty from the blind crack. A desperate mantel follows (no arête allowed).

❽ Force Nine
V6 (6c)

The high slabby wall is a scary E4. Even gaining the flake is a sporty problem.

❾ The Finger
V0– (4b)

Mount the finger.

⑩ Jamless VI (5c)
The perfect hand crack fortunately demands no jamming skills.

⑪ Arête on Left
VI (5b)

⑫ Project
The holdless arête, climbed on its right side, is a tough proposition.

⑬ Epilogue V5 (6b)
Reachy, and with a desperate top-out.

⑭ The Rammer
VI (5b)
One of the Peak's better chimney problems. Squirm up the constricted fissure, using heads, shoulders, knees and toes. A real undresser.

⑮ Monologue
VI0 (6c)
The right arête of The Rammer is minging hard.

⑯ The Pinches
V4 (6a)
Climb the features on the overhanging arête.

⑰ Practice Chimney
V0– (4a)
A much friendlier chimney.

⑱ Dialogue V9 (6c)
Crucify your way up the front of the block using a good deal of power. A modern classic.

⑲ Cracked Arête
VI (5c)

⑳ V2 (5c)
The steep crack to a rounded finish.

㉑ The Harder Mantel V5 (6b)
The flake just right of the arête has a rounded top-out and a dodgy landing.

㉒ The Mantel
V2 (6a)
Step up and mantel the block.

The Pinnacle

Another pointed outcrop lies across the wide gully.

⑩⑥ Great Scene Baby S ★   pre-1973
10m The smart crack to the left is gained from 2m up the groove. Climb the crack on good jams onto a slab and finish over a small neb. A direct start is a painful 5b. *Crack School no. 2.*

⑩⑦ Groovy Baby HS 4b   pre-1973
10m Guess where this goes? Not as good as its name; short and green.

⑩⑧ Pile Driver VS 4c ★   pre-1973
17m A very good route with an exposed finish. From the groove, join the crack on the right, which is climbed to its end. A step right leaves one below the final crack.

⑩⑨ The Press E1 5b ★★   1971
15m Another belter, which is solid at the grade. Where Pile Driver goes up, continue right along the obvious break until a beefy pull can be made into the steep crack. This is followed round the arête to an easier finish.

This area also has some superb, powerful bouldering to offer.

⑪⓪ Press Direct V4 (6b)
Climb twin seams dynamically to join the crack. **The obvious bum** start to this problem goes at a mighty V7 (6c).

⑪⑪ Lust Left-Hand V7 (6c)
Follow the crimpy handrail rightwards and into the niche on the right.

⑪⑫ Night of Lust Start V5 (6b)
The first moves, into the niche, make a superb crimpy problem. Starting from the low flat **jug beefs** the difficulties up to V6 (6b).

⑪⑬ Runnel Entry V7 (6b)
From the low, flat hold, head up and enter the shallow water runnel directly above.

A super highball problem would be to climb directly up the bulging arête to the point where Night of Lust meets The Press. Difficulties would be of the highest order, and although it is significantly above bouldering height, the landing, at least, is flat.

⑭ Night of Lust E4 6b ★ 1984

14m A desperate start leads to easier climbing above. Make a series of thin pulls to gain a niche and some gear. Grope over a bulge, then pull up and left to join The Press. Gaining the route from the gully is an exposed E3 5c.

⑮ Curfew HVS 5b ★ pre-1973

12m Very Ramshaw. Another burly pull off the ground is the main feature of the steep corner crack. The rest is merely pleasant.

⑯ Foord's Folly E2 6a ★★★ 1968–73

10m Valiantly attempt to climb the exasperating crack without wrecking digits. If successful, move out to an easier finish up the thin hand crack above. For those carrying and placing gear it's probably E2, for those soloing, a bold E1. The fact remains it's hard 6a for both. *Crack School no. 8.*

⑰ The Swinger HVS 5a 1972

13m Takes the right edge of the buttress with a difficult start on a couple of sloping ramps. From the ledge continue up the arête above. A rather contrived girdle, **Screwy Driver** (VS 4c, 1968–73) crosses the prow at two-thirds height starting from the gully left of Great Scene Baby and finishing right of The Swinger.

Up and behind this section the rocks are smaller, greener and very broken although there may be a little scope for exploration. Fifty metres to the right is an undercut nose with a short wall above and to the left which features an obvious crack at its left end.

⑱ Slow Hand Clap E2 5c 1979

8m The wall 2m right of the crack seems ok until the last move. Easily bottled out to jeers from your mates! **Modesty Crack** (D, pre-1973) can be found shyly climbing the crack left of the nose to finish on the right over blocks.

⑲ California Screamin' V8 (6c)

A brilliant boulder problem over the bulge and arête just right, with hard slappy moves to gain the upper ridge. The top feels high, almost warranting E4 for the final moves.

⑳ The Brag VS 5a pre-1973

9m The short groove to the right has a difficult start to much easier climbing. At the second crack move left to finish up a little prow.

㉑ Shark's Fin V0 (5a)

Another 30m on, up on the ridge, is a short very steep wall/roof. Climb the obvious flake under the roof. A **double dyno** (V5) from the base to the top has also been done (see the first scene in Stone Monkey), as has the **lip traverse**. And it bears repeating, beware the giant frog!

From here the crag becomes very broken with a number of small buttresses separated by awkward steep heather. Of these, the last is by far the most significant, while the others provide some rarely repeated delights of mixed quality. The first of these, after 30m, is more substantial than it first appears.

㉒ Rash Challenge E1 5b ★ 1976

8m A very exciting little number. The main roof is gained from the right or left via a small slab and tackled boldly from slightly left of centre to gain a groove. The groove to the left is **Early Retirement** (D, pre-1973).

㉓ Honking Bank Worker E2 5c 1984

8m The arête that bounds the previous slab is climbed to where the wall steepens and bold moves on smaller crimps commence.

㉔ Extended Credit HVS 4c 1973

9m The flakes to the right are climbed to a short finishing groove. A little loose and overgrown.

㉕ Caramta S 4b pre-1973

12m Another 20m right is a buttress with a leftward-slanting crack. The short jamming crack is taken to twin noses.

⑫⑥ The Prism VD — pre-1973
9m Sort of good in a desperately bad way. Bridge up the horrid corner on the right. Finish left or right.

⑫⑦ Approaching Dark E1 5c — 1984
9m The flake and overhang to the right are tricky but shouldn't keep you all day.

⑫⑧ Lechery HS 4a — pre-1973
9m A short but fun route taking the arête to the right on big holds. Finish over the second prow.

⑫⑨ Ceiling Zero HVS 4c — 1980
6m Forty metres to the right at a slightly higher level is a shelf with an enormous roof. Start direct or from the left and cross the main roof at its widest point.

⑬⓪ Pocket Wall HS 4a — pre-1973
6m From the right-hand end of the shelf, good holds ease a stiff start into the short hanging groove. Move right and climb up via a couple of substantial pockets.

Below and right is a buttress containing a large overhang. **Curver** (HVD, pre-1973) *climbs under the overhang following the slab from left to right, to finish up a flake. Poor. Fifteen metres to the right is another substantial buttress but this time containing a couple of the best routes at Ramshaw.*

⑬① Old Fogey E3 5c ★★★ — 1977
12m An absorbing lead. Starting a little way up the gully, move right on reasonable holds to a standing position on a mini 'horn' on the arête. Boldly climb to a break and finish direct on better holds.

⑬② Old Fogey Direct E5 6b ★★★ — 1980
15m A superb and much fallen-off route. Climb the lower wall on pebbles to reach better holds. Swing left to join the original at the arête. Luckily the ground below is fairly soft.

⑬③ King Harold S ★ — pre-1973
9m The wide chimney to the right is much better than a poke in the eye.

⑬④ Little Giraffe Man HS 4a ★ — 1968–73
12m A worthwhile route which takes the arête right of the chimney to where an exciting step across leads on to the main buttress. Move left and finish up the thin crack.

The Lady Stone

This is the last real buttress at Ramshaw. Separated by a couple of hundred metres from the main crag, it is unfortunately neglected, since permission to climb is not forthcoming from the landowners at the present time. Again the routes are included for completeness. On the left of the buttress is a small slab which goes at 4a, and a short overgrown chimney to its right can also be climbed at Diff. The next route is much better.

⑬⑤ Farmhouse Arête HS — pre-1973
9m From one metre up the chimney climb out on the cracks to the arête which is followed by a long reach to finish.

⑬⑥ Childhood's End HVS 5a ★ — 1978
9m Take the overhang 2m right of the arête via a fingery move or jump to a niche. Step up left then go rightwards through the overhangs to a final slab.

⑱ Ladies' Route S   pre-1973
l0m Takes the wide fissure in the centre of the buttress. Climb the small ramp from the right to gain the crack and finish right at the top.

⑱ Evil Crack HVS 5a ★   1973
8m The best route on the buttress. From below the obvious crack climb to a hole then make difficult moves up and left to gain the sloping tongue and enter the wide crack, which gets easier quite quickly. Strenuous.

Ramshaw Rocks First Ascents

1950–65	**Brown's Crack, Don's Crack, Prostration, The Great Zawn, Masochism, The Crank** Joe Brown, Don Whillans, various leads
1964 Sep	**Ramshaw Crack** Joe Brown *Some aid used. Climbed free by Gabe Regan in 1976.*
1968 Oct 9	**Louie Groove, The Untouchable** John Yates, Colin Foord, various leads
1968 Oct 16	**Alcatraz** Dave Salt
1969 Jan 15	**The Watercourse, Dan's Dare** Pete Ruddle
1969 Jan 16	**Bowrosin** Barry Marsden
1969 Feb 5	**The Crippler** John Yates
1971 Oct	**The Press** Bob Hassall
1972 Aug	**Tally Not** (1 pt.) Bob Hassall, Norman Hoskins *Climbed free by Martin Boysen later in the same year.*
1972 Oct 9	**Green Crack** Pete Harrop
1973 Jul 7	**The Undertaker** (1 pt.) Dave Salt, Barry Marsden *Climbed free by Jonny Woodward in 1976.*
1973 Jul 8	**Rubber Crack, Evil Crack, Extended Credit** Steve Dale, Dave Salt, various leads
1972	**The Swinger** Martin Boysen
1968–73	**Screwy Driver** Bob Hassall
1968–73	**Foord's Folly** (2 pts.) Colin Foord *Climbed on a wet day to keep the lads amused. First free ascent by John Allen in 1973.*
1968–73	**Little Nasty** Dave Salt *Only the finish was climbed. The first crack had obviously been done before, probably by Joe Brown.*
	Abdomen, Little Giraffe Man John Yates, Julian Yewdall
pre-1973	**East Face, Southern Crack, Loaf and Cheese, Wall and Groove, The Arête, Leeds Crack, Twin Cracks, Broken Groove, Broken Groove Arête, Wellingtons, Battle**

of the Bulge, The Cannon, Phallic Crack, Corner Crack, The Rippler, Crab Walk, The Comedian, Camelian Crack, Wriggler, Arête and Crack, Assegai, Boomerang, Gully Wall, Four Purists, Green Corner, Imposition, Iron Horse Crack, Tricouni Crack, Darkness, Army Route, Dusk, Flake Gully, Flaky Wall Direct, Flaky Wall Indirect, Cracked Gully, Cracked Arête, Arête Wall, Magic Roundabout Direct, Magic Roundabout, Delectable Deviation, Perched Flake, Port Crack, Starboard Crack, Owl'ole, Middle Route, The Shoulder, South Cheek, North Cheek, Collar Bone, The Veil, Big Richard, Mantrap, Great Scene Baby, Groovy Baby, Pile Driver, Curfew, Modesty Crack, The Brag, Shark's Fin, Early Retirement, Caramta, The Prism, Lechery, Pocket Wall, Curver, King Harold, Farmhouse Arête, Ladies' Route, Chockstone Chimney *These routes marked the publication of the 1973 guidebook which was the first to attempt to describe all of the routes on Ramshaw Rocks. Many of these had almost certainly been climbed before in the past, yet all were named, and some were climbed for the first time, by the North Staffs. M.C. who did as many routes as possible in one frantic weekend.*

1974 Autumn	**Elastic Limit** Andrew Woodward (solo) *Gained from the right. The direct start added by Nick Longland in 1977.*
1975 Oct	**Magic Roundabout Super-Direct** Jonny Woodward (solo)
1976 Spring	**Honest Jonny** Jonny Woodward (solo)
1976 Apr 10	**Crystal Tipps** Andrew Woodward (solo)

1976 Aug	**Rash Challenge**	Jonny Woodward (solo)

Counter-claimed as Overdraught by Martin Boysen in August 1977.

1977 Jun 2   **Traveller in Time**   Andrew Woodward, Jonny Woodward. *Counter-claimed by Martin Boysen as Jumbo in July 1977. The debates still runs over this one and at the time was a big bone of contention between the two.*

1977   **Gumshoe, Trivial Traverse, Overdrive, Handrail, Escape, Old Fogey** Martin Boysen

1978   **Childhood's End, National Acrobat, Electric Savage**   Jonny Woodward   *National Acrobat is still one of the hardest cracks on grit. Climbed by Sean Myles and Johnny Dawes on the same day in 1996, possibly the first repeats after 18 years. Had a number of ascents since, the best being by Patch Hammond, ground-up with falls in early 2001. Only the top pitch of Electric Savage was climbed. The first pitch added by Nick Longland in 1979.*

1978 Apr   **After Eight**   Nick Longland (solo)

1979 Jun 3   **English Towns, Time Out** Gary Gibson, Ian Barker

1979 Jun 28   **The Sneeze**   Nick Longland, Dave Jones

1979 Aug 8   **Tier's End**   Nick Longland

1979 Aug   **Slow Hand Clap**   Gary Gibson (solo)

1979 Aug   **Whilly's Whopper** Dave Jones, Gary Gibson, Nick Longland

1980 Apr 10   **Ceiling Zero**   Gary Gibson, Derek Beetlestone

1980 May 9   **Old Fogey Direct**   Jonny Woodward (solo) *A significant addition. `Three snatches for crystals'. Even more of the crystals have departed but still eminently doable.*

1980 May   **Tierdrop, The Proboscid, Leeds Slab** Nick Longland

1981 Aug 10   **Torture**   Gary Gibson (solo)

1973–81   **Double Chin, Prowler**

1984 Mar 21   **Handrail Direct, Scooped Surprise**   Simon Nadin   *The former with a hanging rope.*

1984 May   **The Honking Bank Worker, Arthur Scargill's Hairpiece is Missing** Allen Williams (solo)   *More bizarre nomenclature from 'Big Al'.*

1984   **Approaching Dark, Dream Fighter, Cold Wind**   Richard Davies (solo)

1984   **Body Pop, Night of Lust, The Ultra Direct** John Allen, Mark Stokes   *The first ascent of the*

latter is something of a bone of contention. Certainly it may have been climbed before by either Allen Williams or Richard Davies.

1985   **Force Nine**   Simon Nadin

1986 May 7   **Dangerous Crocodile Snogging** Simon Nadin (solo)   *Originally finished more directly up the slab on pebbles whereas subsequent ascensionists have gone slightly left. Top-roped first and many times since. The foothold on the arête, however, seems to be wearing badly and maybe we need less of the above.*

1986 May 26   **Never Never Land** Simon Nadin, Richard Davies.

1986   **Assembled Techniques, Gully Arête** Richard Davies   *Right-hand version to the former added by Richie Patterson in 1999 but possibly done before.*

1987 Apr 16   **T'rival Traverse**   Graham Hoey, John Allen, Martin Veale

1987 Apr 16   **Rock Trivia, Maximum Hype** John Allen, Graham Hoey, Martin Veale

1987 Jul 16   **Scout In Situ**   Pete Oxley *Almost certainly done before.*

1987 Aug 6   **Wick Slip**   Nick Dixon, Andy Popp

1987 Sep 28   **Colly Wobble**   Simon Nadin, John Perry *The four drilled holes were not the work of the first ascensionists. They were created well before the advent of bolt protection but luckily accept a small tri-cam. Apparently originally called 'Take Me To Cleveland'.*

1990   **Rollercoaster**   Simon Nadin

1991 Oct   **Clippety Clop Clippety Clop Clippety Clop, Juan Cur**   Seb Grieve   *Clippety Clop was a significant addition as it claimed one of the most outrageous lines on grit as well as introducing Seb Grieve to an unsuspecting public. Climbed by Seb wearing his trademark jeans for better friction for a 'knee mantel' finish. Famously fallen off by Julian Lines on a repeat attempt who gained a break for his troubles. 'On a rope it all seemed easy but on solo it's always more gripping. I was so stretched I couldn't tell if my hands were on the holds, and then....' Since he had also previously fallen off but walked away from Dangerous Crocodiles Snogging, it has to be said one out of two ain't bad. Juan Cur named after the bounder who nicked Seb's gear from the belay while he was top-roping the route!*

1991   **Pat Is Parched**   Pat Quinn

1994 Apr   **Ultimate Sculpture, Antlers Hall** Justin Critchlow   *Ultimate Sculpture has lost*

pebbles since first done but is still eminently climbable by the talented. Where are you?

1994 May	**Sketching Wildly**	Rob Mirfin

Probably unrepeated.

1994	**Paul's Rib**	Paul Higginson
1996 Aug	**Flaky Wall Super-Direct**	

Paul Harrison, Nick Jowett

1990s	**Monty**	Mark Cluer
2000 Sep 23	**Cedez La Passage**	Nik Jennings
2001	**Blockbuster**	Andi Turner
2001 May	**Creep, Leap, Creep, Creep**	Nick Dixon,

Andi Turner *Ramshaw became a very popular venue in 2001, as it was one of the few crags to be opened during a Foot and Mouth crisis that swept the British countryside that year. This line may also have been climbed previously by Rob Mirfin.*

2002 April	**Wheel of Misfortune**	Mark Sharratt
2002 Sep	**Boom Bip**	Tom Briggs *Boom Bip was*

generously donated and belayed by Neil Bentley, the route's original suitor, after an injury in late 2001 precluded an ascent. This is a thoroughly modern effort with possibly the longest dyno on any route. Tom took the fall on his first go and due to the amount of slack needed to complete the move finished only 4 feet off the ground! Possibly undergraded at 6c!

⊘ Ramshaw Rocks Bouldering First Ascents

Be Calmed Graham Hoey, 1986 *Starts on the arête on the left and reached into the scoop but not described clearly in the previous guide.*

California Screamin' Tom Briggs, 2002.

Cleg Nick Longland, 1979.

Epilogue, Monologue, Dialogue Andi Turner, 2001.

Hem Line Nick Longland, 1978.

Johnny's Groove Johnny Dawes.

Midge, Press Direct Martin Boysen, 1977.

Ram Air John Welford, 2000.

Sam's Left Hand Sam Whitaker, 2003.

Sensible Shoes Dave Jones, 1980.

Tier Drop Nick Longland, 1980.

Tit Grip Paul Higginson, 1990s.

Sam Whittaker on the classic Ramshaw highball Tierdrop V7 (page 145). Photo: Dave Simmonite.

Dave Bishop bouldering on the Yawning Stone (page 187). Photo: Niall Grimes.

Newstones
to Back Forest

4

including **Baldstones, Gib Torr,
Wolf Edge** and **The Hanging Stone**

Rested and well-taped, he gained the
hanging slot, spun round using the skills
of years and with abs strengthened
during that period, a leg was pulled up
and placed where so many had been
wedged to such limited effect already
that day. After stacking a fist jam he
emerged from under the ceiling,
grabbed his leg and started to yard
his way up it. Pulling on his boot,
he resembled a coyote caught in a trap
and starting to bite through its own leg...

**Chris Plant describes
Jonny Woodward on Ray's Roof,
On The Edge**

Here are some great crags for boulderers, soloists and leaders with a short rope, all of which lie in the areas surrounding the main crags. The most popular of these is the Newstones, with its friendly bouldering, but the rest are all superb crags, with great routes and problems waiting to be discovered.

Newstones, Baldstones and Gib Torr all lie along the ridge from Ramshaw, and while they each have a different character, they still all suit the same mood. Baldstones and Newstones are often visited in the same session, and despite their size, have masses of problems and routes of all grades to keep climbers entertained for many visits. The scale of the climbs and their accessibility mean that lots can be done during these visits. Gib Torr has similar qualities, and being virtually a roadside crag, climbers won't need much time to get completely thrashed.

Back Forest is a ridgeback of small, fine buttresses that continues along the line of the Skyline. They are short and friendly, and offer gentle bouldering and short routes, best savoured on a summer's evening, ideally with a picnic. Carry on along this ridge to the Hanging Stone, a fairly abrupt little outcrop, with a limited number of obscure classic climbs, with a punch-packing steepness that complements Back Forest well.

Gradbach Hill has all the same charms, and should also appeal to the mid-grade climber seeking good routes, interesting bouldering, solitude and natural beauty, lying, as it does, in a beautiful bracken-covered valley. By contrast, Wolf Edge, a scattering of small outcrops well suited, again, to moderate grade bouldering, has a higher, bleaker moorland setting, with a rugged beauty all its own.

Newstones and Baldstones

by John H Bull

These broken edges present a continuum of scale that encompasses minor problems and substantial routes in almost equal measure. Newstones gives superb bouldering with good landings, as well as climbs that receive fewer roped ascents than they deserve. The rock is very rough Staffordshire grit, which for the most part is sound and clean. In many places unique veins or dykes of dark, tough rock protrude from the parent gritstone, providing positive holds ranging in size from tiny edges to boilerplate jugs. These contrast with the many rasping holds of the granular bedrock that abrade fingertips at an alarming rate.

The rocks at Baldstones are slightly grander in scale, the main buttresses offering substantial and strong lines as well as subtler bouldering charms with a serenely remote feel. The rock here is generally fine-grained and relatively forgiving to human skin. A few fragile flakes and sandy surfaces can be encountered especially after wet weather.

Conditions & aspect

Two clusters of outcrops on a faint moorland ridge running north from Ramshaw Rocks towards Gib Torr. They are fairly exposed and quick drying. East-facing, they get early morning sun, although this goes off Baldstones by the late morning, and off Newstones by early afternoon. Nevertheless, evening sun can be found at both crags.

Routes & bouldering

Newstones

Good for short easy routes, and a few harder ones, all with good character. Many are in the area between routes and bouldering. Brilliant for bouldering, over 60 problems of all grades, some being both hard and high.

Baldstones

About 20 routes, best in the VS-E2 range, with enough classics at each grade. The Pinnacle is a great location for routes, and there's also Ray's Roof. About 25 boulder problems with a good range, some offering good rain protection.

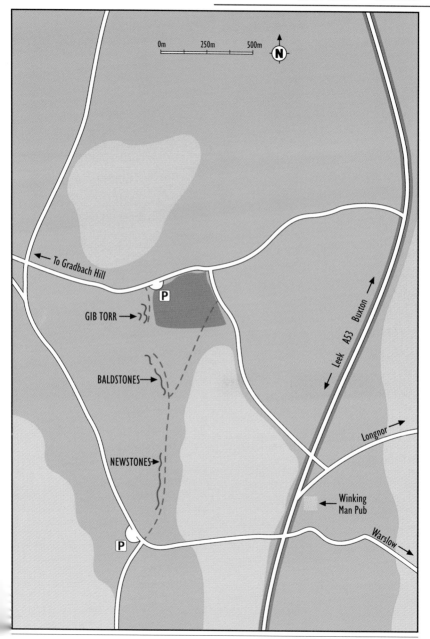

0m 250m 500m

N

To Gradbach Hill

P

GIB TORR →

BALDSTONES →

NEWSTONES →

Leek A53 Buxton

Longnor →

Winking Man Pub →

P

Warslow →

Approaches

Park at the road junction and follow the track past Corner Cottage to Newstones (1–2 minutes). Please have some consideration for the occupants of the cottage, who are very sympathetic to, and tolerant of, climbers. Let's keep it that way. For Baldstones, continue to where a gate and stile lead onto open moorland. Follow the path north for a few hundred metres until Baldstones Pinnacle comes into view. 5–10 minutes.

Access

The estate containing Baldstones is owned by the Staffordshire Wildlife Trust; please respect any seasonal restrictions due to nesting birds in spring. These will be posted on the approach path as appropriate, though the crag was not affected in 2003. Do not walk on the land in front of the outcrops, as it is a highly protected SSSI. For the same reason, do not cross from Baldstones to Gib Torr.

Newstones

O.S. Ref. **SK018638**   Altitude: **420m a.s.l.**

Charlie's Overhang

This is the first small buttress, 100m up the track.

❶ S&M V7 (6c)
From the flake jug, move up to gain the vertical flake-crack and a desperate direct finish. The **left-hand finish** is V6, and the **sit-start** from the flat slot down right adds a grade to the above.

❷ Leather Joy Boys E4 6c ★   1984
6m Gain the all-evil all-sloping diagonal break and scorch across to the right arête. **Ⓥ Highball V7**.

❸ Little Traverse V2 (5c)
From the jug below S&M, traverse nice blobs right to their conclusion.

❹ Charlie's Overhang E2 5c ★   1974
6m The main overhang direct. Many are called but few are chosen. **Ⓥ Highball V3**, but it's a toughie.

❺ Newstones Chimney VD   pre-1973
6m Either of two short cracks leads to the upper chimney, which is climbed insecurely.

❻ Moonshine E1 5b   pre-1981
6m The bulging wall to the right has number of problem starts (around V1) and a steep, bold finish. **Ⓥ Highball V2**, a mini-Charlie's.

❼ Praying Mantel HVS 5a   pre-1981
6m Negotiate the prow on the right, then pay homage to the vague depression via a tantalising stretch. **Ⓥ** A hard **sit-start** would be possible here, slapping up both sides of the low prow, and a **low traverse** of this wall is V2 (5c).

❽ Wraparound Arête V5 (6b)
The undercut bulging arête just right. The small buttress 5m right has some problems at around V1.

Uppermost Outcrop

The superb block packs in a wealth of bouldering. There are many problems and variations, all with low starts that may one day bank out with accumulations of shed epidermis.

9 **Square-Cut Face** V2 (6a)

10 **Arête on Left** V2 (5c)

11 **Wall Past Mono** V3 (6a)
Only a touch harder without the mono.

12 **Varicose** V3 (6a)

13 **Grinding Sloper** V3 (6a)

14 **Easy Slab** V0 (5a)

15 **Uppermost Traverse**
This can be done right to left at various levels with various finishes, from V3 to V5. The **wall** right of the crack is V0– (4a), and the **right arête** is V2 (6a).

Gritstone is to be found in abundance in Yorkshire, Derbyshire and Staffordshire. I have purposefully not mentioned gritstone before, since it requires a special technique of its own. There are many climbers who are brilliant on gritstone, yet cannot do anything on ordinary rock. Severe though many of them are, gritstone climbs are not a very important part of real climbing. So I advise you to leave them alone.
Colin Kirkus, **Let's Go Climbing.**

And now for the hard bit! Mark Sharratt on Charlie's Overhang, E2 5c (page 166), where the big holds run out, and a committing rockover is needed to get to the top. Photo: Dave Garnett.

⑯ Left Twin Arête V0– (4a)
The left of 2 arêtes just below.

⑰ Right Twin Arête V0– (4c)

⑱ Flake Slab V1 (5b)
The delicate slab. A **sit-start** is V4 (6a), while avoiding all holds on the **steep slab** to the right is V2 (6a).

Hazel Barn Buttress

The next main buttress has a distinctive rippled left wall.

⑲ Ripple V3 (6a)
A fingery classic, finger-traversing the unique wafers. **Rocking left** to the top from the start of Ripple is V3 (6a).

⑳ Martin's Traverse V1 (5b)
The lower break leads to the right-hand arête, often meting out comical corporal punishment to knave technicians and optimistic smearers. Avoid ignominy by going **straight up** the wall from a couple of moves along, V3 (6a).

㉑ Crack and Arête V3 (6a)
The overhang leads to an ungainly rightwards exit onto the slab. The excrescent slab itself is **Short Wall** V1 (5b), and after this is **Short Chimney** (D).

㉒ Hazel Barrow Crack HS ★   pre-1973
6m The first main crack-line leads from the toe of the buttress to a protectable exit.

㉓ Hazel Barn S ★   pre-1973
8m The excellent crack and groove just to the right lead to a reachy finish.

㉔ Hazel Groove V4 (6b)
Plenty of holds, just using them's the problem. Baffling. A **low-ish traverse** from the start of Hazel Barn gives a strenuous problem, V2 (5c).

㉕ Nutmeg HS 4b   pre-1981
8m Grind up huge juggy flanges to the upper prow, which is climbed on its left for the full experience.

㉖ Nutmeg Groove V2 (5c)
To the right of Nutmeg, the slight groove in the face is excellent; the **stepped overhang** (low start) gives a tricky V3 (5c). Just to the right, marking the end of the buttress, is an innocuous looking **mantelshelf** V4 (6b). Depressing.

Fingery cranking on unique holds makes Ripple (V3) a memorable Newstones classic (page 169). Luisa Giles concentrating hard. Photo: Niall Grimes.

Scratch Buttress

The next buttress has unfortunately suffered unsightly and irreparable damage. Please do all you can to stop this worsening.

㉗ Scratch Crack V0 (5b)
The steep crack on the left wall. The **wall to the left** can be climbed with an eliminate approach, **V2 (6a)**. A **sit-start** off an undercut and chip is **V4 (6b)**.

㉘ Itchy Groove V4 (6a)
Gain the slim groove direct. Technical. A good powerful problem starts sitting below and swings up and left to climb the **bulging arête**, V5 (6b).

㉙ Itchy Fingers V2 (6a)
The appealing slab gained from the right. The short slab in the recess is **Bridget**, V0– (4c).

Ⓥ The Dyke
The next problems are on a boulder above the crag at this point. It features a distinctive horizontal dyke: **traverse** this leftwards, and keep going past pleasing layback moves to reach the left-hand arête, V2 (5c), or do it hanging from your feet – the **Australian traverse**. The **jam crack** V0– (4c) can be

The **traffic** on these **once quiet** boulders has put great strain on the rock in recent years. In some ways this can't be helped, but please do all you can to preserve this beautiful and superb location. Remember to keep all brushing to the very minimum, and use the softest brush you can find. Or a feather, even. Once the surface goes, the rock below is very soft. This should also be an incentive to climb well, as uncontrolled scuffing tends to be harsh also.

made harder by eliminating the dyke and/or starting low. The **flakes and criss-cross dykes** to the left are V0– (4b).

Rhynose Buttress

This is the bulging buttress opposite Scratch Buttress.

㉚ Drain the Main Vein E1 5b ★   2002
8m Roll up your sleeves, start at the back of the gully and progress rightwards along the skyline dykes. At the last rugosity make a bold mantelshelf. Strangely appealing, despite being escapable upwards at almost any point.

③① Puffed Up E3 6b ★ 1986
8m Slightly left of centre of the wall is a poor under-cut at about 4m. Make use of this to finish direct.

③② Rhynose VS 4b ★ pre-1973
8m Gain and climb the atmospheric groove to the right. Bridge airily left, or finish more easily and logically rightwards (HS).

③③ Ponsified E4 6a† 1989
8m From 3m up Rhynose, climb the bulge on the left to gain a prominent vein in the headwall. Finish up this.

Ⓥ The **low-level traverse** of this face, **VI (5a)**, and the **undercut arête** right of Rhynose from a sit-start, **V2 (5c)** give good problems. The following routes take the pleasant, slabby east face of the buttress.

③④ Hippo VD pre-1973
8m A shallow groove to the right leads to the upper face, which is climbed direct.

③⑤ Rosehip S 4a pre-1981
8m Climb curious projections over the bulge, and the slab above just left of some stacked boulders. **The Witch** (D, 1951–73) is the line formed where the stacked boulders meet the crag, while **Candy Man** (S 4a, 1951–73) takes the easiest line up the stacked boulders to the right.

Sly Buttress

The biggest buttress at Newstones.

③⑥ Trepidation E4 6a ★ 1975
9m The crag's most impressive line takes the steep wall above the gully. Climb cracks to a sloping break and cam protection. Reach up a short groove, and climb the headwall trending first left then right to a bold finish at the apex of the face.

③⑦ Stallone Arête V6 (6b)

③⑧ Sly Stallone V4 (6b)
The dyno for the lip. The **left to right traverse** is V2 (5c), or V6 (6b) without footholds on the lower ramp.

I remember

doing that sort of thing when we were kids. We never used to call it bouldering though, we just used to call it **farting about.**
Ian Dacre, grown-up non-climber, on witnessing his mates' weekend activities

Not just a bouldering crag. Mark Sharratt feeling the height on Trepidation, E4 6a. Photo: Dave Garnett.

③⑨ The Snake S 4a pre-1973
12m An entertaining route that rates an equally worthwhile Difficult if started from the gully. Gain the ledge above the steep wall, and wriggle left-wards until easier climbing gains a ledge. Go up and right to a higher ledge, and a wide finishing crack.

④⓪ The Fox E1 5c pre-1973
9m Give chase to the sly chockstone in the left-hand crack, unless sabotaged by the offwidth start.

④ The Vixen HVS 5b ★ pre-1973

9m The right-hand crack gives short, sharp jamming with good protection.

The striking vein on the face to the right can be gained at several points, which constitute various starts to the parent routes. As the finishing slab poses no serious problem they are given V grades.

④ The Sly Mantelshelf HVS 5a ★ pre-1973

9m Hand-traverse in from the left end of the vein and mantelshelf at its centre. Finish up the weakness in the slab above (V1). **Valley of Ultravixens** (E3 5c ★, 1989) steps left from the vein to take the steep slab between The Vixen and the finish of The Sly Mantelshelf. Ⓥ **Sly Super-Direct**, V2 (5c), gains the centre of the dyke directly, and **Sly Direct**, V0 (5a), gains the original finish by finger-traversing in from the right.

④ Captain Quark V6 (6b)

9m From 2 small crimps at the right-hand end of the buttress front, pull up to the smaller pocket and rock hopefully to the vein. Push onwards direct to the top (E1).

④ Sly Corner VS 4c ★ pre-1973

9m Around to the right is a small, often damp wall. From this, grope leftwards around the arête, and foot-traverse along the vein to finish as for The Sly Mantelshelf.

Ⓥ The sloping right **sidewall** of the buttress is V3 (6a), and the **short wall** above the ramp to the right is V0– (4c). Past the wide crack on the right is a **green wall**. Start on a hold on the left, then traverse right to the arête and up, V2 (5c).

Ⓥ Stegosaurus Bouldering:

Around the back is some distinctive armour plating with good steep, if short, problems. **Tiny Crack**, V0– (4a), is the left-most crack. **Left Crack**, VI (5b), is the crack left of the arête from low pockets. **Cracked Arête** VI (5b), is climbed from a sit-start, and is harder if the lowest boulder is not used for the feet. **Prehistoric Offwidth**, V0– (4c), is climbed from a sit-start on obscenely big holds. **Top Traverse** VI (5a), goes right to left using the crown to finish above Tiny Crack. **Middle Traverse**, V2 (5b), goes the same way, only avoids the top till the very end. Steep and with great holds.

Taking heed of any restrictions posted at the gate, continue for a few hundred metres to reach...

Baldstones

O.S. Ref. **SK019644**   Altitude: **405m a.s.l.**

BALDSTONE

Baldstones Pinnacle

The Pinnacle is composed of superb sculpted gritstone topped with huge fluted jugs. It provides a concentrated selection of high quality routes in the VS-E2 range, with the slight drawback that its tapered shape imposes common finishes on several climbs.

Descent: either rap from an iron stake on the summit, reverse Perambulator Parade, or downclimb the back of the pinnacle and jump off.

The first four routes start above the remains of a dry stone wall.

❶ Perambulator Parade VD ★   pre-1951
11m Climb the short leftwards-slanting ramp starting at the ruined wall, then move right to the summit by the easiest route.

❷ Pants on Fire HVS 5a ★   2001
15m A spiralling ascent of the Pinnacle, starting up Perambulator Parade. Gain the break in the hanging slab and traverse it to join the arête. Step up, gain the higher break on the front face and traverse this to join Baldstones Arête.

❸ Incognito HVS 4c   pre-1981
9m A direct ascent of the hanging slab via a pocket, finishing up a leftwards-slanting groove. Worthwhile.

❹ Baldstones Face VS 4c ★   pre-1973
11m A ramp leads rightwards from the ruined wall to a blunt arête. Climb the arête on its right-hand side, past flutings to finish.

❺ Original Route E2 5c ★★★   1960s
9m A route full of surprises, one of the finest in the area. An overhanging groove leads to a short crack and the lonely upper slab.

❶ The start of Original Route gives an extended problem (V1) that unfortunately leaves you beached on a ledge halfway up the crag. The various starts of the next route can be bouldered out with the same result. From here, probably the easiest way off (deep breath) is to trend left to Baldstones Face, then quit this for the finishing groove of Incognito and descend the back of the Pinnacle. Alternatively, down-climb the start of Baldstones Face or Arête.

❻ Baldstones Arête
HVS 4c ★★★   **pre-1973**

11m Starting below the stepped overhangs a few metres right, yard up juggy flakes to a resting ledge and cam placements. Gain and climb the right arête in a superb position.

Variations
Mongolian Throat Singing (E1 5b, 2001) climbs the arête right of the start of Original Route (V1), trending right to jugs on Baldstones Arête and the halfway ledge, then follows rounded pockets directly up the face to join the arête higher up.

Gallstones (4c) is a variation start that climbs the crack on the right (north) face of the Pinnacle, and traverses awkwardly leftwards under the overhang to the halfway ledge.

❼ Prelude to XB   E4 5c   1992
10m Start directly up the nose under the overhang on the corner of the buttress. Climb the right-hand side of the overhang, aiming for the ledge on the arête above. Pull onto this and finish up the arête.

❽ Tasmanian Tendencies
E2 5b ★   1995

10m Around the arête is a grassy bay. From the top of the easy crack in the corner of the bay, this route hand-traverses the break leftwards using the scoop for footholds, aiming for the arête. Delicate and bold.

Are you a
Staffordshire Obscurist?

One of the great features of Staffordshire climbing is how the blatantly classic and popular can live so close to the delightfully obscure. Venues tucked away in woods or farmland, little pinnacles or bold secret buttresses. All are worth visiting and offer rewards not found on the more popular patches.

Here is a selection of routes to get you started on your obscure journey.

- **Rubberneck** HVS 5a, The Clouds
  Okay, maybe not that obscure, but possibly the best HVS in Staffordshire
- **Hanging Stone Crack** HVS 5b, Hanging Stone
  Some fun brutality on this ignored feature
- **Kaleidoscope** E1 5a, Sharpcliffe
  Churnet weirdness of the first degree
- **Kneewrecker Chimney** HVS 4c, Belmont Hall
  A bold feature with a tree for dessert
- **The Helix** HVS 5a, Harston
  Spiralling up an fine tower, with good length and exposure for grit
- **Atlas** E2 5c, Ina's Rock
  And while you're there, visit Park Banks Crags for more of the same
- **Hot Tin Roof** E1 5a, Bosley
  Slab climbing in this faraway outcrop
- **Top Brick** E2 5c, Dimmings Dale
  Classy wall climbing in this picturesque dale
- **The Yawn** 5a, Gradbach Hill
  One for the boulderers
- **Baldstones Arête** HVS 4c, Baldstones
  Airy climbing, lonely setting – magnifique!
- **Don't go Down to the Woods Today** VS 4b, Roaches Skyline
  A coy Culm Coast slab with a barbed-wire safety net
- **Kipling Arête** E2 5c, Rudyard Pinnacle
  A local climb for local people

Good luck!

With its bold runout, Original Route (page 175) is an unforgettable lead for any E2 leaders. Justin Critchlow nearing easier ground. Photo: Dave Garnett.

Gold Rush Buttress

Ten metres to the right is the face that features a high hanging scoop above an easy slab.

⑨ National Hysteria E5 6b   1997
10m Climb the easy slab to a horizontal break, where RPs can be arranged. Climb the steep wall left of the scoop direct by several hard moves.

⑩ Gold Rush E4 5c   1976
10m Pad easily up to the hanging scoop. Step right into the scoop and aim for the break above, which is capped by a tiny finishing crack. A bold and impressive line but unfortunately rather sandy.

⑪ Goldsitch Crack HVS 4c   pre-1973
12m Above the bouldering area is a proud, unmistakable crack-line (★★), or a repulsive suppurating orifice (•) – you choose. Gain it via an undercut start and a green slab, and squirm up the cleft to scatological fulfilment. Rubber gloves optional; psychiatric help mandatory.

⑫ The Dyno V4 (6b)
Go from the jugs to the prominent blob on the lip.

⑬ Baldstones Traverse V7 (6b)
A very sloping and difficult traverse going right to left along the finger-rail. **Lower variations** are possible at up to V10. A good ever-dry option for those occasional wet days.

⑭ Riding the Gravy Train E6 6c†   1997
11m Takes the bulging territory to the right of Goldsitch Crack. Climb directly to an incipient crack in the roof below a deep horizontal break. Gain the break, traverse right for a few moves, step up to a crimp and RP, then finish via a sloping crux.

⑮ Blackbank Crack HS 4b   pre-1973
12m A few metres right of the bouldering traverse is a short layback crack. Muscle steeply up this (flakes slightly left are also climbable) to gain the wide ledge. Step left to a finish up a wide crack.

The next landmark is a deep chimney starting in a corner.

The **influx** of the **masses** will **degrade** almost any **athletic** activity.

That which becomes popular and saturated with jargon is cheapened by the attendant media influence. That's not to say 'standards' won't increase, for they certainly will, with many more skilled participants; but is an increase of standards, going from V12 to V13 for example, really part of the act of climbing? Or is it not merely a common trait of all athletic competition?

You climb; you learn the ratings; you find at which rating level you climb; you try to advance to the next level, no longer focusing entirely on the climbing, but on its numerical representation. The tail wags the dog. Besides, rating schemes are always flawed. I can no longer tell where genetics ends and 'difficulty' begins. Can you?

John Gill, spiritual father of modern bouldering

⑯ Forking Chimney D ★   pre-1951
9m The chimney provides temporary relief for homesick cavers.

To the right is a green buttress that remains luminous even in the height of summer.

⑰ Bareleg Wall VS 4c   1977
8m Climb the groove 3m right of the chimney and then balance rightwards along a break to the curving finishing crack.

⑱ Morridge Top HVS 4c†   1977
9m Climb the colonised green wall directly up its centre. Sticky rubber will not help. Probably best to wait for hard winter conditions and the inevitable development of dry lichening.

Ray's Buttress

Set at right angles to the green wall, the next face forms the left-hand side of a buttress, and is topped by a small pinnacle.

⑲ Minipin Crack VD · · · · · pre-1973
6m The short dog-leg crack has a wide finish through which the sky beckons.

⑳ Last Banana Before Sunset V2 (5c)
The wall 2m to the right. Check for remaining daylight, then climb past a tiny curved ledge to finish right of the pinnacle.

㉑ All-Stars' Wall HVS 5a ★ · · · · 1970s
6m Starting at the toe of the buttress, climb a rib, then use a small pocket to attain the higher break and the top.

㉒ Ray's Roof E7 6c ★★★ · · · · 1977
8m Gain and climb the impressive roof-crack, using a variety of limb jams and counterintuitive postures. A significant test-piece that has seen only a handful of ascents since 1977, when it was graded definitive 5.11c. However, this is not a route where mere numbers will give you any idea of what to expect.

㉓ Johnny's Indirect Rear Entry
E5 6b† · · · · · · · · · · · · · · · · c.1990
6m This route takes the break in the wall to the right of Ray's Roof gained from the right, and

The surrounding land is owned by the Staffordshire Wildlife Trust and is a SSSI for zoological and botanical reasons. SWT are willing to allow access providing climbers do not stray onto moorland, particularly between Baldstones and Gib Torr. Gib Torr can be accessed by the public footpath running north-east from the south end of Baldstones, then turning left at the road, then left again.

There. That didn't hurt, did it?

followed to finish as for Ray's Roof. Enigmatically compared by its creators to a three-dimensional slug trail. Become one with the rock and all will be revealed. Probably.

24 Hanging Arête V7 (6c)

The small boulder arête right of Ray's Roof, on its left-hand side. Someone has been optimistically trying to climb directly over the overhang to the left of the arête. Good luck. The **arête on the right** is much easier at V2 (5c). **The crack** right again is V0+ (5b).

❂ Elephant's Boulder

The small buttress to the right has some brilliant bouldering.

25 Ganderhole Crack V1– (5a)

The wide crack. The featured wall to the left will never go! Never! Not ever!

26 Fielder's Indirect V1 (5b)

Move right around the rib to climb the wall on pockets.

27 Fielder's Corner V4 (6a)

Classic. The groove above a perplexing start.

28 Fielder's Wall V8 (6c)

The face to the right via a large pocket and a pebble.

29 Elephant's Ear V0 (5a)

The layback flake. **Elephant's Ear Sit-Start** is a classy low start V5 (6b). **Elephant's Eye** V4 (6b) breaks out left to the lower pocket, and up. V1 if you go to the higher pocket.

30 Clever Skin V7 (6c)

The baffling arête on the right is a good test of grit technique. Good conditions help. The wall to the right may have been climbed.

❂ Just right is a little bun of rock. To the left of this, a groove and arête, from a sit-start, is V1 (5b). Manteling the left side of the bun, just to the right, is V3 (6a). **The Wart** gains this from the non-pocket below at a grade of V7 (6c). **Manteling at the Bun** to the right is V3 (6a).

A further 15m right a jutting prow forms the uncanny **Gurning Bulldog**. *To its left is an easy slab and crack.*

31 Lucid Reams E2 6a   **2001**

6m Climb the easy slab for 2m, then step right onto the short wall. Intense moves past mauling hand-jams lead to a rounded finish. Further right, **Pyeclough** (VS 4b, pre-1973) climbs the steep gash slightly to the right of the neck of the buttress.

Next is a slabby face bounded on its right by an easy slanting rampline. **Heathylee** (S 4a, pre-1973), *climbs the faint groove to the left of the easy rampline. At the break move left to a ledge, or finish direct. Alternatively take the easy rampline trending right* (D).

Fifty metres further on is the last buttress. **End Game** (VD, pre-1981) *is an arbitrary route that climbs the wall and prow at its highest point.*

❂ Double Overhang Bouldering

To the right of this tiered roofs marks out some bouldering. This is slightly limited, but its overhanging nature makes it a good option in rain. A **juggy flake** on the left, which is traversed left to easy ground, is V0 (4b). To the right, there is a large flake in the top roof. Gain this by using a pocket and sidepull flake, **Below the Flake**, V2 (5c). A **sit-start** using the mono is V3 (6a). The roof may or may not have been crossed using this flake. **Overhanging Crack** is a significant jamming test, crossing the bulge from a sit-start, V2 (6a). **Short Crack** is on the right, V0– (4c). Traversing **between the cracks** is V2 (5c), while continuing the traverse **between the roofs** as far as the juggy flake is V3 (6a).

Do not go any further!

Gib Torr is prominent across the wooded valley of Black Brook, although access from Baldstones is not permitted, as the area between the two is a highly protected SSSI. Please respect this situation.

Solitude and stunning natural beauty are always just around the corner in Staffordshire. Justin Critchlow on one of his favourite problems, Fielder's Corner, V4 (page 179). Photo: Niall Grimes.

Gib Torr

by Sam Whittaker and Niall Grimes

O.S. Ref. **SK0I8648** | Altitude: **420m a.s.l.**

A small crag with a big personality, a kind of baby Almscliff, containing lots of quality bouldering and a small but significant body of routes. The setting is very friendly, currently sat near a pine forest, yet with a very open aspect, and gives good views across the Baldstones–Newstones ridge-back. A very good little crag.

Conditions & aspect
The crag is very clean, apart from a couple of the routes on the lower buttress. It gets good shelter from winds, and is more sheltered from rain than most crags. It faces east, and gets early morning sun, making it good for cold mornings or hot afternoons.

Routes & bouldering
Fifteen routes, tending to be quite vicious despite a friendly appearance. Best around HVS. About 25 problems, usually bulging sloping action, but with one superb arête and one of Staffordshire's best highballs.

Parking & approach
Park by the gate. See it now? Approach in seconds.

Access
Don't walk from here to Baldstones as the area in-between is an SSSI.

Lower Tier

This is the lower of 2 tiers.

❶ The Fin V5 (6b)
A bold scratchy classic up the front of the jutting prow. A good **sit-start** off pockets is V8 (6c). The crack on the left wall is **Left Fin, V2 (5c)**.

❷ The Fink V7 (6c)
A tough fingery problem up the left side of the steep wall. Scary.

❸ 5c Wall V2 (5c)
The easier wall just right is bold.

❹ Gibbering Left V4 (6a)
From the sloping finger-hold, exit left.

❺ Gibbering Right V6 (6c)
Starts the same, but makes a harder exit up and right. The **Gibbering Lip V8 (6c)**, continues draping right along the hanging lip to pull up above a good hold.

6 Gibby Haines V4 (6a)

From pockets and a sloper, go up to gain the top of the crack. **Gibby Sit-Start** V8 (6c), comes from the sidepull pocket way under the overhang, making very fingery moves to gain the original. Fans of space travel may enjoy trying **Maurice Gib**, a dyno from the good flat hold on the original to a flat jug about 6 miles up and left. Somewhere in the V10 range. Linking this to the sit-start will be a superb challenge.

7 Gibber Crack S   pre-1973

6m The twisting crack leads to a sloping exit.

8 Gibbon Take HVS 5b ★   1977

15m From Gibber Crack, traverse the sandwiched slab. Good delicate moves. Protection may do more harm than good, a bouldering mat being more use. The route originally joined The Gibe, although soloists may prefer to come back down the easy flake.

9 Porridge Wall V2 (6a)

Start in the low finger jug, and yank up to gain the round pocket. The ledge to the left gives a **good mantel**, V1 (5b), avoiding the crack.

Andi Turner letting rip on an attempt on Maurice Gib.
Photo: Turner Collection.

⑩ Porridge at Morridge Top E5 6b ★ 1980s
9m A bold technical climb that usually requires a brushing beforehand. Move up past the flake (last pro) and easily gain round holds under the second overlap. From here, a short but trying sequence leads up the scoop to salvation.

⑪ The Gibe HVS 4c ★ 1974
9m A Gogarth classic. Go up the flake to get stood on the pedestal. Drop down then go steeply up to a big jug (can be reached more easily direct up the groove below). From here, catcrawl right along the sloping gangway and finish round the arête. A fairly serious adventure. The crack above the catcrawl is reported to have been climbed but no-one has, so far, confessed.

⑫ Montezuma's Revenge E4 5c† ★ 1979
9m A good, serious climb that would require a clean. From the pedestal (last possible gear), climb up and left through the overlaps on round holds to the ledge.

⑬ Martin's Problem V5 (6b)
Start low on a big hold and snatch up and right on a series of rounded crimps.

⑭ Stall Arête V6 (6c)
The beautiful hanging arête is a supreme test of gritstone technique, requiring power, balance and a load of stickiness. **Stall Sit-Start V9 (6c)** is just as classic, and requires a bit more of all of the above, especially the power bit. And don't dare use the slab on the right.

⑮ Stall E5 6c† 1989
8m 'Very grisly and esoteric,' according to the first ascensionist. Having done the problem start, move up and left under the bulge and, with what gear you can muster, tackle the 6c bulge above.

⑯ Gibble Gabble Slab D pre-1973
8m The slab and wide crack.

⑰ Little Traverse V2 (5c)
Traverse the lip. The **mantel** through the middle of this is V5 (6b).

Rock-climbing has the advantage

over many other motions in that it has no rules save respect. The rock just seduces you, first by its look, then by its touch and then its moves, finally becoming a warm glow, Each special route for me has a glow almost as reminiscent in extent as a feeling you have for a lover when you shut your eyes and feel what is left when you cannot see them.
Johnny Dawes

⑱ Gary's 5c V3 (6a)
Set back and to the right of this section is a triangular green wall. This problem takes the cracked arête. A V0 (5a) problem is possible to the left.

⑲ Seams Green V4 (6a)
The mossy wall to the right is climbed on poor holds.

Gibbon Buttress

This is the prominent 'boulder' above the Lower Tier.

⑳ Gib Torrture V2 (5c)
Gain the short crack on the left wall, and climb it as quickly as possible. Or continue along the break, **Extended Torrture**, to go up the crack nearer the arête, V4 (6a). Both can be led to prolong the pleasure ⓥ. More bouldering lies down and left from here, especially on a long flat barrel of rock.

㉑ Gibbering Wreck V8 (6c)

A Tierdrop for the year 2000. Great flakes lead to the lip, where a small pocket awaits… One of the best highballs anywhere, although its original grade of E6 6c may well feel warranted if no pads are used.

㉒ Gibe Turkey HVS 5b   1992

6m Lunge for the ledge then pull up and over the overhang direct.

㉓ Gibling Corner S   pre-1973

6m Up the little corner then finish off right, or direct at 4a.

㉔ Gibbon Wall HS 4b   pre-1973

8m A nice route that tackles the steep well-protected bulge on chunky jams.

㉕ Gibeonite Girdle HVS 5b   pre-1973

12m A meaty route that continues past Gibbon Wall to attack (or be attacked by) the horizontal crack to its steep conclusion.

The Upper Tier

This lies just to the right.

㉖ Gibraltar S   pre-1973

8m The wide cracks.

㉗ The Ensign HVS 5a ★   pre-1973

8m The bulging finger-crack.

㉘ Gib E2 6a ★   1970s

9m Desperate bouldering (although there's a trick, apparently) leads to a flake. From here the climbing eases off to the top.

㉙ The Gibbet HVS 5a ★   pre-1973

9m From the wide crack (**Giblet Crack**, VD, pre-1973, that finishes up left), make a delicate diagonal up the wall leftwards to finish at the arête.

Gradbach Hill

by Paul Smith and Robert Lavin

O.S. Ref. **SK001653** | Altitude: **390m a.s.l.**

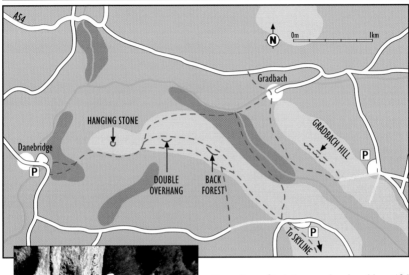

For seekers of isolation, good rock and beautiful views, the small collection of buttresses known as Gradbach Hill is a truly delightful venue. Overlooking a broad pastoral and forested valley, and lying almost dormant behind the thronging ridges of the Roaches, it is a silent and personal crag, which seems incongruous with its short approach and the multitudes of climbers not far away. The rock is high quality grit, and the sunny aspect makes it a very pleasant place to visit.

Conditions & aspect

The crag gets lots of sun and no seepage. It is very clean and suitable for year round climbing. It faces south-west and gets sun from morning to sunset.

Left: Paul Smith on his own route (perhaps), Whose Line Is It Anyway? Photo: Becca Ward.

Staffordshire Grit

Routes & bouldering

25 routes. Easily enough to merit a visit. Mostly up to HVS with one brilliant E4. 20 boulder problems. A superb venue for the more moderate boulderers with good problems on good features and generally friendly landings.

Parking & approach

Park sensibly at the junction. Follow the rough track slightly uphill, and over a stile. Where the path goes downhill, follow the crest rightwards, along a very rough sheep track, directly to the rocks. 10 minutes.

Access

The PDNPA places a high value on the peace and quiet of this area, so does the wildlife, and so should you. No large groups, as this will jeopardise access.

The two most obvious features on the crag are The Pinnacle, the tallest tower at the left side, and The Yawning Stone, a 5m high boulder above the crag, 200m to the right. The climbs are described from left to right.

Cynic's Buttress

The first routes lie on a small buttress 120m left of The Pinnacle.

❶ Fat Old Nick VD   1980
9m Climb a crack on the left of an overhang, then move right and go up the front slab. **Al's Abdominal Start** takes the overhang direct on large rounded holds at E1 5a.

❷ For Tim D   1980
9m The wide central crack. **Whose Line is it Anyway?** (HVS 5a, 2000) climbs the buttress immediately right on small pockets and edges.

❸ Old Son VD   1980
8m Climb the corner-crack and arête above, right of the central crack.

100m right is a square buttress with two 'wings'.

❹ Pot Black E2 6a   1986
9m Climb the wall just right of the left arête to a ledge. From the ledge, climb the left arête passing an obvious snapped flake by some technical moves. Don't fall off rightwards!

❺ The Billiard Table S ★   pre-1973
9m A fine, tall climb. From the lowest point of the buttress, climb a crack to a bulge. Go over this awkwardly to the ledge and exit up the corner-crack.

❻ The Cue VD   pre-1973
6m The crack on the right side of the buttress passing the right edge of the ledge. Thrutchy. Climbing the wall just left of the crack is **The Chalk** (HVS 5a, 1980). A new route could be had up the sharp arête just right and bold slab above.

❼ The Hour Glass E3 6b†   1997
5m The undercut sidewall to the right is climbed, desperately, above a bad landing.

The Pinnacle

One of the best features in the valley is the tall pinnacle 15m right, home to a bold Staffordshire test-piece. The short back side is Difficult and the side just to the left is Severe. A dry-stone wall runs up to its front face.

❽ Cleft Route VD   pre-1973
12m The very traditional crack on the left wall. Follow this past a large moving chockstone and move round to finish up the easy back route. The steeper crack to the right is **Green Crack**, which traverses into Cleft Route to finish (HS 4b, 1973).

⑨ The Phantom E4 5c ★★ 1971

15m A superb and spooky route, a classic Staffordshire head-game. Go up a crack then step left onto a small ledge. Climb the vague rib above, past a ghost of a bolt to a big ledge. Go over the top bulge by a thin crack, or climb direct to the summit from the ledge.

Ⓥ Just round to the right lie a few boulder problems. **Cave Crack** V3 (6a) jams the finger crack over the cave, without recourse to the slab behind. Starting at the back adds a bit more spice. **Little Rib** VI (5a) climbs onto and up the little hanging ridge, above a bad landing. **The Hanging Arête** V0− (4c) is the lovely little arête just above, aided by a flat hold and some flakes. **The wall** left of the arête is V0− (4b). **Thin Crack** (HVS 6a, 1986) is the thin bouldery crack topped by a small roof, 10m right of The Pinnacle. **The Overhang** (HVS 5a, 1986) is a short overhang in the bracken another 15m to the right, while **Pip** (HVS 5c, 1997) is the wall just right of this, using a pebble.

⑩ Little Arête VD ★★ 1980

6m A short but pleasant climb up the arête 60m right. Skirt the overhang to the left. Climbing it on its right side is severe.

Ⓥ *Eighty metres right the rocks re-emerge from the hillside. Before these rocks, a boulder built into the wall below gives a couple of problems. On the face facing The Phantom, the **left arête** is V0 (4a), and the **wall to the right** is V0 (5a), or 4b using the right arête.*

Square Boulder

Returning to the main edge, the next feature is a square bouldery buttress on the top of the crag, 25m left of The Yawning Stone. It contains 3 good problems.

⑪ Tip-Toe Arête V0 (5a)

The delicate left arête on its left side requires concentration.

⑫ Front Crack V0+ (5a)

Superb. Climb the steep crack on the front of the block. This could also be led, as it is a little high. The

crack just right of the arête is also steep, but more awkward, V0+ (5a).

The Yawning Stone

The bulging perched block to the right has a superb concentration of good problems. Some of these feel high, but the landings are generally on your side.

⑬ V0− (4b)

The short wall on the left of the tapering side-wall leads to a sloping mantel.

⑭ Slim Groove V0+ (5a)

The shallow groove to the right is climbed delicately on sloping finger-holds.

⑮ V0− (4a)

The arête is climbed on its left side above a bad landing, finishing on good jugs on the front face.

⑯ Mantel VI (5c)

Below the front face is a cave. Starting low on a pinch, trend left and make a gruesome mantel over the lip. Strenuous.

⑰ The Yawn V0+ (5a)

Classic. Pull straight over the centre of the roof using some short cracks and continue on superb

holds to the top. Always juggy, but strenuous. A fin-gery low start is possible.

⓲ The Arête VI (5b)
Start for The Yawn but ape right to the arête and sur-mount it on rounded holds. A great problem. **Starting low** on small crimps is V2 (5c), but less pleasant.

⓳ The Green Streak V7 (6c)
Gain the green streak direct on unhelpful holds.

⓴ Brown Wall V4 (6b)
The fingery wall just right, passing a hole.

㉑ Chunky VI (5b)
Great holds lead up the leaning wall to a sketchy top-out.

Returning to the edge below, the next route begins behind a tree.

㉒ Oak Tree Crack VD   pre-1973
6m On the edge, below and left, the crack behind the tree leads to an easier finish. **French Connection** (E1 5c, 1985) climbs the slab just right, then over the bulge continue direct.

The **Phantom** Bolt

The classic of the crag once sported a controversial protection bolt. It was said to have been placed by a mysterious Boy Scout on abseil, but he was unable to use it as he had placed it out of reach. Why he wanted to use it is a further mystery. However, the 1981 guide admits that it was placed by 'a known member of the NSMC.' The route was climbed with 2 points of aid by Colin Foord (of the NSMC), 1 point by John Yates, and then no points of aid by Jonny Woodward, all in 1971. They all used the bolt for protection, however, and it remained until it was chopped, and the route led without by Ian Dunn in 1986. The route is still said to be haunted by the bolt, however, and the route is no place to be on a lonely winter night.

㉓ John's Arête HVS 5a ★   1980
9m Climb the arête right of the oak tree, then go directly up the slab. Pleasant climbing.

㉔ Sleepwalker HS 4b   1969
9m Climb the crack to a double overhang. Traverse strenuously left on creaking flakes, then trend right-wards up the delicate slab.

Over the years, many **strange sightings**

have been reported in the Staffordshire area of strange eyes watching climbers from the ferns – the Roaches Wallabies. The wallabies were introduced to the Swythamley Estate by the Earl of Swythamley prior to WW2. They were kept in a zoo underneath Hen Cloud with some yak. When war broke out the gamekeepers were called up and the animals were left to fend for themselves. The yak succumbed to the meat shortages of the '40s but the wallabies bred successfully and became a feral British breed in the '70s. Although no-one can be certain why they have almost died out (only two or three remain, not a breeding population) the sheep overgrazing of the early '80s and the massive increase in public use with roaming dogs certainly hasn't helped. There also was a regular slaughter on the roads backed up by many an amusing tale at Leek Police Station –

'You're not going to believe this, Officer, and I haven't been drinking, but I've just run over a kangaroo…'

dunno who he is but he can't half dyno!

Illustration: Duncan Bourne.

㉕ Barbiturate S ★ 1969
7m Gain the handsome hand-sized corner-crack and climb it direct. The little hanging arête, climbed on its left, is **Morpheus** (E2 6b†, 1997).

㉖ Anniversaire E2 5c ★ 1985
8m Climb directly through the overhang immediately left of Chockstone Crack. Technical. The overgrown crack to the left was once **Marsden's Crack** (VS 4c, 1969).

㉗ Chockstone Crack S ★ 1969
8m The prominent crack. A big jug eases the passage of the overhang.

㉘ The Gape VS 4c ★★ 1980
8m Good climbing in fine situations. Start up the arête, but move left and climb the front face on good features and superb rock.

㉙ Sense of Doubt E2 5c ★ 1980
8m Nicely exposed climbing up the main arête of the pinnacle. Follow the blunt arête closely with a hard move above the horizontal crack. The wall to its right awaits someone with sufficient finger power to climb it.

The last climbs lie on twin slabs 100m to the right. On the left-hand slab the right edge and left side are 4a and 4c respectively, and **Feed the Enemy** *(HS 4b, 1978) is the blunt arête of the right-hand slab (currently overgrown).*

Wolf Edge

by John H Bull

| O.S. Ref. **SK021674** | Altitude: **450m a.s.l.** |

…Magnesium, proverbs and sobs,
Howling the pack in formation appears…

Wolfpack, Syd Barrett

Wolf Edge is situated high on the Staffordshire moorland, and is effectively the first gritstone outcrop to emerge from the ridge that Axe Edge Moor throws off to the south, gradually leading to Ramshaw Rocks. It is host to a multitude of excellent easy and mid-grade problems. The Edge forms the northern boundary of a small valley that drains into the river Dane. It overlooks the sheep pastures and tumbledown stone walls that form the farming hinterland of Flash, a tiny village that claims to be the highest in Britain. A faint air of abandonment permeates the area, perched as it is on the very edge of habitability.

Wolf Edge has somehow escaped documentation in previous editions of Staffordshire Gritstone or any other guide to Peak climbing, presumably due to a combination of its diminutive stature and its invisibility from the A53 Buxton-Leek road. However, the bouldering deserves recognition, and this introductory description hopes to rescue the Edge from unjust obscurity.

Conditions & aspect

This modest edge is the county's highest and, as such, is exposed to the worst of the elements. However, it is sunny of aspect, very pleasant, fast-drying. At the time of writing, the neglected rocks feel gritty and slightly friable, but regular traffic will do much to improve matters. The edge faces south-east, and gets good afternoon sun.

Routes & bouldering

This is basically a bouldering crag, with about 30 problems, mainly in low to mid grades. On the whole the landings are friendly.

Parking & approach

From Flash, a road leads uphill past the New Inn pub. At the edge of the village (very limited parking), walk up a rough lane that leads past the last house on the right, over a brow from which the edge is soon visible. Where the lane forks, take the left branch for the Warren and Fin areas, and the right branch for the Quarry area. 10 minutes.

Access:

The presence of this chapter in the guide does not imply any right to climb at Wolf Edge. The access situation is uncertain and possibly quite delicate. Footpaths lead directly past the foot of the Fin area, and past the Quarry, and it seems unlikely that access issues will arise in these areas. However, the terrain between these outcrops is farmland. Fences and walls can be avoided by staying high or low rather than contouring the hillside. In addition, there is no right of way to the Warren. Keep a low profile and if asked to leave, please do so politely.

Bouldering Areas are described from **left** to **right**. To aid description, the most obvious problems are detailed, being split into 3 areas. The first area is approached from the **right** from the lane that crosses the edge, and is thus described.

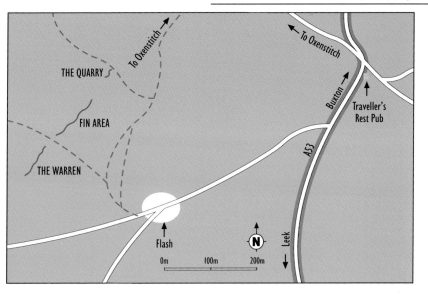

ⓥ The Warren

This is the lowest part of the edge to the left of the lane. Approaching from the right, the first obvious feature is a tower-like buttress with a rounded arête on its right (unclimbed) and a stone-built fold at its foot on the left. Further left is a small **sharp arête** VI (5b); to its left, a **dyno** face problem, V4 (6a). Directly downhill is a boulder with a superb triangular south face: **hand-traverse** left to right from a sitting start to gain the top, V2 (5c); or climb the face past **creases** finishing left, V4 (6b). Up on the main edge, over the wall to the left is a **fine slab**, VI (5a) with an easy **right arête** V0– (4c). To the left is a small bay– traverse into the bay on breaks and move up the crack to give **Hairy Hat Man**, a superb V3 (5c). Just downhill is a boulder with a scooped face above a rabbit hole, **Warren Piece**, V0 (5b).

ⓥ The Fin

This area lies to the right of the lane. Just right of the lane is a small **flying arête** that at present is in need of cleaning, followed by several **easier arêtes** V0–. **The Fin** (VS 4b ★; V0) climbs the arête on its left. On the **left wall** of the arête is a cleaned face problem, **This is My Church** V5 (6b). On its right wall is a distinctive **ear-shaped flake** (HS, 4b; V0–). Right again, set

back is a **steep arête** VI (5a) with a harder sit-start. To the right is a square promontory whose **left arête** VI (5b), **face** V4 (6a), and **right arête** V2 (5c) are excellent. Slightly further right is a **prow** giving a superb V2 (6a) sit-start. Isolated 20m to the right are the distinctive **Twin Arêtes**: left of the first arête is a **mantelshelf** VI (5c); the left arête is small, strange and dirty (**Gollum, V4** 6b). The arêtes are separated by a **deep jam** crack (V0– 4b); the **right-hand face** (sit-start) is V1 (5b); a **low traverse** is V1 (5b). A further 30m to the right is the fine **Ramp Boulder: left arête** V4 (6b); **right arête** from the left V2 (6a), **face** VI (5c), **ramp** V0– (4b), and **face** (no holds on the ramp) V2 (5c).

ⓥ The Quarry

130m to the right of the Ramp Boulder is this square-cut bay. The problems include the **left arête** VI (5b sit-start), **crack** V0– (4a), **face** VI (5c), and to the right of the corner several face and arête problems (V0–V1).

Further documentation of this and other local 'wild' bouldering in the area can be found in the *High Over Buxton* bouldering guide, available from local climbing shops.

Outlying Crags in the Gradbach Area

by Dave Bishop

Ludchurch

O.S. Ref. **SJ987656**

This remarkable ravine, steeped in history (and vegetation), is on the north-eastern slopes of Back Forest Ridge. Receiving practically no sunshine, its side-walls are cloaked in vegetation and most of the rock remains wet and greasy except after a drought. Ludchurch thus affords a rare environment for thirsty plants suffering photophobia and as such is thought to be of greater significance to the botanist and ecologist than to the climber. Although a few routes have been unearthed on the north wall in the past, such as Subterranean Sidewalk and Dead Man's Creek, they should remain as historical epitaphs to the climbers who no longer come here.
Climbers are requested not to climb here.

Castle Cliff Rocks

O.S. Ref. **SJ985658**

There is a group of shattered pinnacles near Ludchurch which offers a few minor problems unworthy of climbers' attention, but makes a nice picnic spot.

Gibbons Cliff

O.S. Ref. **SJ971664**

One kilometre downstream from Allgreave Bridge, Clough Brook winds through a short length of wooded valley with very steep sides. There are a number of outcrops here which are in the main overwhelmed by vegetation. The two cleanest buttresses are situated on the west bank directly above the ruins of an old mill. The old mill provides marginally more attractive problems than these rocks.

The Ballstone

O.S. Ref. **SK013658**

This is a gigantic perched boulder in the grounds of Green Gutter Stake Farm. Whilst it may offer bouldering, the farmer is understandably unwilling to allow climbing since it lies in his back yard!

Flash Bottom Rocks

O.S. Ref. **SK018657**

The name may have Freudian attractions for you; resist them. In the past some climbing has taken place here but in 1999 the BMC agreed a no climbing restriction for this site. The surrounds are vital for the long-term survival of endangered species and you are requested to comply so as not to jeopardise access at much more valuable nearby climbing sites.

The **Hanging Stone** and **Back Forest**

by Paul Smith

The Back Forest crags are a collection of short buttresses widely scattered along the natural continuation of the Roaches ridge that runs from Roach End to Danebridge. The main crag is by far the most extensive and forms a delightful spot for family picnics or an evening's soloing. The aspect is pleasant, the views fine, the rock sound and clean, the routes, almost without exception, friendly and worthwhile. The routes on the Rostrum and on the western outcrop are slightly more dramatic and exposed, whilst those on the Hanging Stone are impressive and imposing.

Conditions & aspect
The main crag is fairly sheltered and can be a pleasant sun-trap in winter. The Hanging Stone can be windy. All the crags dry quickly and are all-year venues. They face south-west to south, and get afternoon and evening sun.

Routes
About 50 short routes, mostly in the VD to HVS range. Many soloable by the competent, with the occasional sterner challenge.

Bouldering
Excellent easier bouldering, currently with pleasant grassy landings. Considerate use of bouldering mats will reduce erosion and would be greatly appreciated by local regulars.

Parking & approach
See the map on page 185. For the main crag and western outcrop, the best approach is from Roach End. Cross the wall to the north of the limited parking area, by the narrow stile, and follow the path along the ridge, initially alongside a wall. Either continue along the ridge to the top of the crag, or take the left fork where it dips down to the left, over a further stile, before reaching a rushy hollow where the main crag is visible. About 15 minutes. The western outcrop lies about 700m farther along the ridge.

Whilst the Hanging Stone can also be approached along the ridge (in 10 minutes), by far the best approach is from Danebridge (OS ref. SJ965652). From the bridge, follow a wide track upstream on the Staffordshire side for 50m. Cross the fence on the right via a stile and follow another path up through the wooded valley, then cross the field to Hanging Stone Farm. Pass between the farm buildings and continue on up the hillside to reach the block (15 minutes). Do not park on the track below the Hanging Stone.

Access
The crag is in an area designated as 'quiet countryside' within the Roaches Management Plan. The Peak Park discourages large groups (such as outdoor centres and groups under instruction) from using the crag. Groups of more than 5 people are likely to be approached by a warden and asked to move to an alternative venue. Access for individual climbers is tolerated and discreet behaviour is unlikely to attract attention. The path that stretches along the ridge from the main crag to the Hanging Stone is concessional, although heavily used by walkers. Climbing at the Hanging Stone itself is somewhat frowned on. If challenged, retreat graciously.

Beneath this rock,
August 1st 1874, lies buried, **BURKE**,
a noble mastiff, black and tan, faithful as
a woman, braver than a man, a gun and
a ramble, his heart's desire, with the friend
of his life, the Swythamley squire.
Commemoration on the Hanging Stone.

The Hanging Stone

O.S. Ref. **SJ974654**   Altitude: **320m a.s.l.**

The impressive hanging block has two plaques on it; the left one commemorates the heart-warming devotion of a dead dog and the other is a memorial to a notable member of the Brocklehurst family.

❶ Left-Hand Crack VS 5a   pre-1973
8m The corner right of the steps leads to a break. Struggle with the crack through the overhang above to gain the top. Amusing.

❷ The Bridge of Sighs E3 5c ★★   1977
12m Hard climbing leads diagonally across the wall (crux) to the uppermost break. Compose yourself and then hand-traverse out across the lip, before rocking over and climbing the final groove to the top. **Jewel of Corruption** (E2 5b ★★★, 1990s) is a much better, more direct and easier variation, climbing the lower arête direct on its left.

❸ Hanging Stone Crack HVS 5b ★★   pre-1973
11m A great muscular and airy struggle. Climb the shallow groove on small holds, one metal, to gain an upper crack, which is followed by tricky jamming, and/or holds out to the right.

❹ Right Bow E1 5b   1977
8m Climb the bulging right wall of the buttress to gain a high flake and finish up it strenuously.

The buttress can be girdled from left to right at three points. **The Low Girdle** is Severe, **The Drifter's Escape**, VS 4c, uses the central break and **The High Girdle**, HS 4a, crawls along the uppermost break.

Back Forest

The Back Forest crags are now strung along the ridge.

The Western Outcrop

O.S. Ref. **SJ981655**   Altitude: **355m a.s.l.**

The first of the Back Forest crags is a double over-hung buttress high on the ridge, 700m past The Hanging Stone, and 600m west from the main Back Forest crag.

❶ Burnham Crack VS 4c   1971
9m The steep green corner left of Double Overhang.

❷ Double Overhang E1 5b ★★   1971
11m A spectacular and not over-protected classic taking the fine overhangs directly. The first is tackled centrally via a long stretch for a super-jug on the lip. Use similar tactics to overcome the second, but slightly to the right.

❸ Mr Creosote HVS 5b   1991
11m Climb the hanging right-hand arête of the buttress.

❹ The Gaping Void D   1971
11m Starting on the left side of the buttress, traverse right with an exposed move across Burnham Crack and sneak between the overhangs to finish right.

Fifty metres after this buttress lies a small isolated crag containing **Suspended Sentence** *(VS 5a, 1974), which climbs the crack through the overhang.*

The Rostrum

O.S. Ref. **SJ986653**   Altitude: **365m a.s.l.**

The main section lies 600m further along. Before this, an outcrop sits on the crest of the ridge, with a smaller outcrop sat to its right.

⑤ The Rostrum VS 4b ★   pre-1973
7m Pull up the very steep wall on good holds until an ungainly exit can be made leftwards onto the great shelf itself. Finish easily above.

⑥ John's Route HVS 5a   1979
7m The bulging wall 3m right of the Rostrum taken direct.

⑦ Bumper Cars VS 4c   2003
7m The pumpy, bulging wall to the right of the holly is climbed direct. **Ruth's Septic Trench** (D, 1999) takes the obvious and often unpleasant chimney on the right side of the outcrop.

⑧ Pinnacle Buttress VS 5a   2001
6m Climb the pinnacle direct.

To the right of the main outcrop is a small buttress; **Racer's Rock** (S 4b, pre-1981).

The Main Crag

O.S. Ref. **SJ987652**   Altitude: **360m a.s.l.**

This lies almost 100m along the ridge (OS ref. SJ987652). The first rock met is Holly Tree Buttress. The first route is the short **Green Crack** (HVD, pre-1973), bounding the left side of the buttress. Good fun can be had by wearing **Action**

Becca Ward on the first ascent of Bumper Cars.
Photo: Paul Smith.

Trousers (VS 4b, 2002), which stride right from the start of Green Crack, along the main, lower, break and round the arête. Finish up Holly Tree Niche left or right.

⑨ Twin Thin S   pre-1973
8m The eponymous vertical cracks 1m right. Finish up the vague groove.

⑩ Eye of Japetus HVS 5a ★   1974
9m Climb a thin crack left of the arête. Make a mighty lunge to gain the break (or pull elegantly over the nose just right). Finish direct via a faint flake. Satisfying.

To the **north**,

Manchester's great glow heralded a vast complexity, while in the same direction but closer by, the homelier presence of Macclesfield could be guessed at. Turning south a myriad of roads, hamlets, villages and towns inexplicably coalesced into the Potteries from where we had come that evening. Alongside the illuminated roads lay the lanes and paths, the canals, rivers and streams, unseen but still felt.

Andy Popp
At the End of an Evening's Climbing in Staffordshire.

⑪ Holly Tree Niche Left Route
S 4a ★   pre-1931
9m The main arête of the buttress on its right side. At the first bulge move left and make awkward moves up the left-hand side of the nose.

⑫ Holly Tree Niche Right Route
D   pre-1931
6m Attain the niche and finish up the corner. The holly is no more, making tweeds redundant. **Blow Hard** (S 4a, pre-1981) is the flaky crack right of the niche.

⑬ The Keeper HVS 5a   1975
6m Gain the middle of the steep left-hand wall of the next buttress by an awkward pull, and then pass

a ledge to finish up the right arête. **Back Forest Gâteau** (E2 6a, 1994) is a desperate, though artificial, problem through the undercut arête to the right.

⑭ Portcullis Crack S 4a ★★   pre-1973
6m Take the steep, technical crack, complete with chockstone, on the front of the buttress. Pass the overhang and finish leftwards to the arête. Excellent.

⑮ Keep Face S 4a   pre-1931
6m Gain a ledge on the right and use an L-shaped crack to move up and left to a mantelshelf finish.

⑯ The Saucer Direct S 4a   pre-1981
6m Past the chasm is a little capped slab. From the right of the slab, climb to the overhang and move right to pass it via a wedged flake. A right-hand start is 4c. **The Saucer** (VD, pre-1931) climbs the slab, then moves left around the corner to finish via a crack.

⑰ Capstone Chimney S 4a   pre-1931
6m A traditional exercise, up the wide chimney line, passing outside the chockstone. **Wrestle Crack** (VS 4b, pre-1931) attacks the horrendous-looking undercut crack, using hidden holds, 1m to the left. Hard for its time.

⑱ Bollard Edge VS 4b ★★★   pre-1931
8m A must-do; well-protected, steep and committing. From the foot of the buttress skirt the overhang to the left by a crack to reach the top of the Bollard.

Try not to think what it's attached to, and press on just left of the spectacular arête to gain the top.

⑲ Toe Rail HVS 5a ★★   1979

8m Excellent. The impressive steep face taken more or less directly on bumper holds and protection. For a consistent route at this grade, step in from slightly right to start. Even better is the **Direct Start**; a big reach and staunch pull using thin flake crack overcomes the initial bulge for a classic HVS 5c.

⑳ Pseudo Crack HVD ★   pre-1931

8m The groove and crack exiting right at the top, or better, finishing left via an airy traverse all the way to the arête.

㉑ Bastion Corner VD   pre-1931

7m On the face just right, follow holds rightwards to finish up the vague arête. **Bastion Face** (D, pre-1931) gains the same point directly via a break and a black flake. A small rounded buttress to the right has a poor Severe arête; **Filler In**.

Broken Nose Buttress

lies 10m to the right.

㉒ Green Shaker VD ★   pre-1973

8m On the front of the buttress, gain a ledge. Step left onto the side-wall and a small flake, then move rightwards to the top. **A Fist Full of Freshers** (S 4a, 2000) goes up the wall to the left, past a black hold to an interesting finish.

㉓ Central Route HS 4b ★   pre-1931

8m From the ledge, follow the ridge to the second overhang and turn this awkwardly to the right.

㉔ Not So Central Route S 4a ★   pre-1981

8m Move right below the initial overhang of Central Route and finish direct.

㉕ Thin Crack HS 4a ★   pre-1973

8m Follow the inviting thin crack, after stepping in from the right. Starting direct is a finger-licking 5b.

The corner is **Hanging Stone Crack**, M. *The next climbs are on the steep wall to the right.*

㉖ Requiem for Tired Fingers
HVS 5b ★   1974

6m Nip up the left side of the wall by a thin pull to reach better holds before finishing slightly right. Not quite as foreboding as the name suggests, but don't blow the top.

㉗ Grasper VS 5a ★★   pre-1973

7m Tackle the centre of the wall to a tough finish up the cracks.

Solitude and natural beauty

are common traits to all the crags in this chapter. While it would be good to see them get more deserved attention, above all, we must respect these areas, and allow them to continue to flourish without the heavy hand of man. Please do all you can to minimise your impact here. Go in small teams, or alone; keep the noise down; stick to the paths, remove any traces of your visit. By doing so, these special areas will remain special for a long time to come.

Kirsty Hamilton Maclaren topping out on Rocking Stone Ridge, VD. Photo: Paul Smith.

㉘ Mustard S 4b   pre-1931
5m Start just left of the arête. Make some thin pulls to get established and then climb easily to finish at the top of the arête.

㉙ Rocking Stone Ridge VD   pre-1931
7m Climb the front of the buttress, after an awkward start and finishing near the top of the left arête. The right edge of the buttress is **Weathered Corner**, D, coming in from the right. The direct start to the left arête is a gut-busting 5c mantel, best savoured as the finishing move of the **low traverse** of the break, V3 (5c).

The final section of the crag offers some shorter routes, whose stature makes them more appropriately seen as tall boulder problems.

㉚ Harrop's Pride V0– (4c)
Strenuously climb the undercut wall and then the arête. **Simple View**, 5a, starts up the thin crack just left, but is rather dirty and indistinct thereafter.

㉛ Dog-Leg Crack VD (3c)

㉜ Armstrain V1 (5c)
The attractive undercut face on good breaks, starting on the left.

㉝ Dog-Leg Corner VD (4a)

㉞ Problem Arête V2 (6a)
Climb the arête on its right-hand side. On its left is V0 (5b).

㉟ Paul's Wall V4 (6b)
The excellent slabby wall, crossing the roof directly.

㊱ Contract Worker V0 (4c)
Climb the obvious thin recessed crack topped by an overhang. Finish excitingly by pulling directly over at the highest point. A mini-classic. The final blunt arête is taken by **Unseen Face** (4b).

Becca Ward on Paul's Wall. Photo: Paul Smith.

Newstones to Back Forest First Ascents

pre-1931 **Rocking Stone Ridge, Central Route, Bastion Face, Bastion Corner, Pseudo Crack, Mustard, Bollard Edge, Capstone Chimney, Wrestle Crack, The Saucer, Keep Face, Holly Tree Niche Right Route, Holly Tree Niche Left Route** *All appeared in the Rucksack Club Journal of 1931.*

pre-1951 **Perambulator Parade, Forking Chimney** *(originally known as Y-chimney)*

1969 **Marsden's Crack, Chockstone Crack, Barbiturate, Sleep Walker** Barry Marsden.

1960s **Original Route** Martin Boysen

1971 **The Phantom** (2 pts. aid) Colin Foord *Climbed free by Jonny Woodward in 1977 with the bolt for protection and without by Ian Dunn and Claudie Dunn in 1986.*

1971 **Burnham Crack, The Gaping Void, Double Overhang** (1 pt.) Dave Salt, Colin Foord *The aid on Double Overhang was a nut on the initial roof. Climbed free by Tony Barley and Robin Brown in May 1974.*

pre-1973 **Baldstones Arête, The Ensign, The Gibbet** North Staffordshire Mountaineering Club members

pre-1973 **Newstones Chimney, Hazel Barrow Crack, Hazel Barn, Rhynose, Hippo, The Witch, Candy Man, The Snake, The Fox, The Vixen, The Sly Mantelshelf, Sly Corner, Baldstones Face, Goldsitch Crack*, Blackbank Crack*, Minipin Crack, Ganderhole Crack, The Brund (later known as Elephant's Ear), Pyeclough, Heathylee, Gibble Gabble Slab, Gibber Crack, Gib Sail, Giblet Crack, Gibraltar, Gibling Corner, Gibbon Wall, Gibeonite Girdle, Contract Worker, Dog-Leg Corner, Dog-Leg Crack, Harrop's Pride, Grasper, Thin Crack, Green Shaker, Portcullis Crack, Twin Thin, Green Crack, The Rostrum, Left-Hand Crack, Hanging**

Stone Crack, Low Girdle, High Girdle, Oak Tree Crack, Cleft Route, The Cue *All appeared for the first time in the 1973 Staffordshire Gritstone guidebook.* **Paul Nunn's selective guide,* **Rock Climbing in the Peak District (1975)** *gave different names: Overhanging Crack and Ferox, respectively.*

1974 May **Charlie's Overhang, The Gibe, Requiem for Tired Fingers, Suspended Sentence** Tony Barley *Charlie's Overhang also known as Barleyman.*

1974 **Eye of Japetus** Jonny Woodward, Andrew Woodward

1975 Jul **The Keeper** Tony Barley

1975 Nov 2 **Trepidation** Jim Campbell, Con Carey

1976 Jun 19 **Gold Rush** Jim Campbell, Nick Colton

1977 Jul **Ray's Roof** Ray Jardine, Clive Jones *In the late 1970s, the man who invented Friends was at the height of his powers, and still took 4 days to climb the route. In 1977 he also climbed the Phoenix, Yosemite's first 5.13. At the time of writing, Ray's Roof still has had only 4 known repeats.*

1977 **Bridge of Sighs** Dave Jones, John Gilbert

1977 **Right Bow, Morridge Top, Bareleg Wall, Gibbon Take** Jonny Woodward (solo) *Bareleg Wall apparently climbed in 1975 as Let Out.*

1978 May **Feed the Enemy** Gary Gibson

1979 **Toe Rail** John Holt

1979 **John's Route** Gary Gibson

1979 **Montezuma's Revenge** Nick Longland

1970s **All-Stars' Wall, Gib** Martin Boysen.

1980 **The Gape, Sense of Doubt, John's Arête, Little Arête, The Chalk, Old Son, For Tim, Fat Old Nick** Nick Longland, John Holt

pre-1981 **Moonshine, Praying Mantel, Nutmeg, Rosehip, Incognito, End Game, Problem Arête, Armstrain, Simple View, Not so Central Route, The Saucer Direct, Blow**

Hard, Racer's Rock, The Drifter's Escape
Appeared for the first time in the 1981 guidebook.

1984	**Leather Joy Boys** Mark Stokes	
early '80s	**Porridge at Morridge Top** Martin Boysen	

Named by Paul Mitchell who believed he had done the first ascent in 1984.

1985   **French Connection, Anniversaire**
Ian Dunn, Claudie Dunn.

1986   **Puffed Up**   Martin Boysen
Named by John Allen from an ascent in 1989. The actual first ascent was unearthed from Boysen's memory in 2003 when he happened upon Neil Pearsons attempting what he believed was to be the first ascent. Pearsons was hanging off a cam when "along shambles an old man. 'Ah, someone trying my new route,' he says. 'I never did write that up. It's about 5c.' This was after a few days effort, thinking it would be English 7a." On The Edge

1986   **Gibbering**   Tom Leppert (solo)

1986   **Pot Black**   Ian Dunn

1989 Jun/Jul **Valley of Ultravixens, Ponsified** John Allen

1989   **Stall**   Johnny Dawes   *The start climbed by Martin Boysen in the early '80s.*

c.1990   **Johnny's Indirect Rear Entry**
Jonny Woodward, Johnny Dawes
Both on-sight solo 'in caravan'.

1991   **Mr Creosote**   Roger Nichols

1992 May 23 **Prelude to XB**
Richard Pickford, Rob Weston.

1992   **Gibe Turkey**   Geoff Hornby, Mark Turnbull

1994   **Back Forest Gâteau**   Rob Mirfin

1995   **Tasmanian Tendencies**   Richard Taylor
Also claimed as Onychophagia by John H Bull.

1997   **Riding the Gravy Train, National Hysteria**
Sean Myles   *Gear placed on the lead. The latter route climbed on the day of Princess Diana's funeral.*

1997   **The Hour Glass, Morpheus, Pip**
Mark Katz

1999   **Ruth's Septic Trench**   Ruth Creamer

1990s   **Jewel of Corruption**   Julian Lines

2000   **Fist Full of Freshers, Whose Line is it Anyway**   Paul Smith, Rob Lavin

2001 July **Pants on Fire, Gallstones, Lucid Reams, Mongolian Throat Singing**   John H Bull, the latter with Kieran McCusker.

2001   **Pinnacle Buttress**   Paul Smith

2002   **Drain the Main Vein**   Justin Critchlow, Mark Sharratt (both led)

2002   **Action Trousers**   John H Bull

2003   **Bumper Cars**   Becca Ward, Paul Smith, Sam Clarke

⊙ Newstones to Back Forest Bouldering First Ascents

Captain Quark   Jon Barton, Rupert Davies, 9th November 2003

Clever Skin   Martin Boysen, early 1980s and called Elephant's Trunk. *Claimed as Clever Skin by Johnny Dawes in 1989, the latter name having stuck.*

Fielder's Wall   Johnny Dawes, March 27, 1989.

The Fin   John Allen, 1984. *Although possibly Martin Boysen, early '80s. Sit-start by John Welford, 1990s.*

Gibbering Left   Tom Leppert, 1986.

Gibbering Wreck   *Previously a top-rope problem, probably the work of Jerry Moffatt, it was soloed and named by Sam Whittaker in 1998. It turned out to have been soloed by Andy Brown in 1994, with the name Gib Torr Roof.*

Last Banana Before Sunset   Chris King, 1989.

Martin's Traverse   Martin Boysen.

Maurice Gib   Pat Rainbird, October 2003. *A long term project of local boy Andi Turner. Pat double-dynoed his way to glory under Turner's nose after making the mistake of trying the problem when out with a strong team.*

Paul's Wall   Paul Smith, 2002.

Stall   Martin Boysen, early 1980s. *Named by Johnny Dawes.*

The Churnet

5

The rock is a Triassic conglomerate.
Large sized pebbles are in abundance and
frequently snap when used, thus making the climbs
occasionally harder. The cracks are very painful
to climb and seem only to suit the masochist.

An obviously impressed crag writer's opinion
of one aspect of the Churnet's personality.

Dave Bishop on Wright's Traverse (page 241). Photo: Alex Ekins.

The Churnet Valley Crags

by Gary Gibson

*A fairytale land of deep, wooded, crag-rimmed dales
containing babbling brooks and rivers, towered over
by castles and halls. A land so Tolkienesque that one
expects Bilbo Baggins to skip round the corner singing
merrily, heading a happy band of pixies, elves and gnomes,
ready to sweep you along on one of their adventures.*

Simon Alsop, On The Edge

The Churnet Area has traditionally been seen in two distinct parts, the Upper and Lower Churnet.

The Upper Churnet Valley

including **Sharpcliffe Rocks, Belmont Hall Crags, Harston Rocks, Oldridge Pinnacle** and **Garston Rocks**

The 5 main crags of the Upper Churnet, packed into a small geographical area around the pretty village of Ipstones, all manage to have vastly different characters, and as such, give entirely different climbing experiences.

Sharpcliffe is possibly the most individual crag in the guide, its main outcrop being a huge cornice of solid conglomerate yielding climbs from VS to E5. While these grades vary a lot, the experience will not, with all the climbs being proper 'leads', calling on reserves of experience and skill, and giving due reward. The crag also has a good mid-grade bouldering circuit. Belmont Hall, while nearby, is vastly different. Two vertical faces nestling in a wooded dale, they offer a good spread of tough routes on sound clean grit. The mystical Harston Rock is also near here, a perched obelisk with a small number of very worthwhile climbs that all climbers should visit. And if you are having an 'obelisk' day out, it is a short hop from here to Oldridge Pinnacle. This rather obscure rock has, besides some easier routes, a merry band of short bold routes or tough highball problems, depending on your outlook. Lastly is the gentle Garston Rock, where the lower-grade climber can pack in a good number of interesting climbs, again, in a unique pastoral setting.

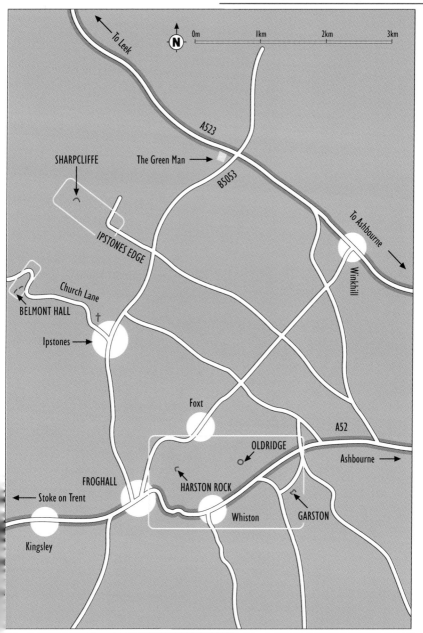

Sharpcliffe Rocks

| O.S. Ref. **SK015521** Altitude: **320m a.s.l.** |

Even for the Churnet Valley this is an eccentric crag. Nicknamed Pebblesville by its original explorers, it is a series of buttresses, some little ones of good gritstone, and one big one made from a readymix of good sandstone and bunter pebbles. The little ones offer good bouldering in good situations, while the big one offers some of the most memorable climbing in the area. Ironically, its weakness is its strength, and the sometimes harrowing nature of the climbing makes the routes memorable out of all proportion to their length.

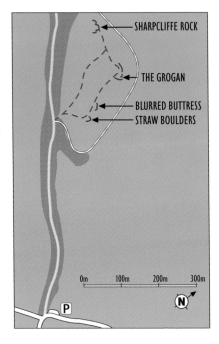

Conditions & aspect

The crag faces generally north with the front face getting early morning sunshine, and the main right wall getting it in the afternoon. Seepage is not a problem. Climbing possible year round though some of the bouldering gets green in winter.

Routes & bouldering

Eleven routes, all worthwhile. Better for extremes. Tend to be bold. Good easier bouldering (25 problems) on interesting rock, as well as one futuristic project.

Parking & approach

Park at a sharp right-hand bend. A metalled road continues straight on here into the grounds of Sharpcliffe Hall itself. Take this for 400m, then break out right over a gate into some rough open ground. 10 minutes.

Access

The rocks lie in the grounds of Sharpcliffe Hall and the owners are none too happy with climbers using these rocks. If you are asked to leave, please do so courteously.

Ⓥ *For the bouldering, turn right off the main path soon after you have crossed the gate. The first problems lie on the far side of the rhododendron ridge. The talented may wish to note a 5m block on the crest of the ridge. This has a beautiful, sharp and gruesomely overhanging arête on it, and a perfect jug at its base. However, it has no holds, and success,*

even on the stand-up version, would be a great achievement. Anyone? Just below is a large block with a through cave at its base, known as the Straw Boulders.

❶ Peep Show V0– (4a)
The left-hand crack and flake on the front face of the block.

❷ Cabana VI (5b)
Superb. The bulging right-hand flake gives a sterner test.

Ⓥ Blurred Buttress

This is the next set of boulders, 40m further on.

❸ Pebblesville V0+ (5b)
To the left of the initial crack lies this excellent problem, pulling over the bulge into a scoop. A problem just left is also possible. **Hush Puppy** V0– (4a) is the awkward wide crack to the right, and **Hot Dog** V0– (4b) is the next slanting groove.

The Sharpcliffe Arête project

④ Johnson'sville VI (5b)
Small knobs and dinks lead up the wall to the right. Gets harder ascent by ascent!

⑤ Bowcock's Chimney V0– (4a)
A classic Leek name: they had something on their mind? The chimney to the right.

⑥ Cannabis Arm V4 (6a)
Technical moves up the overhanging arête to the right.

⑦ Puffed Wheat VI (5b)
The centre of the wall to the right. The attractive right arête, on its right, is unclimbed

Ⓥ The Grogan
This is heavily sculpted, flat wall, 80m along the broad ridge. It lies on the right just before some small boulders on the top.

⑧ Gorgonzola V0 (5a)
Good moves up incipient cracks lead to the left side of the tower. The **awkward crack** to the left is V0 (5a).

⑨ Mr Grogan VI (5b)
The wall taken at its centre via pockets, pebbles and rugosities. Superb climbing.

⑩ Charlie Farley V0– (4c)
Getting even better. The shallow groove in the right-hand side of the buttress. Pockets, pebbles and buckets. An **eliminate** is possible between this problem and the arête, V1 (5b). The bulging arête direct would also be possible.

⑪ Rusks And Rye V2 (5b)
The atrocious, bulging crack on the front face of the buttress. Try it without tape.

Many possibilities lie among the jumbled rocks in the next 30m. After that distance, and around the corner, is a 6m wall with a clean tall arête.

⑫ Genetix VI (5b)
The crack in the sidewall of the buttress.

⑬ Bond It V3 (5c)
The handsome arête itself is exciting, due to its height.

⑭ Blu-Tac V2 (5c)
The left-hand side of the front face.

Ⓥ **Stickfast** V0+ (5b) is the centre of the wall. **Raven** V0– (4a) is just to the right and just left of the arête. **Spirella** V0– (4a) waltzes along the obvious break from right to left. **Meninges** (D) is a slab on the right.

Sharpcliffe Rock

The main rock now lies 100m across the broad grassy area, or is reached directly from the gate by following the main path. Grab a rope, some runners and a tube of glue! The rock is bounded on its left by a deep chimney (**Marsden's Eliminate**, M, 1973). To its left is a little prow. Following the niche through this is **Underhung Chimney** (S 4a, 1973), while climbing the right arête is a pleasant HS (**Konsolation Prize**, 1980). Next lies the main crag, with its bulging pebble infested overhangs. A difficult new route would be possible up the steep pocketed wall right of the chimney. The first route is based on the very steep front face of the rock.

⑮ Knossos E5 5c ★★★   1979
18m An impressive and uncompromising challenge taking the front face head on. Prepare yourself for limited protection and variable stability of holds. Climb up to a vague break and swing left along it before climbing the pink, pebble-dashed wall to reach a wide crack round the left arête – good large nuts. Exit frantically right and upwards on the nose of the wall. A more difficult start at 6a leads directly to the wide crack.

⑯ Krushna E4 6a ★   1980
16m Another fraught experience aiming for the prominent roof crack on the right-hand side of the front face. Climb the pink-coloured wall 5m to the right of Knossos to reach a break and then gain the impressive wide crack above. This provides a mean, hand-crushing finale.

⑰ Kenyatta E4 5c ★   1980
15m Less friable and more amenable than the last route, though more scary, up the vague right-hand arête of the front face. Climb the wall 2m to the right passing a break and awkward bulge to reach flutings. These lead more easily to the top.

⑱ Kaleidoscope E1 5a ★★   1973
16m Another Churnet classic well worth seeking out if visiting the area. Climb from the end of the little platform up and right directly up, over the bulge, and into the narrow square cut groove to finish direct. Moves are reasonable and gear exists. It remains, however, an E1 experience.

⑲ Killjoy E2 5b ★★   1979
14m Climb the wall just to the left of a diagonal crack, to gain a break. Continue slightly leftwards via a scoop to the top.

⑳ Kobold E3 5c ★   1979
14m Climb the obvious diagonal crack to reach the break. Continue directly to the top via a series of small pockets.

㉑ Kudos VS 5a   1979
8m This route starts on the highest platform. Climb a depression on the right side of the wall. A bold eliminate, **Krakatoa** (E3 5c, 1979) climbs the slab to the left, keeping left of easy ground.

㉒ Special K HVS 4c ★★   1973
18m Technically reasonable climbing giving access to some fine situations. From the platform on the right-hand side of the rock, step down to the left and follow a break across the wall to reach flutings leading to the top.

Ⓥ The main mass of Sharpcliffe Rock is bounded on the right by a pleasant undercut buttress. **Golden Sovereign** V0– (4a), is the wall to the left of the obvious undercut arête. **Doubloon** V0 (5a), the undercut arête. **Pieces of Eight** V0– (4a), the slab to the right All 1973. A number of other problems are available in this area although by this time the owner may well have thrown you off!

A small cliff with a big feel. Special K, HVS 4c, traverses the main face of Sharpcliffe Rock, with interesting moves, strange rock and great positions. Photo: Alex Ekins.

Belmont Hall Crags

O.S. Ref. **SK007504** Altitude: **190m a.s.l.**

These are a pair of steep compact buttresses set in a beautiful wooded setting, almost limestone in character, along a tranquil and picturesque little hillside overlooking Collyhole Brook. The rock is sound, and the cleaner routes are good quality. The left-hand buttress in particular has a great collection of tough extremes, and both buttresses sport mighty central crack-lines.

Conditions & aspect

The crag can be somewhat green in parts after bad weather although, as with a lot of crags in the area, a couple of dry days or a quick going over with a soft brush should return them to a climbable state. Easily worth the effort. They face north-west and get little sun. A good cool summer venue.

Routes & bouldering

Twenty three routes on vertical rock. Some good easier cracks but also some dirty ones. The harder routes tend to be better and cleaner, with technical climbing and some runouts. Limited bouldering at the bottom of the routes.

Parking & approach

From Ipstones, follow Church Lane for about 1 mile, past some sharp bends, to park at the bottom of a hill by a stream. Follow the pleasant track for 250m and the buttresses are on the hillside on the left. Five easy minutes.

Left-Hand Buttress

The more northerly of the buttresses provides the best routes on the crag. The harder routes are certainly well worth seeking out and classics of their type.

At the extreme left of the buttress are two north-facing cracks. A dirty slab to the left of these gives **Wild Frontier** *(HS 4b, 1989), and the twin cracks themselves form* **Vertigo** *(VD, 1962).*

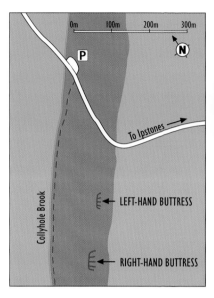

❶ Life In The Left Lane E3 5c   1986

14m Pull over the initial overlaps of Life in the Wrong Lane and continue up the rib and over the third bulge with poor protection back on the ledge below.

❷ Life in the Wrong Lane E1 5b   1979

14m Pull over the double overlap 3m right again onto the rib. Step right and climb the left-hand groove finishing leftwards.

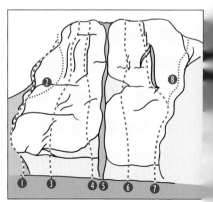

❸ The Clown E2 6a ★★ 1971

15m A fine steep little route with technical climbing and sound protection. Three metres right again a finger-hold over the lip enables access to the wall above via a mighty heave and rockover. Continue via the slabby wall to gain the central groove above, peg runner. Finish directly.

❹ The Jester E5 6a ★★ 1979

15m A superb wall pitch giving sustained and varied climbing. Climb the roof just to the left of the prominent chimney, an easier entry than The Clown. The bold face and arête above lead into the steepening crack in the upper face. This gives a fitting finale.

❺ Kneewrecker Chimney HVS 4c ★★ 1962

15m The powerful central crack of the buttress is a classic of its type. Climb the narrowing cleft between the buttocks of the crag and battle with the holly tree towards its top.

❻ Face E5 6b ★★ 1986

15m Superb. The immaculate clean wall to the right leads boldly to a break and peg runner in the wall above. Difficult moves past this lead onto a flake and a bold finale on the magnificent upper wall.

❼ The Joker E3 6a ★ 1971

15m Another steep and well-protected line. From 6m up the slanting groove, swing up and left into the base of a steeper groove. Climb this with difficulty at first to an easier and exposed finish.

❽ Deadwood Groove HVS 4c 1962

11m The obvious slanting groove is tricky at its finish. Sparsely protected. ☑A difficult problem on the short wall to the right provides **Allen's Fingers** V4 (6a).

❾ Deadwood Crack VS 4c 1962

11m The obvious crack right again. Bypassing the rotten tree leads to a rotten finish.

❿ Crimes of Passion E4 6a 1982

11m A technically testing pitch up the vague rampline to the right. From the obvious hole finish directly up the slab. Bold but dirty. V3.

Right-Hand Buttress

Situated 100m downstream and clearly identified by its central cave. This gives a number of very worthwhile pitches although the first few routes are in a poor state due to an overgrowth of heather and lichen. The rest of the routes here are generally cleaner.

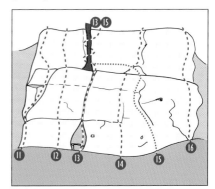

The first routes are situated on the left-hand wall of the buttress. The filthy crack and bulge above a cave at the left-hand side of the buttress give **Sale's Bulge** (VD, 1962). The wide crack to the right of this is **Twisting Crack** (D, 1962). Just to the right a shallow groove, thin crack and nose give **No Pegs Please, We're British** (HVS 4c, 1989), and the crack right again is **Hassall's Crack** (VD, 1962).

⓫ Cave Rib VS 4b 1962

12m The prominent rib finishing right around the overhang.

⓬ Flake Escape E2 5c 1989

8m The wall between Cave Rib and Cave Crack via an obvious flake. Reachy.

⓭ Cave Crack VS 4b ★ 1962

11m From the obvious cave, bridge out and struggle up the prominent crack-line to a difficult exit onto the ledge. The finish necessitates a bizarre manoeuvre involving the tree. The initial crack can be climbed from the back of the cave at 5c.

Matt Ekins delves into the depths of Kneewrecker Chimney, HVS 4c, Belmont Hall Crags (page 211). Photo: Alex Ekins.

⑭ Distant Runners E3 5c ★   1989
11m A very good pitch. The thin crack-line to the right gives access to the ledge. The finishing groove contains a peg runner and is sometimes dirty.

⑮ Flake Traverse HS   1962
15m A flake 3m to the right leads to a ledge. Traverse left and finish via Cave Crack.

⑯ Wigglette HVS 5a   1962
11m The blunt arête to the right. Climbed on its left-hand side to a break from where a bulge and slab lead to the top.

⑰ In Days of Hold E2 6b   1989
6m The short right-hand arête of the flat face to the right has a desperate start but soon eases.

Flintmill Buttress, Consallforge

O.S. Ref. **SK004484**   Altitude: **220m a.s.l.**

This is a large crag bristling with overhangs and cloaked in masses of vegetation from glorious moss beds to large hanging vines. The routes (roots?) now resemble their original state before they were gardened and whilst an impressive venue, the cliff will require major excavations before its routes can be reascended. The best approach is from the A52, Stoke to Ashbourne road. A small lane runs between Kingsley and Kingsley Moor, through the villages of Hollins, Hazles and Hazles Cross. Between the latter two a public footpath runs down to Consallforge and is well marked.

At the left-hand end of the crag, a disjointed groove merges into an overhanging and very vegetated chimney. This is the **Constant Grumble** (HVS, 1970). **Grumbling Wall** (VS, 1977) lies to its left. Two aid routes tackle the overhangs to the right. **Miller's Melody** (A2) is the smaller overhang whilst **Death Wish** (A3, 1974) is the big roof. Nine metres right again are twin grooves. **Full Frontal** (HVS, 1971) follows the right-hand groove, with a point of aid along the

way; **Indecent Exposure** (HVS, 1977) is a more direct version with even more aid; **Manifesto** (HVS, 1970) struggles past the tree to the right; **Peeping Tom** (HVS, 1978) is the line to the right; **Nosey Parker** (E1, 1971) climbs a crack 5m to the right, 2 pegs for aid; 5m right again, **The Missus** (VS, 1971) is based on the slab and chimney; **Spearhead** is the last line (thankfully) taking the buttress right of the gully.

Price's Cave Crag

From the Black Lion Inn at Consallforge, follow the Devil's Staircase, which leads towards Belmont Hall. Part way up these steps a prominent arête is visible: **Here Be Dragons** (E2 5c, 1990) starts from a block on the right; climb the arête mainly on its steeper right-hand side. An in-situ thread in a pocket above an overlap provides the only worthwhile protection although a low side-runner was used to safeguard the initial moves.

Wetley Rocks

These lie on the northern side of the Stone to Leek road. Whilst they have been climbed on over the years, they offer little for the accomplished climber. A good ridge is available at the Difficult standard to the left of the service station.

Harston Rocks

by Stuart Millis and Gary Gibson

O.S. Ref. **SK032477**   Altitude: **185m a.s.l.**

Harston Rock is the Upper Churnet's *pièce de résistance*, offering a handful of very fine routes on good rock with an imposing position above a beautiful and heavily wooded valley floor. The open nature lends itself to cleanliness not seen on the neighbouring buttresses, and its inspiring steepness has caused it to be home to the area's two hardest climbs. The small bluffs littered along the rim of the valley do not get much sunshine and consequently the degrees of moss and greenery that adorn the lesser buttress can be uninspiring.

Conditions & aspect

The crags are north-facing and get little sun, leaving the smaller buttresses unpleasant. The main rock is very clean and gets little seepage, even in winter. Limited sunshine.

Routes & bouldering

Fifty five routes, but mainly in dubious condition. Ten routes on the main rock offer great climbs from HVS to E7. Limited bouldering at the bottom of the routes.

Parking & approach

Park in the small lay-by on the outskirts of Whiston. Walk back down the hill to the sharp bend and follow a farm track to its end at a farmhouse. The commencement of the cliffs lies 25m up the hill to the right and is gained via an obvious path through the woods. Harston Rock is found by carrying on down the main track for 500m, where it can be seen 30m up on the right. Approach: 10–15 minutes.

Access

Access is not a problem as long as a courteous attitude is undertaken and a polite request is made at the farmhouse at the end of the track.

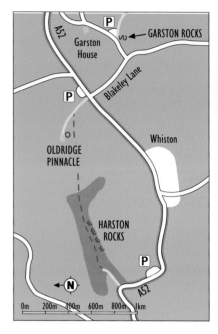

Devil's Rock

An obvious bulging nose protrudes through the trees and offers a tapering wall to its left.

❶ The Nose HVS 5b ★ 1970
8m Two starts, both steep, give access to the broad groove on the front of the nose. This leads to an awkward finish. The overgrown slab to the right once gave **Saunter** (VD, 1952).

❷ The Cheek VS 5a 1970
8m Climb the tricky wall just left of the arête and finish more easily. Originally this was gained via a traverse in from The Nose.

Devil's Crack (S, 1952) is a crack in the tapering wall. **Rugosity** (S 4a, 1952) is just to the left, while **Footpath** (VD, 1952), is the chippings left again. **Alternative**

Ulster (4b, 1978) is the last line. **Saunter** (S, 1952) traversed the rock.

Gib Buttress

This lies 25m beyond the initial buttress, a shelf of rock on the left providing an obvious feature. **Wave** (D) takes the right wall and bulge. **Ripple** (VD) lies just right of the corner via a groove. **Crest** (VD) climbs a crack to the shelf and then the slab above. **Breaks** (VD) takes the corner, then traverses left and up via a crack and wall. **Backwash** (VD) climbs the corner, crack and wall. All 1952.

Biscay Buttress

The buttress below and to the left provides a bay with a prominent protruding nose to its left. The majority of the routes are in disrepair. The bay to the right of the prow contains **Emerald Groove** (VD, 1952), the right corner. The easy groove on the right wall is **As You Like It** (M, 1952). **Flake Wall** (HS, 1952) is the flake to the left, **Original Route** (VS,1952), the major corner to the left again. **The Web** (HS, 1952) is the wall left of the corner finishing left of the prow. The prow itself is **Black Widow** (E3 5c, 1970s), which starts up the right-hand side then swings round left to finish. **Emerald Wall** (VD, 1952) climbs the wall below the prow and then the corner and wall on the right. **Corner Traverse** (D, 1952) traverses the wall at half height.

Pinnacle Buttress

This is the next bottle-shaped buttress. **Moore's Crack** (D, 1952) climbs the crack at the top of the gully, and **The Sting** (E1 5a, 1970s) is the shallow groove to the left. **Titan's Wall** (E2 5a, 1952) is the terrifying front headwall gained from the right. The direct start is 5b. **Ostentation** (E2 5a, 1970) is the even more terrifying wall to the left. **Fandango** (HS, 1952) traverses left from Ostentation to finish on pockets. **Magenta Corner** (HS, 1952) gains and climbs the upper pinnacle from below. **Glyph** (S, 1952) gains the same pinnacle via a crack to the left and **Rotondas** (S, 1952) climbs the wall on pockets left again. In the land to the left are three isolated buttresses, with a single route on each. They are **Oak Spur** (D, 1952), **Moss Rose** (VD, 1952), and **Frequency** (S, 1952). They are of little interest and the land is very overgrown.

Cave Buttress

Cave Buttress comes next. **Vereker's Venture** (VS 5a, 1952) endeavours to climb the wall's right edge. **Taming of the Shrew** (HVS 5c, 1978) steps left from Vereker's Venture to climb the bulge and wall. **Much Ado About Nothing** ★ (E3 6a, 1978) is the thin crack just right of the cave, by far the best climb on this area of rock. **The Cave Crack** (S, 1952), obvious by name and a struggle by nature. **Palsy Wall** (E2 5c, 1970s) is the scooped wall to the left finishing on pockets. **Palpitation** (HVD, 1952) is the corner on the front face to a finish off right. **Shelf Route** (HVD, 1952) climbs direct up the left extremity of the buttress.

Technician's Wall

One hundred metres left again is a small wall cloaked in greenery and hardly worthy of mention. **The Technician** (5a, 1978) climbs the right-hand wall; **Tiptoe** (HVD, 1952) lies just right of the central chimney; **Diagonal Crack** (D, 1952) is the chimney; **Clam** (5b, 1952), the rounded left arête; **Limpet** (4a, 1952), the left-hand face is taken direct; **Megalomania** (5b, 1978) traverses from left to right.

Harston Rock

One hundred metres left (north) of Technician's Wall is the bastion of Upper Churnet climbing, a 20m high tower of the best quality sandstone, set amongst trees on an idyllic bracken-clad hillside. The rock is sound and despite its wooded setting, is generally free from any lichens. The overlaps at the back of the pinnacle lead to the summit and also provide the easiest means of descent.

❸ Via Trita E1 5a ★ 1952
14m A good starting point. Climb the crack in the right-hand side of the south face and make a tricky mantelshelf to gain a ledge, poor protection. The upper wall gives delightful climbing on a series of ripples.

❹ The Helix HVS 5a ★★★ 1952
22m An excellent outing, something of an expedition for gritstone, spiralling around the pinnacle. From a point 3m up Via Trita, traverse left to an overlap. Continue leftwards to a small ledge and then climb a slab to gain a horizontal break. Follow this leftwards across the exposed front face to finish up a groove above the far arête.

❺ EMS E1 5c 1990
18m Climb the wall just to the left continuing through an overlap to a small ledge. The steep wall above via a flake provides the crux.

❻ Melancholy Man E2 5c ★ 1978
14m An eliminate based on the initial part of the Helix leads to a difficult finale. Starting just left of Via Trita, traverse left across a small slab. Pull onto

Leon Zablocki on The Helix, HVS 5a (page 215),
a fine spiral of the mythical Harston Rock,
where imposing territory is covered at
a reasonable standard. Photo: Alex Ekins.

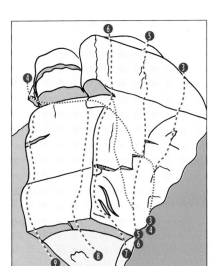

The **Harston crags**

were 'discovered' by members of the Oread Mountaineering Club in the spring of 1951. The second assault on the crags was in early 1952. Under the direction of Penlington and armed with spades and brushes, they cleaned out the majority of the routes.

1973 Staffordshire Grit Guide

the hanging slab above and climb it to a break. Step right to finish via the steepening wall.

7 DNA E4 6a ★★   1977

18m A classic of the late 1970s and a typical sandbag of its time. Fine, scary climbing via the right arête of the front face. Gain the undercut scoop in the prow by a series of awkward moves. Leave the scoop on the left using a horizontal break, then make technical moves up the rib to the next break: protection, though available, does not inspire confidence. Finish via the steepening wall of Melancholy Man.

8 Pair O' Genes E7 6c ★★   1999

18m Superb, technical and bold climbing up the centre of the front face. Start 3m left of DNA. Climb to the overhang and make desperate moves through it to gain the steep slab above. Continue precariously to gain the horizontal break and the sanctuary of an *in-situ* thread runner. Finish directly above this or make a left-hand finish at 7a.

9 One Chromosome's Missing

E7 6b ★★★   1984

18m A gritstone gem to rival any in the Peak District, and one of the first routes of its grade in the country. The right-hand side of the left arête of the front face offers absorbing technical climbing in a serious position. A cunning Rock 3 may or may not protect the upper section.

10 The Boysen-Carrington Route

E6 6b ★★   1990s

20m A high-quality eliminate, combining sections of the previous two desperates to find a more reasonable way up the wall. Climb the arête of One Chromosome to the break. Traverse right to the Weetabix thread on Pair O' Genes to finish up this.

11 The Impending Doom E4 5c ★★   1970

18m A fine steep pitch up the flakes in the left-hand side of the arête leads to a difficult rounded finish. Protection is barely adequate.

12 Old King Cole E5 6b ★★   1990

16m A superb, tough route, featuring steep and powerful climbing up the centre of the clean north wall of the obelisk. The thin discontinuous crack in the steep tower is gained via a long reach and followed with fine moves to its end. The final wall provides a fitting climax.

13 Hatscheck's Groove HVS 5a ★   1952

14m The broken crack to the left leads to a large ledge. The shallow groove above gives a difficult and airy finish.

Harston Quarry exists down and to the left and is not worth visiting.

Oldridge Pinnacle

O.S. Ref. **SK043480** Altitude: **250m a.s.l.**

A strangely-positioned gritstone obelisk standing amidst lush open pasture in fields. There are no easy routes here and the hardest of these are esoteric classics of their type. These tough extremes, however, will give well-spotted and well-padded boulderers a handful of superb highballs, all above a perfect landing. You are certainly going to be on your own here save for a watchful eye from the residents of the local farm whose house you can peer into from atop the pinnacle!

Conditions & aspect

The north-facing side is very green and uninviting. The south gets lots of sun, and is where the better climbing is. Sheltered, and climbable all year.

Routes & bouldering

Eleven routes, of which half are better seen as high boulder problems (i.e. mats and spotters advised).

Parking & approach

Take a left turn a half a mile after passing through the village of Whiston. This track leads to a farm tucked in alongside the pinnacle. Ask the farmer for permission to climb as a matter of courtesy. It will normally be granted. Approach: 10 seconds. An old railway line leads from here to Harston Rock, a few hundred metres away.

① The South-West Crack VS 4b   1952
6m The awkward fissure lying to the left of the dry-stone wall on the west face.

② Boats for Hire E4 6a ★   1984
6m The left-hand arête of the overhanging south face gives a route with a split personality. The initial crack proves very, very steep. Traverse left above the dry-stone wall to finish delicately via the bulging slab. **Ⓥ** Highball V5 for the first half.

③ The Fatalist's Canoe E4 6a ★★   1986
6m From the flake just right, climb upwards and leftwards. Finish just left of the next route. **Ⓥ** Highball V4.

④ The Gateless Gate E3 6a ★★   1978
6m The central line on the face is strenuous and frustrating. Starting at a crack and hole, move up and slightly left to a tough well-protected finish. **Ⓥ** Highball V4. A more direct, though desperate, right-hand finish would also be possible for the over-strong.

⑤ Qui Vive E3 6a ★★   1978
6m The right-hand arête leads, via a series of rock-overs, to a thread runner and obligatory rounded finish, crux. **Ⓥ** Highball V4.

⑦ South-East Crack VS 4a ★   1952
7m The wide corner-crack provides the easiest route on the pinnacle and the best means of descent.

The square-cut arête directly to the right is **Ivanhoe** (VS 4c, 1978). **Nom De Guerre** (E1 5b, 1978) is the thin crack just to the right of the arête. **The North Face** (VS 4b ★, 1952) gains the top of the boulder in the centre of the face. Finish by climbing the thin crack above. **Tour De Force** (E1 5b, 1978) is the very green north face just to the left of Battle Royal. Move up and then right to a hidden hole on the arête. Use this to gain a shelf and finish up the wall above. **Battle Royal** itself (E3 5c, 1978) is the arête facing the farm with the crux leaving the small groove.

Garston Rocks

O.S. Ref. **SKI05476**   Altitude: **240m a.s.l.**

This is a pleasant crag composed of good quality sandstone with weathered features and holds. Although there is the odd friable section, the main interest in this crag lies in its easier routes with the odd problem thrown in for good measure.

Conditions & aspect

Due to its aspect, many of the routes have become rather green during wetter periods. This can be rectified in a good drying wind with a soft brush. The crag faces north-west and gets little sun.

Routes & bouldering

Twenty routes, with the odd problem thrown in. Ideally suited to the lower-grade climber.

Parking & approach

Turn left off Blakeley Lane to limited parking below the crag.

Access

Access is a little protracted but now possible. Continue along the road for 200m to a farm building on the left (Garston House): this is just before a right turn. Ask permission from the farmer, Mr Rawlinson, before climbing and please remember to treat the walls below the cliff with respect (i.e. don't scramble over them, use the gate).

❶ Tequila Sunrise HVS 5a ★   1978
8m The prominent knife-edge arête, starting awkwardly on the right. **Ⓥ** The bouldery wall to the right is **White Widow** V3 (6a).

❷ Runaway E2 5c   1978
8m The difficult bulging left-hand wall of the gully.

❸ Feet of Strength HS 4a   1952
6m The first wide crack on the left-hand side of the gully proves a struggle.

❹ The Arête S ★★   1952
12m A superb route taking the prominent arête with a huge thread runner at half-height. Pass through the initial scoop, starting right or left, and continue past the thread to a mantelshelf finish. Classic stuff.

❺ Hole and Corner Crack S   1952
9m The crack to the left with a cave at half-height. The wall and scoop to the right can be climbed at HVS 5a (**Technocrat**, 1978).

❻ Don Quixote E2 6a ★   1978
11m A super little problem. A porthole to the left enables a scoop to be gained, followed all too briefly by a wall.

❼ Skull Crack S ★   1952
11m Another little gem taking the awkward wide crack.

❽ The Chute VD   1952
8m The pleasant open corner. Moving right from the corner to pass a break to gain the top via a vague rib is **Tricky Woo** (HVS 5a, 1978). **Ⓥ** A **direct start** goes at V2 (6a). The left arête of the corner is **Pillow of Wind** (VS 4b, 1978).

❾ One Knight Stand HVS 5a   1978
6m Climb directly up the centre of the next wall. The start is delicate, the rest much easier.

❿ The Bishop's Move VS 4a ★   1952
9m Move up just to the left and follow the slanting crack rightwards to finish just left of the corner. Excellent.

⓫ All the King's Horses HS 4a   1978
18m Even this cliff gets the girdle-traverse! From the arête of The Bishop's Move continue into Tricky Woo and on into Hole and Corner Crack. Finish just to the right of this.

At the back of the bay is a good bouldering wall full of rugosities and easy problems. The following routes are on the left-hand wall of the bay. **Larva Wall** (VD, 1952) is a slab and overhang on the right extremity of the buttress. **The Stadium** (HVS 5b, 1978) features thin moves over a bulge to the left leading onto an easier short slab. **Left Arête** (S, 1952) has an awkward start leading onto the obvious feature.

⑫ Cave Wall VD   1952
8m Climb up to the obvious cave on the left wall. Exit onto the wall above and use thin cracks to gain a finishing bulge.

⑬ Rainbow Recess VD   1952
8m Gain a ledge 2m to the left, then step right and up to finish.

⑭ Triack HS 4a   1952
6m A series of cracks on the left extremity of the buttress.

Ⓥ *The track running eastwards leads past the farm to a field containing a number of boulders and suitable problems. The largest of the boulders offers* **The Last Post** *V1 (5b), via its arête.*

The Lower Churnet Valley

including **Stoney Dale Quarry, Cotton Bank Crag, Great Gate Buttress, Peakstone Rock, Castle Crag, Park Banks Crags & Ina's Rock, Rake's Dale, Toothill Rock, Dimmings Dale, Wright's Rock, Peakstone Inn Amphitheatre, Ousal Dale, Wootton Lodge**

This is a collection of crags lying roughly along the banks of the River Churnet between the picturesque villages of Oakamoor and Alton, and all within screaming distance of the mighty Alton Towers. The crags vary greatly in height, quality and character, from the towering ferocity of Great Gate Buttress, with powerful climbs of up to E7 calling for the boldest of leads, to small sit-down boulder problems on Cottage Rocks; from the crumbling horror of Castle Crag to the secluded calm of Park Banks Crags. The settings are pretty and varied, being amongst pastoral farmland, wooded hillsides, or rhododendron-jewelled river-banks. Whilst not to everyone's taste, the Lower Churnet has tremendous variety for climbers in search of adventure. We know you're out there!

Routes
Many of the routes, indeed, many of the crags in the area, are overgrown, crumbling, or both. This has caused many to write the whole area off. However every effort has been made to ensure that the descriptions here reflect the current state of routes, not how they were after being cleaned 20 years ago. To this end, routes that are in disrepair have been relegated to mere mentions in order to preserve the

historical record. The best crags to visit for routes are Great Gate Buttress, Stoney Dale Quarry, Ina's Rock, Park Banks Crags and Lord's Buttress.

Ⓥ Bouldering
The Lower Churnet is becoming rightly popular with boulderers. The main crags, Ousal Crag, Cottage Rocks, Wright's Rock, Long Wall Gentleman's Rock and Peakstone Rock, all offer unique fingery bouldering on very unusual rock, with sustained fitness-testing traverses being a speciality. These crags are places that, once visited, tend to be somewhere that boulderers will return to again and again. Many of them are rainproof (while they can also suffer from condensation) and, being north-facing, offer a good alternative on hot weather. The fact that they are free from midges also makes them a good summer option. Most of the crags can be visited in a single session.

Food & accommodation
The Rambler's Retreat serves great food including chips, cake and coffee, and is ideally situated at the bottom of Dimmings Dale. For the thirsty, pubs are available in Alton, Oakamoor as well as the Peakstone Inn. There is a campsite in Cotton, on the B5417 north of Oakamoor.

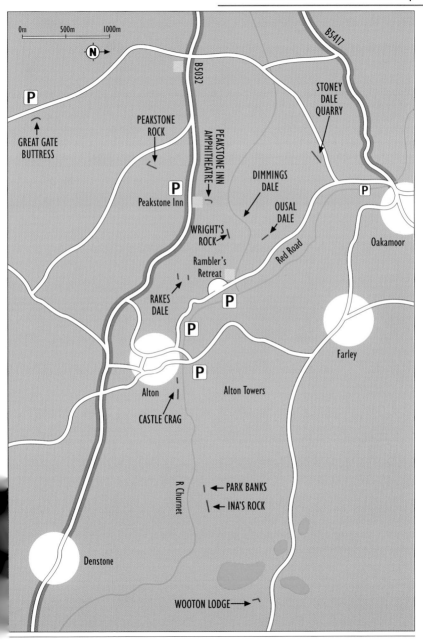

0m   500m   1000m

N

P

GREAT GATE
BUTTRESS

PEAKSTONE
ROCK

B5032

PEAKSTONE INN
AMPHITHEATRE

STONEY
DALE
QUARRY

B5417

P

Peakstone Inn

DIMMINGS
DALE

OUSAL
DALE

P

Oakamoor

WRIGHT'S
ROCK

Red Road

Rambler's
Retreat

P

RAKES
DALE

P

P

Alton

Alton Towers

Farley

CASTLE CRAG

R Churnet

◄— PARK BANKS

◄— INA'S ROCK

Denstone

WOOTON LODGE ——►

Stoney Dale Quarry, Lion Rock

O.S. Ref. **SK048439**   Altitude: **175m a.s.l.**

These two crags, while not very far apart, have very different character. The main quarry is home to a fair number of vertical and technical challenges, both routes and bouldering. It is set amongst trees, and while it has some routes that are unclimbable, it has others that are mainly clean. The latter would need only a quick brushing to return them to a good state. Lion Rock, by contrast, is a small and very overhanging natural buttress. A few easy routes lie either side, but for anyone able of climbing E6, it is a must-visit crag.

holds or fine arêtes. Lion Rock is natural overhanging fare.

Parking & approach

Park at the large car-park at the old station, which is on the south side of Oakamoor. Walk down the road for 200m to the Red Road. Follow this for 50m, then veer uphill on a little track just before the brick wall (built by prisoners from Moor Court in the late 1800s). Go right after 30m and follow a footpath to the quarry, comprising 2 right angled vertical walls, 300m away. Approach 15 minutes. The other venues here are to the left of the main quarry, roughly along the ridge running north-east, but are most easily found with reference to the quarry.

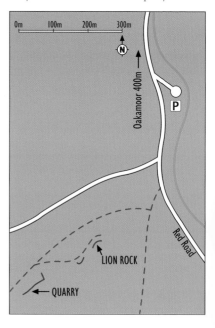

Conditions & aspect

Crags face north-east, and are not very sunny. All the routes that are climbable come into condition quite quickly. A soft brush is useful.

Routes & bouldering

Thirty five routes, with the harder ones generally being better. A number of worthwhile boulder problems on a vertical wall. The main quarry is good vertical sandstone, with climbing on small

The routes are described from left to right, starting at the left of the long flat wall (Robin Hood Wall). **Chiropodist's Nightmare** (D, 1989) is the left arête gained from the right. Moving diagonally rightwards from the arête to gain a ledge is a filthy HVS 5a (**Klangerman**, 1990). **Maid Marion** (E1 5c, 1979) is the wall to the right, starting from the letterbox. Dirty.

The next climbs lie on the attractive vertical wall to the right. These are a combination of routes that go all the way to the top, some of which can be done as boulder problems, and shorter problems. The climbing is more technical and fingery than powerful, featuring poor sloping finger edges and disappointing pockets. The wall doesn't seep much, although a soft brush may be useful.

❶ Gain Entry To Your Soul E3 6b   1990s
9m The superb little wall to the right (and just left of Robin Hood) yields with a difficult start. **Ⓥ** The first moves alone are V4 (6b).

❷ Robin Hood E3 6b ★   1979
9m Gain the bow-shaped crack in the wall below the big tree with difficulty. This gives an easier finish. **Ⓥ** The moves to the break are V4 (6b).

❸ Cad Cam Warrior E5 6a ★   1990
9m E3 if you have a size 6 cam! Starting at a deep slot a few metres right, sustained climbing leads up the wall with trying moves to stand in the break. Step right to reach a good hold, then move up and left to finish.

❹ Friar Muck E1 6b ★   1979
9m Start 12m left of the corner, below a prominent crack. Difficult moves up the very vague rib gain a break. Finish up the crack. **Ⓥ** The moves to the break are V3 (6b). Another problem, in a similarly technical vein, climbs **the wall** 1m left; V3 (6a). A long arduous **traverse** is possible from here to the ledges near the left end of the wall.

The next routes are on the right of the main mucky corner crack, and near a little arête.

❺ Cave Crack E1 5b   1980
12m Dirty holds in the mossy groove to the left gain a cave. The difficult and dirty crack above leads to a sandy finish. **Long Lankin** (E1 5b, 1980) starts up this route, then gains and climbs the repulsive crack to the left. The direct start is also repulsive.

❻ Doina Da J'al E4 6a ★★   1979
9m One of the better routes in the quarry, but still requires cleaning. The arête is taken initially on its right-hand side to the break. Finish boldly on its left-hand side. Taking the arête on its left side has been nicknamed **The Brazilian** (E4 5c, 1987), while climbing it all the way on the right is…

❼ Your Own Undoing E4 6a ★★   2002
9m A thrilling variation on the last route is to climb the arête on its right side all the way. A very enjoyable route, although bold, despite a runner just below half-height.

❽ Longstop E2 5c   1983
10m The corner to the right gives a good pitch but is currently in a filthy condition. Peg runner at half-height. **Little Nikki** (E1 5c, 1980) is the prominent crack 4m right, with easy climbing to an impasse at a peg runner. Once the sandy shelf is gained finish leftwards. Two routes existed to the right, but are now in a state of disrepair: **My Mother is a Rhinoceros** (E3 6a, 1990) is the wall 2m right, and **General Accident** (E1 5a, 1989) is the vaguely scooped wall 6m left of the arête.

❾ Dance of the Flies E2 5c ★★   1979
18m Good edgy climbing. The wall 1m left of the arête, when clean, is one of the best routes in the quarry. A poor peg protects.

❿ Sole Survivor E6 6b ★★★   2002
18m The Master's Edge of Staffordshire. The eye-catching arête taken on its right-hand side. Initially desperate moves gain a good hold, peg – this can be avoided on the left and stepping right. Superb lay-backing gains a good edge, peg, and the final, crux moves to gain good holds and the top. For the tall, the peg on the left can just about be reached.

The bay to the right is bounded by two blank, unclimbed corners. The dirty crack in-between is **Pegger's Original** (A2, pre-1970).

The Little Quarry

On returning back down the track, after 25m, a vague track leads off to the right. This leads into a small quarry.

⑩ Short Ride V0 (5b) is the pleasant left arête. **The Whirling Pit** V0 (5b) is the wall just left of the arête while **Lisa Lust** V0– (4a) is the wall further left via a shallow scoop. **Roger Melly** V0– (4b) is the centre of the wall to the right of the arête. **Billy the Fish** V0– (4b) takes the central corner. **Fat Slags** V3 (6a) climbs the right wall of the corner. The hanging arête above the cave is unclimbed.

Lion Rock

This is a compact, isolated but very impressive piece of rock tucked away in the trees beyond the quarry. It doesn't have many routes, but one is among the best hard routes in Staffordshire. To get there, exit left from The Little Quarry, then go down a slight path leading to the crag, which is just visible, 50m away.

The routes are described from right to left. On the right-hand side of the buttress dirty twin cracks and a wide crack above provide **Evensong** (VD, 1972). Diagonally leftwards and up via a slab left of this is **Psalm** (S, 1972). **Magnificat** (S, 1972) is the overhanging crack bounding the nose on its right-hand side. The corner above is easier. A good problem (V1, 5c) leads to the roof 2m to the left.

⑪ Hand Jive E6 6a ★   1979
18m An incredibly spectacular and bold route with creaking flakes and little by way of worthwhile protection. Reach and follow the flake across the overhang to the right-hand side of the lip. Fingery pulls and a slap lead to a short groove on the left and top.

⑫ The Pride E6 6b ★★★   1988
18m A brilliant pitch of upside-down spacewalking. Reasonable protection and just merits the grade. Climb the flake to the left-hand side of the roof, then make an intimidating series of moves rightwards to, and along the lip and up the headwall to gain the top.

⑬ Rocking Stone Crack HS 4a ★   1972
10m The obvious layback crack to the left. Pleasant. The blunt rib to the left is **Rocket to 'em** (HVS 5c, 2002), while a dirty corner to the left gives **Descant** (HS 4a, 1972). **Canticle** (VS 4c, 1979) takes the steep arête to the left stepping right after 3m and up via the short diagonal crack. Clean and worthwhile. The mossy unprotected wall to the right is **Ex-Lion Tamer** (HVS 5a, 1990).

Well-Hidden Buttress

Another 200m left is a superb buttress well-hidden in the trees. A prominent feature here is the capping overhang with a prominent sloping ledge beneath. Both the routes here are of good quality but will need cleaning before an ascent can be made.

⑭ Monk's Blues E3 5c ★   1988
9m Climb the gently leaning wall to gain the ledge and surmount the final overlap utilising a small sapling.

⑮ The High Priest E4 6a ★   1988
9m The steep wall to the left exiting via a short groove. A good runner in the slot protects the crux.

Cotton Bank Crag

O.S. Ref. **SK058463** Altitude: **260m a.s.l.**

A moss-enveloped boulder lurking in a dark wood on a steep bramble-choked slope. Currently unclimbable. Beneath the upholstery lies what would be quite an impressive slab but unfortunately cleaning would be a Herculean and, probably, ecologically unsound operation.

Conditions & aspect
North facing, and shaded by trees.

Routes & bouldering
More famous for the wit of its names than the quality, or indeed, the possibility of its climbing.

Parking & approach

If you really must see it, approach from Garston Rocks by continuing along the track on the left for approximately 1 mile, passing a farm, until a boulder adjacent to the track is reached on the right, a few hundred metres from Cotton Bank Farm. From here, the keen-eyed will spot the boulder through the trees, although, as mentioned, it is well camouflaged. Oakamoor-based naturalists may also reach it by a 25 minute walk.

From left to right, the routes were: **Rum Punch** (VS 4b), the groove and overhang left of the chimney; **A Scent of Lamb** (D), the narrow slab just right; **Barriers in Slime** (HVS 5a), the left arête of the main slab; **Porkstorm** (E1 5b), the centre of the slab; **Henry Hothead Realises that Being the Author of your Own Broken Ankle Can be Very Embarrassing** (E1 5b), the slab just to the right, passing a small overlap; **Poisonous Pieman** (VS 4c), the slab and crack just right again. All 1990.

Great Gate Buttress

O.S. Ref. **SK047410**   Altitude: **180m a.s.l.**

There's steep, and then there's steep. Then there's Great Gate Buttress. This sickeningly overhanging buttress, nestled among innocent farmland to the south of the River Churnet, has only recently been 'discovered', but already holds a fistful of the most challenging climbs in the area. You better be at least a world champion if you think you're going to have a chance here.

Conditions & aspect

Walls face north and west. The north wall is a little greener, and takes a while to dry. The west wall gets some late afternoon and evening sun, and is usually very clean. It is located among tall trees. A good option in warmer weather.

Routes & bouldering

Only 5 routes, but you are unlikely to run out of things to do. All steep and long, physical and serious. No bouldering.

Parking & approach

On the B5032, go south at Threapwood (by The Highwayman Pub, the ultimate rock venue). Pass 2 farms on the left, and park at a recessed gate 400m after the second (Lightoaks Farm). This gate is by some pools, and 1.3 miles from The Highwayman, and a friendly pony lives in the field. Go over the gate and follow the little stream on the left for 80m. Contour up into the woods to find the buttress. Approach 2 minutes.

Access
The ownership of these crags is unknown and best left undiscovered. Please keep a low profile, and if asked to leave, then do so politely.

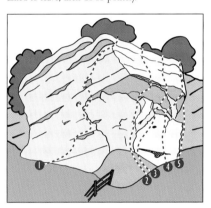

❶ Moov Over   E7 6c   ★★★   1990s

18m The hardest climbing in the area in the most exposed situation in Staffordshire. Gain the obvious left-facing flake from the left, then the break running across the buttress. Traverse right on this until below a peg runner in the next break. Difficult moves above this lead to two pegs below the final bulge. Move gingerly rightwards to pull over.

❷ Pull the Udder One   E6 6b   ★★   1990s

12m Begin on the front face 5m right of the fence and just left of a right-facing flake. A difficult start past a peg runner leads to sustained climbing directly up the wall. Continue direct through the overlap above. Small cams protect.

❸ Black and White E5 5c ★ 1990s

12m Climb the right-facing flake and swing up and left to the break. Ease through the overlap on a dinner-plate hold and with poor protection.

❹ Curd be Cheese E6 6a ★★ 1990s

12m Climbs through the heavily-holed bulge to the right again finishing by a stern pull over from the hanging arête. Limited protection.

❺ John's Route E3 6a ★ 1990s

11m Climb between the breaks on the right-hand side of the crag starting via a short arête. Well-protected.

Peakstone Rock

O.S. Ref. **SK052422** Altitude: **185m a.s.l.**

This is a peculiar group of rocks and buttresses forming a small ridge with a pinnacle halfway along, situated on the south side of a shallow hollow on Alton Common. The eastern side of the right is fairly loose and the west face is a bulging wall. However, interest is concentrated on the south face. The climbing is mainly on pebbles, generally fairly solid, and gives unique and fingery climbing.

Conditions & aspect

The crag dries quickly, and is ideal for an evening visit. It gets sun in afternoon and evening.

Routes & bouldering

The climbs, in the main, are probably best enjoyed as highball boulder problems, i.e. with a mat and spotter. Landings are generally very good.

Parking & approach

The crag is very difficult to locate on the first or subsequent visits! Park in the Peakstone Inn car park (the owners don't seem to mind, especially when you buy a pint afterwards). Walk along the road for 300m (towards Cheadle), then follow a farm track, past a bungalow to a farm at the end. The cliff is across the field to the right some 400m away. Permission at the local farm should be requested and

this has always been granted. Since a public footpath passes the cliff, it would be very difficult not to. Beware electric fences. Climbs are described left to right, starting on the wall left of the central corner-crack (Afrodizzycrack). Approach: 10 minutes.

❶ My Arse E4 6a† ★ 1990s

13m A big route on a little crag. The left-hand side of the buttress leads to the front face of the pinnacle. Start at the arête, being the junction between the overhanging and off vertical, 3m left of an elder tree. A steep start leads to increasingly worrying moves trending rightwards across the wall to a welcome breather below the overhung pinnacle. Attack the right-hand edge of this to an alarming and sandy finish.

❷ Time's Arrow E4 6a 1979

9m Climb the scoop 3m left of the corner moving left to a break below a roof. Step left and pull over the bulge using a jug and finish up the slab above. Hard.

❸ Afrodizzycrack HVS 5a 1971

8m The corner proves awkward.

❹ Five Thousand Volts E1 5c ★ 1979

7m Worthwhile. Starting 3m right of the corner, climb direct with difficulty. (V2). **◊** The **sharp wall** to the right can be climbed at V3 (6a), jumping off on easy ground.

❺ Plebble E1 5c 1971

8m On the front face, climb the obvious scoops into the fat crack. **◊** V2 to the break. The **overhanging arête** itself can be climbed at V4 (6a).

❻ Dimetrodon E3 6a 1971

8m The shallow groove left of the bush leads to a break. Step left and climb the face using small holds. **◊** V2 to the break, but award yourself V8 if you break through the thorny cornice. A crack once lived under the gorse to the right (**Peakstone Crack**, VS, 1971).

❼ Stumblehead HVS 5a 1971

8m From the obvious wall, climb the face moving leftwards. Stepping right at half-height and following a hairline crack to the top can make an alternative finish: E1 5b.

8 Back Side VS 4b ★   1959–63
5m This route gains the summit of the pinnacle. Climb the short side on large holds to an awkward finish. To descend, either reverse the route or abseil from a lone tree.

Crags in the **Alton** Area

For the next three crags, **Castle Crag**, **Park Banks Crags** and **Ina's Rock**, park at the bottom of the hill on the outskirts of Alton.

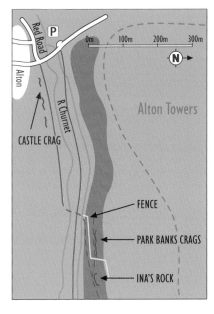

Castle Crag

O.S. Ref. **SK173425**   Altitude: **120m a.s.l.**

This is one of the easiest cliffs in the Lower Churnet valley to find. It lies directly below the walls of the old castle in Alton. A strange cliff, its construction and character is dominated by the infamous bunter pebbles. The rock on the right-hand side of the walls is more compact sandstone whilst in its centre it has a paler complexion. Scaling the walls of the castle above is now much more difficult since the demise of the scaffolding.

Character & aspect
The rock quality varies from okay to poor, mainly depending on pebble soundness. Some routes are overgrown. Crag faces north and gets little sun, but seepage is not a problem.

Routes & bouldering
20 routes, mainly at easier grades. The better ones give a unique climbing experience. No bouldering.

Parking & approach
Park carefully in the end of the Red Road and strike up the hillside above the track to reach the main cliff (5 minutes). For the remainder of the cliffs, follow the track and the buttresses will be seen on its right-hand side (10 minutes).

The climbs are described from right to left beginning at an old metal pipe running down a corner at the right-hand side of the walls.

1 Daedalus VS 4a   1970
9m The pleasant, open and bold arête. **Minos** (VS 4c, 1970) is the crack-line to the left.

2 Minotaur VS 4c ★   1970
15m The twisting crack left again leads past a thread runner to its end. Move right into a chimney complete with tree to finish.

3 Theseus HVS 5b ★   1970
18m Climb the wall 7m to the left, step right and go up via a vague crack-line to a ledge. Continue up a crack via its retaining groove to the top.

Thirty metres to the left, and past an open scoop, is a wide, left-facing crack. **Icarus** (E1 5b, 1971) is the wide crack to the left until moves gain a ledge on the left, finishing up a flake. On the left side of the bay is a through cave. **Zeus** (E2 5b, 1971) bridges up the right side of the cave then the overhanging crack and dirty gully above. Sound appealing? **Pasiphae**

(VS 4c, 1970) goes right from the tree, to then go a long and very random way left. The opposite side of the through cave around to the left gives the start of **The Gallows** (E1 5b, 1970), the vertical cracks above the cave. **The Labyrinth** (HVS 5a, 1970) is the obvious traverse of the buttress from right to left taking belays as you see fit. Finish at The Gallows before abseiling off. Once said to be the Churnet's version of Chee Tor Girdle but now the equivalent to a visit to the Lost World. At the far end of the wall, just before a series of slabs, is a short wall. **Death Mask** (VS 4c, 2002) is a small nose and wall via a break gains a twisted tree.

One hundred metres beyond the main bulk of Castle Cliff is another buttress. This is best approached from the track below, assuming, of course, that you can see it. Left of a block overhang on the right-hand side of the cliff is a ledge at 9m. **The Prodigal** (E1 5c, 1971) has hard moves beneath the ledge to a smaller ledge on the right. From the top of the crack above, traverse left with difficulty to a second ledge. Finish up the dirty corner above, tree roots and vegetation de rigueur. **The Graduate** (VS 4a, 1971) is a slab and crack above a ledge to the left.

Four hundred metres left again is a more easily identifiable buttress known as **Alton Cliff**. Routes are described this time from left to right. In the centre of the cliff is a prominent roof. **The Molegrip Kid** (HVS 5c, 1990) climbs the wall to the left of the overhang to continue directly up the dirty slab. **Rig A Dig Dig** (E2 5c, 1971) was said to be worth the walk in earlier guidebooks, although the increasingly dirty nature of this pitch may make that statement obsolete. From a short groove at the left end of the buttress, traverse right beneath the overhang to an easier finish via a crack. **Restless Natives** (E1 5c, 1990) is the undercut rib to the right with a peg runner. The top bulge requires a strategically placed tree root to exit. **The Brothers** (E1 5b, 1971) is the pebble-dashed arête to the right. The steep wall to the right contains an obvious crack. **To Live Again** (E3 5c, 1978) is an undercut arête left of the crack. **Transit Crack** (S, 1971) is the crack itself. **Down To The Elbows** (E3 6a, 1978) is the vicious overhanging offwidth crack to the right of the gully. **Pull Johnny** (E1 5b, 1978) is a pleasant route up the crack 9m to the right. Step right at its top and finish at a tree.

Park Bank Crags & Ina's Rock

These two crags are two of the best and most important crags in the Lower Churnet. With their similar characteristics, aspects and approaches, as well as being only a couple of hundred metres apart, they can be dealt with together. It makes sense to visit both when in the area, although you will most likely come back again.

The crags manage to combine the unique wooded setting of the Churnet, with the quality more usually found on the main Staffordshire crags, and the routes are of consistently higher quality than that found elsewhere in the neighbourhood. Both cliffs are of the finest quality sandstone. Bunter pebbles, the Curse of the Churnet, do exist but they are infrequent, and rarely present a problem. The crags are never busy, which make the area a superb place to see lots of bird and mammal life not often seen on busier venues.

Conditions & aspect

Crags face south-west. Both get good sun in the afternoon and evening, and dry relatively quickly. They are sheltered by trees, but even so, do not become too green in the darker months. As such, they are suitable after dry periods in winter. They both are sat on the edge of an old footpath, The Rock Walk, which makes the bottoms friendly, adding to the relaxed nature, although nettles can be a problem in summer for Ina's.

Routes and bouldering

Almost 50 routes. The climbs are on tall vertical walls, giving bold faces and arêtes, and some steep, stiff cracks. Routes of all grades are on offer, but a good Extreme leader will find more here than the lower grade climber. Climbs are generally clean, although some routes may benefit from a soft brushing beforehand. No bouldering.

Parking & approach (see map on page 229)

Park just across the north side of the river and follow the railway track for 1km until a kissing gate is located on the left-hand side of the track. Go through this, the remnants of Gig Cottage lies in the

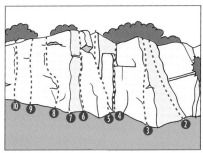

undergrowth just to the right, and be confronted with the huge fence protecting Alton Towers from the outside world.

For Park Bank, follow the right edge of this fence along then steeply up the gully. If there is a gap in the fence here, go through it and contour leftwards towards the crag, 100m away. The biggest problem is that the cliff lies within the grounds of Alton Towers and access is denied to the faces without the purchase of a ticket; even then the owners of the Towers may not be too happy about you climbing. Should you decide to climb here, any of the approaches and route descriptions are only for information and do not indicate any right to climb here.

For Ina's Rock, don't go up the gully, but follow an obvious angled track rising gently up the hillside for 400m to the crag. This crag has no access issues. The obvious walkway leads between both venues.

Park Bank Crags

O.S. Ref. **SK082429**   Altitude: **145m a.s.l.**

The routes are described from right to left when approaching from the fence. When walking along the broad path, The Rock Walk, the first buttress contains **Coelred's Crack** (HVS 5c, pre-1951), which is the obvious crack through a roof. Moving on 50m to the main crag, the first main feature of the crag is a huge roof above head-height.

❶ Fast and Bulbous E2 5b   1984
10m The right-hand arête of the crack to the left of the roof. Start on the left and move right onto a ledge at 4m. Finish on the arête's right-hand side. A direct start is 5c.

Hollybush Hell (S, 1959–63) once lay up the crack under this holly, while **Hopeless Holly** (E1 5b, 1988) climbing the slabby arête to the left, is similarly uninviting.

❷ Defiance VS 4a ★★   1959–63
9m A narrow slab to the left gained from an obvious corner below. Good.

❸ Chilton's Superdirect VS 4b   1959–63
9m Start just to the left again. A short corner and groove lead onto the arête of Defiance.

❹ Right Twin Crack S 4a ★   1959–63
9m A fine jamming pitch via the obvious crack. **Aliens** (E3 6b, 1988) is an excellent problem up the vague flake and crack to the right, avoiding the main crack, while **Alien Wall** (HVS 5b, 1970) is the shallow scoop right again, leading, with difficulty, to the ledge. Finish into Right Twin.

❺ Left Twin Crack S 3c   1959–63
9m The left-hand crack. There are two exits. Starting 2m left to gain the next route is **The Height Below** (E1 5c, 1977).

❻ The Renaissance VS 4c ★★   1970
9m A classic of the Churnet. The prominent thin crack gives fine climbing and protection. Wouldn't be out of place on the Roaches.

⑦ You'll Always Reap What You Sow
E5 6a† ★   1988

9m Nor would this. The elegant round arête to the left taken directly and with no protection.

⑧ Anthem for a Doomed Youth   E4 5c   1975

9m From 5m to the left, move up and slightly rightwards. Step back left to a sandy ledge and finish directly.

⑨ No Future   E6 6b† ★   1988

9m You may not have if you fall off. The centre of the bald wall to the left above the remains of 'Mark Capper'.

⑩ Grounded   E5 6b† ★   1989

7m Marginally easier up the wall to the left past a hole and debilitating reach.

To the left lies a forest of descents, whilst the layback provides **Blunder** (D, 1959–63) with wooden holds. The thin filthy crack to the left is **Uchimata** (D). **Four Horsemen** (E2 5c, 1977) is 10m left again. An awkward crack on the left gains a break. The nose above has small holds and loads of lichen. Fifty metres left, the fine rock reappears with a prominent chimney and striking arête. The buttress to the right of these provides **Honest John** (E1 5a, 1971), which starts at the right side of the wall before traversing left and move up to a flourishing rhododendron. Another bush and slab leads to the top.

⑪ Open All Hours   E4 6a†   1989

15m From just right of the main chimney line, climb a shallow groove and step right at the roof. Pull over into a worrying red corner and from its apex finish via the headwall on the left. Typical Churnet runners and typical Churnet E4.

⑫ Brad's Chimney   VD ★★   pre-1951

18m An atmospheric journey up the magnificent chimney.

⑬ Miss Understood   E6 6a ★★   1989

20m A bigger white knuckle ride than any in the nearby theme park. The main arête to the left of the chimney is taken direct low down, and on its left-hand side above one-third height. Protection is very limited but the rock is sound throughout. A significant pitch.

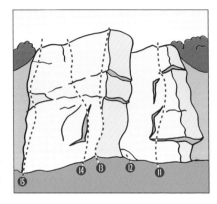

⑭ Patient Weaver   E5 6a ★★   1978

20m More of the same. Climb the shallow corner to the left and exit left via some fingery moves. Continue up the wall above moving leftwards via a shallow depression to a good hold and a long reach to finish.

A significant variation on the climb is **The Humble Potter** (E6 6a, 1989). This climbs Patient Weaver to the rest ledge, then follows the obvious traverse line, right under the headwall to climb the arête on its left side.

⑮ Time Flies By   E4 5c   1986

20m The hanging arête to the left. Climb the wall on its left-hand side and swing right on the right-hand side of the arête. Climb the wall on dirty holds to a break and swing left to finish up the arête. **The Overhang**, (E1 5b, 1970) is an awful route up the tree infested face to the right of a blocky overhang on the wall to the left. Best forgotten.

The next series of buttresses lie 100m further along the Rock Walk. A steep groove on the right-hand of the buttress, to the right of its main nose, is the first landmark. The groove line gives **Tre Cime** (VS 4b, 1971) to a routine finish. The layback crack to the left is **Per Rectum** (VS 4b, 1971). The usually wet wall left again with the use of a lassoed stump for aid is **Extractum** (HVS 5b, 1971). The corner around to the left gives **Mark** (S, 1971) and an exit left and up from Mark gives **Stark** (VD, 1970). The corner left again is **Stephen** (VS 4a, 1971), reserving its hardest to last. The final and best route here **Dark Star** (E3 5c,1975), goes up the arête to the left. The crags continue in the direction of Alton Towers but diminish in height.

Ina's Rock

O.S. Ref. **SK087429**   Altitude: **145m a.s.l.**

See previous section for approach information. Having done everything at Park Bank Crag, it is now a short stroll across to Ina's Rock. The routes are described from left to right. The first routes are quite minor and overgrown. They are **Rawhide** (S, 1970), a chimney near the left, **Gladiator** (VS 4b, 1970), a bulging crack to the right, **Donor** (S, 1971), a scoop and corner to the right, and **Amazing Grace** (VS 4c, 1971), a chimney right again. However, the next batch of routes are probably the best pitches worth carrying a rope for in the Lower Churnet Valley. They are all on very compact rock.

❶ Ina's Chimney S 4a ★★   pre-1951
18m A confident line providing a deep journey into the bowels of the earth, in the recess left of the strange pillar.

To the right is a massive overhang with a bulging nose above. Hopefully the brick pillar is not supporting it. The next routes begin in the wide crack right nose. Lying beneath this are the remnants of an impressive stone shelter above which lie old bolts which presumably helped some form of covering material.

❷ Inaccessible E5 6a† ★★★   1990s
20m Brilliant rock and good gear make this a new classic of the cliff. Climb the wide crack (Atlas) to the half-height break. Move left and pull through the bulge at a good pocket and vertical crack. Continue directly up the wall via breaks and numerous 'nobbles', to the final bulge. A Tri-cam 2 protects the final awkward moves. **Big Mike and the Deadfall of Doom** (E3 6a†, 1990s) is a possible direct start up the hanging rib - left of the cave.

❸ Atlas E2 5c ★★   1970
15m A good chunky classic, although this crack is a more helpful size. In the centre of the crag is an amphitheatre, centred by a deep cave. Exit the cave

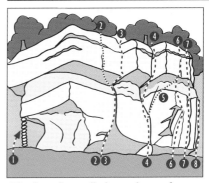

The long flat wall above the roof right of the strange pillar tells an interesting geological story. If you look closely, you will see that the top is concave. This is a cross-section of a stream bed, worn away by the flow of water and stones many millions of years ago. The stones in question are now what make up the layer above. The stream and its contents have settled and solidified, the result being Ina's Rock.

(awkward) and follow the crack. The bulge from the mid-height ledge provides the crux.

❹ Ground Support E1 5b ★★   1970
15m Another excellent pitch. Follow the thin crack just right of the cave. The wide crack above gives fine climbing and positions.

❺ Whispering Myth E3 6a   1979
20m From 3m up Ground Support, traverse right to reach a vague leftwards line. This gives initial hard and quite scary moves to reach a bolt from where moves right gain a ledge (possible stance). Finish up the thin crack to the left of a wider crack on the right (Tactical Weapon).

A tree to the right obscures an old mileage plaque hewn into the rock.

⑥ Lethal Weapon E5 6a ★   1989

15m Fine, technical and bold. From the plaque below the arête to the right, climb the perfectly formed arête and tiny right-facing groove to a rounded ledge. Tackle the face above moving leftwards to finish up the upper arête.

⑦ Tactical Weapon E1 5b ★   1970

15m Climb the crack and rugosities to the right pleasantly to the ledge. Finish via the crack above.

⑧ Ina City Riot E5 6b ★   1990

9m Superb bold moves on the right-hand side of the arête to the right.

The dirty groove around the corner gives **Initiation Groove** (VS 4b, 1970). A girdle traverse of the crag has been done from left to right taking stances as and when required – **Crud on the Tracks** (E1 5b, 1978). Forty-five metres to the right an isolated buttress gives: **Bloody Crack** (VS 4b, 1970). The lower crack to the ledge – escape right to avoid the upper crack (unclimbed).

The **Red Road**

A tree-lined road running between Alton and Oakamoor is the access for Rakes Dale, as well as all the Dimmings Dale crags, and eventually runs underneath Stoney Dale Quarry.

Rakes Dale

O.S. Ref. **SK066424** Altitude: **170m a.s.l.**

This is the wide and fairly open dale with two pleasant crags on either side.

Conditions & aspect

Both crags are fairly open, sitting high on the dale, but get little sun. Can be slow to dry.

Routes & bouldering

Twelve routes. Mainly technical and bold wall climbs. No bouldering.

Parking & approach

Park on the horseshoe bend on The Red Road, 500m from Alton. A path marked Toothill Wood goes steeply uphill. Don't take this – unless you want to go to Toothill Rock – which you don't – unless you are a weirdo – which you probably are – in which case you probably should become a guidebook fieldworker. Marginally less weird people should instead take the unmetalled road just right of this, leading to Rakes Dale House. After 150m, a sharp left turn leads past the house into an open grassy dale. The crags lie on the flanks of this dale. Approach 5 minutes.

Austin's Crag

A fine little face, lying on the left side of the dale that has a number of pleasant routes. It dries relatively quickly but gets little sunshine due to its north-westerly aspect. It lies at the upper end of the dale, directly above the wooden building at its head.

① Dust Storm E1 5b   1979

9m Start 5m right of the left-hand edge of the wall. Gain a flake at 3m and traverse left for 3m. Continue over a tricky little bulge past a tree to reach a short finishing crack.

② Castles of Sand E3 5c ★   1991

12m To the right is a shrub. Start 4m right of this and climb directly via peculiar moves to gain easier moves leftwards to finish.

Sandbagger (HVS 5a) takes the tree-lined crack to the right. **Austin's Chimney** (M) is obvious by name on the right. **Desert Rat** (HVS 5a) is a hanging corner in the right wall. **White Mouse** (VD) starts on the front face and traverses into the chimney. All 1979.

Rakes Dale Wall

A fine wall, steep and featureless, and covered in pebbles sitting high on the right side of the dale. The climbs here are generally very bold and would benefit from prior inspection. It can stay

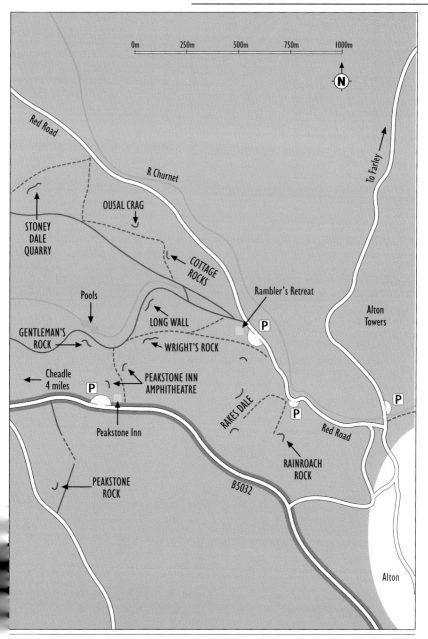

wet during the winter period and, facing north-east, gets little sunshine unless you arrive early in the morning. One criticism of the climbs could be their 'saminess', although you are unlikely to be doing them all. Unique Churnet. It lies directly above the house at the lower end of the dale. There is an overgrown flake at the left side. Routes start from here.

❶ Legosaurus Rex E4 5c   1991
10m Twenty metres right of the flake is a massive pebble at 5m. Intricate and technical move past this, the bunter of all bunters. Unprotected.

❷ Duplo Magic E4 6a   1991
9m Starting 3m to the right of the pebble climb directly up the wall. Marginally harder than Legosaurus Rex but still no protection.

❸ The Plastics Factory E5 6b ★   1991
12m A fine little route. Starting 5m right of Duplo Magic, climb up to the bulge, runner! Lunge around this and stand up somewhat precariously. Finish more easily.

❹ Raiders of the Lost Bark E5 6b ★   1991
12m Start just to the right of a recess 5m to the right, small arrow. After a technical start on pebbles the climbing above eases significantly.

❺ Stickle Brick Wall E6 6b ★   1991
12m Start 4m to the right. Move up to gain a series of poor slots and pebbles leading leftwards via a slight bulge. Continue leftwards to finish at a tree. Superb intricacies.

❻ Legoland E5 6a ★   1989
12m Serious and very unusual climbing with just sufficient protection. At the far right-hand side of the wall a peculiar brown 'lump' adorns the face. Start 15m to the left of the lump. Climb the bulge and slab to reach a break. Step right to a hole and make hard moves to reach a tiny tree that aids a worrying exit. **Rakes Dale Chimney** (HVS 5a, 1979) is to the right.

The buttresses continue to the right and around the corner (into Rakes Dale proper) for quite some distance. There are many worthwhile sections of rock, not least the fine wall at the end of the escarpment. Access to this area is best from the Cheadle to Alton road, 500m to the east of the Peakstone Inn.

Toothill Rock

O.S. Ref. **SK068425**   Altitude: **215m a.s.l.**

The rock commands an impressive position overlooking the valley, although the climbing is relatively poor, with an abundance of those famous bunter pebbles and copious amounts of vegetation. Most of the routes may still be awaiting second ascents. It is best regarded as a superior vantage point for Alton Tower's fireworks or as a picnic site.

To approach, park at the sharp bend on the Red Road (as for Rakes Dale), and strike steeply up the path (marked Toothill Wood). The crag can then be seen on the left. Approach 5 minutes. Toothill Rock itself has a huge overhang. The climbs are described from this point and from right to left. **The Highwayman** (VS 4b,1970) takes the crack left of a roof and finishes up the wall behind the ledge. **Hot Pants** (VS 4c, 1970), walls just right of the next arête and a groove above the ledge. **Droopy Draws** (HS 4a, 1978) climbs the jamming crack to the left. On the upper tier of the crag **Tyre Pressure** (S, 1978) takes a short corner, swings right and up the wall escaping left to ledges. **Parking Fine** (VS 4b, 1978) climbs the wall to the left. **Ant's Corner** (VS 4a, 1978) lies further to the left via a corner left of a pebbly-dashed roof (sounds like someone's house?). **Uncles Arête** (VS 4b, 1978) takes the arête on the left. Another 200m on past several awful buttresses is a less awful buttress! **Daddy Long Legs** (HVS 5b, 1979), climbs a crumbling wall to exit via a jamming roof crack and nasty finish – bet you can't wait?

Illustration: Duncan Bourne.

Churnet Valley: The Lost World

The **Dimmings Dale** Area

The next crags are situated in and around the beautiful wooded valleys of Dimmings Dale, running west from the Rambler's Retreat. It is home to a select number of quality routes, but is most noteworthy because of its bouldering. The setting is unique.

Dimmings Dale

O.S. Ref. **SK062432** to **SK045436**
Altitude: **105m a.s.l.**

A beautiful dale of woods and waterfalls running away from the Rambler's Retreat. Amid much overgrown rock there are three buttresses of significant worth. Lord's Buttress offers a handful of excellent routes on good quality sandstone making them worth carrying a rope for. The Long Wall and Gentleman's Rock have become the domain of the boulderer and offer many good problems, most especially of the horizontal nature.

Conditions & aspect

Most of the crags face north and get little sun. Some crags are overgrown, but those that are treated as such in the text. Some routes can be subject to dampness, especially in the humid summer weather and after long periods of rain. In crisp dry weather in the autumn or spring this is an ideal climbing venue. The bouldering venues suffer similar but usually remain dry after short spells of rain.

Routes & bouldering

The good routes are concentrated on Lord's Buttress, with 8 good steep, clean routes on interesting rock. There are many other overgrown routes. A good selection of good bouldering on Long Wall and Gentleman's Rock that is well worth seeking out.

Parking & approach

Simply park at the Rambler's Retreat and walk up the broad track leading up the dale. Routes are describes as they are encountered. Approach up to 15 minutes. No access problems.

Smelting Mill Buttress

Level with the top end of the first pool on the left is a buttress with a red left-hand wall. Climbing on this buttress is not very worthwhile. In the centre is an awful-looking wide crack complete with holly tree. **Slip Knot** (E2 5c) traversed the red wall. **Dimmingsdale Crack** (E1 5b) climbs the awful wide crack. **Iron Ore** (E1 5b) a flake and slab just right, **Green Slab** (HVS 5b), a slab higher up, **The Mexican** (E1 5b) is a good problem climbing a roof crack higher up and round on the right, **Chocolate Orange** (VS 4c), a groove to the right, **Twiggy** (S), a crack to the right, **Fagan** (S), another crack further right. Fifty metres to the right is an isolated buttress alongside a prominent large fur tree. **Christmas Tree Crack** (VS 4b) is here. All these 1979.

Lord's Buttress

Two hundred metres further up the path lies the most imposing crag in this dale. It is easily recognised by its striking central pillar with a crack running up the middle. It has a limited number of quality extremes which are well worth seeking out in anything other than muggy summer weather. It is generally very clean, although it gets little sun.

At the left-hand side of the crag is a small wall with some good problems on perfect pockets. To the right lies a gully with a protruding nose to the right again. **Slippery Caramel (E3 5c, 1979)** climbs the gully then the right wall of the tower via a couple of cracks.

❶ Overlord E3 6a ★★ 1992
20m Brilliant, varied crack climbing in a great situation. Climb the short hand-crack on the front of the buttress to a ledge and possible belay (4c). The fine thin crack above the ledge gives sustained interest with good protection to a sapling. Traverse right to finish up the arête.

❷ Lord's Arête E4 6a ★★ 1979
18m Tricky climbing in an exposed setting. Climb the groove just to the right of the main arête of the buttress to a ledge (or if this is dirty, climb the gully). Continue up the wall with difficulty, sling runner. to gain a break, peg. Swing back left onto the arête and finish up this.

❸ Top Brick E2 5c ★★ 1979
15m A Churnet classic, with good wall climbing. From the foot of the chimney around to the right, move out left onto the face, thread runner, and pull up to the cave (peg on left). From the cave, climb steeply to a wide break, then finish up the wall above.

❹ Toast Rack HVS 4c ★★ 1979
18m A good traversing line with an exposed crux. From high up the chimney, cross the left wall on good holds to reach the front face. Traverse delicately across the slab to a ledge and walk off to the left.

❺ Mental Traveller E1 5b 1981
9m The right arête of the chimney **(Lord's Chimney**, VD, 1979) is climbed using a fragile fin and several fragile pockets.

❻ Travelling Light E2 5b ★ 2002
9m The centre of the front face provides a stern test of nerve with steep climbing on varied and unusual holds. Very worthwhile.

❼ Travelling Bag E4 5c 2002
9m The even bolder right arête of the wall gained via the undercut prow below.

Nine metres to the right of the chimney is a dirty corner. **Reverse Charge (VS 4b)** follows a break rightwards from the corner and climb the arête via a flake. Step left and finish direct. Thirty metres to the right lies the next small buttress. This contains **Rhody Crack (VD)**, climbing via two prows. Another 150m on lies a notably vile buttress: **Pebble Buttress**. The slab and crack on its right-hand side is **Grott (D)** – bet you can't wait. All 1979.

Long Wall

Continue along the path to the crown of the second left-hand bend and alongside a small bridge over the stream. This marks the approaches up to the wall. At its left-hand side via a start in the gully and the arête to the right is **Root Slab** (S, 1979). The best reason to visit Long Wall, however is its boulder problem traverse. Up problems would be possible, but are curtailed by a mossy band.

❶ The Long Traverse V4 (6a)
Usually done from the large tree on the right-hand side of the crag at a low-level and finishes at the first step up on the left-hand side of the crag. The traverse can be extended at both ends. Leftwards and slightly upward via pebbles and crimps is V6 (6b). Beginning the traverse 8m right of the tree and moving leftwards to gain the original traverse is V8 (6c).

Dave Bishop going for it on Top Brick, E2 5c (page 237), deep in the wooded valley of Dimmings Dale. Photo: Alex Ekins.

Even longer than Long Wall. John H Bull traversing on the amazing Gentleman's Rock. Photo: Dave Garnett.

Shepherd's Delight (E4 6b(†), 1993) *climbs the highest part of the wall. At a lower level, a groove in the roof gives* **Drop Leaf** (HS 4a, 1979).

Gentleman's Rock

Continuing along the drive and around a right-hand bend leads to the lower of another series of pools and waterfalls. This buttress lies to the left of the first waterfall. It is a small steep crag, best suited to bouldering, featuring a massively long traverse, and some powerful up problems. Bits tend to be damp in muggy weather, while other sections will stay dry in a downpour. In the centre there is a sacrificial altar.

❶ Jill the Traverse V4 (5c)
The safer, lower traverse from the shelf on the left to the central crack. At the start of the left-hand traverse a good move **goes up** the vague arête from low-level jugs to a sloper and pocket V5 (6b).

❷ V5 (6a)
From 4m right of the arête, use a rounded green finger-pocket to climb the overhanging wall.

❸ Fifty Pence Project
From just left of the altar, use a coin shaped pebble to gain a good pocket up and left.

❹ Gentleman John V4 (6a)
The savage finger crack towards the right side. The jugs feel high enough, but the disturbed will continue to the top at E4.

❺ High Speed Imp Act V7 (6b)
A superb problem up the leaning wall to the right yields to power, a long reach and a slap. Jump off, or continue. The moves to the ledge will feel very committing.

❻ The Nose V5 (6b)
Start low and crank rightwards to finish over the bulging nose.

❼ Low Traverse V6 (6b)
Start on the very low shelf on the right, and move left and up, to finish up any (or all) of the last 3 problems, which will add one or two grades to the originals.

❽ The Mega Traverse V7 (6b)
Get fit quick by doing Jill the Traverse, drop down the flake, and continue to finish up the bulging nose.

❾ Jack the Traverse E5 6a ★   1978
30m A physical and very worrying traverse of the upper break from a boulder on the left to the central crack (Gentleman John). Possible to be seen as a boulder problem, although the altar may demand a sacrifice.

Hermit's Rock

Returning back to the Rambler's Retreat, a broad track follows the right-hand side of the dale past the lowest pool. Follow this, always keeping alongside the pool and keeping left where it forks. Continue past the Earl's Rock cottage. Just beyond this, a path cuts up through the trees. Take this and after 50m, go rightwards up the hill. Here will clearly be seen a large buttress complete with Hermit's Cave. **Maloof** (HVS 5b, 1979) is the wide crack above the cave. Awkward to say the least.

Rainroach Rock

O.S. Ref. **SK063430** Altitude: **260m a.s.l.**

One of the tallest crags in the area this cliff occupies an imposing position on the hillside slightly to the south of the Rambler's Retreat and 1km north-west of Alton Castle. The climbing here is relatively poor since the regrowth of the dense undergrowth that was cut back to reveal the climbs many years ago. Park at the Rambler's Retreat and follow the track that runs parallel to the road for 100m – this eventually leads to Holm Cottage on the far side of the track. From here strike directly up the hillside and more through misfortune than judgement, land at the foot of the buttress. The land is owned by Mrs Tideswell who owns Rainroach Farm above the cliffs. She is quite happy for climbing to take place here.

The climbs are described from right to left beginning at the obvious groove at the right-hand end of the cliff. **Five Bar Crack** (HVS 5b, 1983) climbs the thin crack right of the groove and the overhanging crack above. **Spreadeagle** (S, 1969) is the groove and from a ledge continue up the corner above. **The Taxman** (HVS 5a, 1969) goes from the first ledge of Spreadeagle, then left for 5m. Swing across a corner and move onto a ledge.

Climb up to yet another ledge and stomach-traverse right to gain an overhanging corner. **The Unveiling** (VS 4c, 1969) climbs a wall to a ledge. Walk left to climb a crack. Move right and finish. **Pebble Drop** (VD, 1976) starts at the base of a slab in the centre of the crag. Climb this to gain a tree at 6m and finish via the crack at the back of the ledge. **Climb To The Lost World** (S and A1, 1976) is a vegetated crack to a ledge. Use aid to climb the crack above, then traverse left for 9m to finish via another crack. **The Fly** (E1 5b, 1969) is up the overhanging wall at the extreme left-hand side of the crag. A flake is gained with difficulty.

Wright's Rock

O.S. Ref. **SK058430** Altitude: **185m a.s.l.**

The rock and climbing, and specifically, the bouldering, is the best the Churnet has to offer. Steep powerful up-problems, many over large roofs, as well as brilliant traversing. It has the ambience of many of the more open crags of the area, and the views of the surrounding countryside, including Alton Towers, are superb.

Conditions & aspect
Wright's Rock stands proudly overlooking farmland on the southern rim of Dimmings Dale. Its aspect is very open. It faces north and gets virtually no sun. The crag dries quickly and can be climbed on most of the year round. Avoid the crag after spells of wet or humid weather, the latter enticing clouds of midges. It stays dry in the rain. Good in hot summers.

Routes & bouldering
Seventeen routes, but many overgrown. A couple of desperates that would need little cleaning. Very good for bouldering, 13 problems.

Parking & approach

From the Rambler's Retreat, follow the path up the left-hand side of Dimmings Dale. At the foot of the first pool a track runs up the hillside on the left via an obvious shallow valley to the fields below the cliff. Direct access is then obvious. 10 minutes.

The climbs are described from left to right starting at the prominent cave. **Stonemason's Route** (S, 1959–63) is a pleasant climb up the wall left of the cave. The next three climbs are on the bulging walls right of the cave. While they are worthwhile, they would need some cleaning before an ascent. **Cherry Rare** (E5 6b, 1990) pulls through the right-hand side of the cave to a break. Worrying moves using a flake then gain the ledge above. **The Clumsy Too** (E5 6a, 1990) moves straight up from the break on Cherry Rare to continue using a huge pebble and poor undercut. **Never Never** (E4 6a, 1990) climbs the right arête of the cave to a break. Step left and make a difficult move to gain the short, flared crack. The ledge lies just above but the floor may feel much closer! **Puppet Life** (E2 5c, 1988) goes from 3m right of the cave over the bulge and traverses right and up past a peg runner to gain a rounded break. Move left and up to finish at a tree.

Ⓥ Two good problems can be had in this cave. The desperate **undercutting and finger-jamming** roof crack to the left is unclimbed. Crossing the **roof on pockets** just right is V4 (6b).

❶ The Niche Traverse V2 (5c)

To the right is a square-cut niche. Traverse the back wall from left to right. Technical.

❷ Sauron HVS 5b ★   1970

9m A super little route up the right-hand corner of the square niche. **Saur Off** (E2 5b, 1979) is the green and rounded arête to the right of the corner, with the occasionally rounded hold. A fine solo. Ⓥ The sit-start to the Saur Off is a good dynamic V3 (6a), while rocking right after the first move, using the unusual 'pebble' is a fingery V2 (6a). **Sculptor's Wall** (VS 4a, 1959–63) is the wall right again, using the occasional 'bevelled' hold. From the large ledge finish up the wall. The obvious deep fissure dividing the centre of the buttress is **Central Crack** (D, 1959–63).

The Main Crag

Wright's Rock bouldering

❸ Wright's Traverse V8 (6b)

The superb traverse on pebbles and pockets is sustained and fingery. Usually done left to wright, from the niche on the left and finishing up the niche on the right.

❹ Thorns Start V0– (4c)

❺ V2 (5c)

Climb directly to the roof and cross this. An alternative goes a little further right, then pulls over **at a flake** V2 (5c).

❻ Fireman Indirect V5 (6b)

From the previous problem, continue to gain the base of the curving finger-ramp.

❼ Simple Simon V7 (6c)

A desperate brute of a thing, with all the odds stacked against you. From a good jug on the lip, launch upwards on visionary holds to gain the ramp. Starting on the porthole under the roof doesn't add much to the grade, but **gaining the lip** from here is a good V3 (6b) in its own right.

❽ V6 (6b)

From small pockets and flakes under the roof, climb up and left to gain the Fireman jug on the lip. Avoid the porthole pocket out left.

❾ Fingers Start V8 (6c)

From good pockets under the roof, gain a hole over the lip. Move upwards (highly unlikely) to eventually gain a break. If, in your dreams, you get here, either jump off or, even harder, traverse left to the bottom of the Fireman ramp and sell your boots. Gaining the **first pocket** over the roof is an established V1 (5c).

❿ Alternative Start V3 (6a)

Climb up and rightwards to the roof. Using a flake in its underside, gain the break above.

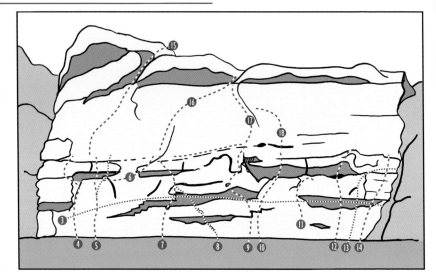

⓫ The Undercut V7 (6c)

From the round pocket, undercut up to get established on the square flake.

⓬ V7 (6b)

Cross the roof on tiny diagonal flakes to get established in the sloping break. While you're there, try going over the bulge above using the twisting undercut feature.

⓭ Little Groove VI (5c)

⓮ V2 (5c)

Crimps up the little wall right of the groove.

The main crag is also home to a small number of very challenging routes:

⓯ Thorns E4 5c ★   1979

12m An impressive little route, especially considering the friable nature of the holds. From the ledge, climb the thin flakes just right of the tree. The bulge and wide crack relent above. Avoiding use of the tree, which has grown much bigger than when the first ascent was done, may prove problematic.

⓰ The Leading Firemen E2 5b ★   1988

11m From the the recess on Thorns, move right and up, via a rounded crack, to the break below the capping roof. Traverse this rightwards to an exit on the slabs above. A gripper.

⓱ Fingers in Every Pie E6 6c ★★   1988

9m Desperate bouldering at an unfriendly height, forming a direct entry to the hanging flake high on the vague nose of the crag. From Fingers Start, pass a peg runner with extreme difficulty. The upper flake is easier.

⓲ Alternative Three E5 6a† ★   1979

12m Gain and use the flake to reach the lip (Alternative Start). Moving left and then up to the Finger's flake proves even more difficult. Impressive for its time.

Tunnel Chimney (D, 1959–63), is the dirty chimney just right. **Ⓥ** The next section on the right has **a flake** on its left side. Gain this with difficulty, and climb to the top. The top-out is uninviting V5 (6a). **Traversing this buttress** is V1 (5b). **The Hob** (VS 4c, 1970), begins 8m right and gains a ledge, finishing right. A left finish is 5a. Further to the right and above an old ricketty fence lies the upper tier.

Tiger's Wall (VS 4b, 1970), climbs the highest part of the wall and **Ugly Puss** (VS 4b, 1970), the flake to its left. ❂ **Motorbike** V7 (6b) is a hideous little problem at the right-hand end of the wall and on a small isolated wall. Pad the boulder below.

Painter's Rock

Returning to the left-hand side of the cliff and 300m to the left again is a little crag. This lies within a small patch of forest and can be difficult to find in the summer months when foliage is on the trees. The rock is nowhere near as good as its neighbours and the increase in vegetation both on the crag and below it over recent years has made it completely unclimbable. **The first buttress is the poorer of the two and the second buttress provides the routes. The routes are described from right to left.**

Recess Corner (VD) takes a short corner left of the first buttress. **Working Hunter** (HVS 5b) climbs the slabs of the next buttress. **Rabbit Stew** (E3 5c) takes a delicate groove on the left and bulge, peg runner, to a finish in the corner of the next route. **Bright Eyes** (E2 5c) climbs a faint crack and corner left again. Left of the next more vegetated section is an upper tier. **Glossy Finish** (VS 4c) climbs the wall just left of centre via a ledge and **Undercoat** (HVS 5b) takes the roof on the right traversing right to finish just right of the arête. All 1979.

Peakstone Inn Amphitheatre

O.S. Ref. **SK055428**   Altitude: **160m a.s.l.**

This is a collection of crags lying on each side of a deepening wooded vale leading into Dimmings Dale. The rock, like on many local crags, varies in quality: crags on the left-hand, shadier side, are generally poor and unattractive. Those on the right-hand side offer a handful of good harder routes, and are a pleasant place to be when the sun shines.

Conditions & aspect
The left-hand crags don't get much sun, so tend to be dank. The right, north-west facing side, gets afternoon sun, and combined with its more open aspect, has some perfectly clean rock.

Routes & bouldering
The right-hand side has a handful of good, fingery extremes, some with in-situ protection. Although short, these give a good day out. Limited bouldering.

Parking & approach
Park in the Peakstone Inn car park (the owners don't seem to mind especially when you buy a pint afterwards). From here, a series of steps lead down the hillside where a small track leads to Dimmings Dale – of course this point can be gained from the Rambler's Retreat. The crags are either side of the small track. Approach, under 5 minutes.

Left-Hand Side of the Amphitheatre

From the pub car park, follow the steps until a bridge is reached. From here the first buttress will be seen through the undergrowth up and to the left.

Northern Lights (S, 1978) is the obvious left to right line gaining a ledge. Finish via the dirty arête. One hundred metres further on and to the right, past more vegetation and beer cans, beyond a small

steep buttress, is **Back Wall**. At the right side of the cliff is a slabby groove: this is **Dancing Bear** (E1 4b, 5b,, 1978), a two-pitch route climbing the slabby groove then a steep wall above.

The final buttress is situated across a gully and fern clad bank on the most northerly point of the amphitheatre. **Scoop Wall** (HVS 5a, 1971) is the centre of the clean wall left of the overhanging arête to a break. The short **overhanging wall** gives a good V5 (6b) problem. **Chockstone Crack** (S, pre-1951) is the obvious crack to the right. **Rock Around The Chock** (HS,1990) is the arête to the right. **Right Wall** (HVS 5a, 1971) goes from a vegetated ledge 9m to the right, to climb the wall to a flake. A small buttress 200m further on gives **BJM** (VS 4b, 1971), a steep crack and narrow chimney, and **Scout Wall** (VS 4c, 1971), the wall left of the crack.

Right-Hand Side of the Amphitheatre

From the far side of the bridge at the foot of the steps, strike diagonally rightwards across the bank to reach a small group of crags, visible on the crest of the hill.

The right-hand part of this has an overlap at 5m and offers a number of short problems including a good fingery traverse V4 (6a). Towards its left side a thin crack splits the roof, **Supermac V5** (6b) 1988, mat essential. To the left, the rock becomes a lot more attractive. **One Dunne** (VD, pre-1951) is the pleasant arête at the left-hand of the overlap.

❶ All Day and All of the Night
E5 6b ★★   1988
9m Superb fingery climbing on steep clean rock. From 5m left of the large block to the left, tackle the centre of the leaning wall with a hard start, past a rounded break to the top. Two thread runners protect.

❷ Suckin' Pebbles E4 6b ★★   1990
9m Another fierce and technical climb, thankfully well protected by in-situ runners. The thin crack and leaning arête to the left gives a series of fingery moves. Two pegs and one thread runner.

❸ Pocket Hercules E3 5c ★ 1990
7m Steep positive moves in an exciting setting. From atop the block to the left move up via a pocket to a break. Swing merrily right along this to finish via the vague arête on distant holds.

❹ Ripples E1 5a 1990
6m Continue directly up the wall above the start of Pocket Hercules and finish rightwards via an 'ear' on a short prow.

❺ Dead Tree Slab D pre-1951
9m The pleasant slab at the left-hand end of the wall. **Dead Tree Crack** (VD, pre-1951) is the crack to the left with a finish via the arête.

Ousal Dale

This is the right-hand tributary of Dimmings Dale and offers a number of smaller buttresses, giving a few routes and lots of very good bouldering. To reach the dale follow the right-hand path from the Rambler's Retreat. Branch off right up a track from halfway along the first pool.

The first buttress lies at footpath level within 80m. **Footpath Chimney** *(D, pre-1970) tackles the flake in the centre of the buttress and* **No Veranda** *(VS 4c, 1991) the centre of the overhanging wall to the left.*

Cottage Rocks

The first good bouldering lies a couple of hundred metres along the path, just at a sharp right-hand bend (*see page 250*).

Lone Buttress

Continue along the main track and around a sharp left-hand bend complete with picnic table. This next buttress lies after 150m and on the right-hand side of the track.

Lone Wall *(E1 5b, 1979) takes the right-hand side of the buttress past a thin crack.* **Even Lonelier** *(E1 5c, 1979) starts*

from a ledge 1m to the left then traverses right to tackle an overhang above a ledge.

ⓥ Fifty metres along is a small steep wall by the path. **Bizarre**, V7 (6c), is the obvious problem from a sit-start. The **stand-up** is V5.

Ousal Crag

Continue along the path for another 150m, keeping a good watch through the trees for this next crag, lying about 25m up the right bank. The up problems are quite good here, but the two traverses are mega-classics.

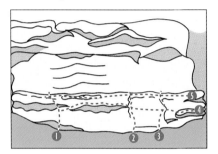

A note on conditions: the lower part of the cliff can remain damp through the winter months but generally the cliff is useful as an all-year round venue. Avoid humid weather in summer, and after periods of heavy rain.

❶ V1 (5c)
Start low and pull over the roof to the higher break.

❷ Little Rib V0 (5a)

❸ V0− (5a)
Start low and climb the blunt arête. A variation starts the same but climbs **rightwards on pockets** V1 (5c).

❹ Ousal Low V6 (6b)
A classic crossing the crag in either, or both directions. It can be started on the sloping shelf at the extreme right, or the blunt arête just left.

Deep in the heart of Hobbit country. Allen Williams on Bizarre V7 (page 245) in Ousal Dale. Photo: Ian Parnell.

Cottage Rocks Bouldering

A lovely little venue, up to 6m high with perfect landings. While it gets the sun, the trees afford a lot of shade. Problems are a combination of steep fingery yarding on positive holds, or delicate slabby walls.

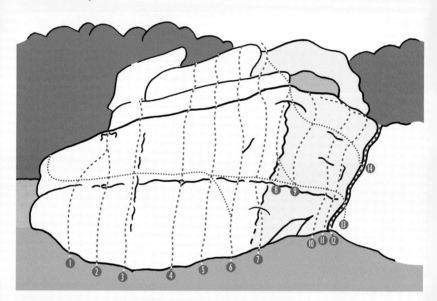

1 V0+ (5b)
Climb to the right-hand end of the wide break, then move right to finish as for the next problem. **Going left** is V1 (5b).

2 Billy Bunter
V0+ (5a)
Climb the wall, passing a large pebble.

3 Crusty V0− (4c)
Climb the dotty crack to the top.

4 Sid the Sexist
V0 (5a)
Climb the wall past a pebbly pock.

5 V2 (5c)
Go up the wall just right to gain a high hole.

The next 7 routes all finish by gaining the flake above problem 7.

6 V4 (6a)
Tricky moves past the bulging right side of the wall, with the finger-ramp for the right hand.

7 Sapling Bugle
V4 (6b)
From the low jug, climb directly to the baby tree (finger-ramp for left hand).

8 Tufa V2 (5c)
Pinch up the good feature on the arête.

9 V2 (5c)
Good pocket-pulling leads to the top break.

10 Pocket Wall
V0+ (5b)
A good problem up the centre of the steep wall. A good **sit-start** is V4 (6a).

11 The Wafer
V2 (5c)
Ascend the steep wall direct from the little fin as far as the big break. A stiff **sit-start** is V3 (6a).

12 Strenuosity
V0+ (5a)
A wide voyage up the mean crack-line. At the

top, move left to finish as for the previous problems.

⑬ Cottaging V5 (6b)
From the bottom of the crack, traverse left with some difficulty. Either finish up tufa, or adventurous cottagers will go all the way. A pleasant easier variant starts up Problem 6 at VI (5b).

⑭ Cottage Cheese
VI (5b)
From the crack, traverse the wall on good holds to finish up the flake.

Pine Buttress

Three more good problems lie on a bulging right-facing wall on an outcrop 10m right.

⑮ Left Pine V6 (6c)
On the left side of the bulging wall, start sitting at the back of the recess. From a small crimp, crank upwards on edges to reach a rounded feature at half-height.

⑯ Pine Wall V3 (6a)
Just right, start sitting with hand in a hole. Move left and up through a groovy feature to get established in a flake crack higher up. Retreat from here.

⑰ Right Pine V5 (6b)
From the same start, move up and right to eventually gain the top of the thin crack at the top of the rock. Bail out from here.

Winter warmer. Justin Critchlow on a variation on the Ousal Traverse. Photo: Andi Turner.

⑤ Ousal High V3 (5c)
The upper traverse has bigger holds, and is every bit as classic. The obvious circuit is linking the high and low traverses at their ends and doing laps. The low has a hands-off rest, which feels a bit like cheating. However, this can be missed out by coming down Little Rib.

And a few routes to look at. **Impacted Bowel** (VS 4c, 4b★, 1978) is a good high-level girdle of the crag starting high on the left. Follow a break rightwards into the chimney and move around the arête. Continue across the face to a belay below the finishing crack of Moto Perpetuo. The break leads to a corner at the right-hand end of the crag and the finish to an entertaining climb. **Solo Chimney** (VD, pre-1970) is the chimney on the left side of the face and **Thum** (VD, 1979) the wall and crack through the overhang to the left. **Prowler** (E5 5c, 2002) is a direct line through the prow at the right-hand side of the crag. Good moves but utilising a creaky flake of suspect strength. **Moto Perpetuo** (E2 5c, 1979) gains the scoop to the left of Prowler with difficulty and on unsettling pebbles. Once gained, move leftwards along the break to a finishing crack.

The final crag in the Lower Churnet lies 2 miles east of Farley.

Wootton Lodge Crags

O.S. Ref. **SK095435**   Altitude: **125m a.s.l.**

These crags, which consist of two main buttresses, lie overlooking the Bamford's test track on a wooded hillside 2 miles along the lane running from Farley to Ellastone. The old Wootton Lodge gates, which the crags lie beyond, have now become somewhat overgrown but can just be made out on the right-hand side of the road.

Conditions & aspect
Good, pebbly rock, steep, and while some of it is crumbly, the majority of it is very good.

Routes & bouldering
The crag consists of two separate buttresses that offer a host of excellent bouldering opportunities, more so than the routes that are described. For the most part both buttresses are undercut and the rock is solid.

Parking & approach
Follow the road from Farley, running behind Alton Towers, past the Towers itself and down into a hollow. Continue along this road until the gates can just be made out on the right-hand side of the road. Locate a public footpath sign and follow the track through the gates. The cliffs will be seen on the left 300m along this track.

Access
The land hereabouts is owned by JCB and climbing over recent years has become actively discouraged.

By keeping a low profile and a courteous behaviour this may be overcome.

The routes are described as you approach them, from left to right.

Left-Hand Buttress

❶ Ungodly Groove   E1 5b   1970
9m The hanging groove on the left-hand side of the first buttress. Strenuous.

❷ Central Route   VS 4c   1970
12m The steep wall just to the right leads rightwards to a ledge. Move right to a crack and finish up this. Worthwhile.

❸ Pull John   E5 6a   1971
15m The nasty crumbling arête to the right gains a ledge on the right. Continue up the wall 5m right of the overhanging upper arête, gradually moving left towards the top.

❹ Quasimodo   E2 6a   1971
12m The desperate crack on the right. Finish up the crack above the ledge.

❺ Cripple's Corner   VS 4c   1971
11m Start at the far right-hand side of the buttress. Traverse leftwards across the wall to reach a ledge. Finish via the crack on the right.

❻ Wootton Wanderer   HVS 5a   1971
25m Starting from the left-hand side of the crag, traverse right to the large ledge on the arête. From the left end of this, continue diagonally rightwards to the finish of Quasimodo.

Right-Hand Buttress

❼ The Long Traverse   VD ★★   1970
34m As fine a pitch at the grade in the Lower Churnet. Starting from the left-hand side of the crag, traverse right at a height of 6m.

To the right is an obvious hanging crack.

8 A Phoenix Too Frequent E3 6a ★ 1975
12m From just left of the crack, make a fingery traverse leftwards from where the easier upper wall can be gained. The line immediately left of this is **Premature Evacuation** (E2 5b, 1990s).

9 Hanging Crack HVS 5b ★ 1971
9m Good strenuous climbing via the obvious crack.

V To the right, walls get shorter, allowing a handful of superb problems in the V3–V6 range.

The Churnet First Ascents

pre-1951 **Ina's Chimney, Brad's Chimney, Coelred's Crack, Chockstone Crack, Himac, One Dunne, Dead Tree Slab, Dead Tree Crack** Unknown *Himac was climbed free as Supermac by Gary Gibson on April 6th 1988.*

1951 Spring **Original Route** Dave Penlington, Michael Harby

1951 Aug **Cave Crack, Magenta Crack, Flake Crack, Devil's Crack** Dave Penlington, P Gardener, M Moore

1952 Spring **Hatschek's Groove** John Fisher

1952 Spring **Glyph** Ernie Marshall

1952 Spring **Via Trita** Martin Ridges

1952 Spring **Introduction, Rugosity, Footpath, Saunter, Wave, Ripple, Crest, Backwash, As You Like It, Emerald Groove, Flake Wall, Emerald Wall, Corner Traverse, Moore's Crack, Rotandas, Oak Spur, Moss Rose, Frequency, Vereker's Venture, The Cave Crack, Palpitation, Shelf Route, Tiptoe, Diagonal Crack, The Clam, Limpet** Oread Mountaineering Club members

1952 Jun **The Arête, Hole and Corner Crack, Feet of Strength, Skull Crack, The Chute, The Bishop's Move, Lava Wall, Left Arête, Cave Wall, Rainbow Recess, Triack** Alan Simpson, Martin Ridges

1952 **The South-East Crack, The South-West Crack, The North Face, The Helix, Titan's Wall, The Web, Fandango** Dave Penlington

1962 June **Vertigo, Deadwood Crack, Deadwood Groove, Cave Rib, Cave Crack, The Flake Traverse** Midland Association of Mountaineers members

1962 Autumn **Twisting Crack, Hassell's Crack, Wigglette, Sale's Bulge, Kneewrecker Chimney**

Combination of Bob Hassall, Dave Sales, Graham Martin, John Wilding

1959–63 **Hollybush Hell, Defiance, Chilton's Superdirect, Left Twin Crack, Right Twin Crack, Central Crack, Tunnel Chimney, Blunder** David Hudson and some members from Denstone College Climbing Club

1959–63 **Stonemason's Crack, Sculptor's Wall, Back Side** unknown

1969 **Spreadeagle** Austin Plant, J Stubbs

1969 **The Taxman, The Unveiling, The Fly** (some aid used) Austin Plant, Bob Hassall *The Fly was climbed free by Andrew and Jonny Woodward in 1975.*

pre-1970 **Pine Tree Wall, Footpath Climb, Solo Chimney, Pegger's Original** D Hewitt

1970 Jan **Sauron, The Hob, Tiger's Wall, The Highwayman, Hot Pants, Ugly Puss** John Yates, Barry Marsden, various leads

1970 **The Gallows, Pasihpae, Daedalus, Theseus, Minotaur, Labyrinth, Long Traverse, Central Route, Tactical Weapon** (1 pt.), **Initiation Groove, Ground Support, Rawhide, Bloody Crack, The Renaissance, Ungodly Groove, Gladiator, Atlas** (1 pt.) John Yates, Norman Hoskins, Austin Plant, Bob Hassall, various leads *The Gallows was finished via the castle walls. Only the upper half of Theseus was climbed, the route was started on the right. Direct start added in 1971 by the same climber. Tactical Weapon climbed free by Andrew and Jonny Woodward in October 1975. Atlas climbed free by Jonny and Andrew Woodward in September 1977. Only a partial ascent of Ungodly Groove was made, a complete ascent coming from John Yates in 1971.*

1970 **Alien Wall, The Overhang, Minos** North Staffordshire Mountaineering Club

| 1970 Spring | **The Nose, The Cheek, Ostentation, The Impending Doom** (2 pts)   Austin Plant
Impending Doom climbed free in 1970 by John Yates. |
| 1970 June | **The Constant Grumble**   Norman Hoskins |
| 1970 June | **Manifesto**   Bob Hassall, Ralph Fawcett |
| 1971 | **Mark, Stephen, The Brothers, Transit Crack, Stark, Zeus** (I pt.)   Norman Hoskins
Zeus climbed free by Andrew and Jonny Woodward in July 1978. |
| 1971 Feb | **The Prodigal, Per Rectum, The Graduate**   Dave Salt |
| 1971 | **Extractum, Tre Cime, Honest John, Peakstone Crack, Stumblehead, Plebble, Afrodizzy Crack, Scoop Wall, Right Wall, Scout Wall, B.J.M., Cripples Corner, Pull John, Gentleman John** (I pt.)
John Yates, Barry Marsden, various leads
Gentleman John climbed free by Jonny and Andrew Woodward in 1978. |
| 1971 Apr | **Donor, Amazing Grace, The Missus, Full Frontal**   Bob Hassall, Dave Salt   *A new finish added to The Missus in 1978 by Steve Dale.* |
| 1971 | **Quasimodo** (some aid used)   John Yates, Barry Marsden   *Climbed free by Andrew and Jonny Woodward in 1973.* |
| 1971 | **Wootton Wanderer, Hanging Crack** (I pt.)
Pete Ruddle, Barry Marsden, Chris Cartlidge
Hanging Crack climbed free by Andrew Woodward in 1975. |
1971	**Rig a Dig Dig** (4 pts.) Pete Ruddle, Dave Salt, Norman Hoskins *Climbed free by Jonny Woodward in 1975.*
1971 May	**The Clown** (I pt.), **The Joker** (I pt.) Norman Hoskins *Both climbed free by Jonny Woodward in 1975.*
1971	**Nosey Parker** Ralph Fawcett, Barry Marsden, Pete Harrop, Jeff Wincott
1972 Mar	**Rocking Stone Crack, Magnificat, Evensons, Psalm, Descant** Bob Hassall
1973	**Special K, Kaleidoscope** John Yates (solo)
1974	**Death Wish** Barry Marsden
1975	**Dark Star, Anthem for Doomed Youth, A Phoenix too Frequent, Much Ado About Nothing** Jonny Woodward, unseconded, or with Andrew Woodward
1976	**Pebble Drop, Climb to the Lost World** Unknown

1977 Sep 17	**The Height Below, Four Horsemen** Andrew Woodward, Jonny Woodward, various leads
1977	**Grumbling Wall, Indecent Exposure** Steve and Brian Dale
1977 Aug	**DNA** Steve Bancroft, Nicky Stokes
1978	**Ant's Corner, Uncle's Arête, Dancing Bear, Impacted Bowl, Northern Lights, Peeping Tom** Steve Dale, Brian Dale, Barry Marsden, various leads
1978	**Droopy Draws, Tyre Pressure, Parking Fine, Crud on the Tracks, Tequila Sunrise** Ewan Murray, Sharon Tonks
1978 Oct	**Jack the Traverse, To Live Again, Down to the Elbows, Pull Jonny, Patient Weaver** Jonny Woodward, Andrew Woodward. *Twenty-five years on, Jack the Traverse has still not had a known repeat.*
1978	**Runaway** Mike Hernon
1978	**Technocrat, Don Quixote, Tricky Woo, The Gateless Gate, Ivanhoe, Taming of the Shrew, Tour de Force, Qui Vive, Nom de Guerre, Battle Royal, Melancholy Man** John Codling (solo)
1978	**Pillow of Winds, One Knight Stand, All the King's Horses, The Stadium, The Last Post, Megalomania, Alternative Ulster** Gary Gibson (solo)
1979	**Daddy Long Legs, The Mexican** Ewan Murray
1979	**Rhody Crack, Lord's Chimney, Reverse Charge, Iron Ore, Dimmings Dale Crack, Slip Knot, Green Slab, Tope Brick, Slippery Caramel, Toast Rack, Lord's Arête** (I pt.), **Working Hunter, Rabbit Stew, Bright Eyes, Recess Corner, Glossy Finish, Undercoat, Christmas Tree Crack, Grott, Roof Slab, Drop Leaf, Desert Rat, White Mouse, Dust Storm, Sandbagger, Canticle, Dance of the Flies, Austin's Chimney, Rakes Dale Chimney, Crusty, Lone Wall, Even lonelier, Thum, Maloof, Bubble, Squeak** Steve Dale, Brian Dale, various leads *Lord's Arête freed by Ian Barker in 1986. Dance of the Flies was top-roped first and named after a cloud of midges that accompanied the ascent. Some of the routes may have been climbed before.*
1979	**Moto Perpetuo, Whispering Myth, Five Thousand Volts, Dimetrodon, Time's Arrow,**

Soar Off, Thorns, Alternative Three, Doina Da J'al, Robin Hood, Friar Muck, Hand Jive Jonny Woodward, Andrew Woodward

1979 Jul 26 **Chocolate Orange, Twiggy, Fagan** T Salt

1979 **Killjoy, Kudos, Knossos, Kobold, Krakatoa, The Jester, Life in the Wrong Lane** Gary Gibson, solo, or with a combination of John Perry, Kons Nowak, Mark 'Ralph' Hewitt *Knossos was top-roped three times before a lead was made after an on-sight failure resulted in a frightening fall. Kons Nowak was a local lad who was led to believe that climbing was fun and was lured from college to hold the ropes. He soon changed his mind to find that music and alcohol were more fun!*

1970s **Black Widow, Palsy Wall, The Sting** Martin Boysen *Palsey Wall soloed by Tony Barley, May 9, 1974, which may have been the first ascent.*

1980 May **Cave Crack, Long Lankin, Little Nikki** Steve Dale, Brian Dale

1980 May **Konsolation Prize, Krushna, Kenyatta** Gary Gibson, solo, or with Dave Williams

1982 **Crimes of Passion** Paul Pepperday

1983 Mar **Longstop, Five Bar Crack** Steve Dale, Barry Marsden *Longstop led originally with a peg for aid but climbed free by the same pair on the same day.*

1983 **Mental Traveller** Paddy Gaunt

1984 May 16 **Boats for Hire** Nick Dixon, Steve Lowe

1984 May 22 **One Chromosome's Missing** Nick Dixon, Andy Popp *A major addition. An impressive show of boldness on these esoteric outcrops, one of the country's first E7s. The route was flashed by Ben Tetler in 1999, having been there while friends top-roped it, although…. "Ben was there when we were on it, but I don't recall him paying much attention." Surprisingly, Tetler also decided to solo it, despite the fact that protection is fairly hopeful. In the afternoon, he made the 2nd ascent of Pair O' Genes.*

1984 Dec 16 **Fast and Bulbous** Brian Davison, Richard Jones, Neil Horn

1986 Jul 27 **Time Flies By** Brian Davison, Richard Jones

1986 **The Fatalist's Canoe, Face** Nick Dixon *The Fatalist's Canoe climbed on-sight after many attempts in the rain.*

1986 **Life in the Left Lane** Ian Dun

1987 Apr 20 **The Brazilian** Simon Alsop (solo)

1988 Feb 15 **Hopeless Holly, Aliens, You'll Always Reap What You Sow** Gary Gibson (solo)

1988 Apr 6 **Supermac, All Day and All of the Night** Gary Gibson *Supermac was a free ascent of Himac.*

1988 Apr 23 **Fingers in Every Pie** Simon Nadin

1988 Apr **The Leading Fireman** John Perry, Simon Nadin

1988 Jul 21 **The Pride** Martin Boysen, Alan Hubbard

1988 Sep 10 **Puppet Life** Jim Nicholls, Roger Nicholls

1988 Oct **Monk's Blues, The High Priest** Rab Carrington, Martin Boysen

1989 Apr 22 **Distant Summers** Simon Alsop, Tim Twentymen, Dave Whittles *Two peg runners were used on the first ascent. The route was reclimbed without these by Jim and Roger Nicholls on 2nd August 1989. An alternative name of Distant Runners was offered.*

1989 **Legoland, Grounded, Lethal Weapon, Open All Hours, Miss Understood** Gary Gibson, alone or with Hazel Gibson

1989 **General Accident, Chiropodist's Nightmare, No Pegs Please, We're British, Wild Frontier, Flake Escape** Roger Nicholls, Jim Nicholls, various leads

1989 Spring **In Days of Hold, The Humble Potter** Andy Popp

1990 **Pocket Hercules, Ripples, Cherry Rare, Never, Never, Suckin' Pebbles, Motorbike** Gary Gibson, either solo, or with Hazel Gibson

1990 Apr 4 **Ina City Riot** Andy Popp (solo)

1990 Apr 22 **The Molegrip Kid, Restless Natives** Simon Alsop, Brian Edmonds, Rob Hilditch

1990 **Kangerman, Cad Cam Warrior, Ex-Lion Tamer, Feast of Blaze, Poisonous Pie-Man, Rum Punch, Here Be Dragons** Roger Nicholls, Jim Nicholls, various leads *A home-made cam provided half-height protection on Cad Cam Warrior.*

1990 Apr 29 **Rock Around the Chock** Mark Haselgrove

1990 May 1 **The Clumsy Too** Simon Bartram (solo)

1990 Jul 10 **My Mother is a Rhinoceros** Colin Cheetham (solo)

1990 Mar **Barriers in Slime, Porkstorm** John Perry, Colin Cheetham, Rob Barnett, S Birch

1990 May 31 **Old King Cole** Andy Popp, on sight

1990 Jul 22 **Henry Hothead realises that being the author of your Own Broken Ankle can be very Embarrassing, A Scent of Lamb** Simon Alsop

1990 Oct 7	**EMS**	Mike Grinder, Lee Swinson, John Emery
1991 Sep/Oct	**Legosaurus Rex, Duplo Magic, The Plastics Factory, Stickle Brick Wall, Raiders of the Lost Bark, Castles of Sand**	Gary Gibson (solo)
1991 Sep 9	**No Veranda**	Roger Nicholls (solo)
1992 Sep 13	**Overlord**	John Yates, Martin Boysen
1994 Sep	**Unnamed** (Wootton Lodge)	Justin Critchlow
1999	**Pair o' Genes**	Sam Whittaker *Second ascent by Ben Tetler, 1999. See One Chromosome first ascent note.*
1990s	**Moov Over, Pull the Udder One, Black and White, Curd be Cheese, Inaccessible, My Arse**	Simon Nadin

1990s	**John's Route**	John Perry, Simon Nadin
1990s	**Big Mike and the Dead Lift of Doom, Shepherd's Delight**	Julian Lines
1990s	**The Boyson-Carrington Route**	Martin Boyson, Rab Carrington
1990s	**Premature Evacuation**	Justin Critchlow, Julian Lines
2002	**Travelling Light, Travelling, Rocket to 'em, Prowler, Death Mask, Your Own Undoing, Sole Survivor**	Gary Gibson

❺ The Churnet Bouldering First Ascents

Allen's Fingers Allen Williams, 1986.

Billy Bunter, Sid the Sexist Roger & Jim Nicholls, 1989.

Blu-Tac, Bowcock's Chimney, Cabana, Charlie Farley, Doubloon, Golden Sovereign, Hot Dog, Hush Puppy, Marsden's Eliminate, Meninges, Mr Grogan, Peep Show, Pieces of Eight, Puffed Wheat, Raven, Spirella, Stickfast, Underhung Chimney Combination of Steve Dale, Brian Dale, Barry Marsden, John Yates, 1973.

Bond It Jonny Woodward, 1981.

Cannabis Arm Ian Dunn, 1986.

Fat Slags Gary Gibson, 2002.

Genetix, Pebblesville, Rusks and Rye Gary Gibson, 1979.

Johnson'sville Ian Johnson, 1979.

Lisa Lust Jim Nicholls, 1990.

Motorbike Gary Gibson, 1990.

Roger Melly, Billy the Fish Jim & Roger Nicholls, May, 1989.

Short Ride Jonny Woodward, 1979.

Simple Simon Andy Brown, Kelvin Grice, Lucy Ellis, Oct. 6, 1992.

Strenuosity, Pocket Wall Steve Dale, Brian Dale, 1979.

High Speed Imp Act Martin Veale. *Also claimed as Ungentlemanly Conduct by Gary Gibson.*

The Whirling Pit Simon Alsop, 1991.

White Widow Justin Critchlow, 2001.

Pockets O'Donnell bouldering on The Grogan at
Sharpcliffe (page 207). Photo: Alex Ekins.

In an effort to do something new, Alf Bridge set out straight from work one Saturday lunchtime [in 1927]. His plan was to make a climbing and walking excursion of the Peak...

...It was 6.30 p.m. before he arrived at Castle Naze and could gaze down at the promised land of Chinley. The A.P. Chimney seemed much harder than usual, and blistered heels forced a gingerly tread across The Scoop. For the final climb of the weekend he had planned to do Castle Naze Crack, but realised that in his worn out condition it was beyond him, so instead he struggled wearily up the safe but clinging cleft of Deep Chimney.

From **High Peak**, by Eric Byne

Outlying *Crags*

including **Windgather, Castle Naze** and **Bosley Cloud**

Castle Naze, the perfect evening venue.
Niall Grimes soloing on Combs Edge
(page 277), just south of the main edge.
Photo: Ken Wilson.

Outlying Crags

Windgather, Castle Naze, Bosley Cloud, Knypersley Rocks, Heighley Castle, Mow Cop, Rudyard Pinnacle and **The Wicken Stones**

Here, in the final chapter, is a round up of all the other crags dispersed throughout the area. They are scattered across the furthest reaches of Staffordshire, and often beyond. Here again, you will find something for everyone. The two star crags of this section, Windgather and Castle Naze, are both natural crags of the highest order. Windgather must surely be one of the most suitable beginner's crags in the country, with steep exciting climbs in the lowest of grades. Castle

Naze is a good next step up, with more serious outings in a fine moorland setting, only minutes from the road.

Conversely, crags such as Knypersley Rocks, Rudyard Pinnacle or Bosley Cloud are more suited to the lover of the esoteric. All have good routes in quirky settings, and most can guarantee a good day's adventure to anyone who possesses the exploratory urge.

Windgather

by Martin Kocsis

| O.S. Ref. **SJ997783** | Altitude: **400m a.s.l.** |

This is a beginners' crag *par excellence,* where the number of good quality, low-grade climbs on steep, juggy rock is unmatched throughout the Peak District. The crag, which sits on the Shining Tor ridge, commands an excellent view over much of the Goyt Valley.

Conditions & aspect

The name tells you pretty much all you need to know about the usual weather conditions around here! The rock is very clean and sound, and is quick drying. Being west-facing, it gets the sun from the afternoon, and is a suitable venue for year-round climbing.

Routes & bouldering

Superb. Seventy routes, mainly from Diff to VS, with a couple of harder ones as well. The crag as a whole

looks as if it is pushing up (or sinking) through the moorland. This has the pleasing result that the angle of the crag is friendly, and the holds are juggy where it matters. In fact, it probably has some of the steepest easy routes anywhere! As an inevitable result of its great character, Windgather nearly always has a team or two on it, and this has contributed to the smooth nature of some of the holds. Stoney Middleton though, this isn't, and there's very little reason why a foot should slip, other than as a result of the usual 'Elvis' impersonation at moments of extreme stress! For those with a discerning eye, the bouldering possibilities up to 5c/6a are extensive. The *High over Buxton* bouldering guide (available from local climbing shops) details 50 problems at the crag.

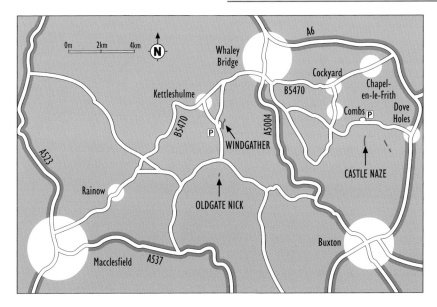

Parking & approach

Approaches come in three flavours: from Buxton, Whaley Bridge and Macclesfield. If you're coming from Buxton, the Shining Tor ridge can be reached by turning left off the Long Hill Road (Buxton to Whaley Bridge, A5004). This you do at the left-hand junction signposted for the Goyt about a mile out of Buxton on a right-hand bend. After crossing the Errwood reservoir dam, turn right and follow the road to the ridge top. Here, turn right into the lane which eventually runs below the crag.

Between Macclesfield and Whaley Bridge on the B5470, turn south in Kettleshulme near the Black Bull pub and, after two miles, the crag will be obvious on the skyline. Parking below the crag. Tractors and other agricultural car-wreckers use the lane beneath the crag, so you're advised to park well into the lay-by. There's space for a dozen cars, eight minibuses, or three coaches (not a pretty sight). Approach is less than a minute.

Access

After opposition to climbers using the crag from a previous owner, the crag is now owned by the Peak Park Planning Board, and the crag must ONLY be approached from the lane via the two stiles and the fenced alley. Climbers have access to the area within the fences above and below the crag, and they are asked not to damage them or the walls which limit the access area at either end of the crag. The lower fence, denoting the boundary, runs to the right (south) under the crag towards the quarry to meet one of these transverse walls. **Please do not climb over this fence.** There is a stone stile giving access to the quarry hidden a little higher up the slope.

On approaching the crag along the fenced alley, the first buttress in front of you is Buttress One. However, the climbs described start way off to the left, the best reference point being a dry-stone wall almost 200m away in that direction. In the first hundred metres from the alley lie the majority of the crag's routes. After North Buttress, the diminishing stature of the rock means that it holds more interest for boulderers.

V There is a wealth of bouldering at Windgather. Some of it is described here, some is left for you to discover on your own. Lots of bouldering can be had along the first low rocks, on good quality rounded gritstone, with lots of arêtes, slabs and overhangs. Not quite big enough to be routes, these little buttresses are almost the same size as some of the crags they climb on in North Yorkshire! The problems start far to the left, where the path that skirts the base of the crag bends up, through a pair of old gateposts and onto the top of the crag. This is about 20m right of the boundary dry stone wall.

◐ The first few problems to the right of the gateposts are obvious. They take a variety of slabs, ribs and cracks in the lower grades starting with a buttress with a projecting 'gun' at its top. **The gun** itself is split by a crack: this is an excellent but exposed 5a, whilst **the face** to the right is about 5b. To the right is an easy crack at VD, then a narrow, bulging buttress. **The direct** is a steep 4c. Just right again is a **low cave**. Climbing out of its left side and up the face above apparently involves a dyno and comes in at about 5a. All these V0. **Direct** through the lip is 5c (V1), and up and out of the **right-hand** side is 5a. Just right of this buttress is a short crack through a low roof: **Pure Crackling**, is a frustrating 5b (V1) that sticks purely to the crack and which will, most likely, spit you out several times!

◐ Further right is a quarry. The north-facing wall is fingery, steep and green. The **left** and **right-hand** lines are 4c, whilst the **central** one is V0 (5b). Not far right are some small undercut slabs, with jamming cracks in the middle. The **right-hand slab** is 4c and the **left-hand** one is 5a. The cracks themselves are most entertaining. Forty metres to the right of the slabs there is a steep, compact face with a niche near the top. The **right-hand side** of the face, then traversing into the niche, or climbing direct to the top is a fingery 4c. **Direct to the niche** is 5b, the **jinking crack** to the left is 4b and the **scooped face** left again is a tricky 5c. All V0–V1. Other, harder eliminates up to 6a are possible.
  The first routes start from two small grassy bays almost opposite a dry stone wall running up to the road on its other side. To the left, there is a concave wall above the first grassy bay. Climb the shallow angle at its centre, moving left at the bulge. **Bay Wall (S★)**. Worthwhile. **Christmas Nose (VS 5a)** goes up the staircase on the left, then moves gymnasti-

cally over the nose. **Red Nose Route (D)** climbs the corner on the left. Best done in the wet (and at night) for full satisfaction. **Christmas Arête (VD★)** climbs a short wall on the right-hand side of the second grassy bay to a ledge, then the sharp arête on satisfying holds. **◐** The traverse across the short wall, using the obvious sloping shelf is a short but hard 5c (V2). Down and right of this bay is a small bulging buttress. A fun V0– (5a) problem tackles the most bulging line. Further fillers-in lie in the next 10m.

North Buttress

Forty metres right of Christmas Arête is a prominent buttress. The first route is a fairly technical offering (for Windgather!) up a narrow buttress, set forward from the main bulk of the crag.

❶ The Rib VS 5a
9m A hard step off a block leads directly up the centre on small crimps. Tricky to protect. Use of the arêtes makes it 4c.

❷ The Rib Right-Hand S
9m Start at the same place as The Rib, but climb up and right to a small flake. Use this to gain the side face of the buttress, and climb it until you can step round onto the front face about ten feet below the top.

❸ Staircase M ★
9m A fine beginner's lead with both good moves and good protection.

❹ Green Slab S ★
9m Start just to the left of the wide flake-crack (or cheat up the crack). Make an awkward but well-protected move off the flake and go up the wall above.

❺ Black Slab S ★
9m A tricky start leads to more steep climbing. Cross the bulge, then go up a flake to finish 1m left of Green Crack.

6 Green Crack S ★★
9m A thrilling lead, with great three dimensional climbing on steep rock. Follow the steep groove to the wide, leaning upper crack.

7 North Buttress Arête VS 4c ★★
9m A steep and bold climb, but with great holds. Surmount the undercut left side of the arête (rumoured to be 5a), then continue up the left-hand side of the arête. A Windgather classic.

8 North Buttress Arête Indirect S ★
9m Follow the arête on its right-hand side, pulling round left onto the front face near the top. Exposed.

9 Chimney and Crack VD
9m Climb to the ledge and move up leftwards into the chimney, to finish with some difficulty up the wide crack on the left.

10 Heather Buttress VD ★
8m This route lies 15m right of North Buttress. A broken arête leads to a gap below an overhang. Climb the arête and the wall above the overhang. Opinions about the grade vary considerably; consequently *perhaps* a soft touch at this grade.

Windgather

is a very popular crag for top-roping on. However, it should be remembered that, for those new to the game, there is no finer place to learn one's leading skills.

In the text, every effort has been made to point out less well-protected routes that inexperienced leaders may wish to avoid. Also, a list of well-protected routes is given here:

- **Staircase**
- **Slant Start**
- **Chockstone Chimney**
- **Mississippi Crack**
- **The Corner**
- **High Buttress Arête**
- **Buttress Two Gully**
- **Squashed Finger**

All these routes can be well-protected with a modest beginner's rack, consisting of a set of nuts, a few larger hexes, a couple of slings and a few quickdraws. Once you are comfortable with these, then check out the suggestions for beginners on the Roaches, then the list of advanced beginner's routes at Hen Cloud and Ramshaw. After that, you will be a skilled leader ready for anything.

Great holds make the routes at Windgather surprisingly easy for their steepness. Ronan Browner soloing North Buttress Arête, VS 4c (page 261). Photo: Niall Grimes.

Middle Buttress

This is the next blocky buttress 15m right of Heather Buttress. Tricky descents are possible on either side of it.

⓫ Taller Overhang VS 5b
8m This takes the double overhangs as centrally as possible. More technical than strenuous, and as hard as Portfolio but nowhere near as entertaining.

Small Wall (S 4b) is the low and short square-cut wall. **The Corner** (M) is the obvious corner. Stepping out of it leftwards onto the platform gives an easy way up (or down).

⓬ Portfolio HVS 5b ★
8m A steep local test-piece. Avoiding the holds on Wall Climb, ascend direct to the overhang. This is surmounted via a crucial series of strenuous pulls. Be **very** aware of the polish on the initial slab.

⓭ Wall Climb VD
9m Strangely named… Climb the parallel cracks (polished) to the final chimney. This is steep, deep and exciting.

⓮ Central Route HVD ★
9m Start below a thin crack in the crag top and climb direct to it. For **Slant Start** (VD) climb diagonally to the top crack from the start of Chockstone Chimney.

John Laycock recorded that routes such as **High Buttress Arête** and **Middle Buttress Arête** were climbed prior to 1913. Other routes were done but were not deemed important enough to be named. Later, in 1935, C D Milner produced the first guidebook to the rocks in the Mountaineering Journal, and eighteen routes were reported. However it is likely that many of these were first climbed years before 1914 by Stanley Jeffcoat, a resident of Buxton. By 1948 there were still only 24 recorded routes, and **Portfolio** (often credited to Joe Brown) was the most significant ascent. First ascents are recorded as 'Traditional', as these rocks have been climbed on for well over a hundred years. First ascent dates and details are not given, since every route described, plus those that aren't, will have been climbed repeatedly since time immemorial.

⓯ Chockstone Chimney D ★
9m The ragged crack gives a well-protected lead.

⓰ Mississippi (or Straight) **Crack** S ★
9m The fine bottomless crack is long and sustained, and a good first Severe lead.

⓱ Mississippi Crack Variant VD ★★
9m Start up The Medicine and traverse left under the overlap to join the Mississippi crack above its crux. An excellent, sustained combination.

⓲ The Medicine HS 4a ★
9m Take the juggy bulges direct. Poorly protected and with some worryingly long reaches: testing!

⓳ M.B. Arête D
9m Climb up to an awkward move into a corner. This leads to the broad platform. Step left and climb the right edge of the face above.

High Buttress

This is the next buttress along, with a prominent right arête, and a brown, slightly sandy 'footprint' halfway up the face. This is the most popular buttress hereabouts, with a fine selection of quality offerings.

⓴ Bulging Arête S
9m Set forward from the main buttress, this climb takes the small overhang on its right. Demanding on the arms and with a serious feel, until you find the hidden hold.

㉑ The Corner D
9m A route to consider as both an early lead and an introduction to the delights of polished holds!

㉒ Toe Nail VD ★
9m Go directly through the 'toes'. Protection is a little distant above the bulge.

㉓ Zigzag D
9m Start as for Toe Nail and climb diagonally right to a position above the nose, then finish direct. A long route on this little crag.

㉔ Footprint VD
9m Climb direct through the heel of the footprint.

㉕ Nose Direct HVD ★★
9m Start at the small recess just left of the arête, and climb direct to the nose. Pull over it, step left, and continue direct. A problematic route, but with great protection. Climbing 1m to the right gives the myopic **Director**, (VS 4c).

㉖ High Buttress Arête D ★★
9m Start at the foot of the arête and follow it almost direct. An excellent route at this grade, perhaps one of the best in the Peak.

㉗ Heather Face VD ★
9m Similar in nature to Side Face (poor gear and rounded holds) and with an excellent (but protected) 'sting in the tail' at the overlap. **Broken Cracks** (HD), the climb just right, is better protected, but vegetated and loose.

Buttress Two

This is the nearest buttress to the road. Very popular, with a good selection of routes and at least one beefy struggle!

㉘ Rib and Slab M
9m Clean climbing just left of the gully.

㉙ Buttress Two Gully M ★
9m A very traditional climb (for your first lead!)

㉚ Leg Stump D
9m Bowl up the easiest (but unprotected) line up the slab.

㉛ Middle and Leg D
9m Good climbing and protection.

㉜ The Centre VD
9m Fine climbing but without any gear until near the top.

㉝ Squashed Finger VD ★
9m Good climbing; quite stiff but well-protected.

34 Struggle HS 4b ★
9m The crack through the nose. A hard but well-protected little problem that gives 'full value' at this grade.

35 Corner Crack VD ★
9m For those who need an explanation, none is possible.

36 Aged Crack HS 4a ★
9m Climb direct to the crack. Moving into the crack from Corner Crack makes the route VD.

37 Traditional HS 4a ★
9m Step off the block and climb directly past the blunt flake. Small cams are useful.

38 The Broken Groove in the Arête D
9m Steep and well-protected: an excellent first lead.

39 Cheek HVS 5a
9m Start from a block below the right-hand side-wall and climb up to meet the arête at the top. Short and sharp. The protection is there for those with the cunning to place it!

Buttress One

The next compact buttress past broken rocks.

40 Face Route 2 M
9m Follow the broken cracks.

41 Face Route I VD
9m Easy climbing but gearless where it matters the most. Pull over the small overhang, then climb more easily up the face.

42 First's Arête D
9m Follow the right-hand side of the arête.

43 Side Face S
9m Climb directly up the right-hand side face on sloping holds and limited gear, keeping to the left of the holly.

The small walls within the next 30m offer many problems and possibilities. The flat, quarried face in the middle of these walls offers blinkered eliminates at about Severe.

South Buttress

Thirty five metres to the right of the entrance to the crag is a large undercut buttress with a cave at the right-hand end and a pulpit at about the same level under its left-hand end.

44 Overhanging Arête VD
9m Hard moves lead from the gully on the left of the buttress. Move rightwards to join and follow Leg Up.

45 Leg Up HVS 5a
9m From the pulpit, make a bold and strenuous pull over the nose. A strenuous arête problem, easi-

It may no longer be the hardest route in the Peak, but it is still one of the finest routes of its grade. The famous Crack at Castle Naze. VS 4b (page 265). Photo: Niall Grimes.

ly protected although this is not initially obvious. If you stray too far right then the problem is almost two grades harder due to a broken hold.

㊻ Route 2 VS 4b ★
9m From the pulpit, step right and climb the steep crack through the overhang. Quite hard considering its shortness.

㊼ Route 1.5 HVS 5a ★
9m A route with adequate protection, if you have the strength and cunning to place it.

㊽ Editor's Note VS 5a
9m Pull out and up to join and follow Route 1 on rapidly improving jugs. Small wires may help for the one and only hard move.

㊾ Arête Direct E1 5b ★
9m A fun climb with very good moves but effectively a solo, as the finish is much easier. Stretch from the ledge for good holds on the lip left of the arête and cut loose! If you are unsure, side-runners can be placed on the right wall from the ledge, reducing the climb to HVS 5b. Some locals will tell you that even heel hooking on the right is cheating!

㊿ Route 1 S ★★
9m Climb part way up South Crack, and then traverse leftwards round the arête onto a ledge above the cave. Pull past blocks and continue to the top.
Variation: The left-hand side of the arête, from the right-hand side of the ledge, is VS 4c.

51 Route 1 Direct HVS 5a
9m The right-hand side of the arête, followed direct, is good value.

52 South Crack M
9m Wide crack climbing.

To the right of South Crack are three short cracks, all of which are less easy than you would think! They are the **Triplet Cracks**. **Left Triplet Crack** is D, **Middle Triplet Crack** is S, as is **Right Triplet Crack**. **Overlapping Wall** (HS 4b) climbs the small bulging buttress just right. Two very minor routes climb rock to the right of Overlapping Wall. **Discontinuous Rib** and **Groove**, both M.

V The Quarry 100m to the right of the main crag is an excellent and sheltered venue for both amenable boulder problems and steady traverses. There are many, many variations and so nothing is described, just find out for yourself!

Oldgate Nick

by John H Bull

| O.S. Ref. **SJ996764** | Altitude: **400m a.s.l.** |

Hear the howl of the rope, a question:

Did we miss anything? Did we miss anything?

'Catapult' (Berry, Buck, Mills, Stipe)

This pleasant isolated buttress, also known as Cat's Tor, is visible from the road junction about half a mile south of Windgather Rocks. Approach from the junction via the path that leads along the to ridge to Cat's Tor proper and Shining Tor. The crag's main feature is the impressive triangular overhang taken by Catapult. The arête composed of bedding planes 25m left of the main overhang gives **Stilted** (VD); the similar rib 10m left of the overhang is **Jilted (D)**. The main slab above the overhang is gained by a bouldery start up a steep rib to give **Rib and Slab** (HVD). All 2000. At the time of writing there is a belay peg above the main overhanging section of the crag.

1 Nine Tales VS 4c   2000
10m Under the left side of the main overhang is a bulging flake at 4m. Climb direct to the bulging flake, and hand-traverse it steeply leftwards to join the slab. Finish direct.

2 Original Route HVD ★   pre-1990
12m Climb up a rightward-leaning groove to a ledge under the roof. Traverse awkwardly rightwards to gain twin cracks, and finish up these with reverence.

3 Catapult E5 6a ★   2003
12m A committing traverse of the vertical tiered face under the roof. Climb to the ledge under the right-hand side of the roof, and reach from a wobbly flake to good incuts above. Follow holds leftwards under the roof until, feet on the flake of Nine Tales, it is possible to pull onto the slab. The unsuccessful become ammunition for an ancient weapon used to hurl large objects.

4 Crime Gene VS 4b   2000
10m Climb a steep rib to gain the ledge of Original Route. Pull around the right side of the overhang just left of the twin cracks of Original Route, and steal up the stratified face directly.

5 The Cat Inside VD   1997
12m Start at a groove studded with large hemispherical holes, and gain the traverse line in the face above the overhang. Slink leftwards to finish up the easy-angled arête past a loose block. The small overhanging buttress to the right gives some steep problems (V0–V1).

Castle Naze

by Martin Kocsis

O.S. Ref. **SJ054785** | Altitude: **400m a.s.l.**

Highly underrated for many years, Castle Naze has often been dismissed as a beginners' crag, perhaps next on the syllabus after Windgather. This is something of a misconception, for, while it may be true that it is a beginners' crag, there are enough routes in the Extreme category to interest and baffle any competent leader. Most of the crag consists of natural rock and is therefore fairly solid, though lumps do fly off the top both frequently and without warning.

Conditions & aspect

The crag faces west, is fairly sheltered, and is consequently clean and quick drying. It is also an excellent evening venue with great views and a reasonably sheltered nature.

Routes & bouldering

A great selection of routes, best suited to the low- and mid-grade leader. Many of the VS and HVS routes are less than easy, and have been known to cause both broken bones and damaged egos. Routes up to VS are also generally regarded as 'good value' (whatever that may mean!). The quarried section at the right-hand end is home to some suspect rock above the routes, but the routes themselves have been well-cleaned recently and are as solid as you could expect. Belays are occasionally hard to find, though assorted metal stakes and fence posts are more than adequate in most cases. Not a great crag for bouldering, although some problems are documented in the bouldering guide *High over Buxton*.

Parking & approach

The Naze is on the moorland above the High Peak village of Combs, reached by a minor road off the B5470 between Whaley Bridge and Chapel en le Frith. From The Beehive pub in Combs follow the road towards the crag, seen above the village to the east. The road is narrow and steep in places. Once

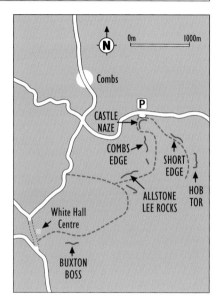

the road levels out at the top of the moor, two lay-bys will be obvious with spaces for bout six cars. If they're full please go elsewhere, since wing mirrors are, on occasion, easily removed by passing tractors.

If you're coming from Buxton, turn left in Dove Holes ("Twinned with Siberia", according to infamous local graffiti) down Station Road, following signs to the railway station. Go over the railway bridge, and a couple of hundred metres later, turn left up Cowlow Lane. After a couple of miles, the lay-bys previously mentioned will be seen. There's an obvious, but strangely exhausting, path up to the rocks. 5 minutes.

Pubs

The Beehive Inn in Combs is excellent for food, beer and a warm fire.

The recorded routes start on the first substantial piece of rock you come to on your approach. Here you will find a short face, split by a crack that begins life as a wide crack, but then splits into two. This is **Double Crack**.

❶ Double Crack D · pre-1913
4m Climb the crack. ❤ **The face** to the right, avoiding the crack and arête, is an exciting V0 (5a). **The Arête** (HS 4a), is the fine slabby arête. A small cam protects the easier but still exposed finish. Climbing the arête on its right is V1 (5c).

Just right is a small bay, containing a few short, easy cracks of about D. The next recorded routes are based around the obvious pinnacle.

❷ Pinnacle Arête VD · pre-1913
5m Climb the outer edge of the pinnacle to the summit. The top block is wobbly and the block that used to be above this now lies beneath you amongst the scree. **Pinnacle Crack** (VD, pre-1913) climbs the wall to the left, finishing behind the pinnacle.

❸ Sheltered Crack D ★ · pre-1913
5m This crack is behind and right of the pinnacle. Avoid use of the pinnacle for the full tick. **Bow Crack** (S, 1984) starts as for the previous route, but breaks out rightwards to a perched block.

❹ Overhanging Chockstone Crack
VD · pre-1913
6m A good traditional tweed-wrecker. Start up the gully, and somehow climb over the huge chockstone. You may also wish to do the through route for full value at a slightly easier grade. **Slanting Crack** (S, 1960s) climbs a crack to the left, finishing leftwards past a triangular block.

❺ The Fifth Horseman HVS 5a ★ · 1984
6m Take the easiest line up the left-hand side of the wall. Quite bold for its size.

❻ Icebreaker E2 5b · 2002
6m This takes a bold but enjoyable line up the slab right of the last route. You should head for, and use, the obvious big pebble. A small wire provides limited protection for the few short moves on the slab. Taller climbers will find this much easier.

To the right, five short problems make their way to the ledge above, with two exits from that ledge (both Severe).

❼ Muscle Crack VS 4c · pre-1913
4m The blocky crack leads to the ledge. Climb the flake on the right. **Thin Crack** (4c, 1960s) is a good alternative start following the brisk crack just left, while **V-Corner** (4b, pre-1913) uses awkward thrutching or precarious layaways to gain the ledge via the short corner left again.

As is **the case**

with many of the gritstone crags, the origins of climbing here are somewhat obscure but it can be assumed that a good number of the routes included in Laycock's 1913 **Some Gritstone Climbs** were done well before the turn of the century. This guidebook, that reads more like a novel than a climbing guidebook, contained some 32 named routes and mentioned numerous other possibilities and sporting problems. By 1923, Fergus Graham, in his **Recent Developments on Gritstone**, reported that Jeffcoat was the 'original exploiter of Castle Naze' and that even then 'the rocks were so thoroughly explored by their discoverers, that very little scope remains for further additions'.

⑧ Block Crack Left-Hand S   1960s
6m The thick crack leads to the ledge. Take the flake above. **Bloody Crack** (S, 1960s) is the well-named alternative start up the fist-crack to the left.

⑨ The Nose HS 4b   1960s
12m Technical and committing bridging leads up the recess, and then into the sentry box. Go back up and right from there.

⑩ The Nithin S 4a   pre-1913
12m The steep right-hand crack of the recess leads strenuously to the ledge. Finish up the chimney crack.

⑪ Flake Crack HS 4a   pre-1913
12m Start in the corner to the right, and climb the obvious crack to the ledge on The Nithin. Layback the propped flakes to get to a leftwards finish.

⑫ Main Corner S   1960s
12m A deeply traditional struggle.

⑬ The Fly Walk S   pre-1913
10m The well worn crack right of Main Corner.

⑭ The Niche S ★★   pre-1913
10m Steep jamming on good rough rock. Leave the niche via jams and the jammed block.

⑮ Niche Arête VS 4c ★★   pre-1913
10m Rounded, bold and satisfying. Climb the arête directly via long reaches and a pull up or two.

⑯ Orm and Cheep E1 6a ★   1989
10m The right slanting groove is climbed to a ledge (V3). Climb the wall above directly via several shallow pockets. Originally climbed with a side-runner to the right.

⑰ Studio HS 4a ★   pre-1913
9m Climb the major crack.

⑱ Nursery Arête HVS 5b ★   2003
10m The hanging arête. Step off a boulder and make tricky moves to a ledge. Climb the arête above

using the breaks (but not the right-hand wall). Surprisingly independent.

⑲ A.P. Chimney S ★   pre-1913
10m A classic chimney that needs no description. The AP stands for Absolutely Perpendicular.

⑳ Pod Crack E1 5c ★   1984
11m The thin crack with the pod halfway up it. Criminally undergraded… if you cruise this, go straight past 'Regent Street' and on to something much harder.

㉑ Pilgrim's Progress HS 4a ★   pre-1935
11m Climb the crack at the right end of the wall. Use of the right arête will not be frowned upon. **Pitoned Crack** (HVS 5b, 1960s) is the barely independent crack to the left. If you stick to the crack, award yourself a pat on the back, but it's very hard to keep a hand or foot out of Pilgrim's Progress.

㉒ Little Pillar HS 4b   pre-1913
11m Climb the crack in the right hand side of a rib. From the platform above, climb the continuation of the crack to the top.

㉓ Ledgeway HVS 5a   1970s
11m Climb to the ledge any way you chose, then use a flake on the back wall to reach a left slanting crack. **Ⓥ Short and Sweet** V3 (6a) climbs the arête to the left of the start.

㉔ No Name HVD   pre-1948
11m Climb the awkward crack to reach the ledge. Continue directly.

㉕ Keep Buttress HVS 5a   1970s
11m Climb the crack in the rib to the right and then finish up the right-hand side of the rib above.

㉖ Keep Corner HVD ★   pre-1913
11m A good route up the corner right of Keep Buttress.

The next buttress is home to the 'world famous' Scoop. Originally, bare feet were considered appropriate for an ascent; these days, a blizzard of chalk and a load of sliding around on the first few moves seems more usual!

㉗ Keep Arête VS 4b ★   pre-1948
11m After some good steep moves, follow the arête of the buttress as closely as you can. A short sling may be found useful en route.

㉘ Scoop Direct HVS 5a   1970s
11m Climb into the left-hand end of the scoop, and continue directly via a thin crack.

㉙ Scoop Face HVS 5a ★★   1914
13m An inspirational achievement for the year it was climbed. Start 3m right of Keep Arête, and using polished holds and clean technique, climb into the scoop above. Traverse delicately up and right to a useful pocket and thin crack. Go up and left to finish. **The Direct Start** (E1 5c) steps off a little ledge 3m right of the normal start, and uses all available means to gain the scoop via the obvious pocket below the centre of the scoop itself. Various other 'directs' have been done, all at about 6a.

㉚ Scoop Wall E1 5b   1988
11m Climb directly to the right edge of the scoop. From there, take a more or less direct line to the top. You might have to turn the bulge slightly on the left

㉛ Footstool Left S   pre-1913
11m The corner just right is a bit of a struggle. The arête to the right, **Piano Stool** (E1 5b, 1988), is a bold undertaking, not helped by pointy boulders beneath.

㉜ Footstool Right VD   1964
11m Another struggle up the corner on the right side of the arête.

*The rock to the right is easy angled, and the features are all too close together to be independent. It can be climbed anywhere up to Severe, the best route being the thin finger-crack (**Combs Climb**, 1984).*

The Crack Area

The gully to the right is an easy scrambling way down. The next routes start on the wall to the right. The first, **The Two-Step** (D, 1960s) is a poor route up the left side of the ridge. **Fat Man's Chimney** (M, pre-1913), is a short but entertaining problem up the first chimney. The next face contained what was, for nearly 30 years, the hardest route at the Naze. The true line up the centre of the Plankton wall is still unclimbed.

㉝ Come On Eileen E2 5c   1999
9m A bouldery and committing route up the left side of the wall. Climb to the porthole, and use the arête to climb to the top. **Plankton (E4 6a†, 1984)** is a serious and artificial line up the centre of the wall, finishing rightwards,

㉞ Assorted Pond Life HVS 5a   1997
9m Climb directly up the face just to the left of Deep Crack. Quite independent, and not all that easy.

㉟ Deep Crack VD   1984
9m Guess where this goes…

㊱ Deep Chimney VD   pre-1913
9m The next fissure to the right. If you cruise this without raising a sweat, head for The Beehive and a cream tea (or two).

㊲ Birthday Climb HVS 5b ★   1968
16m Climb the crack in the lower wall to the sentry box. Leave this by climbing up and left to the base of a flake, then follow this to the top. Underrated.

㊳ The Crack VS 4b ★★   pre-1913
14m Once one of the hardest routes in the Peak. From the sentry box, follow the alluring crack through the overhang.

㊳ Nozag VS 4c ★★★   pre-1948
14m Testing climbing in a superb position. Climb a crack until a step left leads onto the bold face. Climb this directly using the thin crack and all your bottle.

㊵ Zigzag Crack HS 4b ★   pre-1913
16m As for Nozag, but follow the crack to a wider crack and an easy finish.

㊶ Zig-a-Zag-a D   1984
14m A long and easy climb. Follow a corner system and wall above.

Later, after extensive research (during which time the encyclopaedic brains of both Keith Ashton and Gary Gibson were quizzed), it was realised that the lines in the quarried section near Peg Crack had been neither climbed nor claimed. This was immediately remedied to give ***Stoke the Engine***s by Laurie Carefoot, and then a few days later ***Keith George: The Movie*** by Martin Kocsis. The remaining two (harder) lines were then offered to certain 'big cheeses' within the climbing world. Neil Foster and Olly Allen were somehow recruited and, with publication deadlines looming, they bagged what are now the two hardest routes at Castle Naze.

㊷ Long Climb VD **pre-1913**
16m Take the easiest direct line to the top.

㊸ Central Tower VD ★ **pre-1913**
16m Better than it looks! Follow the green corner to the terrace. Move back right again and climb the lett-hand groove to the top.

㊹ Atropine HS 4b ★ **1977**
16m A good sustained route. Right of Central Tower, there's a projecting flake. Climb over this to a bay, then climb a ramp and crack near the left end of the bay to ledges. From here, take the tough flake to the right-hand finishing crack.

㊺ The Ugly Bloke E3 6a **1997**
16m Follow the next route (Belladonna) to the top of the rampline. Step left and move directly up the wall above, finishing via a blind pocket. Very bold, needing great care and cunning to place adequate gear.

㊻ Belladonna E1 5c ★ **1977**
17m A good route, despite the strangeness of the line. Follow Atropine to the ledge and continue up the right side of the arête above, until the obvious overlap is reached. Go right beneath this and then up to the next overlap. From here, traverse back left to the upper part of the original arête and an excellent finish. **Belladonna Direct** (E3 5c★, 1990), climbs the short section of arête avoided by Belladonna.

㊼ The Green Crack S **pre-1913**
16m Take the obvious series of corners. The top is somewhat dodgy, so take care. **The Blusher** (VS, 1984), climbs rocks down and to the right.Always loose and utterly dangerous: try tiger baiting as a safer alternative.

The next routes are in the quarried section, starting to the right of an obvious area of damaged rock.The first routes are on a steep slab with obvious cracks in it.

㊽ Morocc'n Roll E1 5b ★ **1986**
14m A good route. After a tricky start, follow the right slanting crack to a junction with Syringe Benefit.

㊾ Syringe Benefit E1 5c **1986**
14m The obvious, harder crack to the right. The chimney to the right (**Columbal Convenience**, S, 1986) is full of both jammed blocks and certain death.

The quarried face to the right is home to some climbs that, were they elsewhere in the Peak, would be extremely popular.

㊿ Chamonaze Blues E4 6b ★ **2003**
14m The first crack in the face ends it's usefulness at half height. From there, hard crimping, technical moves and some very small wires may be of some use!

(51) Peg Crack E1 5c ★ **1960s**
14m A good route up the crack in the middle of the face. The start is the hardest part of the climb.

(52) Iron Age Fortitude E4 6b ★★ **2003**
14m The striking crack-line. Hard moves will get you to the first jam; from there only determination will see you to the top. Well-protected and extremely good value.

(53) Keith George: The Movie E1 5b ★ **2003**
14m Climb directly to the niche at the right end of the quarried face, and then make a couple of hard

buttress. **South Crack** (D, 1986) is a right slanting crack just right. **South Buttress** (D, pre-1913) climbs the steps of the buttress from a lower level, finishing up the V-groove in the headwall. **V-Chimney** (D★, pre-1913) is a quality route taking the obvious major groove containing two flakes. **Southern Arête** (HS, 1986), is the right arête of V-Chimney.

Across the descent gully is an enticing, rippled buttress. **Bubbly Wall** (HVS 5a, 1970s) climbs the sidewall of the buttress, just left of the right arête. **Vanishing Crack** (HS 4a★, pre-1913) climbs the V-shaped corner and crack above. Another good little route. **The Vice** (D, pre-1948) is broken crack to the right, finishing up the cleft. **Struggle** (HS, 1950s) is the final route, up the chimney and twin cracks.

The Cluster of Ribs

Ten metres right of the last route is a small cluster of ribs and grooves.

There are three short lines here that have somehow acquired route status: **Boomerang** (M) is the obvious wide crack on the left of the first rib; **Boomerang Buttress** (VS 4b) is the arête to the right with a grim landing; **Overhanging Chimney** (VD) is, well… All pre-1913. Beyond these last three routes are further areas of ribs, corners and arêtes. These are not described here, and are best enjoyed as an evening's soloing in the lower grades

Finally, there is the 'ultra classic' that is alleged to have been the forerunner of every single girdle traverse in the world. It is actually much better than you would think!

55 Herford's Girdle Traverse HS ★ 1910–1912

miles A classic expedition which is less easy than you might imagine. The route starts at Double Crack, and finishes, some time later at the top of Overhanging Chimney. Many variations can be done to either raise or lower the difficulty. Certainly worth doing.

Beyond these routes are further areas of assorted ribs, corners and arêtes. It feels so 'remote' here that it has become known as Australia Buttress! A great place to solo in the last of the evening's light. Most routes are about 4 or 5m in height. **Duck-Billed**

pulls up and left from a scary undercut onto the face. Finish up the thin crack above. Like Keith, better than it looks.

54 Stoke the Engines E1 5b ★ 2003

14m Just to the right of the previous route climb easily into the corner. From here, step up and left onto the base of the clean slab, and boldly climb it to a steeper finish.

South Buttress

About 15m right of this last route is a short, natural buttress. It has a fine collection of short routes, which are of very different character to the main face, on weathered, heavily-featured sound rock.

One of the biggest problems of climbing here is the exposed start positions where belays are a sensible idea, especially if there is any dampness around. The rock is good, weathered moorland grit, and although the climbs are very short, they are good problems nonetheless. There is an exposed but easy grassy descent slope on its left, which requires care in wet conditions, especially given the steep slope below. The first route is **Hodgkinson's Chimney** (M, pre-1913), the easy chimney in the left wall of the

A **girdle** traverse

of some 250 feet by Herford was included in the 1913 guidebook and the description informs us that a party of two good 'average climbers' knowing the rock could complete the course in one hour. A strange inclusion however is *The Girdle Traverse Reversed*, which will appeal most to those who have first made the passage in the original direction; the various difficulties were said to present a novel aspect.

Platypus (HS 4c) is the arête right of Overhanging Chimney climbed with blinkers. **Koala** (M) is the chimney gully to the right, which is worthwhile despite some vegetation. **Wombat** (VD) is the hanging corner crack right again. **Kangaroo** (VS 5a) is a very good micro-route up the steep prow using sidepulls on both sides to finish on jugs. **Opossum** (D) is the cracks and chimney right again. **Tasmanian Devil** (HD) is the corner right again, preferably starting up the front of the detached block below. Better than its green appearance would suggest. **Wallaby** (S 4b) is the arête right again on good holds. **Bandicoot** (M) is the broken corner right again. **Dingo** (S 4b) is the arête right again is a little dirty. Right again, at the end of the crag is another grassy descent that requires care.

Castle Naze – Surrounding Crags

by John H Bull

I remember my body. It was a metropolis of worms deep in a black hole. Candles appeared on my hands, feet and stomach. The candles became needles and stuck out of my grey corpse like beacons. And it was at this point that my luck began to change…"MOSS ELIXIR – out now!"

Robyn Hitchcock

Combs Moss, is an extensive expanse of grouse moorland lying between Buxton and Chapel en le Frith. Castle Naze forms its north-westerly apex and, above it, ancient earthworks delineate the missing side of a triangle of natural fortification; the remains of a hill fort that was first constructed in the Iron Age. Dotted about on the edges of the moor are several small outcrops whose neglected atmosphere, with a little imagination, is redolent of forgotten Celtic myth. Hob was here: the horned god; the green man; and probably the individual responsible for the copious moss on many routes at Short Edge and the Tor that bears his name. For those who might enjoy the walk needed to reach them, the crags provide a smattering of mostly easy climbing in unfrequented situations, with the added attractions of Combs' excellent Beehive Inn in at the end of the day.

Western Combs
OS ref. SK054780

This lies 300m south along the ridge from Castle Naze, about 5 minutes' further walk. It has some great micro-routes making it well worth the visit. It is recognisable by a prominent detached pillar at the right-hand side.

The left-hand buttress contains 3 routes: **Eeny** (S) is the face and crack on the left of the buttress; **Meeny** (HVS 4c) is a direct up the front face from the rock platform; **Miny** (VD) is the right arête of the buttress. On the pinnacle, **Mo** (VS 5a) is the ragged crack up the left face. **Frank's Route** (HVS 5a) is the right arête. All 2003.

Allstone Lee Rocks
OS ref. SK051773

The rocks are reached about in 15 minutes from Castle Naze. Follow the edge of the moor south, past the deep gash of Pyegreave Brook. Just past Pyegreave Brook is a tiny outcrop (O.S. ref SK054777), set in the slope between two minor stream gullies.

Insects from Hell (VS 5a) climbs the striking crack. Further along the edge, pass some minor north-facing outcrops with scrambling possibilities, to reach the far side of a moorland promontory. The crag comprises three south-facing buttresses that bask in any available sunshine. The first is the most substantial and is characterised by a steep arête above a flat grassy ledge. **Waggledunce** (D) is the minor arête a few metres left of the main buttress. **Bees** (VD) climbs the crack and face 1m left of the arête past a small ledge, while the more substantial **Honeycomb** (S) ascends the central crack system past some steep moves. The next outcrop is at a lower level: **Thorax** (D) climbs the stepped crest. The third buttress is small but interesting, comprising several easy micro-routes and some bouldering that is currently rather friable. The best feature is **Cyber Insekt** (HS 4b), an alluring crack set into the prow of the left-hand arête.

South-Western Combs
OS ref. SK035764

Approach by road from Whaley Bridge via Buxton Old Road, or from the road leading south from the village of Combs. The crags are best approached from behind the White Hall outdoor centre, via a squelchy footpath that leads past stiles to open moorland.

White Hall Rocks
OS ref. SK035764

White Hall Rocks are visible from the road (5 minutes). This north-facing crag is unwelcoming and green for most of the year. Despite its relatively large size, it has few continuous lines and no route details are known.

Buxton Boss
OS ref. SK040757

This tiny craglet, visible from the Buxton-Whaley Bridge road, sits near an old unmetalled road of alleged Roman origin. Approach as for White Hall Rocks then follow the moor edge in a southerly direction until the rocks come into view (10 minutes). The rock is better that average for Combs, the routes are worthwhile, and as a pleasant picnic spot it's worth an hour's visit if you're passing.

Several problems (Diff to S) lie to the left of the first route; **Aquae Arnemetiaie** (VD): the chimney and rib. **Respectable Street** (HS 4c) is the first steep crack: gain the halfway ledge finishing direct over the bulge above. **Geography of Power** (HS 4b) climbs the second steep crack, finishing as for Respectable Street. The arête to the right can also be climbed (V0). The main feature of the outcrop, the excellent clean slab of **Crushed Pagan God** (VS 4c), is started on the right: gain pebbles and pockets that lead to a large ledge, and climb the crack above. The slab can be climbed direct (V0). The low level traverse from route 1 to 4 is a good V1 problem. Right of the main buttress is a **gully** (M) a **slab** (D), and some easy problems.

Northern Combs

Short Edge and Hob Tor can be reached from Castle Naze by following a rough path along the northern edge of the moor.

Short Edge

OS ref. SK060782

Short Edge is situated 600m to the south-east of Castle Naze. Follow the footpath along the moor edge until the crag, consisting of three small north-facing buttresses, comes into view (10 minutes). The main buttress is the most visible, and is set at a slightly lower level. The crag suffers more than most from vegetation, but nevertheless dries fairly quickly. Most of the lines are clean enough to be enjoyable, but one or two routes would benefit from some judicial denudement prior to an ascent.

Flies of Ambition, Windshields of Fate (VD, 2000) climbs the short crack and narrow buttress 10m left of the main buttress. On the main buttress itself, **Earthquake Crack** (VS 4b★, 1984) gains a curving crack from a grassy recess, which leads to a short arête. **Richter 5** (HVS 5b, 1984) climbs an overhang just right it at its centre to the easy slab above. **Off The Scale** (HVS 5a, 1988) ascends the short corner 2m to the right, pulling over the overhang, and traversing left along the lip to the left edge of the buttress. Finish up the arête. **Quaking All Over** (S, 1984) is the right-hand arête direct from the toe of the buttress. Set back to the right is the unmistakable if unappealing **Corner Crack** (VD, 1988). The slab to its right of the corner gives: **Framed** (VS 5a, 1988) is a flake and **Shockwave** (HVS 5b, 1988) is the green groove and flake to the right.

Another 30m to the right is a square-cut buttress at a higher level (stake belays above). Although small, the routes start above a steeply sloping hillside that drops away alarmingly as height is gained, giving a good sense of exposure. The first route is **Slanting Crack** (VD, 1988). **Fat Man Burger Overdose** (E1 5b, 2000) is based on the clean arête to the right (rather friable) that has yet to be led direct. This route climbs the face right of Slanting Crack (side-runner) to get started until a swing right around the arête can be made to finish. **Seismic Wall** (HVS 5a, 1984) gains

the broad sloping ledge in the centre of the wall, then quakes upwards on holds that are very overgrown. **Inspector Remorse** (E1 5c★, 1993) is the rippled arête to the right of Seismic Wall giving a worthwhile climb on unhelpful holds. Start on the right past a tiny crack. Very small cams are useful higher up. The corner-crack just to the right (**Andy's Crack** VD, 1984) features some interesting plant life. **Short Arête** (HVD, 1984) is the appealing arête to the right.

The next buttress 15m to the right has a large overhang on its front. **Carpet Crack** (HS, 1984) is the overhanging block-filled crack 2m from the left-hand end of the wall. **Hooverville** (HVS 4c, 1988) ascends the broken wall and makes worrying moves, just to the left of a big jug, over the obvious overhang. **Tremor** (VS 4c, 1984) climbs the slabby wall on the right-hand side of the buttress, moving left at the top.

Hob Tor

O.S. ref. SK063778

This diminutive crag is reached by walking along the edge of the moor past Short Edge. Continue for a few hundred metres, passing a stone wall that eventually parts company with the moor edge, until the rocks become visible (15 minutes from the road). Facing east overlooking one of the more ravaged areas of the Peak, it nevertheless feels remote from the quarries that defile its aspect. It is probably best approached with some out-of-the-way soloing in mind, yet protection is nevertheless available on most of the routes. The rock is variable, and there is copious lichen. However, the jugs are generous and the landings good.

The first small outcrop/boulder has some good problems including a V3 face, then the main buttress, upon which the unmistakable **Hob Crack** is a good landmark, is 40m beyond. The crag continues in the shape of two clusters of small buttresses lying between grassy gullies. Routes are described from right to left. **Hobjection Overruled** (S 4b) is the juggy rib to the right of Hob Crack giving a good route on solid rock. **Hob Crack** (VS 4c) is the obvious splitter crack, the best line at the crag, but dirtier than appearances would suggest. Lunging for the enticing jug at the top is not to be recommended. **N.E. Hobbs**

(HS 4c) is the problem rib 3m left of Hob Crack with an overhanging start. **Imperfect Lichenous** (S) is the promising wide crack that precedes the rather dirty and precarious wall that forms the left-hand side of the buttress. Fifteen metres left is a blunt rib with a bulge at half height, taken by **Furry Green Atom Bowl** (HS 4b).

Ten metres left again is the second main buttress, characterised by 3 overhanging prows. **Hobs of Hell** (HS 4c★) is the appealing crack between the jutting arêtes and the best route here. Gain it direct, or better, from the left. **City Hobgoblins** (VS 5a) is the undercut arête to the left of an easy gully with a

tricky start. **Uncorrected Personality Traits** (D) takes the slab just left. Twenty metres left again is the final broken outcrop. **The Mixer** (D) climbs the best rock on its right-hand side, between 2 grassy gullies. **High Tension Line** (D) takes a line 2m right, on the right arête of a buttress past a grassy ledge. Better is **A Past Gone Mad** (VD), which takes a more continuous line up the left side of the buttress. The final slabby face lies a few m to the left. **City Dweller** (VD) climbs the right arête to a crack. **Rose** (S) takes the centre of the face past an overhang. **Antidote** (VD) climbs the left arête.

Bosley Cloud
by Simon Wilson

O.S. Ref. **SJ904638** | Altitude: **310m a.s.l.**

Bosley Cloud is the prominent hill 5km east of Congleton, marking the boundary between the hills of North Staffordshire and the Cheshire Plain, the boundary between the two counties running through the summit trig point. Locally famous for its dramatic skyline and the curious 'double sunset' visible from St Edward's churchyard in Leek on midsummer's day, the Cloud is less well-known to climbers, other than the local cognoscenti. The climbing is of two distinct, contrasting styles; natural and quarried rock.

The routes on the small natural grit buttresses scattered around the hill are as solid as any and are well worth the trouble of seeking out. Many are short enough to provide excellent soloing for the competent, complementing some bouldering. The Catstone is on rather a different scale, presenting an impressive slabby pillar giving one of the finest routes of its grade in the Peak.

The North Quarry is more of an acquired taste: grimly north-facing, with rock that is worryingly friable in places and rarely completely above suspicion anywhere, and routes tending to the uncompromising and bold. To those of the right temperament, of course, this all adds to the adventure!

Conditions & aspect
The crags line the Cloud from east to north and can be very green after a wet winter, but on a warm summer's day can be delightful. The Catstone, being west-facing, tends to be in better condition earlier in the season and is especially suitable for a sunny evening.

Routes & bouldering
Over 50 routes from rambling VDiff slabs to the most serious of E7s, with an out-of-the-way atmosphere. Enough to give anyone a memorable day's

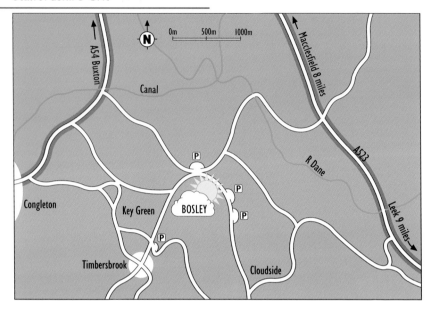

climbing. A popular bouldering venue with locals with some especially good problems in the easier grades, particularly in the Summit Rocks area, plus, of course, one famous desperate.

Parking & approach

Visible from afar, the Cloud can be approached from Congleton, Bosley, or Rushton Spencer, but can be surprisingly frustrating to reach without a map. Those unfamiliar with the area will probably approach from the A523 Leek–Macclesfield road, whence the simplest approach is probably from Rushton Spencer. Just south of the Royal Oak pub, take the Congleton road (Beat Lane) for about two miles to a junction, where 'Cloudside' is signposted to the right. From here, the map should indicate the most convenient parking for each buttress.

Access

Bosley Cloud is owned by the National Trust and there have been no objections to climbing. Climbers on the Catstone are asked to respect the peace and quiet of the residents of the house just below the crag, particularly on summer evenings.

The climbs are described from LEFT to RIGHT

The Nose

The first routes lie on a buttress 50m east of, and at a lower level than the trig point, bounded on its left by a large green wall.

Corner Route (VD, pre-1951) takes an indistinct line up the green, ledgy wall on the left-hand side of the buttress. An alternative, and better, finish climbs the right wall of the hanging groove at the top, Severe.

❶ Left Nostril VD   pre-1951
15m Picks its way up the obvious chimney, which is reached by an awkward scrabble onto the slab and a crack to a ledge.

❷ Right Nostril S   pre-1951
15m The steep crack just to the right is sharp but short, leading to a junction with the previous route.

❸ V-Chimney E1 5b ★   1940s
15m The acute groove provides a compelling line, which would probably give excellent climbing

following a good cleaning during an exceptional summer. A thoroughly untrustworthy peg runner at 8m is unlikely to be of much comfort. Finish leftwards across the overhanging wall to the top.

④ Why Kill Time When You Can Kill a Friend? E5 6a ★ 1985

14m The left arête of the imposing blank wall just to the right gives a superb, but precarious, route. There is no gear until the hard climbing is completed, but a mat and spotter would make all the difference.

⑤ Stuck Behind a Yellow Metro E5 6b† 1995

15m A bold route directly up to the shallow scoop just right of the centre of the seemingly blank wall to the right. Leaving the scoop even hard. A mat and spotter may not make enough of a difference. Very green at present.

⑥ Green Gully Direct HS 4a pre-1951

11m The well-named corner 6m to the right to the large grassy ledge. Step back left, up the corner and mantel on the right to the top.

The next two climbs are on a small face 30m to the left of a bigger buttress, further along the bottom path.

⑦ Envy Face S 4a pre-1951

8m Pull awkwardly into the thin crack in the wall, finishing on the left arête.

⑧ Mr Magoo E1 6a, 5c† 1986

6m Essentially two extended boulder problems one above the other, about 15m right of Envy Face. The first is up a steep thin slab to the grass while the next continues up the upper slab to the small overhang and over this directly. Unfortunately rather dirty.

North Buttress

The aforementioned bigger buttress, 30m right.

⑨ Contraception on Demand E2 5c ★ 1985

6m A good solo up the left-most slab of the buttress, behind the rowan, to a nerve-wracking

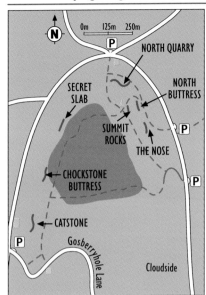

top-out. Short, but surprisingly committing - with a bad landing. Try not to fall off rightwards!

⑩ Fertility Rite Left-Hand E1 5c 1977

8m The blind crack to the left of the undercut corner is hard to enter, but eases with height.

⑪ Fertility Rite HVS 5a pre-1973

8m The hanging corner is gained from the slab on the right and is climbed direct to a bold finish.

⑫ Slab Wall HVS 4c ★★ 1973

8m The steep slab left of the arête gives a delicate and rewarding route. Small wires protect the crucial middle section.

⑬ Kremlin Wall E4 6b 1985

8m The steep flaky wall to the right of the arête is powerful, with a worryingly technical upper half.

⑭ Bulldog Flake E1 5b 1963

8m Aggressive and unpredictable. Strenuous and poorly protected laybacking, and precarious unless perfectly dry.

Adam Long climbing the mythical Summit Arête,
Bosley Cloud's famous desperate. Grades start at
E2 6b. Photo: Adam Long.

⑮ White House Crack VD   pre-1963
8m The classic right-hand flake is a much friendlier affair. Quite reachy.... to retrieve some of the gear that is!

⑯ Solitaire E6 6b ★★   1985
8m The unprotected wall to the right is crossed diagonally, from right to left, with the scary, insecure crux coming just below the top.

⑰ Deception HS 4b   pre-1973
6m The undercut crack has a steep start on good flakes. Once the upper crack is gained good jams lead to the top. **Tin Tin** (HVS 6a, 1985) is the slab immediately right of the last route.

Summit Rocks

The next climbs are on the biggest buttress on the right-hand end of the edge. The rest of this edge provides good bouldering above generally excellent landings.

⑱ Summit Arête E2 6b ★   1980
8m The undercut arête. From a standing start from the bank, a long slap off poor holds gains a jug, another long stretch brings a finger slot and easier climbing above ❶ **V5**. Famously given E5 7a in the previous guide. The first ascensionists may have started lower down. An indirect start using the left wall, dubbed **Summit Bypass** (E4 6b†, pre-1991), gains the upper arête by traversing the runnel.

⑲ Drystone Wall E1 5a   pre-1965
9m The crack to the right is climbed by steep pulls until the blocky break is reached. Step left on big (but not entirely sound) footholds until the top can be reached.

At a much lower level and 50m to the right is a vertical rectangular wall:

⑳ Death Crack E2 6a   1986
6m The obvious thin crack is somehow much more technical than it should be. **Living Wall** (E3 6a, 1986) is a hard sequence on crimps and undercuts up the wall to the left.

The next buttress, 20m to the right contains one route, the prominent curving arête.

㉑ Big Red Rock Eater E1 5c   1984
7m The arête on the front on the buttress is lay-backed with assistance from the pocket on the right wall.

Another 20m right is a bigger buttress with two obvious grooves.

㉒ Death Wish E3 6a   1983
8m The shallow corner, which is thin and scary, leads to better holds up right. The green wall to the left is **Everdance** (VS 4b, pre-1965).

㉓ Thin Finger Corner VS 4b   pre-1965
8m The sharp corner to the right. After a ledgy introduction, make some hard moves using the left arête to get established in the groove. Finish up and left.

㉔ Existentialist Arête E3 6a ★   1984
8m I crimp therefore I am. The arête to the right provides a superb series of committing moves. The climbing eases after the ledge but the rock becomes less reliable to compensate!

*The quarry now becomes much larger but unfortunately the rock is very poor. There have been rockfalls in the past: a huge block came tumbling down the cliff in December 1999. Given this and the seriousness of the routes hereabouts, a Culm coast, rather than a gritstone cragging, attitude is probably wise. At the very least, an abseil inspection of the harder routes is advised. The buttress is bounded on its left by a Y-shaped crack. **The Lubricant** (VS 4b) is the left branch, while **Wet and Warm** is the right. Both pre-1965.*

㉕ The Couch Potato E7 6b   2000
15m A miscalculation is likely to result in an even more unfortunate vegetative state. From the start of the previous route, make a committing series of long reaches to gain the hanging flake on the upper wall and the dubious protection behind it. Press on to the top before strength fades. A bold route made even more serious by the nature of the rock.

26 Main Wall E5 6a† pre-1973

15m The steep crack on the right side of the wall provides a strenuous and serious route. The peg runners are now very old, and should probably be replaced before an ascent.

27 Impact Two E5 5c 1977

13m The soaring arête to the right is less strenuous than Main Wall but no less scary. Traverse to the arête at half height from the right. Layback the heart-stopping edge with conviction.

The rest of the climbs are on the western side of the hill and at a lower level. The majority of the routes are in the trees and unfortunately this means an abundance of lichen, especially during the winter months, when the area is probably best avoided. However, when dry, the routes here are superb.

Secret Slab

The first buttress in the woods when coming from the summit is home to two of the best hard routes on the crag.

28 Herbivacious E4 6a 1984

9m The blunt arête on the left of the slab is unprotected, and all the holds point the wrong way!

29 Slender Thread E5 6b ★★ 1979

9m The hairline crack in the centre of the buttress gives a bold and sustained route. From the top of the crack, which doesn't take protection as easily as it should, trend leftwards up the steep slab above.

30 Crystal Voyager E3 6a ★★ 1979

9m Starting below the smooth groove, climb steadily up the slab on good edges until bold moves allow a good hold to be grasped. Place protection in the crack above before a precarious step gains the groove to the left. A superb route, on which good balance and a cool head are essential.

31 Pretentious? Moi? E1 6a ★ 1984

7m The shorter wall to the right is home to a technical, bouldery route. The good landing is likely to be tested.

The next four routes are on a smaller buttress 50m to the right of Secret Slab, and at the same level.

32 Birch Tree Climb S 4a pre-1965

8m Grovel up the dirty corner to the left of the overhang until escape is possible via some exposed moves are required step right onto the hanging arête.

33 Sirloin S 4a pre-1965

8m From the large block under the overhang make a hard move to get established on the front face, then continue up the cracks above.

34 Anticlimax HVS 5b ★ pre-1981

8m The short wall to the right. A precarious rock-over from the obvious pocket provides the crux.

35 Bottle Crack D pre-1965

8m Thrash through the holly-filled gully until the sanctuary of the alcove is reached. The route finishes up the attractive but miniscule crack on the left wall.

Chockstone Buttress

The next buttress is best reached by going back up to the path and following it 250m to the right then heading down the hillside again, past a low flat boulder right of the path. It is easily recognised by a prominent chockstone in the central crack.

Sirloin Climb – (severe)

With moderate handholds, the climber swings to the right and a prominent nose is overcome. The left hand is then raised on high and jammed in a narrow crack. To continue up the very steep crack is exceedingly difficult; a possible alternative is on the right, involving the use of very sloping holds.

From Some Gritstone Climbs
by John Laycock, 1913

36 Minute Wall HVD   **pre-1965**
6m Starting 2m to the left of the crack, head for the obvious jug. An awkward move to stand up on it leads to easier climbing.

37 Key Green Crack VD ★   **pre-1965**
8m The central crack. Once the chockstone has been mounted, either continue up the wide crack or move left to gain a ledge.

38 April Showers HVS 5a   **1984**
8m A hard start to get established on the thin wall to the right, soon leads to a double pocket. Finish up the thin slanting crack above. The **Direct Start** (HVS 5b, 1990) climbs direct to the left-hand pocket

39 May Day HVS 5c   **1984**
7m A line of leftward trending pockets further right are followed until the double pocket can be gained and a common finish with April Showers.

40 Hotter Than July HVS 5c ★   **1990**
7m The arête just to the right is climbed on its left-hand side.

Another 300m to the right, the path comes out of the woods and joins the main track. Thirty metres after the gate marking the end of the woods, a small path rightwards leads to the next buttress, which has some pleasant little slab routes.

41 The Crafty Cockney HVS 5b   **1985**
8m The slab on the left is climbed by committing moves on small edges. The upper arête is much easier.

42 Cool in a Crisis HVS 5c ★   **1985**
8m The central arête involves thin, balancy climbing to gain and leave the pocket to the right. **Crying Wolf** (VS 4c, 1985) is the crack system to the right.

43 Prescription for the Poor VS 4c   **1985**
8m The groove on the right of the buttress is topped by a bulge, the route tackles this direct.

The Catstone

Twenty metres right of this buttress, a tower-like buttress springs from the hillside. This is home to one of the best E1s in Staffordshire.

Termination Crack (S, pre-1973) is the crack left of the main face.

44 The Cat Crawl S 4a ★★   **1920s**
18m The superb left arête. An easy start gains the arête from where holds on both sides of the arête lead to the exhilarating upper section.

45 Hot Tin Roof E1 5a ★★★   **1973**
8m The centre of the buttress is magnificent, but bold. Starting up a crack to the left, traverse rightwards along parallel ledges. Continue up and place gear in the pockets and then storm confidently (or wobble!) through the crux above. Finish directly, then sit back and enjoy the view. A more direct start straight to the end of the traverse is also 5a.

46 Mutiny Chimney VS 5a   **1920s**
18m The chimney to the right is gained from the lower wall, crux. Easier moves up the wide crack enable the pleasant arête above to be gained.

47 Hollybush Wall VS 4c   **pre-1973**
10m The thin curving crack is climbed with difficulty, and is followed by more hard moves to get established on the sharp arête to the right, this is then laybacked. A good finish can be made up the arête of the previous route.

Timbersbrook Quarry

These quarries to the south of the Cloud are no longer climbed. They are very overgrown and unstable at the top, with tree roots forcing blocks off the top making them dangerous. Also, unsurprisingly, the landowners are not happy to allow access.

For those willing to seek it out, the Catstone on Bosley Cloud has one of the finest slab routes in the county. Claire Fennel going for it on Hot Tin Roof, E1 5a (page 285). Photo: Mark Crampton.

The hill in front of **Bosley** is called **Gun.**

It was recorded that Oliver Cromwell fired a cannon from here and hit Leek church. The Cloud is also the site of the famous double sunset, which used to be seen from St Edward's churchyard in Leek. However, due to the Chandler effect this is no longer possible, and you have to walk down the hill a bit.

Mow Cop

by Gary Gibson and Dave Garnett

O.S. Ref. **SJ858576**	Altitude: **330m a.s.l.**

This craggy outcrop is a prominent feature on the Cheshire-Staffordshire border and is clearly visible from miles around. The Folly Castle is a well-known local landmark some 7 miles north of Stoke-on-Trent. However, don't let the apparent gentrification of the area and the nice National Trust car-park fool you. This is still a venue for the desperate and/or very local and transportless only. The Old Man itself is an impressive feature and might exert a deviant fascination for some. However, access to climbers is refused on grounds of alleged instability (of the Old Man). For the rest, the rock is as uninviting as the worst Knypersley can throw at you, without its compensatory sylvan charms.

Conditions & aspect

As the highest point for miles around, Mow Cop tends to attract the worst of the available weather. Faces mostly east.

Routes & bouldering

Mostly in the middle grades, but serious and rarely repeated. Not a place for beginners, those pushing their grade, or sensitive aesthetes. No bouldering of note.

Parking & approach

Mow Cop is well-signposted from Biddulph and Kidsgrove and there is a convenient car-park on its western side. A useful landmark is the Mow Cop Inn, from which Castle Road leads up to the top of the Cop and a left turn leads to the Folly car-park. The Folly Cliff and nearby quarries lie on the eastern side of the Folly, whilst the Old Man lies 200m to the north-west, back across Castle Road and along a sign-posted footpath.

Access

Currently the National Trust allows no climbing on the Folly Cliff, Hawk's Hole Quarry or the Old Man. Access to Millstone Quarry is tolerated, although rarely exercised.

The Old Man of Mow

Half a dozen climbs have been described on the Old Man itself. Starting at the low platform at the back (i.e. facing the hillside) and proceeding clockwise they are as follows:

The Spiral Route (VS 4a, pre-1960) moves up left to gain a ledge at the base of a slab, leads left and down round the corner under the chin, and moves up another slab to the left shoulder. Step up, then move out right onto the forehead and finish direct. **The Direct Route** (HVS 5a, pre-1960) starts at the Old Man's feet and climbs the steep frontal groove to pull over the overhang to meet the Spiral Route. It then steps up and then left onto the face to finish as the previous route. **Alsager Route** (HVS 5a, pre-1960) trends left from the start of the Direct Route to climb direct to the left shoulder to finish up the tight groove in the arête above. **The Lee Side** (E1 5a, 1973) starts at the right-hand side of a pedestal forming the left arête of the front face of the buttress (or the outside of the Old Man's right leg in more anatomical terms). From the top of the pedestal, move out rightwards across the leaning wall and go round the arête onto the shoulder. Finish diagonally back leftwards. **Cambridge Crack** (VS 4c, pre-1960) climbs the prominent steep green crack just left, to any convenient finish. Finally, **Piton Route** (pre-1960) ascends the series of steps on the left skyline as viewed from the Cambridge Crack side, to finish by the Old Man's left ear.

It should be noted that descent from this pinnacle is by a very precarious abseil; not advised for the inexperienced. The geriatric summit bolt may or may not increase confidence. Numerous problems and routes of varying grades are possible in the adjacent quarry. None has any particular merit, though in the past two climbs of Very Difficult standard have been recorded up the left-hand side of the face.

The Folly Cliff

This double-faced quarry is divided centrally by the obvious arête, lying directly beneath the castle.

Cioch Groove (VD, pre-1973) is the leaning chimney/groove at the right-hand end of the cliff. **Crystal Voyager** (HVS 5a, 1979) is the slabby wall just left, and **Initiation Wall** (VS 4b, pre-1973) is the loose overhanging wall 3m left again. **B.S. Mow** (E1 5c, 1960s) is the once-pegged crack another 3m left again with a rightwards finish up the wall above, and **The Arête** (E3 5c, 1960s) is climbed by the sandy peg-scarred cracks. **Man Mow** (E1 5a, 1960s) starts just left and climbs to The Arête before swinging right to and finishing directly past a Damoclean spike. **Folly Berger** (HVS 5a,1960s) moves diagonally left from the ledge on Man Mow to regain The Arête before stepping back right to finish direct. **Right Tot** (HVS 4c, 1960s) climbs the wall to the right of the scoop left of The Arête, moves left to a rotten flake and finishes up this and the wall above (bet you can't wait). Even more beguilingly, **Rot** and **Tot** lie up the wall to the left. Both should delight the connoisseur of loose rock and poor climbing. A girdle traverse is of equally fine quality.

Hawk's Hole Quarry

This the large hole slightly to the south of the castle.

Its upper right wall sports two V-shaped notches, which are climbed by **Double Vee** (HS 4a, pre-1973). **Three Steps** (S, pre-1973) gains the stepped, broken corner left of Double Vee from that route. A harder start lies below, up the obvious short ramp (HVS 5a). The overhanging prow just to the left sports the dynamic aid-climbing duo, **Batman** and **Robin**. Both are A2. **Hawk's Hell** (VS 4c, 1960s) ascends the back right-hand corner of the quarry, gaining the half-height ledge via a large flake. The two cracks springing from the half-height ledge of Hawk's Hell are **Right Eliminate** (A1, pre-1973) and, spookily, **Left Eliminate** (VS 5a,1960s). **Vee Diff** (S, pre-1973!) starts just left of Hawk's Hell and climb leftwards to reach a large ledge, to continue up the arête or the slab above. **Square Buttress** (HS 4a, pre-1973) is the centre of the square buttress 5m to the left. To the left is an obvious scooped face, which gives **The Captain's Blood** (E2 6a, 1979) up the blank-looking right-hand side, and **Captain Skyhook** (E1 5c, 1976) up the centre with a step right to finish.

Millstone Quarry

The largest, and only accessible, quarry lies round to the left again.

1 The Reach HS 4a   pre-1973
11m Climb the right arête until a step left leads to a groove and the top. Carbonel (VS 4c, 1960) goes left from this to the vegetated rampline.

2 Silent Scream E3 6a   1979
13m Start below the mid-point of the traverse of Carbonel. Climb directly up the crystalline wall by difficult moves to reach Carbonel and a finish up the shallow groove above. **Bow and Arrow** (VS 4c, 1960) is the beautifully disgusting bird-limed crack 10m to the left. **Special Branch** (E1 5b, 1978) is the vague crack-line just left of the appalling gully.

3 Castle Crack VS 4b ★   1960s
18m Climb the conspicuous wide crack in the face to the left, gained from a small rib below. Attractive,

by local standards, although falling victim to re-afforestation.

4 Crystine E2 5b   1979
18m Climb the wall 3m left of Castle Crack to easy ground and finish up the arête directly above.

5 Arête and Slab Climb S   pre-1973
25m Follow a vague line 3m left again, by-passing a tricky section to the left. Move rightwards on the obvious line and finish as for the upper section of Castle Crack.

Numerous problems exist on the smaller walls of the quarry. A short slab gives pleasant climbing for beginners but otherwise there is little of worth.

Nick I' Th' Hill   OS ref. SJ881607

There are several quarries along the crest of this ridge, 3 miles north-east of Mow Cop. Many overlook gardens (or are gardens themselves!) and are therefore not worthy of attention.

Knypersley Rocks

by Dave Garnett

O.S. Ref. **SJ901558**   Altitude: **230m a.s.l.**

Conditions & aspect
The rock is allegedly gritstone, but hidden in a damp valley and shrouded by trees, it tends to be very green. Indeed, so green is Green Slab that first-time visitors may not recognise it.

Routes & bouldering
Twenty one routes, mostly poor. It's not destined to become one of the Peak's top venues, but there are one or two routes that might make it worth an evening's exploration.

Approaches & access
The rocks are best approached from the A527 cross-roads at Knypersley. Follow the Biddulph Moor road (Park Lane) for almost 1½ miles and turn right into the concreted Lodge Barn Road (ignoring signs discouraging access). Follow this for 300m until it forks. Take the right fork and park immediately. From the parking place a footpath leads downhill into the woods, keeping to the right-hand side of a dry-stone wall. Follow this, ignoring a stile on the left, to the point where the path leads through a gap

Staffordshire Grit

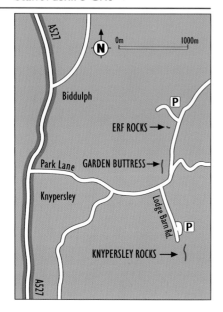

in the wall. Green Slab is up the hillside close to the wall with Little Slab about 50m across to the right. The Pinnacle is about 150m further left at a similar level, but is best reached by following the main path through the wall for about 50m (indigenous trackers will notice a small rectangular moss-covered block beside the track on the right and a pair of Scots pines) before trekking diagonally right into the woods. The buttress is quite striking and should appear within a minute or so.

A further 50m down the valley on the main path, on the left, is a large boulder perched on top of several blocks. This affords the possibility of boulder problems with not just sit-down, but lie-underneath, starts. Hermit's Buttress is beyond this, up the bank. This is the most extensive area of crag, with a natural arch bounding its right-hand side; although this sounds considerably more inspiring than it actually is. Finally, there are few boulder problems on the small outcrops well to the right of the Pinnacle, by the pond on the left-hand side of the track about 100m beyond the parking place

Access

This has not been a problem, but it might be diplomatic to ask permission at the closest house if doing the routes in the Pinnacle area that end close to its garden.

The first routes are described from RIGHT to LEFT.

Little Slab

Escaped the last edition of the guide and now more or less feral.

Right It (VD) climbs up the centre and **Left It** (VD), predictably, climbs up to the left via a ledge.

Green Slab

This heavily camouflaged little gem is probably best left as an ungardened offering to bryologists.

For the record, **Twinkletoes** (VD) picks its way across the upholstered slab diagonally rightwards to reach the right arête, which is followed to the top. **Two Step** (S) ascends the left edge directly.

The Pinnacle

The impressively overhanging front face is split by a chimney. Believe it or not this is the best bit.

❶ Cold Shoulder HVS 5b pre-1989
11m A tasty prospect spoiled by its algal garnish. Gain the right arête from the right by a diagonal weakness, and climb it to the short finishing crack on the left.

❷ The Jug Jam VD ★★ pre-1973
12m Climb the central corner to reach twin cracks. Pull awkwardly over the bulge to gain the chimney. Worth doing.

❸ Scorpion VS 4c   pre-1973
11m Start on the left wall of the buttress and traverse boldly right to gain the arête and a delicate finish. Poorly-protected.

❹ Logos VS 4c   pre-1973
9m The shallow groove left of Scorpion is climbed to another bold move onto the arête. Move slightly right and finish direct. A few metres left of the Pinnacle is a scruffy bit of slab that gives a VD ramble (**Grassy Slabs**).

Hermit's Buttress

From the boulder the first rock encountered is compact square wall with a small slot at two-thirds height.

But for the slime, this might well make a neat little route. Some 20m right of this is a slanting crack, **Keep Left** (VS 5a), which is quite fingery but very close to **Danera** (VD), which climbs the narrow ramp and horrid crack just right. **The Common Good**

(VS 4b) laybacks through the overhang a few metres right on good flakes to a scary move onto a rounded ledge with heather cornice. **Prometheus** (M) is the green alcove and crack to the right. Definitely not worth having your liver pecked out for. Down and right is a dismal corner and dirty crack, **Northern Lights** (D), which is a waste of a good route name. **Halcyone** (VD) climbs just left of the bulge to the right to an awkward finish, whilst down a step is the appropriately unpleasant **Misogynist** (VD), a miserable chimney. Slightly more substantial, if hardly more attractive, is the cracked damp wall to the right. This is **Christmas Cracker** (HVS 5b, pre-1973), reaching the upper crack by slippery moves from slightly right. Really quite nasty. The cracks just left of the arch can sometimes be gained by slippery moves up the appalling bilious wall, **Briar** (VS). The charms of the arch itself seem to have been unaccountably ignored so far. On the buttress to the right, however, **Gryphon** (VD) climbs out of the left side of the overhang to a faint crack. Go up this until level with the arch, then traverse right to a large ledge and then up a steep corner.

The Wicken Stones
by Dave Garnett

O.S. Ref. **SJ898568**   Altitude: **250m a.s.l.**

The dinosaur's spine of gritstone outcrops obvious from the Knypersley to Biddulph Moor road, 2km east of Biddulph, near the hamlet of Rock End. Composed of hard fine-grained gritstone, these buttresses give excellent micro-routes and bouldering and it is surprising that they are not more popular.

There are two main outcrops where climbing is currently allowed, marking the extreme ends of the chain of buttresses. Unfortunately, the conspicuous and attractive crags in-between are denied to climbers.

Conditions & aspect
East-facing keeping the sun until lunchtime. Clean and quick-drying, although the whole area is often swathed in low cloud in poor weather.

Routes & bouldering
A couple of dozen decent routes or substantial problems with some sustained traverses and excellent flat landings. Titan is worth a special visit for scoffing roof specialists.

Garden Buttress

Parking and Approach

The best landmark is the fork in the road at the north end of Rock End. Heading north, the right-hand fork leads to Lask Edge and cars are best left here, near the junction, before walking for a few metres back up the main road towards Biddulph Moor. Garden Buttress is approached through the garden of the last house on the left (The Woodlands).

Obviously, permission to climb must always be sought at the house, whose occupants are surprisingly co-operative as long as numbers are kept to a minimum and visits are not too frequent. Please be sensitive to this and, above all, park considerately, well away from the drive.

The climbs are described from left to right starting with the outcrop situated at the left-hand side of the crag.

❶ Tube Snake VS 4c   pre-1989
9m The obvious jutting prow on the left arête may be gained from the left by a series of sandy pockets. Squirm painfully along the prow until it is possible to gain a standing position, then layback the huge flake above to finish. The final flake can also be gained direct at 5a.

❷ Joshua HVS 5b   pre-1989
9m Four metres right is a shallow water-worn runnel below a whitish flake. Hard starting moves enable some extraordinary holds to be reached at the top of the runnel. Continue direct past the flake to an awkward move to gain the headwall. Finish straight up.

❸ Cherry Hill E1 5b   pre-1989
9m The ramp 2m right is followed until it is possible to swing left under the roof. Tackle this direct using a long reach for hidden holds.

❺ Brick Bank Crack VD   pre-1989
9m The wide central crack is climbed using holds on the right past a difficult section at mid-height.

❻ The Friends of Eddie Coil E2 6a ★   pre-1989
9m The undercut slab right of Brick Bank Crack. Start just left of centre and move up then right to make desperate moves over the overlap, small wires, to gain easy ground above a poor pocket. Continue, stunned, to the top.

❼ Hot Digital Dog HVS 5c ★   pre-1989
8m The right arête. Use pockets in the right wall to gain the arête proper. Balance up this to reach the top. Short and sharp.

The crag continues farther right, but decreases in height, to give some entertaining boulder problems. The vandalised slab in the field 200m right again yields many excellent and hard friction test-pieces. The two large outcrops, which can be seen 200m farther along the ridge, are on private land and the owners have made it clear that they **do not wish** *climbing to take place.*

ERF Rocks

Parking and Approach

At the opposite end of the chain, the largest of the outcrops is situated in a field behind and to the left of the Mitras Composites factory (but named after a previous incarnation of the factory), some 500m further north, towards Biddulph Moor.

Discreet parking in the lay-by part-way down the factory access road is advisable and climbing seems to be tolerated. Approach along a public footpath (signposted) to the right through the yard in front of the factory (follow the yellow hatched path) to a stile. Go left and then carefully cross a rickety gate into another field. Diagonally cross this and the remains of a dry stone wall to reach the right end of the crag.

The left end wall of the main buttress is split by a deep chimney. The bulging rocks to the left give some interesting problems.

Ⓥ The **wall** left of the chimney gives a fingery V3 (6b) up sloping scoops to ripples and the top. The **left arête** of the chimney is a worthwhile V1 (5c).

⑦ Beam Me Up Scotty VD   c1992
5m The tight chimney is convenient (and easier) in descent.

Ⓥ Simon's Wall V2 (6a) is the balancy wall right of the chimney via the break and a just-good-enough pocket. No sneaking onto the arête.

⑧ Farmer Barlimow VS 4b   c1992
5m From the slab just right of the arête, pull over the bulge on good holds.

⑨ Enterprise HVS 5c   pre-1989
5m Climb the overhanging scoop just to the right on disappearing flakes to a bold pull onto the slab above. The finish is currently rather dirty.

⑩ Titan E2 6b ★★   pre-1989
6m The innocuous-looking roof-crack provides a short but intense problem for all but the very tall. A sharp start leads to a desperate struggle to gain improving jams in the unfriendly crack. Ramshaw awaits successful applicants!

⑪ Up to the Elbows HVS 4c   pre-1989
6m The gruesome orifice to the right requires a baffling combination of laybacking, bridging, arm-barring and body-jamming, as well as industrial-sized cams to protect it.

Ⓥ An excellent sustained **low traverse** leads from Farmer Barlimow to Up to the Elbows at V5 (6b).

⑫ Spiderman Meets the Carlsberg Club
VS 5b   2003
6m The steep rounded arête to the right. An entertaining start leads to a blinkered finish up the slab directly above.

⑬ The Fruit Palace VS 4b ★★   pre-1989
6m The excellent, but unprotected, pocketed slab on the right. The starting moves are hard, but persevere to reach the easier-than-it-looks slab and climb it direct.

⑭ Way Purple Splat Balloon VS 4b   2003
6m The rib bounding the Fruit Palace slab on the right.

Ⓥ The traverse of the lowest break across the Fruit Palace slab is a satisfying V3 (5c).

⑮ Harvest Moon HS 4a   pre-1989
6m The gritty groove to a precarious exit.

⑯ Sickle Moon HVS 5a ★   pre-1989
6m A worthwhile eliminate taking the right-hand of two sickle-shaped flakes, over the bulge just to the right, starting with a mantel and pulling over using a good finger flake.

⑰ The Blackpool Trip S 4a ★   pre-1989
6m Roll up and try your luck on the towering crack. Perfect jams make it a pushover.

⑱ Bilberry Slab VD   pre-1989
6m Amble up the centre of the large slab to the right.

⑲ Desert Head HS   pre-1989
6m The bottomless vertical crack halfway along to the end of the crag.

Ⓥ Around the corner, the slabby end wall gives some good balancy problems, including the **tenuous groove**, V3 (6a).

Rudyard Pinnacle

by Dave Garnett

O.S. Ref. **SJ945588**   Altitude: **225m a.s.l.**

A tiny piece of the genuinely obscure; a secret pillar of sculpted gritstone in the woods above Rudyard Lake, but with a couple of worthwhile routes, one of them very good indeed.

Conditions & aspect
North-east facing and in a wooded area, the pillar can be rather green in winter. However, the rock is of excellent quality and, if necessary, a quick (but gentle) brush will quickly clean it up.

Routes & bouldering
Two-nil.

Parking & approach
From the A523 Leek–Macclesfield road, about a mile north of Leek, take the B5331 to Rudyard, turning right at the mini-roundabout at the dormant pub and following the road uphill for about half a mile to Horton St Michael's School on the left. Limited parking here (be considerate). Cross the road to a cunningly hidden public footpath between two houses ('Oakwood' and Wit's End'), invisible to muggles. Head down here, over and through several stiles and gates, past the pony paddocks, following the path round to the right. From the last gate a number of yellow striped posts mark the path. At the fourth post step off the path on the left, onto the top of the hidden pillar. Less than 5 minutes easy walk.

Access
Rights are indeterminate, but keeping a low profile and approaching by abseil from the footpath are probably safest.

❶ Moss Side Story E1 5a   2003
12m The left arête has good, if sometimes well-upholstered, holds leading to a bold and delicate finale.

❷ Kipling Arête E2 5c ★★   2003
12m Delectable climbing, first technical then bold. Climb the steep right arête to a friendly break at half height. Move up to good hold (awkward protection round to the right) and then balance up the narrowing prow until a precarious move round to the left gains a prominent hold, and junction with Moss Side Story, on the slab just below the top.

Heighley Castle Quarries

by Dave Bishop

O.S. Ref. **SJ774471**	Altitude: **170m a.s.l.**

Heighley Castle Quarries, named from the remains of the medieval castle close by, are a line of four sandstone quarries set in mixed coniferous and deciduous woodland, high on an escarpment overlooking the M6.

Routes & bouldering

Traditionally recorded as routes, but best seen as a bouldering venue — topping out on many of the awful finishes is an esoteric risk. The bouldering consists of traverses, arêtes and walls, and is very fingery on generally sound rock. There are a significant number of vital pebbles, vulnerable to misuse, that make for crucial holds on some of the problems. Thirty problems are recorded here, but more potential exists.

Conditions & aspect

The quarries can be vivid green and damp on occasions so the best times to climb are when there is no leaf cover on the trees, November through May. Unfortunately these times also coincide with the pheasant shooting and breeding season. The Fourth Quarry is usually dry at low level even on damp days. Faces east, getting some morning sun.

Parking & approach

To park, use the three passing places on either side of the public highway beyond the farm access lane. **Do not park in this gateway entrance.** Better still is to park elsewhere and walk or cycle so as to not alert the farmer. The No 85 Bus from Chester to The Potteries stops at the Madeley turn, less than a mile away. Approach 1 minute.

Access

The farmer does not want anyone in the woods as it disturbs the pheasants. We as climbers are not prepared to pay for access to compensate any 'losses'. If asked to leave, do so, and come back at a more

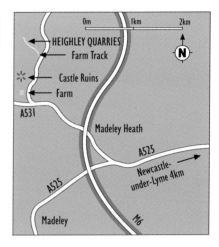

convenient time. A discrete level of use seems to be tolerated and you can encourage this by parking as advised, keeping numbers and noise down, not bringing dogs, removing litter and leaving politely if asked to do so. The woods do get used for other purposes whose practices are a little less savoury, so beware of half-bottles, silver paper, and other sub-culture paraphernalia.

First Quarry

Characterised by a long wall with an inviting rising traverse line.

❶ Ivy League VI (5c)

❷ Long Wall Traverse V2 (5c)
Follow the main, upper break. Usually done from left to right but goes either way. Can be continued around the short wall.

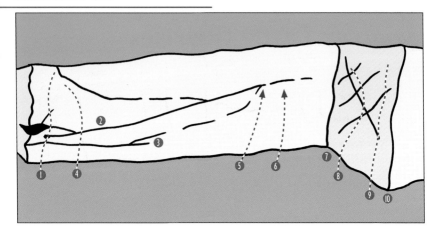

③ Low Traverse V4 (6b)

The much harder bottom line. Keep as low as possible, avoiding the upper line. Done left to right. It is much easier, and normal, if you move up to the higher traverse line at about one third distance, but it is still very fingery.

④ Dixon's Dart Board V3 (6a)

⑤ V3 (6a)

⑥ PPG V4 (6b)

⑦ Little Cenotaph V0 (5b)

Cenotaph Variant traverses the foot-ledge out from the corner to the arête.

⑧ Right Wall V0 (5a)

⑨ Bill's XS V4 (6b)

⑩ Ecstasy I VI (5c)

Second Quarry

This is found at a slightly lower level 10m on the right.

⑪ Punch Arête V5 (6b)

⑫ The Serpent V5 (6b)

Traverse right from the arête, along the obvious line, all the way to beyond Jess's Arête.

⑬ The Heighley Nightmare V4 (6b)

⑭ Killer Wall V3 (6a)

⑮ Jess's Corner VI (5b)

⑯ Alan's Variant VI (5c)

⑰ Jess's Arête V2 (6a)

Done on either side but easier on the left. Not using the pocket close to the arête on its right is the standard. Finishing not recommended.

Third Quarry

The next quarry lies 40m to the right.

⑱ Mark of Zorro V0 (5b)

Traverse the break rightwards.

⑲ Southern Sloper V0 (5b)

A lower traverse.

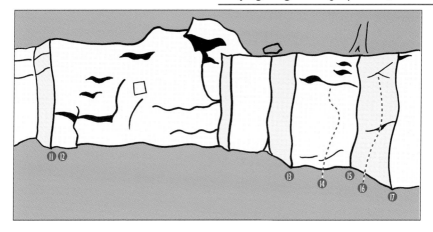

20 5b Arête VI (5b)

21 Fresher's Arête VI (5b)

22 Stepped Arête V0 (5b)

Fourth Quarry

The final quarry is another 50m right again, down a large bank. It is for big boulderers only.

23 Slim Corner 5c

E3 really, so be warned.

24 Suicide Wall 6a

The wall to the right is far too big to ever be a boulder problem. It has been led sometime before 1973, perhaps the only ascent. E5.

25 Suicide Arête 6a

The dominating arête to the right has also been led, sometime before 1973. It was recorded in a Keele University climbing guide from that year that a member of the South Cheshire Climbing Club had led the route (graded 5d). It has subsequently been led once again at E5. As such it must have been one of the hardest routes of its day.

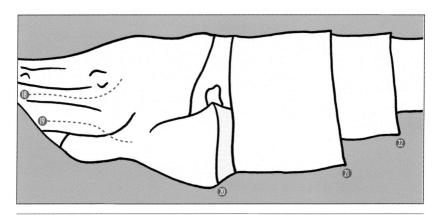

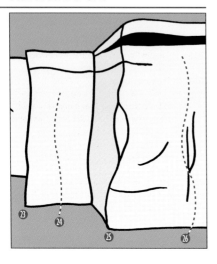

㉖ Hilti Gunner 6b
The wall to the right is another E5.

Ⓥ There are at least three traverses at different heights moving right from Suicide Arête to the main corner of the bay. The lowest with the hands at about head height is the hardest. It is more common to combine bits of all three to your own taste and ability, and to traverse in either direction. Numerous up and down problems can be deduced and the main corner of the bay provides **tough bridging** with an exit left at the first break, V4 (6b). To the right of the bay the height of the crag diminishes and the curved small bay gives entertaining traverses that get harder the more holds you miss out.

Outlying Crags First Ascents

The history of many of the minor crags in the area has not been meticulously maintained and in many cases the only indication of even the era in which the routes were done comes from the publication date of the first guide in which they appear and often the first ascensionists are unrecorded.

1910–1912 **Herford's Girdle Traverse**
Siegfried Herford, John Laycock 'At Castle Naze Herford originated the idea of traversing horizontally along a line of cliff, so was born the Girdle Traverse.'

pre-1913 **Pinnacle Crack, Pinnacle Arête, Sheltered Crack, Overhanging Chockstone Crack, V-Corner, Muscle Crack, The Nithin, Flake Crack, The Fly Walk, The Niche, Niche Arête, Studio, A.P.** (Absolutely Perpendicular) **Chimney, Little Pillar, Keep Corner, Footstool, Left Zigzag Crack, Fat Man's Chimney, Deep Chimney, The Crack,**

Zigzag Crack, Long Climb, Central Tower, Green Crack, Hodgkinson's Chimney, South Buttress, V-Chimney, Vanishing Crack, Boomerang, Overhanging Chimney
Stanley Jeffcoat and friends

1914 **Scoop Face** Stanley Jeffcoat

1915 Jun 13 **The Crack** HM Kelly (first descent) 'Most exhilarating and exciting and taxes the climber's powers to the uttermost.'

1924 **Castle Naze Girdle Extension**
Patrick Monkhouse, M de Selincourt, Miss R Monkhouse

1920s **Mutiny Chimney, The Cat Crawl**
Morley Wood, Fred Piggott, Harry Kelly

1930s **Pilgrim's Progress**
Morley Wood and Rucksack Club friends

pre-1948 **No Name, Keep Arête, Scoop Face Direct Start, Nozag, The Vice, Boomerang Buttress**

1940s **V-Chimney** Eric Byne, M Holland

pre-1951	**Green Gully Direct, Left Nostril, Right Nostril, Corner Route** *Mentioned briefly in the 1951 guidebook.*
1958 Jun	**Birthday Climb**
1950s	**The Two-Step, Struggle**
pre-1960	**Spiral Route** K Maskery
	Alsager Route Harold Drasdo, K Finlay
	Cambridge Crack, Direct Route J Sutton, Harold Drasdo, Bob Downes, Tony Moulam
	Piton Route Harold Drasdo
	At least one peg was used for aid but it was probably fully aided. Climbed free by persons unknown in the 1970s.
1960	**Carbonel, Bow and Arrow** A Taylor, Paul Williams
1963	**Bulldog Flake** Ed Drummond
pre-1965	**Envy Face, Dry-Stone Wall, Thin Finger Corner, Everdance, The Lubricant, Birch Tree Climb, Bottle Climb, Minute Wall, Key Green Crack** *All appeared in Peter Bamfield's notes in the Midland Association of Mountaineers club journal but were lost for the 1973 guide.*
1960s	**Hawks Hell, Left Eliminate** (aid)**, Folly Berger, Man Mow, Right Tot** P Kenway, John Amies, John Lockett
	Castle Crack
	B.S. Mow *Some aid, climbed free and solo by Jonny and Andrew Woodward in 1975.*
	The Arête (some aid) *Climbed free by Jonny and Andrew Woodward in 1976.*
	Slanting Crack, The Bloody Crack, Block Cracks, The Nose, Main Corner, Pitoned Crack, Peg Crack
pre-1973	**Cioch Groove, Initiation Wall, Double Vee, Three Steps, Right Eliminate, Vee Diff, Square Buttress, The Reach, Oak Tree Crack, The Cleft Route, The Cue, Fertility Rite, White House Crack, Deception, Wet and Warm, Main Wall** (aided)**, Hollybush Wall, Termination Crack, Right It, Left It, Twinkle Toes, Two Step, Jug Jam, Scorpion, Logos, Grassy Slabs, Gryphon, Briar, Christmas Crack, Misogynist, Halcyone, Northern Lights, Prometheus, Common Good, Danera, Keep Left** *Main Wall free in 1978 by Jonny and Andrew Woodward.*
1973	**Hot Tin Roof, Slab Wall** Paul Williams, John Amies, P. King
	The Lee Side
1976 Jun	**Captain Skyhook** Andrew Woodward (solo)
1977 Jul	**Plankton, Belladonna** Al Evans *"Plankton was practised on a rope every time I went up to The Naze. Finally I had it wired one day and soloed it straight after a top rope ascent. I guess these days you'd call it a 'headpoint'."*
1977 Jul	**Atropine** Lew Hardy and friend
1977 Oct	**Fertility Rite Left-Hand, Impact Two, Death Wish** Jonny Woodward
1978	**Special Branch** John Holt
1978 May	**Feed the Enemy** Gary Gibson (solo)
1979	**Slender Thread, Crystal Voyager** (Bosley) Jonny Woodward, Andrew Woodward
	Silent Scream Andrew Woodward
1979 Sep	**Crystal Voyager** (Mow Cop)**, The Captain's Blood, Crystine** Gary Gibson (solo)
1970s	**Ledgeway, Bubbly Wall, Scoop Wall, Keep Buttress, Scoop Direct**
1980	**Summit Arête** Jonny Woodward *First free ascent. Originally graded E2 6b but given E5 7a in the last guide. The discrepancy was partly down to the start used.*
pre-1981	**Anticlimax** probably Jonny Woodward
1984 Apr 30	**April Showers** Mark Stokes, John Allen
	May Day John Allen, Mark Stokes
1984 May 31	**Big Red Rock Eater, Pretentious? Moi?** Allen Williams (solo)
	Existentialist Arête Andy Popp (on-sight solo)
	Herbivacious Nick Dixon (solo)
	A very productive day!
1984	**Double Crack, The Arête, Bow Crack, The Fifth Horseman** Jim Rubery, Dave Gregory
	Pod Crack Jim Rubery, Dave Gregory
	Scoop Direct Alastair Ferguson, Jim Rubery
	Footstool Right, Combs Climb, Deep Crack, Zig-a-zag-a Dave Gregory, Jim Rubery
	The Blusher Jim Rubery, Dave Spencer
	Earthquake Crack, Quaking all Over Malc Baxter, Al Parker, Andy French
	Andy's Crack Andy French, Al Parker, Malc Baxter

Carpet Crack, Tremor, Short Arête
Al Parker, Malc Baxter, Andy French
Richter 5, Seismic Wall   Malc Baxter,
Al Parker

1985   **Solitaire, Contraception on Demand,
Kremlin Wall**   Ian Dunn (solo)
Tin Tin   Ian Dunn, Claudie Dunn
Why Kill Time...   Nick Dixon, Ian Dunn

1985 Dec 21   **The Crafty Cockney, Prescription for the
Poor, Crying Wolf**   Keith Ashton,
Malc Baxter
Cool in a Crisis
Malc Baxter, Keith Ashton

1986 Apr   **Death Crack**   Nick Dixon, Mark 'Face'
McGowan, Simon Oaker, Denise Arkless,
Allen Williams
Living Wall
Nick Dixon, Allen Williams
Mr Magoo   Simon Oaker, Nick Dixon,
Allen Williams

1986 Sep 14   **Morocc'n Roll, Syringe Benefit, Columbal
Convenience, South Crack, Southern Arête**
Jim Rubery, Dave Gregory

1988   **Shockwave**   Malc Baxter, Al Parker
Slanting Crack   Al Parker (solo)
Framed   Keith Ashton, Peter Frame
An earthquake had recently occurred in the area
Hooverville, Off The Scale, Corner Crack
Keith Aston
Piano Stool, Short but Sweet   Malc Baxter

pre-1989   **Cold Shoulder, Tube Snake, Joshua, Cherry
Hill, Brick Bank Crack, Friends of Eddie
Coil, Hot Digital Dog, Enterprise, Titan,
Up to the Elbows, Fruit Palace,
Harvest Moon, Sickle Moon, Blackpool
Trip, Bilberry Slab, Desert Head**

1989 May   **Orm and Cheep**   Al Evans   *"Orm and Cheep
were stars in a kids' TV programme around the time
of the first ascent. James was crying in his buggy as
Andrea belayed me, so she sang the theme tune to it.
That did the trick long enough for me to get the
hard bit done!"*

pre-1990   **Original Route** (Oldgate Nick)
1990   **Belladonna Direct**
Malc Baxter, Jim Perrin, Harry Venables
*Also claimed as Primadonna by Joe Bawden
in 1977.*

1990 May 3   **April Showers Direct**
Dave Whittles (solo)
Hotter Than July   Simon Allsop (solo)
pre-1991   **Summit Bypass**   Mike Cluer (solo)
1991 Jul 27   **Sleeping with Sarah**   Tim McLean
c1992   **Beam Me Up Scotty**   Justin Critchlow (solo)
*Very likely to have been done before, but then Justin
was destined for greater things!*
Farmer Barlimow   Antony Hall (solo)
1993   **Fat Man Burger Overdose, Inspector
Remorse**   Keith Ashton, Dave Whitely.
1994 Spring   **Stuck Behind a Yellow Metro**   Ed Jackson
*The route was named with reference to the
frustrating journey to the crag.*
1995 May 7   **Come on Eileen**   Malc Baxter,
Harry Venables, Matt Rhodes
1997   **The Cat Inside**   Ben Tye
1997   **The Ugly Bloke**   Joe Bawden, Paul Knowles
Primadonna   Joe Bawden, Paul Knowles
Essentially the way Belladonna should have gone
Assorted Pond Life
Sandy Sanderson, Tony Edwards
2000   **Flies of Ambition, Windshields of Fate**
John H Bull, Karen Dalkin (solo). Routes on
Buxton Moss, Hob Tor and Allstone Lee
Rocks recorded John H Bull, although some
will have been climbed previously.
2000 Jul 19   **The Couch Potato**   Ed Jackson, Dan Taylor
*E7 reaches Bosley Cloud in the form of an utterly
serious route. "Dubious protection is available behind
the flake, at two thirds height, but it creaks when
you pull on it so I didn't bother on the first ascent. I
first top roped it in the winter of '94 but couldn't
climb it in one go." Repeated October 2000 by
Chris Hutchins.*
2001   **Simon's Wall**   Simon Wilson
2002 Jun   **Ice Breaker**   Paul Fitzsimmons,
Helena Garnard
2003 Apr 6   **Spiderman Meets the Carlsberg Club**
Dave Garnett (solo), John H Bull (solo)
*The local under-age drinking club were very easily
impressed*
Way Purple Splat Balloon
John H Bull (solo)
2003   **Nursery Arête**   Paul Messenger,
Rob Moran   *Climbed (whilst Paul's son was at
nursery) after a chance conversation with the crag
writer revealed this overlooked line.*

2003   **Stoke the Engines**
Laurie Carefoot, Martin Kocsis
Keith George: The Movie   Martin Kocsis,
Laurie Carefoot   *Named after a local climbing*
legend who's catchphrase is "If that's not a jug, I'm
off!" usually in extremis, usually with rising
concern in his voice. There may, or may not, be a
hidden jug on this route! Laurie's first new route
Iron Age Fortitude   Neil Foster,
Graham Hoey, Clare Reading, Martin Kocsis
Enticed to the crag by the promise of tea and cakes
once the route was in the bag, Neil lost more blood
on this route than on any other in the previous six
months!
Chamonaze Blues   Olly Allen, Martin
Kocsis   *The penultimate line on Castle Naze falls to*
a leader jaded from three months of hard alpine
climbing and even harder Chamonix living.

2003 Jul 12   **Kipling Arête**   Dave Garnett, John H Bull
A birthday ascent powered by celebratory chocolate
orange
Moss Side Story   John H Bull, Dave Garnett
2003   **Stilted, Jilted, Rib and Slab, Nine Tales,**
Crime Gene   John H Bull, solo or with
Karen Dalkin   *Some, if not all, had certainly been*
done before.
Catapult   Andrew Healey, Simon Wren,
both solo
2003   **Eeny, Meeny, Miny, Mo, Frank's Route**
Frank Loftus, John Jones, Ken Wilson,
Martin Kocsis, Niall Grimes

Graded List

E8
Judge Jules
Final Destination
Ultimate Sculpture
Young Pretender
Doug

E7
Obsession Fatale
Clippety Clop
Moov Over
Logical Progression
Paralgism
Boom Bip
Pair o' Genes
The Driven Bow
B4 XS
Ray's Roof
The Couch Potato
Never Never Land
Dangerous Crocodile
  Snogging
One Chromosome's
  Missing

E6
A Little Peculiar
Thing on a Spring
Against the Grain
Pull the Udder One
Sole Survivor
Piece of Mind
Destination Earth
Miss Understood
Master of Reality
Arêtenophobia
Solitaire
Art Nouveau
A Fist Full of Crystals
National Acrobat
Barriers in Time
Painted Rumour
Judge Dread
Northern Comfort

The Pride
Bloodspeed

E5
Gillted
Knossos
Nature Trail
Inaccessible
Caricature
Antithesis
Patient Weaver
Slender Thread
Apache Dawn
Bloodstone
The Thin Air
Entropy's Jaw
Counterstroke of Equity
Old Fogey Direct
Catastrophe
  Internationale
Track of the Cat

E4
Crystal Voyager, N^{th} Cloud
Fast Piping
Mirror, Mirror
Ramshaw Crack
DNA
Chameleon
The Super Girdle
Space Probe
The Impending Doom
Secrets of Dance
Bareback Rider
Caesarian
Borstal Breakout
Icarus Allsorts
Metaphysical Scoop
Willow Farm
Trepidation
Iron Age Fortitude
The Phantom
Licence to Run
The Death Knell

Anthrax
Acid Drop
The High Priest
Gypfast
The Pillar of Judgement
Wings of Unreason
Cloudbusting
Traveller in Time

E3
A Phoenix Too Frequent
Ascent of Man
Corinthian
Hunky Dory
Comedian
Crystal Voyager,
  Bosley Cloud
Old Fogey
Bordello
The Swan
The Joker
Appaloosa Sunset
The Bridge of Sighs
Entente Cordiale
Starlight and Storm
Qui Vive
The Sorcerer
The Undertaker
The Better End
San Melas
Smear Test

E2
Gib
Electric Chair
Gumshoe
Charlie's Overhang
Gallows
Elegy
Commander Energy
Finger of Fate
Titan
Walleroo
Ruby Tuesday

Topaz
Enchanted Forest
The Clown
Heart of Gold
Boysen's Arête
Wombat
Kipling Arête
Crack of Gloom
Sense of Doubt
The Perp
Original Route, Baldstones

E1
Pod Crack
Brown's Crack
The Fox
Enigma Variations
Shortcomings
Hawkwing
Safety Net
The Untouchable
Tower Face
Chicken
Keith George:
  The Movie
The Press
Dorothy's Dilemma
Slowhand
Drain the Main Vein
Hypothesis
Morocc'n Roll
Hot Tin Roof
Round Table
Ground Support
Encouragement
Kaleidoscope
Double Overhang

Hard Very Severe
Masochism
Teck Crack
Hen Cloud Eliminate
Bengal Buttress
Saul's Crack

Delstree
Boysen's Delight
The Mincer
Bachelor's Left-Hand
The Sloth
The Helix
Don's Crack
Matinee
Rubberneck
Second's Advance
The Great Zawn
Valkyrie Direct
Prostration
Cave Crack
Baldstones Arête
Roscoe's Wall
Scoop Face
Fifth Horseman
Portfolio
Crispin's Crack
Special K
Kneewrecker Chimney
En Rappel
Toe Rail
Eye of Japetus

Very Severe
Devotoed
Crabbie's Crack
Valkyrie
West's Wallaby
Central Climb Direct
Bachelor's Buttress
The Gape
The Crank
Pincer
Reunion Crack
Rainbow Crack
Pinnacle Face
Niche Arête
Bachelor's Climb
Main Crack
Condor Slab
Hedgehog Crack

Battle of the Bulge
Smun
The Crack, Castle Naze
North Buttress Arête
Via Dolorosa
Keep Arête
Baldstones Face
Central Climb
The Fruit Palace
Aqua
Cave Crack
Defiance
Little Crack
Nozag
The Neb Finish
Rhynose
Roof Climb
Bollard Edge

Hard Severe
Kestrel Crack
Jeffcoat's Buttress
Calcutta Crab Dance
Technical Slab
Herford's Girdle
  Traverse
Sifta's Quid
Damascus Crack
Honky Tonk
Ogden Arête
Slab and Arête
Struggle
Little Giraffe Man
Final Crack
Tricouni Crack
Traditional
Zig-Zag Crack
Hazel Barrow Crack
Thin Crack, Back Forest

Severe
Modern
Crack and Corner
Right-Hand Route

Calcutta Crack
Fledgling's Climb
Rib Chimney
The Niche, Castle Naze
Via Dolorosa Variation
K2
Portcullis Crack
The Blackpool Trip
The Arête, Garston
The Cat Crawl
Great Chimney
Thompson's Buttress
  Route I
Crab Walk
Camelian Crack
Billiard Table
Black and Tans
Runner Route
Hazel Barn
Green Crack, Windgather
Chockstone Crack,
  Gradbach
Route I, Windgather
Hollybush Crack

Hard Very Difficult
Fern Crack
Yong
Black Velvet
The Arête, Hen Cloud
Keep Corner
Original Route,
  Oldgate Nick
Pedestal Route
Cave Arête
Pseudo Crack

Very Difficult
Maud's Garden
Jeffcoat's Chimney
Squashed Finger
Perambulator Parade
Brad's Chimney

Central Tower, Castle Naze
Prow Corner
Squash Balls
Boomerang
Green Shaker
Right Route, Upper Tier
Lighthouse
Jug Jam
Beckermet Slab

Difficult
Inverted Staircase
Raven Rock Gully
Flake Chimney, Lower Tier
Steeplechaser
Prow Cracks
Mantelshelf Route
High Buttress Arête
Mild Thing
Chockstone Chimney,
  Windgather

Moderate
Staircase
Buttress Two Gully

Graded List – Bouldering

V12
Inertia Reel Traverse

V10
Inertia Reel Sitter
Mushin'
Grand Theft
Who Needs Ready Brek?
Nadin's Traverse,
Doxey's Pool
Monologue
Maurice Gib

V9
Dialogue
Stall Arête Sit-Start
Higginson's Arm
The Cube Direct

V8
California Screamin'
Ram Air
Boba Fett
Wright's Traverse
Crystal Voyager
Mean Ol' Bastard
The Fin (Sitter)
The Gutter
Gibbering Wreck
Undercut Dyno
Milky Buttons

V7
Pipe Entry
Leather Joy Boys
The Fly (Sitter)
Hanging Slab, Clouds
Triptych Groove
Hard Arête, Clouds
Nadin's Traverse,
Upper Tier
The Leading
Fireman Direct
(Simple Simon)

The Drowning Pool
Baldstones Traverse
The Fink
Press Sit-Start
Tierdrop
Clever Skin

V6
Stall Arête
Limbless Limbo Dancer
Acne Arête
Ousal Low Traverse
Starlight and Storm
Dignity of Labour
Ant Lives

V5
Summit Arête
Night of Lust Start
The Cube
Elephant's Ear Sit-Start
The Downpipe
Martin's Problem,
Gib Torr
The Nose, Upper Tier
Crinkles Wall
Stretch and Mantel
Left Slab, Spring Boulders
The Boss, Upper Tier

V4
The Pinches, Ramshaw
Teck Crack Direct
The Fly
The Virgin Traverse
Finger of Fate
Jackpot, Piece of Mind
Jump
Soggy Bottom Crack
The Staffs Flyer
The Gateless Gate
Itchy Groove
Sly Stallone
Fielder's Corner

Elephants Eye

V3
Persistence
Crack and Arête,
Art Nouveau
Three Pocket Slab
The Pube
Joe's Arête
Scratchy Scoop,
Dougless Boulder
Cooper's Traverse
Ripple
Greener Traverse
Swivel Finger
Varicose

V2
Crystal Tipps
Off Work
Gromit Arête
The Tufa, Cottage Rocks
The Scoops,
Spring Boulders
Lazy Trout
Holdless Slab, Clouds
Scab
Sly Super-Direct
Itchy Fingers
Croissant Groove

V1
The Rammer
Sensible Shoes
Risky Runnel
Babbacombe Start
Bombay Overhang
Right Vein, Hen Cloud
Mr Grogan
The Blob, Piece of Mind
Chunky, Gradbach
Summit Slab, The Cube

V0
Flight Exam,
Very Far Boulders
Front Crack, Gradbach
The Yawn
Elephant's Ear
Shark's Fin
Classic Arête, Lower Tier
Flaky Romp, Art Nouveau
Rounded Arête,
Very Far Boulders
Don's Crack
Prehistoric Offwidth,
Newstones
Hanging Arête, Gradbach

Bouldering Index

5b Arête 297
5c Wall 181

A
Acne Arête 69
Alan's Variant 296
Allen's Fingers 211
Alternative Start 241
Annie's Egg 29
Another Nadin Traverse 66
Ant Lives 9
Appocaliss 126
Arête, The 188
Armstrain 198
Art Nouveau Boulders
71, 72

B
Baldstones Traverse 177
Be Calmed 154
Below the Flake 179
Bill's XS 296
Billy Bunter 248
Bizarre 245
Blind Flake 11
Blob, The 29
Blu-Tac 207
Boba Fett 11
Bobarête 11
Bombay Overhang 53
Bond It 207
Boozy Traverse, The 13
Boss Slab 8
Boss, The 45
Bowcock's Chimney 207
Bridget 171
Broken Wing 44
Brown Wall 188
Buster 29

C
Cabana 206
Calcutta Crimp 53
Calcutta Problems 53
Calcutta Rib 53
Calcutta Traverse 53
California Screamin' 156
Calmed Left-Hand 154
Cannabis Arm 207
Captain Quark 173
Cellar and Attic
Bouldering 50, 51
Cellar Dwella 51
Chasm Boulders 69

Chasm Crinkle Project 69
Chips Ahoy 28
Chunky 188
Classic Arête 9
Clever Skin 179
Contract Worker 198
Cooper's Traverse 45
Cottage Rocks Bouldering
248
Crab Walk Direct 144
Crack and Arête 72, 169
Crinkles Wall 29
Crinkly Wall 51
Croissant Groove 28
Crusty 248
Crystal Tipps 154
Cube Crack 54
Cube Traverse 54
Cube, The 54

D
Dangerous Crocodile
Bouldering 147
Dialogue 155
Dignity of Labour, The 13
Dirtnap 53
Dish Grab 53
Dixon's Dart Board 296
Dog-Leg Corner 198
Dog-Leg Crack 198
Doubloon 208
Doug-less 13
Downpipe, The 51
Doxey's Pool 66, 67
Dreadful 91
Drowning Pool 66
Drunk Enough 52
Dyno, The 177

E
Ecstasy 1 296
Elephant's Ear 179
Epilogue 155

F
Fielder's Corner 179
Fielder's Indirect 179
Fielder's Wall 179
Fifty Pence Project 239
Fin, The (Gibb Torr) 181
Fin, The (Wolf Edge) 191
Finger, The 50
Fingers Start 241
Fink, The 181

Fireman Indirect 241
Flake Slab 169
Flake, The
(Lower Tier Boulders) 8
Flakes, The 90
Flaky Romp 72
Flight Exam 78
Fly, The 12
Fresher's Arête 297
Front Crack 187

G
Ganderhole Crack 179
Gary's 5c 183
Gates, The 51
Genetix 207
Gentle Slab 10
Gentleman John 239
Gibbering Left 181
Gibbering Lip 181
Gibbering Right 181
Gibbering Wreck 184
Gibby Haines 182
Gibby Sit-Start 182
GibTorrture 183
Glued Up 45
Golden Sovereign 208
Gollum 191
Gorgonzola 207
Grand Theft 45
Green Rib 12
Green Streak, The 188
Greener Mantel 8
Greener Traverse, The 8
Grewsome 29
Grind, The 11
Grinding Sloper 167
Gritstone Pimple 69
Gromit Arête 89
Gutter, The 17

H
Hairy Hat Man 191
Hanging Arête 179
Hanging Slab, The 86
Hanging Start
(Babbacombe) 49
Hard Arête, The 87
Harrop's Pride 198
Hazel Groove 169
Heave Ho 12
Heighley Nightmare, The
296
Hem Line 145
Higginson's Arm 44

Hilti Gunner 298
Holdless Slab 87
Holly Mantel 29
Hot Dog 206
Hush Puppy 206

I
Impotence 11
Inertia Reel 13
Inertia Reel Traverse 7
Inner Tube 77
Itchy Fingers 171
Itchy Groove 171
Ivy League 295

J
Jackpot 29
James Slab 9
Jamless 155
Jams, The 29
Jess's Arête 296
Jess's Corner 296
Jill the Traverse 239
Joe's Arête 45
Joe's Portholes 45
Johnson'sville 207
Jug Up 45
Juggy Flakeline 72
Juggy Groove 44
Jump 54

K
Killer Wall 296
Knees Up 45

L
Last Banana Before Sunset
178
Last Post, The 220
Lazy Trout 77
Leaky Traverse 90
Left Arête (Fifth Cloud) 87
Left Cheek 66
Left Off 29
Left Twin Arête 169
Limbless Limbo Dancer 53
Little Cenotaph 296
Little Groove 242
Little Rib 245
Little Traverse 166, 183
Long Traverse, The 237
Long Wall Traverse 295
Low Traverse (Dimmings
Dale) 239

Staffordshire Grit

Low Traverse
  (Heighley Castle Q.) 296
Lower Tier Boulders 8, 9
Lurch, The 12
Lust Left-Hand 155

M

Magic Arête 154
**Magic Roundabout
  Boulders** 154, 155
Mantel 187
Mantel and Pocket 28
Mark of Zorro 296
Martin's Problem 183
Martin's Traverse 169
Maurice Gib 182
Mega Traverse, The 240
Meninges 207
Milky Buttons 85
Mistral Start 53
Mono Slab 72
Monologue 155
Motorbike 243
Mr Grogan 207
Mr Nice 12
Mushin' 13

N

Nadin's Secret Finger 80
Nadin's Traverse 45
Niche Traverse, The 241
Night of Lust Area 155
Night of Lust Start 155
Nose, The 44, 239
Nother Mantel, A 11
Nutmeg Groove 169

O

Off Work 29
Off-Fingers Crack 77
One Inch Punch 44
Open Groove 77
Ousal Bouldering 247
Ousal High 249
Ousal Low 245
Overlap 144

P

Particle Exchange 13
Paul's Wall 198
Pebbles and Seam 11
Pebblesville 206
Pebbly Wall 11
Peep Show 206
Period Drama 54
Persistence 85
Piece of Mind Bouldering
  28, 29
Pieces of Eight 208
Pinches, The 155

Pinkies to Perkies 77
Pipe Entry 51
Pocket Wall 248
Porridge Wall 182
Potty, The 28
PPG 296
Practice Chimney 155
Prehistoric Offwidth 173
Press Direct 155
Problem Arête 198
Pube, The 54
Puffed Wheat 207
Punch Arête 296
Pussin' Boots 69

R

Radical Runnel 29
Rammer, The 155
Raven 207
Right Twin Arête 169
Right Wall 296
Ripple 169
Risky Runnel 50
Roll Off 145
Roundabout Direct 154
Rumour, The 13
Runnel 11
Runnel Entry 155
Rupert's Sitdown 13
Rusks And Rye 207

S

S Arête 29
S&M 166
Sapling Bugle 248
Scab 29
Scoops 11
Scrack 50
Scratch Crack 171
Scratchy Scoop 12
Seams Green 183
Seams Polished 44
Seconds Out 11
Sensible Shoes 144
Serpent, The 296
Sexy Steve 50
Shark's Fin 156
Sid the Sexist 248
Sidepull Wall 72
Sign Start 53
Simon's Slab 105
Simple Simon 241
Sketchy Rib 12
Sketchy Wall 9
Skinned Rabbit 11
Skydivin 13
Slim Corner 297
Slim Groove 187
Slippery Groove 44
Sly Direct 173
Sly Stallone 172

Smoothment Traverse 144
Soggy Bottom Crack 66
Southern Sloper 296
Spankasaurus Does Chicago
  91
Spirella 207
Spotter's Slop 69
Spotters Pop 69
Spring Boulders 10–13
Spring Roll 10
Squirm, The 50
Staffordshire Flyer 66
Staircase (Upper Tier
  Boulders) 45
Stall Arête 183
Stallone Arête 172
Starlight Left 105
Stepped Arête 297
Strenuosity 248
Stretch and Mantel 9
Stretch Left 9
Suicide Arête 297
Suicide Wall 297
Summit Slab 54
Super Direct Start 154
Swivel Finger 90

T

Teck Crack Direct 13
Teck Crack Super-Direct 13
This is My Church 191
Thorns Start 241
Three Pocket Slab 9
Tip-Toe Arête 187
Tit Grip 145
Too Drunk 52
Triptych Groove 69
Tufa 248
Twisted Crack 29
Two Pocket Slab 77

U

Ultra Direct Start 154
Undercut Dyno 9
Undercut Traverse, The 9
Undercut, The 242
Ungentlemanly Conduct
  239
Upper Tier Boulders, The
  44, 45
Uppermost Traverse 167

V

Varicose 167
Very Far Boulders 77, 78
Violence 11

W

Wafer, The 248
Warren Piece 191

Wavy Slab 10
Weird Little 5c 28
Who Needs Ready Brek?
  85
Wildy's Arête 29
Wildy's Right 29
Wraparound Arête 166
Wright's Traverse 241

Y

Yawn, The 187
Yawning Stone 187

Crag Index

A

Aiguille, The 105
Allstone Lee Rocks 277
Alpha Buttress 65
Amphitheatre Walls 117
Austin's Crag 232

B

Bachelor's Area 119
Baldstones Pinnacle 174
Bengal Buttress 15
Biscay Buttress 214
Biscuit Buttress 128
Black and Tans Area 39
Black Wall 108
Blushing Buttress 49
Bordello Area, The 126
Bosley Cloud 279
Bottom Buttresses, The 127
Boxing Gloves, The 123
Broken Nose Buttress 197
Buttress One 265
Buttress Two 264
Buxton Boss 277

C

Calcutta Buttress 52
Castle Crag 227
Castle Naze 269
Catstone, The 285
Cave Buttress 61, 215
Central Area 112
Central Massif, The 38
Charlie's Overhang 166
Chockstone Buttress 285
Cluster of Ribs, The 275
Condor Buttress 56
Consallforge 213
Cottage Rocks 245
Cotton Bank Crag 224
Crack Area, The 273
Cynic's Buttress 186

D

Delstree Area 109
Devil's Rock 214
Dimmings Dale 236

E

Elegy Slab 22

F

Far Skyline Buttress 70
Fifth Cloud, The 87
First Cloud, The 80
Flaky Buttress 151

Flintmill Buttress 213
Folly Cliff, The 288
Fourth Cloud, The 85

G

Garden Buttress 292
Garston Rocks 219
Gentleman's Rock 239
Gib Buttress 214
Gibbon Buttress 183
Gold Rush Buttress 177
Great Gate Buttress 225
Great Slab, The 41
Green Slab 290

H

Hanging Stone, The 194
Hard Very Far Skyline
  Buttress 75
Harston Rock 215
Hawk's Hole Quarry 288
Hazel Barn Buttress 169
Hermit's Buttress 291
Hermit's Rock 240
High Buttress 264
Hob Tor 278

I

Ina's Rock 231
Inaccessible Pinnacle 123

K

Kestrel Buttress 23

L

Lady Stone, The 157
Left-Hand Buttress 210
Left-Hand Buttress
  (Wootton Lodge) 250
Left-Hand Section (Roaches
  Lower Tier) 6
Left-Hand Section (Roaches
  Upper Tier) 32
Left-Hand Side of the
  Amphitheatre 244
Lion Rock 222, 224
Little Slab 290
Lone Buttress 245
Long Wall 237
Lord's Buttress 236
Lower Buttress, The 125
Lower Tier (Gib Torr) 181
Lower Tier Girdle Traverses
  31
Lower Tier, The (Ramshaw)
  144

Magic Roundabout Buttress
  152

M

Magical Bouldery Wood
  126
Main Crag, The (Back
  Forest) 195
Main Crag, The (Ramshaw)
  136
Main Crag, The (Wright's
  Rock) 241
Main Face, The 91
Maud's Garden Area 35
Middle Buttress 263
Millstone Quarry 289
Mow Cop 287

N

Nick I' Th' Hill 289
North Buttress 260, 281
Northern Combs 278
Nose, The 280
Not So Far Skyline
  Buttress 68

O

Old Man of Mow, The 288
Oldgate Nick 268
Oldridge Pinnacle 218
Ousal Crag 245

P

Painter's Rock 243
Park Bank Crags 229
Peakstone Rock 226
Piece of Mind Slab 27
Pinnacle Buttress 215
Pinnacle, The 155
Pinnacle, The (Gradbach
  Hill) 186
Pinnacle, The (Knypersley)
  290
Pinnacle, The (Skyline) 64
Pinnacles, The (Hen Cloud)
  105
Price's Cave Crag 213

R

Rainroach Rock 240
Rakes Dale 232
Rakes Dale Wall 232
Ramshaw Buttress 150
Raven Rock 16
Ray's Buttress 178
Rhynose Buttress 171

Right-Hand Buttress 211
Right-Hand Buttress
  (Wooton Lodge) 250
Right-Hand Section
  (Roaches Lower Tier) 14
Right-Hand Side of the
  Amphitheatre 244
Roman Nose Buttress 153
Rostrum, The 195

S

Scratch Buttress 171
Second Cloud, The 80
Secret Slab 284
Sharpcliffe Rock 207
Short Edge 278
Skyline Buttress 62
Sly Buttress 172
Smear Test Slab 20
Smelting Mill Buttress 236
South Buttress 142, 265
South Buttress (Castle
  Naze) 275
South-Western Combs 277
Square Boulder 187
Stoney Dale Quarry 222
Summit Rocks 283
Swan Wall, The 18

T

Technician's Wall 215
Third Cloud, The 82
Timbersbrook Quarry 287
Toothill Rock 234
Tower Buttress 60
Trio Buttress 58

U

Upper Tier, The (Gib Torr)
  184
Uppermost Outcrop 167
Very Far Skyline Buttress 71

W

Well Hidden Buttress 224
West's Wallaby Area 34
Western Combs 277
Western Outcrop, The 194
Wetley Rocks 213
White Hall Rocks 277
Wicken Stones, The 291
Wright's Rock 240

Y

Yawning Stone, The 187

Route Index

39th Step 65
7 of 9 117
99% of Gargoyles Look
  Like Bob Todd 42

A

A.M. Anaesthetic 57
A.P. Chimney 272
Abdomen 145
Abstract 64
Acid Drop 62
Ackit 7
Action Trousers 195
Afrodizzycrack 226
After Eight 136
Against the Grain 19
Aged Crack 265
Ageing Adolescents 91
Aiguillette, The 105
Alcatraz 143
Alien Wall 229
Aliens 229
All Day and All of the
  Night 244
All the King's Horses 219
All-Stars' Wall 178
Alpha 68
Alpha Arête 68
Alsager Route 288
Alternative Three 242
Alternative Ulster 214
Alton Cliff 228
Always Dreaming 87
Amazing Grace 231
Anaconda 112
Anaconda Variation 113
Ancient 117
Andrei's Route 119
Andy's Crack 278
Anniversaire 189
Ant's Corner 234
Anthem for a Doomed
  Youth 230
Anthrax 109
Anticlimax 285
Antidote 279
Antithesis 43
Antlers Hall 151
Apache Dawn 6
Ape, The 112
Aperitif 49
Appaloosa Sunset 83
Approaching Dark 157
April Showers 285
Aqua 38

Aquae Arnemetiaie 277
Arête and Crack 149
Arête and Slab Climb 289
Arête Direct 267
Arête Wall (Hen Cloud)
  117
Arête Wall (Ramshaw
  Rocks) 152
Arête, The (Castle Naze)
  270
Arête, The (Garston Rocks)
  219
Arête, The (Hen Cloud
  Central Area) 117
Arête, The (Mow Cop) 288
Arête, The (Ramshaw Rocks
  Main Crag) 139
Arêtenophobia 122
Army Route 151
Art Nouveau 72
Arthur Scargill's Hairpiece
  is Missing 150
As You Like It 215
Ascent of Man 7
Ascent of Woman 7
Aspirant, The 7
Assegai 149
Assembled Techniques 136
Assorted Pond Life 273
Atlas 231
Atropine 274
Attempted Moustache, The
  38
Austin's Chimney 232
Automatix 62

B

B.S. Mow 288
B4XS 113
Babbacombe Lee 49
Bachelor's Buttress 39
Bachelor's Climb 122
Bachelor's Left-Hand 121
Back Forest Gâteau 196
Back Side 227
Back Wall 244
Backwash 214
Bad Joke 108
Bad Poynt 60
Bad Sneakers 59
Bakewell Tart 83
Baldstones Arête 175
Baldstones Face 174
Bandicoot 276
Bantam Crack 109

Barbecue Corners 91
Barbiturate 189
Bareback Rider 6
Bareleg Wall 177
Barriers in Time 7
Bastion Corner 197
Bastion Face 197
Batman 288
Battery Crack 23
Battle of the Bulge 142
Battle Royal 218
Bay Wall 260
Beam Me Up Scotty 293
Beckermet Slab 35
Bed of Nails 43
Bees 277
Belladonna 274
Belladonna Direct 274
Bender, The 82
Bengal Buttress 16
Better End, The 109
Between the Lines 35
Between the Tiles 52
Beware Coconuts 6
Bewhiskered Behemoth
  127
Big Flake, The 82
Big Red Rock Eater 283
Big Richard 153
Bilberry Slab 293
Bilberry Traverse 64
Billiard Table, The 186
Billy the Barbel Busts Loose
  231
Birch Tree Climb 284
Birthday Climb 273
Bishop's Move, The 219
Bitching 119
BJM 244
Black and Tans 40
Black and Tans Variations 41
Black and White 226
Black Eyed Dog 108
Black Pig, The 60
Black Ram Arête 70
Black Ram, The 70
Black Slab 260
Black Velvet 41
Black Widow 215
Blackbank Crack 177
Blackpool Trip, The 293
Blizzard Buttress 110
Block Crack Left-Hand 271
Blockbuster 146
Blood Blisters 108
Bloodspeed 22

Bloodstone 22
Bloody Crack (Castle Naze)
  271
Bloody Crack (Churnet)
  232
Blue Bandanna 85
Blunder 230
Blusher, The 274
Boats for Hire 218
Boboon 126
Body Pop 139
Bollard Edge 196
Bone Idol 68
Boom Bip 151
Boomerang (Castle Naze)
  275
Boomerang (Ramshaw)
  149
Boomerang Buttress 275
Bordello 126
Border Skirmish 126
Borstal Breakout 113
Boston Strangler, The 86
Bottle Crack 285

Bounty Killer 65
Bow and Arrow 289
Bow Buttress 119
Bow Crack 270
Bowrosin 149
Boysen's Arête 125
Boysen's Delight 85
Boysen-Carrington Route,
  The 217
Brad's Chimney 230
Brag, The 156
Brazilian, The 223
Breakfast Problem 68
Breaks 214
Breathless 56
Briar 291
Brick Bank Crack 292
Bridge of Sighs, The 194
Broken Arrow 112
Broken Cracks 264
Broken Groove 141
Broken Groove Arête 141
Broken Groove in the Arête,
  The 265
Broken Slab 36
Brothers, The 228
Brown's Crack 144
Bruno Flake 56
Bubbly Wall 275
Bud Love 49
Bulger, The 23

Bulging Arête 264
Bulldog Flake 281
Bulwark 105
Bumper Cars 195
Burnham Crack 194
Burrito Deluxe 6
Buster the Cat 108
Buttress Two Gully 264

C

Cad Cam Warrior 223
Caesarian 110
Calcutta Buttress 52
Calcutta Crab Dance 52
Calcutta Crack 52
Calf Path, The 73
Cambridge Crack 288
Camelian Crack 145
Cannon, The 143
Cannonball Crack 15
Canticle 224
Capitol Climb 34
Capstan's Corner 62
Capstone Chimney 196
Captain Lethargy 26
Captain Skyhook 289
Captain's Blood, The 288
Caramta 156
Caricature 121
Carpet Crack 278
Carrion 23
Castle Crack 289
Castles of Sand 232
Cat Crawl, The 285
Cat Inside, The 268
Catapult 268
Catastrophe Internationale 6
Cave Arête 62
Cave Buttress 62
Cave Crack (Belmont Hall Crags) 211
Cave Crack (Stoney Dale Q.) 223
Cave Crack (The Roaches) 61
Cave Crack, The (Harston Rocks) 215
Cave Rib 211
Cave Wall 220
Cedez le Passage 149
Ceiling Zero 157
Central Climb 115
Central Climb Direct 113
Central Crack 241
Central Massif 38
Central Route 197
Central Route (The Roaches) 42
Central Route (Windgather) 263

Central Tower (Castle Naze) 274
Central Tower (Hen Cloud) 124
Central Traverse 59
Centre, The 264
Chalkstorm 26
Chameleon 122
Chamonaze Blues 274
Charlie's Overhang 166
Cheek 265
Cheek, The 214
Cherry Hill 292
Cherry Rare 241
Chiaroscuro 121
Chicane 56
Chicane Destination 57
Chicanery 56
Chicken 107
Chicken Direct 107
Chicken Run 33
Childhood's End 157
Chilton's Superdirect 229
Chimney and Crack 261
Chimney, The 70
Chiropodist's Nightmare 222
Chockstone Chimney (Hen Cloud The Pinnacles) 107
Chockstone Chimney (Ramshaw Rocks South Buttress) 142
Chockstone Chimney (Windgather) 264
Chockstone Corner 85
Chockstone Crack (Gradbach Hill) 189
Chockstone Crack (Hen Cloud) 108
Chockstone Crack (Peakstone Inn Amphitheatre) 244
Chocolate Orange 236
Choka 25
Christmas Arête 260
Christmas Cracker 291
Christmas Nose 260
Christmas Tree Crack 236
Chronicle 71
Chute, The 219
Cioch Groove 288
Circuit Breaker 26
City Dweller 279
City Hobgoblins 279
Clam 215
Cleft Route 186
Climb To The Lost World 240
Clippety Clop, Clippety Clop, Clippety Clop 148

Clive Coolhead Realises the Excitement of Knowing You May Be the Author of Your Own Death is More Intense Than Orgasm 22
Cloud Nine 87
Cloudbusting 85
Clown, The 211
Clumsy Too, The 241
Coelred's Crack 229
Cold Bone Forgotten 17
Cold Man's Finger 60
Cold Shoulder 290
Cold Sweat 123
Cold Wind 144
Coldfinger 36
CollyWobble 145
Columbal Convenience 274
Coma Sutra 71
Combs Climb 272
Come Girl 64
Come On Eileen 273
Comedian 120
Comedian, The 145
Commander Energy 26
Common Good, The 291
Communist Crack 80
Condor Chimney 57
Condor Slab 57
Connector 61
Constant Grumble 213
Contraception on Demand 281
Contrary Mary 36
Cool Fool 120
Cool in a Crisis 285
Corinthian 120
Corner Crack (Ramshaw) 143
Corner Crack (Short Edge) 278
Corner Crack (Windgather) 265
Corner Route 280
Corner Traverse 215
Corner, The 264
Cornflake 38
Couch Potato, The 284
Counterstroke Direct 76
Counterstroke of Equity 76
Crab Walk 144
Crabbie's Crack 83
Crabbie's Crack Left-Hand 83
Crack and Corner 47
Crack of Gloom 16
Crack, The (Castle Naze) 273
Cracked Arête (Ramshaw) 152

Cracked Arête (The Roaches) 57
Cracked Gully 152
Crafty Cockney, The 285
Crank, The 142
Creep, Leap, Creep, Creep 149
Crenation 34
Crest 214
Crevasse, The 17
Crime Gene 268
Crimes of Passion 211
Crippler, The 153
Crispin's Crack 126
Crud on the Tracks 232
Crushed Pagan God 277
Crying Wolf 285
Crystal Grazer 14
Crystal Tipps 152
Crystal Voyager (Bosley Cloud) 284
Crystal Voyager (Mow Cop) 288
Crystal Voyager (The Nth Cloud) 91
Crystine 289
Cue, The 186
Curd be Cheese 226
Curfew 156
Curvature 73
Curver 157
Cyber Insekt 277

D

Daddy Long Legs 234
Daedalus 227
Damascus Crack 36
Dan's Dare 150
Dance of the Flies 223
Dancing Bear 244
Danera 291
Dangerous Crocodile Snogging 146
Dangler 70
Dark Star 230
Darkness 151
Dawn Piper 36
Day at the Seaside, A 38
Days Gone By 67
Days of Future Passed 7
Dazed and Confused 52
Dazzler 70
Dead Banana Slab 122
Dead Tree Crack 245
Dead Tree Slab 245
Deadwood Crack 211
Deadwood Groove 211
Death Crack 283
Death Knell, The 25
Death Mask 228
Death Wish 213, 283

Staffordshire Grit

Deceiver, The 124
Deception 283
Deep Chimney 273
Deep Crack 273
Deep in Mystery 70
Defiance 229
Definitive Gaze 65
Delectable Deviation, The 152
Delstree 110
Delusion 123
Demon Wall 33
Descant 224
Desert Head 293
Desert Rat 232
Desperado 122
Destination Earth 15
Destination Venus 49
Devil's Crack 214
Devotoed 68
Diagonal Crack 215
Diagonal Route 123
Diamond Wednesday 41
Dimetrodon 226
Dimmingsdale Crack 236
Dingo 276
Direct Route, The (Mow Cop) 288
Director 264
Dirty Wee Rouge 23
Discontinuous Rib 267
Distant Runners 213
DNA 217
Doina Da J'al 223
Don Quixote 219
Don's Crack 145
Don't Go Down to the Woods Today 70
Donor 231
Dorothy's Dilemma 16
Double Chin 139
Double Crack 270
Double Overhang 194
Double Vee 288
Doug 14
Dougie Returns Home 26
Down To The Elbows 228
Drain the Main Vein 171
Dream Fighter 136
Drifter's Escape, The 194
Driven Bow, The 119
Droopy Draws 234
Drop Acid 64
Drop Leaf 239
Drystone Wall 283
Duck Soup 126
Duck-Billed Platypus 275
Dusk 151
Dust Storm 232

E

Early Retirement 156
Earthquake Crack 278
East Face 136
Easy Come 117
Easy Gully 117
Easy Gully Wall 43
Eclipsed Peach Start, The 83
Editor's Note 267
Eeny 277
Elastic Arm 85
Elastic Limit 149
Electric Chair 108
Electric Savage 150
Elegy 22
Emerald Groove 214
Emerald Wall 215
EMS 215
En Rappel 110
Enchanted Forest 76
Encouragement 115
End Game 179
English Towns 149
Enigma Variation 64
Ensign, The 184
Entente Cordiale 70
Enterprise 293
Entropy's Jaw 73
Envy Face 281
ERF Rocks 292
Escape 153
Eugene's Axe 18
Even Lonelier 245
Even Smaller Buttress 119
Evensong 224
Everdance 283
Evil Crack 158
Ex-Lion Tamer 224
Existentialist Arête 283
Extended Credit 156
Extractum 230
Eye of Japetus 195

F

Face 211
Face Route 1 265
Face Route 2 265
Face Value 123
Fagan 236
False Chicane 56
Fandango 215
Fantasy Finish 33
Farmer Barlimow 293
Farmhouse Arête 157
Fast and Bulbous 229
Fast Piping 120
Fat Man Burger Overdose 278
Fat Man's Chimney 273
Fat Old Nick 186
Fat Old Sun 112

Fatalist's Canoe, The 218
Feed the Enemy 189
Feet of Strength 219
Fern Crack 33
Fertility Rite 281
Fertility Rite Left-Hand 281
Fifth Cloud Eliminate 87
Fifth Horseman, The 270
Filler In 197
Final Crack 113
Final Destination 27
Finger of Fate 80
Fingers in Every Pie 242
Fire Down Below 126
First Quarry 295
First's Arête 265
Fist Full of Crystals, A 14
Fist Full of Freshers, A 197
Five Bar Crack 240
Five Thousand Volts 226
Flabby Crack, A 109
Flake Chimney 25
Flake Crack 271
Flake Escape 211
Flake Traverse 213
Flake Wall 215
Flaky Gully 151
Flaky Wall Direct 151
Flaky Wall Finish 83
Flaky Wall Indirect 152
Flaky Wall Super Direct 152
Fledgling's Climb 23
Flies of Ambition, Windshields of Fate 278
Flimney 25
Flour Wall 122
Flower Power Arête 83
Fluorescent Stripper 26
Flutterbye Grooves 71
Fly Walk, The 271
Fly, The 240
Folly Berger 288
Foord's Folly 156
Footpath 214
Footpath Chimney (Hen Cloud) 122
Footpath Chimney (Ousal Dale) 245
Footprint 264
Footstool Left 272
Footstool Right 272
For Tim 186
Force Nine 152
Forking Chimney 177
Formative Years 68
Four Horsemen 230
Four Purists 150
Fourth Quarry 297
Fox, The 172
Foxy Lady 87
Framed 278
Frank's Route 277

Frayed Nerve 120
Freak Out 33
Fred's Café 14
Frequency 215
Friar Muck 223
Friends of Eddie Coil, The 292
Fruit Palace, The 293
Full Frontal 213
Furry Green Atom Bowl 279

G

Gain Entry To Your Soul 223
Gallows 108
Gallows, The 228
Gallstones 175
Gape, The 189
Gaping Void, The 194
Garden Buttress 292
Garlic 52
Gateless Gate, The 218
General Accident 223
Genetix 52
Geography of Power 277
Geordie Girl 82
Gib 184
Gibber Crack 182
Gibbet, The 184
Gibble Gabble Slab 183
Gibbon Take 182
Gibbon Wall 184
Gibe Turkey 184
Gibe, The 183
Gibeonite Girdle 184
Giblet Crack 184
Gibling Corner 184
Gibraltar 184
Gillted 41
Ging 36
Ginger Biscuit 128
Gingerbread 128
Girdle Traverse, The (Roaches Lower Tier) 31
Girdle Traverse, The (Roaches Skyline) 71
Gladiator 231
Glass Back 85
Glyph (S 215
Go Girl 64
Gold Rush 177
Goldsitch Crack 177
Graduate, The 228
Graffiti 15
Grasper 197
Grassy Slabs 291
Great Chimney 122
Great Scene Baby 155
Great Zawn, The 141
Green Chimney 90

Green Corner (Hen Cloud) 108
Green Corner (Ramshaw Buttress) 150
Green Crack (Back Forest) 195
Green Crack (Gradbach Hill) 186
Green Crack (Ramshaw Main Crag) 136
Green Crack (Windgather) 261
Green Crack, The (Castle Naze) 274
Green Gully Direct 281
Green Shaker 197
Green Slab (Churnet) 236
Green Slab (Windgather) 260
Grenadier 90
Grilled Fingers 51
Gromit 89
Groove 267
Groovy Baby 155
Grott 237
Ground Support 231
Grounded 230
Grumbling Wall 213
Gryphon 291
Guano Gully 22
Gully Arête 141
Gully Wall (Ramshaw Buttress) 150
Gully Wall (The Roaches Upper Tier) 51
Gumshoe 142
Gypfast 39

H

Hal's Ridge 125
Halcyone 291
Hallow to our Men 67
Hand Jive 224
Handrail 149
Handrail Direct 149
Hanging Around 40
Hanging Stone Crack 194, 197
Hangman's Crack 49
Hank's Horror 59
Happiness from Outer Space 90
Harvest Moon 293
Hassall's Crack 211
Hatscheck's Groove 217
Hawk's Hell 288
Hawkwing 23
Hazel Barn 169
Hazel Barrow Crack 169
Headless Horseman 25
Heart of Gold 124

Heartbleed 33
Heather Buttress 261
Heather Face 264
Heather Slab 34
Heathylee 179
Hedgehog Crack 120
Height Below 229
Helix, The 215
Helter Skelter 122
Hen Cloud Eliminate 120
Henry Hothead Realises that Being the Author of your Own Broken Ankle Can be Very Embarrassing 225
Hens Dropping 115
Herbivacious 284
Here Be Dragons 213
Heredity 14
Herford's Girdle Traverse 276
High Buttress Arête 264
High Energy Plan 128
High Girdle, The 194
High Priest, The 224
High Tensile Crack 108
High Tension Line 279
Highwayman, The 234
Hippo 172
Hob Crack 278
Hob, The 242
Hobjection Overruled 278
Hobs of Hell 279
Hodgkinson's Chimney 275
Hole and Corner Crack 219
Holly Tree Niche Left Route 196
Holly Tree Niche Right Route 196
Hollybush Crack 41
Hollybush Hell 229
Hollybush Wall 285
Honest John 230
Honest Jonny 139
Honeycomb 277
Honking Bank Worker 156
Honky Tonk 70
Hooverville 278
Hopeless Holly 229
Hot Digital Dog 292
Hot Pants 234
Hot Tin Roof 285
Hotter Than July 285
Hour Glass, The 186
Humble Potter, The 230
Humdinger 39
Hunky Dory 26
Hypothesis 15

I

Icarus 227
Icarus Allsorts 83
Icebreaker 270
Impact Two 284
Impacted Bowel 249
Impending Doom, The 217
Imperfect Lichenous 279
Imposition 151
In Days of Hold 213
In Passing 55
Ina City Rot 232
Ina's Chimney 231
Inaccessible 231
Incognito 174
Indecent Exposure 213
Inexplicably Anonymous 90
Initiation Groove 232
Initiation Wall 288
Insects from Hell 277
Inspector Remorse 278
Inverted Staircase 33
Iron Age Fortitude 274
Iron Horse Crack 151
Iron Ore 236
Ivanhoe 218

J

Jack the Traverse 240
Jean the Bean 115
Jeffcoat's Buttress 40
Jeffcoat's Chimney 39
Jeffcoat's Chimney Variations 40
Jelly Roll 43
Jellyfish 124
Jester, The 211
Jetez le Pantalon 127
Jewel of Corruption 194
Jimmy Carter 82
Joe Public 38
Jog 36
John's Arête 188
John's Route (Back Forest) 195
John's Route (Churnet) 195
Johnny Pooh Poohed 57
Johnny's Indirect Rear Entry 178
Joiner 61
Joker, The 211
Josephina 89
Joshua 292
Juan Cur 143
Judge Dread 91
Judge Jules 91
Jug Jam, The 290
Just For Today 7
Just Thirteen 122

K

K.P. Nuts 7
K2 115
Kaleidoscope 208
Kangaroo 275
Karabiner Chimney 64
Karabiner Cracks 64
Karabiner Slab 64
Keep Arête 272
Keep Buttress 272
Keep Corner 272
Keep Face 196
Keep Left 291
Keeper, The 196
Keith George:The Movie 274
Kelly's Connection 42
Kelly's Direct 43
Kelly's Shelf 43
Kenyatta 208
Kestrel Crack 25
Key Green Crack 285
KGB 80
Kicking Bird 22
Killjoy 208
King Harold 157
King Swing 61
Kipling Arête 294
Klangerman 222
Kneewrecker Chimney 211
Knossos 208
Koala 275
Kobold 208
Konsolation Prize 207
Krakatoa 208
Kremlin Wall 281
Krushna 208
Kudos 208

L

Labyrinth, The 228
Ladies' Route 158
Laguna Sunrise 83
Larva Wall 219
Last View 128
Late Night Final 35
Laughing all the way to the Blank 43
Leading Firemen, The 242
Leather Joy Boys 166
Lechery 157
Ledgeway 272
Lee Side, The 288
Leeds Crack 139
Leeds Slab 139
Left Arête 219
Left Eliminate 288
Left It 290
Left Nostril 280
Left Triplet Crack 267
Left Twin Crack 229

Left Twin Crack (Hen Cloud Bachelor's Area) 122
Left Twin Crack (The Roaches Skyline) 58
Left-Hand Block Crack 86
Left-Hand Crack 194
Left-Hand Route 49
Leg Stump 264
Leg Up 265
Legends of Lost Leaders 82
Legoland 234
Legosaurus Rex 234
Lenin 82
Lethal Weapon 232
Letter Box Cracks 59
Letter Box Gully 59
Levitation 110
Libra 38
Licence to Lust 18
Licence to Run 18
Licensed to Fill 57
Life In The Left Lane 210
Life in the Wrong Lane 210
Lighthouse 58
Lightning Crack 13
Limpet 215
Little Arête 187
Little Chimney 23
Little Crack 91
Little Flake, The 82
Little Giraffe Man 157
Little Nasty 150
Little Nikki 223
Little Peculiar, A 22
Little Perforations 38
Little Pillar 272
Little Pinnacle Climb 105
Live Bait 34
Living Wall 283
Loaf and Cheese 136
Loculus Lie 42
Logical Progression 25
Logos 291
Lone Ascent 38
Lone Wall 245
Long and the Short, The 112
Long Climb 274
Long Lankin 223
Longstop 223
Looking for Today 65
Loose Fingers 117
Lord's Arête 237
Lord's Chimney 237
Lost Girl 64
Louie Groove 139
Low Girdle, The 194
Lubricant, The 284
Lucas Chimney 23
Lucid Reams 179
Lum, The 109

Lung Cancer 56
Lybstep 36

M
M.B. Arête 264
Mad Lines 127
Magenta Corner 215
Magic Child 47
Magic Roundabout 152
Magic Roundabout Direct 152
Magic Roundabout Super Direct 152
Magnificat 224
Maid Marion 222
Main Corner 271
Main Crack 110
Main Wall 284
Maloof 240
Man Mow 288
Man oh Man 107
Mandrake, The 107
Mandrill 107
Manifesto 213
Mantelshelf Route 85
Mantelshelf Slab 64
Mantis 65
Mantrap 153
Mark 230
Mark of Zorro 126
Marsden's Crack 189
Marsden's Eliminate 207
Marxist Undertones 80
Masochism 141
Master of Puppets 107
Master of Reality 107
Matinee 17
Maud's Garden 35
Maximum Hype 142
May Day 285
Mayhem 90
Meander 86
Meander Variation 86
Medicine, The 264
Meeny 277
Megalomania 215
Melaleucion 68
Melancholy Man 215
Mental Traveller 237
Metaphysical Scoop 92
Mexican, The 236
Mick's Metaphor 126
Micro Storm 26
Microcosm 71
Middle and Leg 264
Middle Triplet Crack 267
Middleton's Motion 59
Mild Thing 71
Miller's Melody 213
Mincer, The 20
Mindbridge 107

Minipin Crack 178
Minotaur 227
Minute Wall 285
Miny 277
Mirror, Mirror 85
Misogynist 291
Miss Understood 230
Mississippi (or Straight) Crack 264
Mississippi Crack Variant 264
Missus, The 213
Mistaken Identity 62
Mistral 52
Mixer, The 279
Mo 277
Modern 117
Modesty Crack 156
Molegrip Kid, The 228
Mongolian Throat Singing 175
Monk's Blues 224
Monkey in your Soul, The 112
Monstrous Angel 68
Montezuma's Revenge 183
Monty 150
Moonshine 166
Moore's Crack 215
Moov Over 225
Morocc'n Roll 274
Morpheus 189
Morridge Top 177
Moss Rose 215
Moss Side Story 294
Moto Perpetuo 250
Mousey's Mistake 22
Mr Creosote 194
Mr Decisive 73
Mr Magoo 281
Much Ado About Nothing 215
Mudhopper 70
Muscle Crack 270
Mustard 198
Mutiny Chimney 285
My Mother is a Rhinoceros 223

N
N.E. Hobbs 278
National Acrobat 137
National Hero 6
National Hysteria 177
Nature Trail 76
Navy Cut 56
Neb Finish, The 41
Never Never 241
Never Never Land 150
New Fi' nial 42
Newstones Chimney 166

Niche Arête 271
Niche, The 271
Night of Lust 156
Nine Tales 268
Nithin, The 271
No Future 230
No Name 272
No Pegs Please, We're British 211
No Veranda 245
Nom De Guerre 218
North Buttress Arête 261
North Buttress Arête Indirect 261
North Face, The 218
Northern Comfort 18
Northern Lights 244, 291
Nose Direct 264
Nose, The (Castle Naze) 271
Nose, The (Churnet) 214
Nosepicker 57
Nosey Parker 213
Not Much Further 68
Not So Central Route 197
Not So Fast 68
Not So Steep 68
Notch, The 107
November Cracks 105
Nozag 273
Nursery Arête 271
Nutcracker, The 124
Nutmeg 169
Nutted by Reality 105

O
Oak Spur 215
Oak Tree Crack 188
Obsession Fatale 27
Off The Scale 278
Ogden 60
Ogden Arête 60
Ogden Recess 60
Old Fogey 157
Old Fogey Direct 157
Old King Cole 217
Old Son 186
Old Statesman, The 25
Omega 68
One Chromosome's Missing 217
One Dunne 244
One Knight Stand 219
Open All Hours 230
Opossum 275
Original Route 268
Original Route (Baldstones) 174
Original Route (Churnet) 215
Orm and Cheep 271

Ostentation 215
Ou est le Spit? 53
Outdoor Pursuits Cooperative, The 80
Outflanked 144
Overdrive 139
Overhang, The 230
Overhanging Arête 265
Overhanging Chimney 275
Overhanging Chockstone Crack 270
Overlapping Wall 267
Overlord 237
Oversight 60

P

Painted Rumour 41
Pair O' Genes 217
Palpitation 215
Palsy Wall 215
Pants on Fire 174
Parallel Lines 121
Paralogism 43
Parking Fine 234
Parrot and the Balaclava, The 73
Pasiphae 227
Past Gone Mad, A 279
Pat is Parched 145
Patient Weaver 230
Paul's Puffer 59
Peakstone Crack 226
Pebble Buttress 237
Pebble Drop 240
Pebbledash 18
Pebbles on a Wessex Beach 59
Ped X-ing 47
Pedestal Route 41
Peeping Tom 213
Peg Crack 274
Pegger's Original 223
Pepper 52
Per Rectum 230
Perambulator Parade 174
Perched Block Arête 61
Perched Flake 152
Perp, The 91
Perverted Staircase 33
Pete's Back Side 124
Peter and the Wolf 120
Phallic Crack 143
Phantom, The 187
Piano Stool 272
Piece of Mind 27
Pile Driver 155
Pilgrim's Progress 272
Pillar of Judgement 91
Pincer 20
Pinch, The 112
Pindles Numb 13

Pink Flake 139
Pinnacle Arête (Castle Naze) 270
Pinnacle Arête (The Roaches) 64
Pinnacle Buttress 195
Pinnacle Crack (Castle Naze) 270
Pinnacle Crack (The Roaches) 65
Pinnacle Face 123
Pinnacle Rib 123
Pinnacle Slab 64
Pinnacle Start and Shaun's End, The 92
Pip 187
Piston Groove 107
Piton Route 288
Pitoned Crack 272
Plankton 273
Plastics Factory, The 234
Plebble 226
Plumb-Line 91
Pluto's Ring 127
Pocket Hercules 245
Pocket Wall 157
Pod Crack 272
Pointless Arête 82
Pointless but Pumpy 110
Poison Gift 23
Poisonous Python 14
Ponsified 172
Poodle Vindaloo 64
Pop Art 71
Porkstorm 225
Porridge at Morridge Top 183
Port Crack 152
Portcullis Crack 196
Portfolio 263
Pot Black 186
Prayers, Poems and Promises 117
Praying Mantel 166
Prelude to Space 75
Prelude to XB 175
Prescription for the Poor 285
Press On Regardless 112
Press, The 155
Pretentious? Moi? 284
Pride, The 224
Prism, The 157
Private Display 86
Probably Boysen's Arête 126
Proboscid, The 153
Prodigal, The 228
Prometheus 291
Prostration 145
Prow Corner 26
Prow Cracks 26

Prowler (Churnet) 250
Prowler (Ramshaw) 139
Psalm 224
Pseudo Crack 197
Public Enemy Number One 38
Puffed Up 172
Pug 109
Pugilist, The 55
Pull Johnny 228
Pull the Udder One 225
Pullet 107
Punch 25
Puppet Life 241
Pyeclough 179

Q

Qantas 112
Quaking All Over 278
Qui Vive 218
Quickbrew 38

R

Racer's Rock 195
Raid, The 109
Raiders of the Lost Bark 234
Rainbow Crack 122
Rainbow Reces 220
Rakes Dale Chimney 234
Ralph's Direct 58
Ralph's Mantelshelves 58
Ramshaw Crack 150
Rash Challenge 156
Rassp! 58
Raven Rock Gully 16
Raven Rock Gully Left-Hand 16
Rawhide 231
Ray's Roof 178
Reach, The 289
Recess Chimney 108
Recess Wall and Arête 58
Red Nose Route 260
Renaissance, The 229
Requiem for Tired Fingers 197
Reset Portion of Galley 37 36
Respectable Street 277
Restless Natives 228
Reunion Crack 111
Reverse Charge 237
Rhodren 25
Rhody Crack 237
Rhynose 172
Rib and Slab 264
Rib Chimney 120
Rib Crack 120
Rib Right-Hand, The 260
Rib Wall 51

Rib, The (The Roaches) 51
Rib, The (Windgather) 260
Richter 5 278
Riding the Gravy Train 177
Rig A Dig Dig 228
Right Bow 194
Right Eliminate 288
Right It 290
Right Nostril 280
Right Route 42
Right Route Right 43
Right Tot 288
Right Triplet Crack 267
Right Twin Crack (Churnet) 229
Right Twin Crack (Hen Cloud) 122
Right-Hand Block Crack 86
Right-Hand Route (The Roaches Skyline) 65
Right-Hand Route (The Roaches Upper Tier) 49
Ripple 214
Rippler, The 143
Ripples 245
Robin 288
Robin Hood 223
Rock Around The Chock 244
Rock Trivia 142
Rocket to 'em 224
Rocking Stone Crack 224
Rocking Stone Gully 26
Rocking Stone Ridge 198
Rodeo 68
Rollercoaster 151
Roman Candle 85
Roman Nose 85
Roof Climb 112
Rooster 32
Root Slab 237
Roscoe's Wall 47
Rose 279
Rosehip 172
Rostrum, The 195
Rot 288
Rotondas 215
Rotunda Buttress 39
Rotunda Gully 39
Round Table 49
Route 1 267
Route 1 Direct 267
Route 1.5 267
Route 2 267
Rowan Tree Crack 91
Rowan Tree Traverse 59
Rubber Crack 151
Rubberneck 83
Ruby Tuesday 40
Rudyard Pinnacle 294
Rugosity 214
Runaway 219

Runner Route 36
Ruth's Septic Trench 195

S

Safety Net 58
Sale's Bulge 211
Sally James 62
San Melas 67
Sandbagger 232
Sands of Time 85
Sanitarium 127
Saucer Direct, The 196
Saucer, The 196
Saul's Crack 39
Saunter 214
Saur Off 241
Sauria 122
Sauron 241
Scarlet Wall 49
Scent of Lamb, A 225
Schoolies 16
Scoop Direct 272
Scoop Face 272
Direct Start 272
Scoop Wall 244, 272
Scooped Surprise 151
Scorpion 291
Scout In Situ 151
Scout Wall 244
Scrabble 124
Screwy Driver 156
Script for a Tear 71
Sculptor's Wall 241
Second Quarry 296
Second's Advance 120
Second's Retreat 120
Secrets of Dance 18
Sedition and Alchemy 126
Seismic Wall 278
Sennapod 65
Sennapod Crack 65
Sense of Doubt 189
Shaun's Other End 90
Shelf Route 215
Sheltered Crack 270
Shelty 52
Shining Path, The 86
Shockwave 278
Shoe Shine Shuffle 123
Short Arête 278
Short Man's Misery 126
Short Trip to a
    Transylvanian Brain
    Surgery, A 38
Shortbread 128
Shortcake 128
Shortcomings 58
Shrug 60
Sickle Moon 293
Side Face 265
Sidewinder 16

Sifta's Quid 26
Sign of the Times 52
Silent Scream 289
Simpkins' Overhang 33
Sirloin 284
Skallagrigg 36
Sketching Wildly 144
Skull Crack 219
Skytrain 62
Slab and Arête 62
Slab Wall 281
Slant Start 263
Slanting Crack (Castle
    Naze) 270
Slanting Crack (Short Edge)
    278
Slanting Crack (The
    Roaches) 90
Sleepwalker 188
Slender Thread 284
Slimline 120
Slip Knot 236
Slippery Caramel 237
Slippery Jim 6
Slips 62
Slipstreams 105
Slither 71
Sloth, The 42
Slow Hand Clap 156
Slowhand 105
Sly Corner 173
Sly Mantelshelf, The 173
Small Buttress 119
Small Wall 263
Smear Test 20
Smun 86
Snake, The 172
Snap, Crackle and Andy
    Popp 6
Sneeze 142
Sole Survivor 223
Solid Geometry 119
Solitaire 283
Solo Chimney 250
Something Better Change
    15
Something Biblical 39
Songs of Praise 117
Sorcerer's Apprentice 61
Sorcerer, The 108
South Buttress 275
South Crack (Castle Naze)
    275
South Crack (Windgather)
    267
South-East Crack 218
South-West Crack, The 218
Southern Arête 275
Southern Crack 136
Southpaw 55
Space Probe 122

Spacepube 127
Spanish Fly 149
Spare Rib 60
Sparkle 51
Spearhead 213
Special Branch 289
Special K 208
Spectrum 59
Spiderman Meets the
    Carlsberg Club 293
Spiral Route, The 288
Split Personality 65
Spreadeagle 240
Square Buttress 288
Square Chimney 58
Squash Balls 85
Squashed Finger 264
Stadium, The 219
Staircase 260
Stalin 82
Stall 183
Standing Tall 115
Starboard Crack 153
Stark 230
Starlight and Storm 105
Steeplechase Crack 70
Steeplechaser 71
Stephen (Churnet) 230
Stephen (The Roaches) 61
Steps 16
Stickle Brick Wall 234
Sting, The 215
Stoke the Engines 275
Stokesline 120
Stomach Punch 55
Stone Loach, The 109
Stonemason's Route 241
Stop... Carry on! 52
Straight Crack 25
Strain Station 59
Stranglehold 86
Struggle 265, 275
Stuck Behind a Yellow
    Metro 281
Studio 271
Stumblehead 226
Sublime, The 34
Substance 58
Suckin' Pebbles 244
Summit Arête 283
Summit Bypass 283
Sumo Cellulite 26
Sunday at Chapel 9
Super Girdle, The 31
Supermac 244
Suspended Sentence 194
Swan Bank 20
Swan, The 19
Swinger 16
Syringe Benefit 274

T

T'rival Traverse 142
Tactical Weapon 232
Take Her Under 139
Taller Overhang 263
Tally Not 142
Taming of the Shrew 215
Tasmanian Devil 275
Tasmanian Tendencies 175
Taxman, The 240
Tealeaf Crack 38
Technical Slab 41
Technician, The 215
Technocrat 219
Teck Crack 7
Tequila Sunrise 219
Termination Crack 285
The Emergency Exit 27
Theseus 187
Thin Air, The 31
Thin Crack 197
Thin Crack (Castle Naze)
    270
Thin Finger Corner 283
Thing on a Spring 19
Third Degree Burn 38
Third Quarry 296
This Poison 120
Thompson's Buttress Route
    One 123
Thompson's Buttress Route
    Two 123
Thorax 277
Thorns 242
Three Steps 288
Three-Tiered Buttress 68
Thrug 60
Thum 250
Tier's End 145
Tierdrop 145
Tiger's Wall 243
Tim Benzadrino 82
Time Flies By 230
Time Out 152
Time to be Had 57
Time's Arrow 226
Tin Tin 283
Tip Toe 85
Tiptoe 215
Titan 293
Titan's Wal 215
To Live Again 228
Toast Rack 237
Tobacco Road 57
Toe Nail 264
Toe Rail 197
Top Brick 237
Topaz 59
Torture 143
Tot 288
Totally Unprecedented 90

Touch 124
Tour De Force 218
Tower Chimney 61
Tower Eliminate 61
Tower Face 61
Tower of Bizarre Delights, The 34
Toxic Socks 57
Track of the Cat 76
Traditional 265
Transcendental Medication 71
Transit Crack 228
Trap Door Finish, The 108
Traveller in Time 136
Travelling Bag 237
Travelling Light 237
Tre Cime 230
Trebia 49
Tree Chimney 123
Tree Corner 71
Tree Grooves 71
Tremor 278
Trepidation 172
Triack 220
Tricky Woo 219
Tricouni Crack 151
Trio Chimney 58
Triple Point 73
Triplet Cracks 267
Triumph of the Good City 124
Trivial Traverse 142
Trouble at t'Mill 126
Tube Snake 292
Tunnel Chimney 242
Tunnel Vision 123
Twiggy 236
Twin Cracks 139
Twin Thin 195
Twinkletoes 290
Twisting Crack 211
Two Step 290
Two-Step, The 273
Tyre Pressure 234

U

Uchimata 230
Ugly Bloke, The 274
Ugly Puss 243
Ultimate Sculpture 142
Ultra Direct, The 152
Uncles Arête 234
Uncorrected Personality Traits 279
Underhung Chimney 207
Underpass, The 31
Undertaker, The 139
Untouchable, The 143
Unveiling, The 240
Up The Swanee 20

Up to the Elbows 293
Up Your Slip 150

V

V-Chimney (Bosley Cloud) 280
V-Chimney (Castle Naze) 275
V-Corner 270
Valkyrie 18
Valkyrie Corner 18
Valkyrie Direct 17
Valley of Ultravixens 173
Valve, The 35
Vanishing Crack 275
Vee Diff 288
Vereker's Venture 215
Vertigo 210
Very Connoisseurish 73
Via Dolorosa 17
Via Dolorosa Variations 17
Via Trita 215
Vice, The 275
Victory 108
Vixen, The 173
Voila 3 26

W

Wad Man Slang 60
Waggledunce 277
Walking on Sunshin 83
Wall and Groove 139
Wall Climb 263
Wallaby 276
Wallaby Wall 65
Walleroo 34
Wander 86
War Wound 49
Watercourse, The 150
Wave 214
Wavelength 122
Waxwing 83
Way Purple Splat Balloon 293
Weathered Corner 198
Web, The 215
Weirdy, The 128
Wellingtons 141
West's Wallaby 34
Wet and Warm 284
Wheel of Misfortun 153
Wheeze 56
Whilly's Whopper 143
Whispering Myth 231
White House Crack 283
White Mouse 232
White Widow 219
Why Kill Time When You
  Can Kill a Friend? 281
Wick Slip 150

Wicked Wind 65
Wigglette 213
Wild Frontier 210
Wild Thing 71
Willow Farm 76
Wine Gums 142
Wings of Unreason 75
Winter in Combat 86
Wipers 38
Wisecrack 15
Wolfman of the KGB 53
Wombat (Castle Naze) 275
Wombat (The Roaches) 34
Wrestle Crack 196
Wriggler 149
Wrong Way Round 34

Y

Yankee Jam 80
Yong 14
Yong Arête 14
You'll Always Reap What
  You Sow 230
Young Pretender, The 125
Your Own Undoing 223

Z

Zeus 227
Zig-a-Zag-a 273
Zigzag 264
Zigzag Crack 273

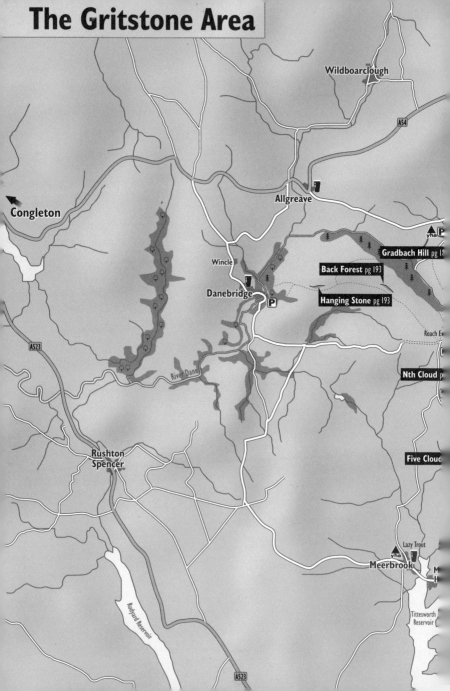

The Gritstone Area

Wildboarclough

A54

Congleton

Allgreave

yha P

Gradbach Hill pg 1⁹

Wincle

Back Forest pg 193

Danebridge

P

Hanging Stone pg 193

Roach E⁵

A523

River Dane

Nth Cloud p

Rushton
Spencer

Five Cloud

Lazy Trout

yha

Meerbrook

M
H

Rudyard Reservoir

Tittesworth
Reservoir

A523